Praise for Charles King's

GODS *of the* UPPER AIR

"Thoughtful, deeply intelligent, and immensely readable."
                                                    —*The Atlantic*

"[King] succeeds in bringing Mead and her fellow travelers into sharp focus as they pioneered a new field and documented mankind's many-splendored diversity in a positive, rather than a divisive, light."   —*USA Today*

"[*Gods of the Upper Air*] offers a vitally relevant way to frame the ugly spectre of racism as it resurfaces in our politics. . . . Now, more than ever, we need to recognise how Boas and others developed an alternative vision of humanity. Understanding this oft-ignored intellectual history is a first step towards defending it."
                                                    —*Financial Times*

"A masterful history of a group of maverick thinkers in the early twentieth century who aimed to dethrone the eugenicists dominating racial thought. With eugenics ascendant again, King's story is a vital book for our times."   —Ibram X. Kendi,
        author of *Stamped from the Beginning: The Definitive History of
        Racist Ideas in America*, winner of the 2016 National Book Award

"[King's] absorbing book makes a compelling case that the struggle to see other cultures' and people's points of view is worth the effort."   —*The Boston Globe*

"Deeply engaging. . . . King offers captivating, exquisitely detailed portraits of these remarkable individuals."
—*Kirkus Reviews* (starred review)

"Deeply thought-provoking and brilliantly written, *Gods of the Upper Air* is a walk in the shoes of giants. Charles King takes you on an unforgettable journey as daring anthropologists unravel the profound mysteries of culture and mankind and discover that they, too, were only human."
—David Hoffman,
Pulitzer Prize–winning author of
The Dead Hand and *The Billion Dollar Spy*

"King's prose is energetic, enlivened with delicious quotations, juicy personal details, and witty turns of phrase. . . . This complex, delightful book will get readers thinking and keep them turning the pages."
—*Publishers Weekly* (starred review)

"This exciting—even entrancing—story traces the birth of a new science in the early twentieth century, championed by a scrappy genius who trained a cadre of bold women for the work. Charles King writes with verve and authority as he follows the nation's first cultural anthropologists to far-flung field sites that suggested antidotes to the racism and xenophobia of American society."
—Dava Sobel, author of *The Glass Universe* and *Longitude*

"King's engrossing look at these extraordinary trailblazers deftly illustrates how crucial their research and work remain today."
—*Booklist*

"An intellectual adventure story of the best sort—elegantly written, thought-provoking, and full of biographical riches."
—Sarah Bakewell, author of
How to Live and *At the Existentialist Café*

"Charles King has written a sweeping and dynamic history of Americanist anthropology through its origins, shaky institutionalization, and creation of ideas that upended common wisdom and challenged the dominant power structure."

—*New York Journal of Books*

"In any era, *Gods of the Upper Air* would be a scholarly masterpiece—an elegantly written, wickedly perceptive account of Franz Boas, the father of cultural anthropology, and his impact upon the key moral issues of his time and ours. Mentoring the likes of Margaret Mead and Zora Neale Hurston, Boas employed the skills of scientific observation to argue that all societies are part of a single, undivided humanity guided by circumstance and history, but none superior to another. In today's deeply polarized world, Charles King's stunning new book reminds us of the brilliance of these renegade anthropologists and the work still to be done."

—David Oshinsky,
Pulitzer Prize–winning author of *Polio* and *Bellevue*

CHARLES KING

GODS *of the* UPPER AIR

Charles King is the author of seven books, including *Midnight at the Pera Palace* and *Odessa*, winner of a National Jewish Book Award. His essays and articles have appeared in *The New York Times*, *The Washington Post*, *Foreign Affairs*, and *The New Republic*. He is a professor of international affairs and government at Georgetown University.

www.charleskingauthor.com

GODS OF THE UPPER AIR

ANCHOR BOOKS

A Division of Penguin Random House LLC

New York

GODS
of the
UPPER AIR

·············

How a Circle of Renegade Anthropologists
Reinvented Race, Sex, and Gender
in the Twentieth Century

······

CHARLES KING

FIRST ANCHOR BOOKS EDITION, JULY 2020

Copyright © 2019 by Charles King

All rights reserved. Published in the United States by Anchor Books,
a division of Penguin Random House LLC, New York, and distributed in Canada
by Penguin Random House Canada Limited, Toronto. Originally published in
hardcover in the United States by Doubleday, a division of Penguin
Random House LLC, New York, in 2019.

Anchor Books and colophon are registered trademarks of
Penguin Random House LLC.

The Library of Congress has cataloged the Doubleday edition as follows:
Names: King, Charles, 1967– author.
Title: Gods of the upper air : how a circle of renegade anthropologists reinvented
race, sex, and gender in the twentieth century / Charles King.
Description: First edition. | New York : Doubleday, 2019. | Includes
bibliographical references (pages 387–406) and index.
Identifiers: LCCN 2019014081
Subjects: Boas, Franz, 1858–1942—Influence. | Ethnology—Study and teaching—
United States—History—20th century. | Culture—Study and teaching—United
States—History—20th century. | Anthropologists—United States—Biography.
Classification: LCC GN308.3.U6 K55 2019 | DDC 306—dc23
LC record available at https://lccn.loc.gov/2019014081

Anchor Books Trade Paperback ISBN: 978-0-525-43232-6
eBook ISBN: 978-0-385-54220-3

Author photograph © Miriam Lomaskin
Book design by Maria Carella

www.anchorbooks.com

Printed in the United States of America
10 9 8 7 6 5 4

FOR MAGGIE,

who else?

I do not say that my conclusions about anything are true for the Universe, but I have lived in many ways, sweet and bitter, and they feel right for me. . . . I have walked in storms with a crown of clouds about my head and the zig zag lightning playing through my fingers. The gods of the upper air have uncovered their faces to my eyes.

—ZORA NEALE HURSTON, anthropologist, 1942

A new scientific truth does not triumph by convincing its opponents and making them see the light, but rather because its opponents eventually die, and a new generation grows up that is familiar with it.

—MAX PLANCK, physicist, 1948

CONTENTS

GODS OF THE UPPER AIR

AWAY

....

On the last day of August 1925, the triple-deck steamship *Sonoma*, midway through its regular run from San Francisco to Sydney, slipped into a harbor formed by an extinct volcano. The island of Tutuila had been scorched by drought, but the hillsides were still a tangle of avocado trees and blooming ginger. Black cliffs loomed over a white sandy beach. Behind a line of spindly palms lay a cluster of open-sided thatched houses, the local building style on the string of Pacific islands known as American Samoa.

On board *Sonoma* was a twenty-three-year-old Pennsylvanian, slight but square-built, unable to swim, given to conjunctivitis, with a broken ankle and a chronic ailment that sometimes rendered her right arm useless. She had left behind a husband in New York and a boyfriend in Chicago, and had spent the transcontinental train ride in the arms of a woman. In her steamer trunk she carried reporters' notebooks, a typewriter, evening dresses, and a photograph of an aging, wild-haired man she called Papa Franz, his face sliced by saber cuts and melted from the nerve damage of a botched surgery. He was the reason for Margaret Mead's journey.

Mead had recently written her doctoral dissertation under his direction. She had been one of the first women to complete the demanding course of study in Columbia University's department of anthropology. So far her writing had drawn more from the library stacks than from real life. But Papa Franz—as Professor Franz Boas, the department chair, was known to his students—had urged her to get out into the field, to find someplace where she could make her mark as an anthropologist. With the right planning and some luck, her research could become "the first serious attempt to enter into the mental attitude of a group in a primitive society," he would write to her a few months later. "I believe that your success would mark a beginning of a new era of methodological investigation of native tribes."

Now, as she looked out over the guardrails, her heart sank.

Gray cruisers, destroyers, and support vessels clogged the harbor. The surface of the water was an oily rainbow. American Samoa and its harbor on Tutuila—Pago Pago—had been controlled by the United States since the 1890s. Only three years before Mead arrived, the navy had shifted most of its seagoing vessels from the Atlantic to the Pacific, a strategic reorientation that took account of America's growing interests in Asia. The islands quickly became a coaling station and repair center for the reorganized fleet—which, as it happened, was steaming into Pago Pago on exactly the same day as Mead. It was the largest naval deployment since Theodore Roosevelt had sent the Great White Fleet around the world as a display of American sea power.

Airplanes screamed overhead. Below, a dozen Fords sputtered along a narrow concrete road. In the *malae*, the open-air common at the center of Pago Pago, Samoans had laid out an impromptu bazaar of wooden bowls, bead necklaces, woven baskets, grass skirts, and toy outrigger canoes. Families were spread around the green, enjoying an early lunch. "The band of some ship is constantly playing ragtime," Mead complained. This was no way to study primitive tribes. She vowed to get as far away from Pago Pago as possible.

Her research topic had been suggested by Papa Franz. Was the transition from childhood to adulthood, with young women and men rebelling against their stultifying parents, the product of a purely biological change, the onset of puberty? Or was adolescence a *thing* simply because a particular society decided to treat it as such? To find out, Mead spent the next several months trekking across mountains, decamping to remote villages, drawing up life histories of local children and teenagers, and quizzing adults about their most intimate experiences of love and sex.

It didn't take her long to conclude that Samoa seemed to have few rebellious adolescents. But that was largely because there was little for them to rebel against. Sexual norms were fluid. Virginity was celebrated in theory but underprized in practice. Strict fidelity in relationships was foreign. Samoan ways, Mead reported, were not so much primitive and backward as intensely modern. Samoans already seemed comfortable with many of the values of her own generation: the American youth of the 1920s who were going to petting parties, downing bootleg gin, and dancing the Charleston. Mead's goal became to work out how Samoans managed to avoid the slammed doors, the Boys Town delinquents, and the fear of civilizational collapse that obsessed commentators back home. How had they produced teenagers without the typically American angst?

Or had they really? "And oh how sick I am of talking sex, sex, sex," she wrote to her closest friend, Ruth Benedict, a few months into her stay. She had filled entire notebooks, written out index cards, and typed up reams of field reports, sending them by canoe through the breakers and over the reef to the mail boat. She watched with her stomach in knots, afraid that the outrigger would capsize and destroy the only reason she had for being on the far side of the world—or for that matter, the only evidence she had of something that could vaguely be called a career. "I've got lots of nice significant facts," she wrote, the sarcasm wafting off the page, but she doubted that they added up to much. "I'm feeling perfectly pathological about my time, my thoughts. . . . I'm going to get a job giving change in the subway when I get home."

She could not have known it at the time, but there among the welcoming feasts and the reef fishing, on humid afternoons and in the lashing winds of a tropical storm, Mead was in the middle of a revolution. It had begun with a set of vexing questions at the heart of philosophy, religion, and the human sciences: What are the natural divisions of human society? Is morality universal? How should we treat people whose beliefs and habits are different from our own? It would end with a root-and-branch reconsideration of what it means to be social animals and the surrender of an easy confidence in the superiority of our own civilization. At stake were the consequences of an astonishing discovery: that our distant ancestors, at some point in their evolution, invented a thing we call culture.

THIS BOOK IS ABOUT women and men who found themselves on the front lines of the greatest moral battle of our time: the struggle to prove that—despite differences of skin color, gender, ability, or custom—humanity is one undivided thing. It tells the story of globalists in an era of nationalism and social division and the origins of an outlook that we now label modern and open-minded. It is a prehistory of the seismic social changes of the last hundred years, from women's suffrage and the civil rights movement to the sexual revolution and marriage equality, as well as of the forces that push in the opposite direction, toward chauvinism and bigotry.

But this is not a book about politics, ethics, or theology. It is not a lesson in tolerance. It is instead a story about science and scientists.

A little over a century ago, any educated person knew that the world worked in certain obvious ways. Humans were individuals, but each was also representative of a specific type, itself the summation of a distinct set of racial, national, and sexual characteristics. Each type was fated to be more or less intelligent, idle, rule-bound, or warlike. Politics properly belonged to men, while women, when they were admitted to public life, were thought to be most productive in charitable organizations, missionary work, and the instruction of children. Immigrants tended to dilute a country's natural vigor and breed political extremism. Animals deserved kindness, and backward peoples, a few rungs above animals, were owed our help but not our respect. Criminals were born to a life beyond the law but might be reformed. Sapphists and sodomites chose their depravities but were probably irredeemable. It was an age of improvement: an era that had moved beyond justifying slavery, that had begun to shake off the strictures of class, and that might eventually do away with empires. But the reminders of humanity's defects—individuals referred to as the blind, the deaf and dumb, cripples, idiots, morons, the insane, and mongoloids—were best left to lead quiet lives behind a wall.

Experience confirmed these natural truths. No sovereign country permitted women both to vote and to hold national office. In the United States, censuses divided society into clear and exclusive racial types, including white, Negro, Chinese, and American Indian. The 1890 census added the terms *mulatto, quadroon,* and *octoroon* to distinguish different shades of the colored. Your proper category was so obvious that it was not what *you* said it was but what *someone else,* the census enumerator—usually a white man—said it was.

If you walked into any major library, from Paris to London to Washington, D.C., you could pull down learned volumes that agreed on all of these points. The twentieth century's first full edition of the *Encyclopaedia Britannica,* completed in 1911, defined "race" as a group of individuals "descended from a common ancestor," which implied that white people and black people, among others, had wholly separate lineages going back through evolutionary time. *Civilization* was defined as that period since "the most highly developed races of men have used systems of writing." The century's earliest version of the *Oxford English Dictionary,* the concise edition published in 1911, contained no entries for *racism, colonialism,* or *homosexuality.*

The standard view of human society was that differences of belief and practice were matters of development and deviance. A more or less straight line ran from primitive societies to advanced ones. In New York City, you could retrace this natural odyssey just by walking from one side of Central Park to the other. Exhibits on Africans, Pacific Islanders, and Native Americans were housed (as they are today) under the same roof as dioramas of elk and grizzlies in the American Museum of Natural History. You had to go across the park, to the Metropolitan Museum of Art, to see what real achievement looked like. Contemporary society still had its flaws: the poor, the sexually aberrant, the feebleminded, overly ambitious women. But these were simply evidence of the work yet to be done in perfecting an already advanced civilization.

The idea of a natural ranking of human types shaped everything: school and university curricula, court decisions and policing strategies, health policy and popular culture, the work of the Bureau of

Indian Affairs and U.S. colonial administrators in the Philippines, as well as their equivalents in Britain, France, Germany, and many other empires, countries, and territories. The poor were poor because of their own inadequacies. Nature favored the robust colonizer over the benighted native. Differences in physical appearance, customs, and language were reflections of a deeper, innate otherness. Progressives, too, accepted these ideas, adding only that it was possible, with enough missionaries, teachers, and physicians on hand, to eradicate primitive and unnatural practices and replace them with enlightened ways. That was why America's foremost periodical on world politics and international relations, published since 1922 and now the influential *Foreign Affairs*, was originally called the *Journal of Race Development*. Primitive races were simply those that had yet to enjoy the benefits of muscular Christianity, flush toilets, and the Ford Motor Company.

About all of these things, however, we have since begun to change our minds.

Concepts such as race, ethnicity, nationality, gender, sexuality, and disability remain some of the most basic categories that we use to make sense of the social world. We ask about some of them on job applications. We measure others on census forms. We talk about all of them—incessantly in twenty-first-century America—in liberal arts classrooms and on social media. But what we mean by them is no longer the same as in the past.

In the 2000 census, for the first time Americans were allowed to report multiple answers to questions about their racial or ethnic identity. The Common Application, the admissions form used by over six hundred American colleges and universities, requires that an applicant's sex match the legal description on a birth certificate but now permits further elaboration of how one perceives or represents that fact. In 2015 a majority of U.S. Supreme Court justices ruled that federal protection of the institution of marriage did not require that a couple consist of a chromosomal female and male. In schools, public buildings, universities, and workplaces, things that were not long ago seen as defects—from deafness to being a wheelchair user to having a particular style of learning—are now treated as differences that should be accommodated, the better to ensure that no ideas, skills, or talents go unexpressed merely because of a sound wave or a staircase.

We usually narrate these changes as an expansion or contraction of our moral universe. In the United States, the political left tends to trace a long, necessary arc from the dismantling of racial authoritarianism in the era of Jim Crow, through the Stonewall riots and the Americans with Disabilities Act, toward the first major female candidate for U.S. president. The narrative is one of progress, of an ever greater fulfillment of the rights enshrined in the nation's founding documents. On the political right, some of these changes are said to constrict a community's ability to determine its own social mores. A new form of state-sanctioned intolerance, protected in safe spaces and monitored by language police from public schools to workplaces, insists that we should all agree on what constitutes marriage, a good joke, or a flourishing society. The narrative is one of overreach and unreasonableness, of an overweening state's infringing on individual speech, thought, and sincerely held values. Similar battle lines exist in other countries—between celebrating certain kinds of difference and preserving the time-honored values of past generations.

Yet a more fundamental shift preceded any of these debates. It was the result of a body of discoveries made by a small band of contrarian researchers whom Franz Boas modestly called "our little group." Real, evidence-driven analysis, they believed, would overturn one of modernity's most deeply held principles: that science will tell us which individuals and groups are naturally smarter, abler, more upstanding, and fitter to rule. Their response was that science pointed in precisely the opposite direction, toward a theory of humanity that embraces all the many ways we humans have devised for living. The social categories into which we typically divide ourselves, including labels such as race and gender, are at base artificial—the products of human artifice, residing in the mental frameworks and unconscious habits of a given society. We are cultural animals, they claimed, bound by rules of our own making, even if these rules are often invisible or taken for granted by the societies that craft them.

The Boas circle's story is worth knowing not because they were the only people ever to challenge old misconceptions. The oneness of humankind is an idea braided through the world's religions, ethical systems, art, and literature. But if Boas and his students were especially adept at sensing the distance between what is real and what we say is real, it was because they were living inside a case study. The United States in the first half of the twentieth century proclaimed its origins in enlightened values but perfected a vast system of racial disenfranchisement. Its inhabitants believed themselves to be uniquely endowed as a nation but insisted on the universal applicability of their idea of a good society. Their government worked hard to keep out certain types of foreigners while expending unprecedented wealth and military power to refashion the countries that sent them. The science of the Boas circle was born of a time and a place that seemed in special need of it.

They called themselves cultural anthropologists—a term they invented—and they named their animating theory cultural relativity, now often known as cultural relativism. For nearly a century, their critics have accused them of everything from justifying immorality to chipping away at the foundations of civilization itself. Today cultural relativism is usually listed among the enemies of tradition and good behavior, along with such terms as postmodernism and multiculturalism. The work of the Boas circle makes appearances as bugbears and objects of derision in conservative media and on alt-right websites, among campaigners against diversity programs and political correctness, and on such lists as "Ten Books That Screwed Up the World." How can we make any judgments about right and wrong, critics ask, if everything is relative to the time, place, and context in which our judgments occur?

The belief that our ways are the only commonsensical, moral ones has a powerful allure, especially when expressed in the language of science, rationality, religion, or tradition. All societies are predisposed to see their own traits as achievements and others' as shortcomings. But the core message of the Boas circle was that, in order to live intelligently in the world, we should view the lives of others through an empathetic lens. We ought to suspend our judgment about other ways of seeing social reality until we really understand them, and in turn we should look at our own society with the same dispassion and skepticism with which we study far-flung peoples.

Culture, as Boas and his students understood it, is the ultimate source for what we think constitutes common sense. It defines what is obvious or beyond question. It tells us how to raise a child, how to pick a leader, how to find good things to eat, how to marry well. Over time these things change, sometimes slowly, sometimes rapidly. Yet there is no more fundamental reality in the social world than the one that humans themselves in some measure create.

The implications of the idea that we make our own agreed-upon truths were profound. It undermined the claim that social development is linear, running from allegedly primitive societies to so-called civilized ones. It called into question some of the building blocks of political and social order, from the belief in the obviousness of race to the conviction that gender and sex are simply the same thing. The concept of race, Boas believed, should be seen as a social reality, not a biological one—no different from the other deeply felt, human-made dividing lines, from caste to tribe to sect, that snake through societies around the world. In the arena of sex, too, the lives of women and men are shaped not by fixed, exclusive sexualities but by flexible ideas of gender, attraction, and eroticism that differ from place to place. The valuing of purity—an unsullied race, a chaste body, a nation that sprang fully formed from its ancestral soil—should give way to the view, validated by observation, that mixing is the natural state of the world.

In time these shifts would inform how sociologists understand immigrant integration or exclusion; how public health officials think about endemic illnesses from diabetes to drug addiction; how police and criminologists seek out the root causes of crime; and how economists model the seemingly irrational actions of buyers and sellers. Belief in the normality of "mixed-race" identity, gender as something beyond either/or, the sheer variety of human sexuality, the fact that social norms color our sense of right and wrong—these things had to be imagined and, in a way, *proven* before they could begin to shape law, government, and public policy. When you visit a museum or fill out a census form, or when your child walks into her eighth-grade health class, the effects of this intellectual revolution are there. If it is now unremarkable for a gay couple to kiss goodbye on a train platform, for a college student to read the *Bhagavad Gita* in a Great Books class, for racism to be rejected as both morally bankrupt and self-evidently stupid, and for anyone, regardless of their gender expression, to claim workplaces and boardrooms as fully theirs—if all of these things are not innovations or aspirations but the regular, taken-for-granted way of organizing a society, then we have the ideas championed by the Boas circle to thank for it.

WITH HIS UNRULY HAIR and thick German accent, Papa Franz was the very image of a mad scientist. In the 1930s he had the distinction of appearing on the cover of *Time* magazine, photographed as usual from the right to hide the drooping left side of his face, and receiving birthday greetings from public figures such as Franklin Roosevelt and Orson Welles. After Adolf Hitler's rise to power in his native Germany, Boas's books were among the first to be tossed into the flames by Nazi zealots, along with those of Einstein, Freud, and Lenin. When he died, in 1942, the *New York Times* published a special note commemorating the loss. It now devolved to his former students, the *Times* wrote, to carry on "the work of enlightenment in which he was a daring pioneer."

They would go on to become some of the century's intellectual stars and might-have-beens: Mead, the outspoken field researcher and one of America's greatest public scientists; Ruth Benedict, Boas's chief assistant and the love of Mead's life, whose research for the U.S. government helped shape the future of post–Second World War Japan; Ella Cara Deloria, who preserved the traditions of Plains Indians but spent most of her life in poverty and obscurity; Zora Neale Hurston, the preeminent contrarian of the Harlem Renaissance, whose ethnographic studies under Boas fed directly into her now-classic novel,

Their Eyes Were Watching God; and a handful of other academics and researchers who created some of the world's foremost departments of anthropology, from Yale to Chicago to Berkeley.

They were scientists and thinkers in love with the challenge of understanding other human beings. The deepest science of humanity, they believed, was not one that taught us what was rooted and unchangeable about human nature. Rather, it was the one that revealed the wide variation in human societies—the immense and diverse vocabulary of propriety, custom, morals, and rectitude. Our most cherished traditions, they insisted, are only a tiny fraction of the many ways humans have devised for solving basic problems, from how to order society to how to mark the passage from childhood to adulthood. Just as the cure for a fatal disease might lie in an undiscovered plant in some remote jungle, so too the solution to social problems might be found in how other people in other places have worked out humanity's common challenges. And there is urgency in this work: as countries change and the world becomes ever more connected, the catalog of human solutions necessarily gets thinner and thinner.

What's more, in going away, you learn something profound about your own backyard—that it doesn't have to be the way it is. Ruth Benedict called it the "illumination that comes of envisaging very different possible ways of handling invariable problems." That was the whole point of the day-to-day work Boas pushed his students to take on—the foreign travel, the museum exhibits, and the technical articles on native languages and sexual mores: to show we aren't the first people to get married, raise a child, mourn the loss of a parent, or decide who makes the rules.

Boas and his students weren't skeptics when it came to the possibility of truth and our ability to know reality. They believed that the scientific method—the assumption that our conclusions are provisional and always subject to contradiction by new data—was in fact one of the greatest advances in human history. It had reshaped our understanding of the natural world and, in their view, could revolutionize our conceptions of the social world as well.

A science of society had to be a kind of salvage operation, they believed. We became who we are through a monumental effort at forgetting: what to call this kind of tree, when to plant this seed, how the gods prefer to be addressed. We may revere our ancestors, but none of us would truly recognize them. Knowing human society, past and present, is a race against oblivion. You have to gather in the treasury of human cultures before people forget—or, worse, misremember—the specifics of who they once were.

Old ways of doing things have passed away. Ours will, too, someday. Our great-grandchildren will wonder how we ever could have believed and behaved as we do. They will marvel at our ignorance and fault our moral judgment. That is why "culture" only makes sense in the plural—a usage that Boas popularized. Van Gogh and Dostoyevsky are part of a culture, but so too are facial tattooing, canoe building, and who counts as kin.

"Courtesy, modesty, good manners, [and] conformity to definite ethical standards are universal," Boas once wrote, "but what constitutes courtesy, modesty, good manners, and ethical standards is not universal." He and his students knew that belief in a timeless human nature sanctifies certain behaviors and sanctions others. Even in an age of scientific discovery, it is hard to shake the conviction that God and tradition are on the side of one type of family or one kind of love—always those with which we happen to be most familiar. But the essential message of the Boas circle was that we are all, in our way, museum pieces. We have our own taboos and totems, our own gods and demons. Since these things are largely our own creations, the choice rests with us to venerate or exorcise them.

More than anyone in his day, Boas understood that his own society's deepest prejudices were grounded not in moral arguments but rather in allegedly scientific ones. Disenfranchised African Americans were intellectually inferior because the latest research said so. Women could not hold positions of influence because their weaknesses and peculiar dispositions were well proven. The feebleminded should be kept to themselves because the key to social betterment lay in reducing their number in the general population. Immigrants carried with them the afflictions of their benighted homelands, from disease to crime to social disorder.

A science that seemed to prove that humanity had unbridgeable divisions had to be countered by a science that showed it didn't. By making Americans in particular see themselves as slightly strange— their tenacious belief in something they call race, their blindness to everyday violence, their stop-and-go attitudes toward sex, their comparative backwardness on women's role in governance—Boas and his circle took a gargantuan step toward seeing the rest of the world as slightly more familiar. This is the discovery of the thinkers in these pages. They taught that no society, including our own, is the endpoint of human social evolution. We aren't even a distinct stage in human development. History moves in loops and circles, not in straight lines, and toward no particular end. Our own vices and blind spots are as readily apparent as those of any society anywhere.

The members of the Boas circle fought and argued, wrote thousands of pages of letters, spent countless nights under mosquito nets and in rain-soaked lodges, and fell in and out of love with one another. For each of them, fame, if it ever arrived, was edged with infamy— their careers became bywords for licentiousness and crudity, or for the batty idea that Americans might not have created the greatest country that has ever existed. They were dismissed from jobs, monitored by the FBI, and hounded in the press, all for making the simple suggestion that the only scientific way to study human societies was to treat them all as parts of one undivided humanity.

A century ago, in jungles and on ice floes, in pueblos and on suburban patios, this band of outsiders began to unearth a dizzying truth that shapes our public and private lives even today.

They discovered that manners do not in fact maketh man.

It's the other way around.

Chapter Two

BAFFIN ISLAND

....

A half-century before Margaret Mead set off for Samoa, Franz Boas nurtured dreams of adventure in his own native land, the hills and fenlands of what would later become northern Germany. The thing that always made him feel the worst was being at home. His favorite book was *Robinson Crusoe*, he declared in a schoolboy memoir, and it had persuaded him to prepare for a future expedition to Africa, "or at any rate to the tropics." He practiced privation by eating great quantities of food he happened to hate. When a schoolmate drowned in a nearby river, he spent days in a rowboat searching, unsuccessfully, for the body.

He was born on July 9, 1858, into an assimilated Jewish household in Minden, a small town in Westphalia, then part of the Kingdom of Prussia. Every schoolchild in Europe knew of Boas's home province. It had given its name to one of the most important wartime accords in history, the Peace of Westphalia, in 1648. The settlement had ended the Thirty Years' War and established the basis for modern diplomacy. It laid the foundation for international law and structured the world as a system of sovereign nation-states. Order, limited power, and rationality were hailed as the foundation of global affairs, just as philosophers were proclaiming the same things as the essence of civilized life in general.

Even in a relatively backward place such as Minden, people of Boas's generation could still glimpse the fading afterglow of the Enlightenment. Schiller and Goethe had died only a few decades earlier. The Prussian naturalist-traveler-philosopher Alexander von

Humboldt—"the greatest man since the Deluge," according to one observer—although incapacitated by a stroke, remained a living link to the *philosophes* of the eighteenth century. The ideas these men had championed—reasoned debate, responsive governance, a life animated by dispassionate inquiry—had inspired the grandest wave of liberal revolutions Europe had ever seen.

Ten years before Boas was born, in 1848, armed uprisings had swept across the continent, challenging autocratic rulers from the Atlantic to the Balkans. Students, workers, intellectuals, and smallholding farmers called for justice and reform. Large public demonstrations in favor of a free press, the right to assemble, and national unification spread across the several German kingdoms and principalities. Barricades rose in Paris and brought down the constitutional monarchy of King Louis-Philippe. Hungarian and Croatian patriots fought their ruler, the Habsburg emperor. The months of disorder, violence, and hope would come to be called the "springtime of peoples." But winter soon set in. Country by country, monarchs reasserted their power. Individuals who had supported the old "Forty-Eighters," both on the cobblestones and in spirit, retreated to the universities and the liberal professions or were pushed into foreign exile. Politics was left to the likes of Otto von Bismarck, Prussia's iron-willed prime minister.

The retreat into local life was especially common if one happened to be Jewish. Prussia was at the time a "kingdom of shreds and patches," according to a contemporary traveler, a country with a complicated array of legal codes, religious restrictions, guild privileges, and municipal and provincial jurisdictions. Minden's Jewish population, as in many northern German towns, was tiny compared to the number of Protestants. Everyday antisemitism, like nearly everywhere in Europe, was a reality. Yet even in an age of renewed autocracy, well-placed Jews could be reasonably confident of their standing in local society. For the family of Meier and Sophie Boas, Franz's parents, being *bürgerlich*—urban, educated, freethinking, bourgeois—was as much a defining feature of life as being members of a minority faith.

Jews were at the literal and figurative heart of municipal affairs, with town houses in the city center and businesses lining the main streets. They were Minden's retailers and bankers, its craftsmen and professionals, and they governed themselves as a distinct community even before Prussia at last granted Jews full civil and citizenship rights in 1869. They paid communal taxes to keep the synagogues going and observed the Jewish holidays but—like the Boas family— also exchanged gifts at Christmas. They were part of a transnational network of commerce, travel, and assumed cosmopolitanism. Meier, formerly a modest grain merchant, had married well enough to enter deeper into that world. He shifted his career to the family business that Sophie, née Meyer, brought along as her dowry: the export of fine linens, tableware, and furniture for the Jacob Meyer firm of New York.

As the only son in a household of sisters, the young Franz was an exasperation to his practical father and an object of worry to his doting mother. He had a tendency to live in his head. He could be depressive and given to headaches, but also adventuresome and brave when something really mattered to him. As part of a reasonably well-to-do family, he eventually enrolled in the local high school, or *Gymnasium*, with its emphasis on classical languages and philosophy. He managed good marks in Latin, French, and arithmetic, even very good ones in geography. But he was the kind of child whom teachers might describe as a fine student though not a diligent one, a boy running from one enthusiasm to the next, rarely settling into anything for very long.

If he had one overarching tendency, he said, summing up his school career, it was to make systematic comparisons between things he observed in nature. When the family returned from a summer holiday in Heligoland, a British-held archipelago in the North Sea, Franz stymied the German customs officer by trying to import an entire trunkload of rocks he had collected for geological research. He saved the carcasses of small animals that he happened to find in the forest. His mother provided a pot so he could boil them up and remove their bones for further study.

When the time came to think about university—where boys in his social class were expected to go if they couldn't be persuaded to join the family firm—he dithered and prevaricated. He rejected his father's suggestion of a medical career. He might study mathematics or physics instead, although he had little sense of what employment those subjects might eventually produce. His guiding principle was that of many talented teenagers: to try to arrange things so that he would not become "unknown and unregarded," as he wrote to one of his sisters. In 1877 he enrolled at Heidelberg University, the Oxford of German institutions, where dreaming spires rose above a medieval city. He celebrated his first evening in town extravagantly by hiring a coach to carry him from the train station and then ordering up a full dinner at a local hotel.

Germany was now an empire, unified only a few years earlier in the wake of the Franco-Prussian War. As a boy, Boas had witnessed a military band leading uniformed soldiers toward the distant front lines in France. Now young men who had heard stories of the glory of combat made their university quads into improvised fields of honor. University students divided themselves almost instantly into associations of friends and confidants whose only real duty was to police the boundaries of the very associations they had made. Lubricated by drink, topped by rakish caps, and occasionally armed with sharp sabers, they lived in a society where personal slights could be rectified only by satisfaction in a staged fight.

On one occasion, when some neighbors complained loudly about a friend's piano playing, Boas escalated the confrontation into an argument and accepted an invitation to a duel. He sliced his opponent's cheek—a lucky blow, since his only instruction in fencing had been some impromptu lessons with two friends—and emerged with a small flap of scalp missing. But it was somehow reckoned he had won. Both duelists walked away with the thing young German men went to university to attain: a *Schmiss,* or dueling scar, worn as proudly as a hussar's brocade tunic. It was the first of at least five such encounters that Boas would have over the course of his university career, knife fights ennobled by a vaguely chivalric code. In later life, the scars would leave him scrimshawed like an old walrus tusk, with *Schmisse* on his forehead, nose, and cheek, a jagged line running from mouth to ear.

It was not unusual for students to make their way around Germany's great universities as itinerants, sitting in on lectures here, attending tutorials with a famous professor there, before finally taking exams for a degree. Boas went from Heidelberg to Bonn and then, in 1879, to Kiel, a good but not outstanding institution located in the northern lowlands along the Baltic Sea. The choice was mainly accidental. One of his sisters, Toni, was recuperating from an illness and under the care of a doctor in the city; Boas moved there to help look after her. He continued his studies in mathematics and physics and gradually began to hope that an independent research project might culminate in the award of a doctorate, the entryway to a career as a scholar and, if he got things right, some renown.

ALL THE INSTITUTIONS IN which Boas studied—and dueled— were heirs to the strain of thought that the philosopher Immanuel Kant had called the *Aufklärung*, the German version of the Enlightenment. French thinkers such as Descartes, Montesquieu, and Diderot speculated about the structure of natural law and the power of reason to shape law and government. They uncovered the mathematical elegance that underlay the apparent chaos of the natural world. Their English and Scottish counterparts, such as John Locke and David Hume, cautioned that true knowledge comes about through direct experience, not abstract speculation. But where these writers were concerned with Man and his ability to know the world, Germans were often concerned with men and their imperfect capacity to imagine it.

For Kant in particular, the human limits on abstract reason should be one of the chief subjects of philosophers, ethicists, and students of the natural world. We may live in a law-governed universe, Kant believed. All of creation may well fit a divine plan of order and perfection. Its deepest secrets, however, are always obscured by the frailty of our own minds. Our ideas about reality come to us through our senses, which should be treated as unreliable informants. Yet rather than being skeptical about everything we claim to perceive, the surest route to true knowledge was to turn our attention toward our perceptions themselves.

After all, while there are plenty of ways we might have wrong ideas about something we claim to see—a mirage, for example, or someone on the street whom we mistake for an old friend—we can't be wrong about our own sense of reality. We are all, by definition, experts in our own experience. The job of philosophers should be to study the space between the sense-perceptions that bombard us and the mental pictures we fashion of things as we believe them to be. The way to understand something about the world was to steer a course between a belief in the universal power of reason and an unbending skepticism about our ability to know anything at all. One of Kant's students, Johann Gottfried von Herder, even suggested that entire peoples could have their own unique frameworks for sense-making—a "genius" that was peculiar to the specific *Kultur* that gave rise to it. Human civilization was a jigsaw puzzle of these distinct ways of being, each adding its own piece, some more rough-edged than others, to the grand picture of human achievement.

No German university student could escape these exhilarating, liberating ideas. Boas read Kant, bought forty volumes of Herder's collected works, and pored over the writings of Alexander von Humboldt, who had proposed that all of nature should be seen as one interconnected system. Kiel turned out to have a particular focus on the practical application of these ideas. The university's faculty stressed scientific rigor, empirical observation, and a concern with the shifting appearances of things in the world. Some of the younger professors were beginning to propose experiments that would get at the relationship between physical reality and human perception. Following their lead, Boas offered a dissertation topic on the photometric properties of liquids. He proposed to study the way light is polarized by water, changing its appearance as it moves through some medium. It was a topic that would allow him to do real observation and to use Kiel's laboratory equipment to conduct original research, a requirement for an advanced degree.

He was soon busy shining light through test tubes containing different types of water and observing the properties on the other side. From a hired boat bobbing in Kiel's busy harbor, he lowered porcelain plates and mirrors into the murky water to try to test the point at which their reflected light changed in the depths. It was all inexpert and improvisational but enough to gain a grudging pass from the examiners. In July 1881, Boas was awarded the title of doctor of philosophy in physics.

At this point, however, he decided to make a shift. He had been bored by this research, as most dissertation writers eventually are, and the middling results of his water experiments—earning a degree magna cum laude but not summa—were never going to impress a fellowship board or hiring committee. Moreover, in order to teach in a German university, he would need a higher doctorate, or *Habilitation*, which would require yet another original research project. It was gradually dawning on Boas that his real interests lay not in working out the timeless laws of physics or in building rigorous mathematical proofs but rather in coming to understand the gulf between his own eye and those porcelain plates he had been dropping into the harbor.

As Boas knew, there is an objective color spectrum that shifts according to predictable laws when light passes through a medium such as water. But it is another thing entirely to try to understand how our minds interpret subtle shifts in light frequencies—the point at which we make the decision that something is no longer blue, say, but aquamarine. These were in fact entirely different research questions, he realized. One concerned the world of concrete reality, while the other had to do with sense perception, or as German university students had learned to name them, channeling Kant, the "noumenal" and "phenomenal" realms. Boas wanted to throw himself into the latter, to figure out not what the natural world *does* but how we determine for ourselves what we *think* it is doing. One way to do that was to begin to understand something about how people very different from yourself might see things. And that, in turn, required getting as far away as possible from familiar places such as Minden and Kiel.

LIKE MANY YOUNG MEN of his generation, Boas had been reared on tales of Arctic adventure. To head north was the cold-weather equivalent of European states' scramble for Africa. But the inhospitable conditions and sparse populations in the Arctic meant that it was usually not soldiers and traders but scientists and patriots who joined the race to the poles. Rather than gobbling up the land and labor of the people who lived there, the goal was exploration in its purest sense. Boas had imbibed the call to duty, instilled in every German schoolchild of means, to add to Germany's national greatness by reaching the ends of the earth before other nations got there.

Forty years earlier a British expedition had fallen victim to shifting ice, scurvy, and starvation. Over the next several decades, other British and American explorers charted the Arctic Sea, collected information on native peoples in the region, and tested the boundaries of human endurance in extreme climates. In the late 1860s and early 1870s, German adventurers and academics joined in as well. Two German polar expeditions fought pack ice, mapped the coast of Greenland, and collected botanical samples for further study by German universities. They never reached the North Pole, but their failure reinforced the enthusiasm for new attempts. A united Germany could now launch itself into the great game of global exploration.

Not long after defending his dissertation, Boas carefully wrote out a plan for his own private expedition: a study of the migration patterns of the native people living on Baffin Island, the fifth-largest island in the world. It was a place already reasonably familiar to German scientific researchers and to the Scottish and American whalers who frequented the coast. Boas spent months thumbing through the scientific literature, learning a smattering of Inuktitut, the language of the indigenous Inuit, and making contacts among geographers and explorers who might assist a young scientist seeking to start afresh in a new area of research. He persuaded a newspaper, the *Berliner Tageblatt,* to allow him to write a series of articles on his adventures. He told his editor that he might well become the German version of Henry Morton Stanley, the journalist who had famously located the explorer David Livingstone in central Africa. Stanley's articles for the *New York Herald* had been a sensation, and Boas reckoned that his could, too—especially if he managed, like Stanley, to write "with the color laid on thick," as he proposed.

Boas had done much of the early planning without telling his family. When he finally broke the news to his father, he also put forward a modest request—that his father foot much of the bill. It was all folly, Meier Boas must have felt, another of the sudden enthusiasms of an only son. Still, it might at least lead to the *Habilitation* degree and, from there, to an actual job. Meier reluctantly agreed, but on one condition: Boas was to take along a family servant, Wilhelm Weike, in the role of assistant and chaperone.

Back in Minden, Boas gathered Weike and said farewells to his family. He trained to confront danger by taking potshots with a revolver, which left him with a ringing in his ears. In mid-June 1883 Boas and Weike arrived in Hamburg, one of the empire's busiest trading centers, where steamships from far-off South America, India, and East Asia traveled up the Elbe River. On the docks, the pair made their way toward the *Germania,* an old sailing ship outfitted by the German Polar Commission, the empire's main coordinating body for Arctic expeditions. Its mission was to pick up another set of researchers who were just completing a yearlong stay on Baffin Island. The commission had agreed to allow two independent travelers to tag along for free.

The men lugged their supplies aboard: scientific instruments, winter clothing, maps, medicines, tents, and as much food as they could manage, along with tobacco, knives, needles, and other goods for barter, the fruit of the Polar Commission's donations and a father's indulgence. They then settled in for the slow journey toward the North Sea. "Farewell, my dear homeland! Dear homeland, adieu!" Boas jotted dramatically in his diary. The twin-masted *Germania,* attached by a cable to a tug, soon weighed anchor and turned its bow toward the open sea. Crowds cheered as it passed. In the age of steam, it was still thrilling to see an old-fashioned ship setting off, even with sails furled. Meier watched from the quay as the *Germania* disappeared downriver.

BOAS HAD ALREADY STARTED calling the people of Baffin Island "*my* Eskimos" that past spring. Over the previous century, the Inuit communities of the region had come into greater contact with European and North American whalers. They were now indispensable players in the surge in polar exploration. As Boas knew, there was no such thing as Arctic travel without their assistance, even though they rarely figured into the accounts that Europeans wrote when they got back home. There were few discoveries to be made that the Inuit hadn't made before. "I shall also engage some Eskimos to help me in my undertakings," he had written confidently in his two-page draft plan.

The Inuit had been well known to Europeans since at least the sixteenth century, when the English privateer Martin Frobisher set out to find the famed Northwest Passage between the Atlantic and the Pacific. Some of the earliest accounts classed them as fierce and crafty, living alongside packs of wolflike dogs. "They eate their meate all rawe, both fleshe, fishe, and foule, or something perboyled with bloud and a little water, whiche they drinke. For lacke of water, they wil eate yce, that is hard frozen, as pleasantly as we will doe Sugar Candie, or other Sugar," reported one of Frobisher's men, Dionyse Settle, in 1577. The crew collected evidence to prove their findings. "Two women, not being so apt to escape as the men were, the one for her age, and the other being incombred with a yong childe," he wrote, "we tooke." Four Inuit—a man, Kalicho; a woman, Arnaq; and her child, Nutaaq; along with another unnamed man—were eventually shipped to England. They became objects of curiosity to gawking Elizabethans before dying from disease and injuries sustained in their capture. They were the first North American aboriginal captives ever to be listed in European sources by name, rather than as just "an Eskimo" or "an Indian."

In the nineteenth century, European travelers found the Inuit to be of less interest than the environment in which they happened to live. The scientists whom the *Germania* was on its way to collect—members of a grand eleven-country effort at polar exploration launched in 1882—were concerned with noting meteorological patterns and understanding the earth's magnetic fields. But Boas had become fascinated by the Inuit themselves—their movement across vast distances, their capacity to survive in a difficult environment, and their ability to make sense of a landscape that could appear, to outsiders, bleak and formless.

He had formulated some initial hypotheses about the relationships among the availability of food, migration patterns, and the environment. But these were hazy, drawn only from reading the available scientific reports and attending a few scholarly seminars. Doing original research, filling notebooks with his own findings gleaned from local sources, he imagined, would launch him far beyond the inexpert experiments he had managed for his doctorate. "I would immediately be accepted among geographical circles," he wrote to his uncle, the exiled Forty-Eighter and prominent New York physician Abraham Jacobi, several months before setting out.

Now, as Boas and Weike hunkered down for a long sail, the North Sea winds screamed as the *Germania* turned toward Heligoland, an archipelago off the mouth of the Elbe. Barely two days into the journey, Boas was already seasick. The captain and the four-man crew set a long arcing course past the Shetland Islands and the Faroes, then Iceland and Greenland, and finally toward Baffin Bay, the gateway to the Canadian Arctic.

Every day became colder, and the sea seemed to change color from morning to afternoon, a phenomenon Boas diligently recorded in his diary. He passed the time by trying to teach Weike some English—"but he has a frightfully hard head," Boas jotted down—and recording the state of his own sea legs: "sick" on many days, "very sick" on others. Weeks passed on the nearly three-thousand-mile journey, with nothing off either side of the ship except calving icebergs that created booms like thunderclaps. Mirages loomed on the frigid sea, tricking the eye and making the two passengers think that a beautiful church had somehow been placed in the middle of the ocean. It was hard to know what was real.

In mid-July Baffin Island finally came into view, but getting to shore was impossible. Another six weeks went by before the captain and sailors could find a way to manage both the shifting winds and the wanderings of deadly icebergs. Finally, on August 26, the *Germania* made its way into Cumberland Sound, just south of the Arctic Circle, and toward the small settlement on Kekerten Island.

Village dogs howled as the ship came into sight. Inuit women, dressed in sealskin jackets covered with cotton petticoats, took to their launches and delivered a cable to the *Germania* for towing to anchor depth. Men of the whaling station hoisted British and American flags in greeting. Once they stepped ashore, Boas and Weike sipped a welcoming tankard of rum and watched as dogs dragged a dead walrus through the smattering of tents that defined the Inuit settlement. "They are not as dirty as I thought," Boas wrote of the tents, once he had been invited inside. "On shore I saw the first flowers; how happy I was." He plucked wild grasses and carefully pressed them in his notebook, squirreling away specimens much as he had done in childhood. "After a few days the ship left us," Boas later recalled, "and I was alone with my servant among the Eskimo."

Boas's plan had originally been to document Inuit movement across the island and map the ice floes, snowdrifts, and habits of seal pods. He quickly realized how difficult this would be in practice. The rough ice and weather forced him and Weike to remain for several months around Cumberland Sound, based mainly at Kekerten. But the time wasn't wasted. Boas had come prepared with a supply of notebooks, bound in leather and with marbled edges, like those he imagined a professional explorer might have. On the voyage out, he had filled pages with numbers, duly noting wind direction and latitude and longitude. Now, by the time he got halfway through his second notebook, he was scribbling down Inuit words, too—a self-created vocabulary list that he developed from long conversations in native tents and houses.

He was surrounded by these people. They far outnumbered the

small whaling community and the two amateur adventurers, and he found as the weeks passed that it was impossible to do anything without them. He spent long winter nights in conversation with Signa, a local Inuit man, in a mixture of foreign languages, while also picking up more and more of Signa's own. Somewhat to Boas's surprise, Signa turned out to have a personal history. He had been born elsewhere, on the coast of the Davis Strait, and had come to Kekerten as a boy. He grew up hunting deer on the great lakes to the west of the sound. His wife, whom the whalers knew as Betty, was generally jolly and accommodating but demanded that Signa bring back seal meat and blubber whenever he went out exploring with the German visitors, much as a Minden housewife might tell her husband to collect a parcel from the butcher. Signa was no timeless native simply struggling for survival on an unchanging shore. He had a past, with wanderings and movement, a family lineage, and remembered moments of hardship and joy.

From Signa and others in the community, Boas heard Inuit stories and began to write them down, just as he had recorded wind speeds and the color of seawater during the sail. His language skills were rudimentary, but he managed well enough in a combination of Inuktitut and pidgin English, the lingua franca of the whaling stations. He remarked on the games the Inuit played in their tents, the structure of their dogsleds, how to wear a caribou-hide suit properly, how to build an igloo, and how to navigate the unexpected frustrations that came with living in an intemperate world. Before long, his vocabulary lists morphed into longer texts in Inuktitut. He drew a family tree, scratching out early attempts with a pencil as he worked to figure out who was related to whom. He used musical notation, the fruit of childhood piano lessons in Minden, to note down songs, transcribing the melodies note by note in the keys of C or G.

He gathered up local expertise, asking people to draw line maps of the places they knew, along with information on sled routes and safe passages. He drew pencil sketches of insects—a mosquito, an ant, a spider in the middle of a gossamer web—and labeled them with their Inuit names. Then he wrote out entire stories, in a phonetically spelled version of Inuktitut. He made a rough census, tent by tent, of everyone who lived around Cumberland Sound. No one in Minden, and only a few of his esteemed professors in Heidelberg or Kiel, could have imagined any of this: that his life would now turn on whether an ice floe was smooth or rough, or whether sufficient dogs were available to pull a sled.

He now knew how hard it was to assemble a crew of boatmen if everyone was away chasing caribou, and how it felt when the sea currents dragged a seal carcass down into an ice hole and, with it, your dinner.

IN LATE OCTOBER an Inuit woman in Kekerten came to Boas with a fever, a cough, and congested lungs. From his supplies, he offered her a turpentine rub for her chest, quinine and opium for the fever and cough, and ammonia to inhale for some relief from the congestion. She took off her shirt, desperately trying to breathe more easily, and Boas placed his own shawl around her shoulders to protect her from the cold. The villagers asked him to check regularly on her condition. He was, after all, the person whom Weike always referred to, both in public and in private, as "Herr Doktor." To the Inuit, he was *Doktoraluk*—big doctor—and the person to whom one would naturally turn for medical advice and a quick cure, despite the fact that he was a trained physicist, not a physician.

Two days later the woman was dead. The next month a young boy died as well. Boas had sat beside him and watched his breathing grow more and more labored. People had always died from exposure or on seal hunts. Sometimes whalers were lost at sea. But this kind of death had never been seen before. Something seemed to be causing healthy women, men, and children to drown on dry land.

Boas was no medical expert, but he knew the symptoms. It was diphtheria, previously unheard of on Cumberland Sound but now racing from settlement to settlement, leaving a string of shattered families in its wake. He saw Inuit rip off their clothes and run wildly among the shacks and tents, screaming, when they discovered a dead relative. He watched them pull down an entire tent if someone had died in it, for fear that the dead person's spirit would infest the living world. "I keep telling myself that I was not to blame for the child's death," he wrote about one victim on November 18, "yet it weighs upon me like a reproach that I was unable to help." Children were now sick in every Inuit household, and in the coming weeks, reports of deaths farther afield filtered back to Kekerten.

The epidemic coincided with the arrival of Boas and Weike, and people made the obvious connection. At best, Boas was a sham doctor. At worst, it was whispered, he had somehow caused the deaths. A native healer named Napekin, living on the western shore of the sound, announced that no Inuit should host him in their homes, work as guides, or offer their sled dogs for travel. In January, Boas traveled across the sound to pay a personal visit and ask to be invited into his igloo. He reminded Napekin that he was his major source for ammunition and other supplies. Boas said he would withhold these goods unless Napekin allowed him to step across his threshold. Napekin relented and, later that spring, paid a return visit with gifts of sealskins and an offer of service on further expeditions on the island.

There were plenty of such encounters—negotiations and cajolings, apologies and amends, gifts offered and rescinded, hurt feelings and mistakes piling up alongside moments of forgiveness, and then finally some peace. To Boas, the inhabitants of Baffin Island had originally been objects of research, a feature of the landscape to be charted and studied. They had never quite been people. But as he actually lived among them, he could feel a change in his own logic, his own outlook on life. "Do you know, I once believed that I myself did not have a heart, because there were many things that I did not feel very intensely, or so I still feel," he wrote that December to Marie Krackowizer, a particular friend and, people might have suspected, even more.

I often ask myself what advantages our "good society" possesses over that of the "savages" and the more I see of their customs, I find that we really have no right to look down upon them contemptuously. Where among us is there such hospitality as here? Where are there people who carry out *any* task requested of them so willingly and without grumbling! We should not censure them for their conventions and superstitions, since we "highly educated" people are relatively much worse.

He had planned to uncover the general principles underlying the interaction of landscape, bad weather, and a hunting economy. He did manage to chart some of the movements of Inuit hunters and to reach stretches of Baffin Island previously unknown to outsiders. But he was also coming around to some realizations about himself. They came not only from listening to Inuit stories and sharing their meals but also from studying himself in interaction with them—perceiving his own perceptions, in a way. Real enlightenment, he began to see, came from owning his foibles and failures, seeing himself as inexpert and power-less, with the wind wailing outside a small hut or a shaman denouncing him as a bearer of evil and death. The environment seemed to demand self-reflection. The only way you could stave off frostbite before it took your nose, he now saw, was to have someone keep an eye on you and tell you when your skin started turning an unnatu-ral shade of white. On long outings with Signa by dogsled, survival depended on using his Inuit guide as a human mirror—looking at him face-to-face—while he returned the favor. "I believe that in every person and every people, renouncing tradition in order to follow the trail of the truth involves a very severe struggle," he wrote to Marie from Anarnitung, an Inuit encampment at the top of Cumberland Sound. The single greatest lesson he was learning, he said, was "my notion of the relativity of all education."

Here among the Inuit, a person with the title of "doctor" couldn't cure an ailing child. A university graduate knew nothing of snow and wind. An explorer was dependent on the whims of a dog team. He had seen it himself—the disorientation that comes with staring at one's own ignorance, as plain as a brown seal on white ice. Being smart was relative to one's circumstances and surroundings. There was even a convenient German word for the sense of regard that his hosts displayed toward him, as well as the reciprocal education that he was gaining from them. Boas had encountered it in the writings of Alexander von Humboldt and other philosophers he had read during his travels through Germany's great universities, and it seemed the perfect way to describe the change of spirit that had overtaken him in the north: *Herʒensbildung*, the training of one's heart to see the humanity of another. Changing his place in the world had changed his perspective on it.

That winter in Anarnitung, then back at Kekerten, and later in the spring, he mapped the areas to the west of the sound and trekked overland to the crystal water of Lake Nettilling, frostbitten and sunburned. Most nights found him inside a tent or an igloo, Weike perhaps on his right, an Inuit woman drying his things to his left, Signa and other Inuit men talking with mouths full of frozen seal meat. In the middle of it all was Boas himself, thawing out his ink and jotting down words in a notebook in the tiny, distinctive handwriting he called his *Krackelfüsse*, his chicken scratches.

IF HE LATER NEEDED proof of these moments of revelation, he had only to look back at the pages where he first recorded them. Even today, the blood from a raw seal liver is still visible on the paper. Boas and Weike remained on Baffin Island until the waning months of 1884. Just as their second Arctic winter was beginning, they hopped a succession of sailing vessels to Halifax, Nova Scotia, and from there caught a fast-moving ship to the United States. Their trunks were full of notebooks and hand-drawn maps, many of them produced by Inuit themselves, along with vocabulary lists, texts, sketches, and other materials. Boas had already sent back photographic plates and had dispatched articles, as promised, to the *Berliner Tageblatt*, which had gained him an avid readership across central Europe.

When the steamer *Ardandhu* arrived in New York on September 21, it had been some fifteen months since Boas set foot inside anything approaching a city. He and Weike had only their caribou hide suits left, so Boas now had to borrow clothes from the ship's captain to make himself presentable to the relatives who met him at the dock—

including Jacob Meyer, owner of the family business that had indirectly subsidized a fair amount of his travels.

They soon shared in the biggest news of all. Throughout his time in the north, Boas had been privately engaged to Marie, a young transatlantic Austrian, daughter of a respected New York physician, and the person to whom he had been pouring out his most intimate thoughts. Boas's cabin on the *Germania* had been decorated with a flag embroidered with her name, and he had left behind on Baffin Island a boat christened *Marie* in her honor. The two had met several years earlier at a mountain resort in Germany. Now she was notably absent from the gaggle on the pier. She was away at Lake George upstate, a favorite vacation spot, and Boas wasted no time catching a train north. He soon received the families' permission to publicize the engagement.

They must have given it reluctantly. Marie's background was impeccable—much closer to that of Sophie, Boas's mother, than to that of his less well-heeled father—and Boas had no real way of supporting a household. His professional life remained only a blueprint. He had no assurance of a professorship in Germany and certainly no route toward anything similar in the United States. He was now proposing to marry someone who lived an ocean away from his immediate family. Even his excursion into journalism had been, once again, subsidized by his father: Meier had given the *Berliner Tageblatt* a financial guarantee that his son would deliver the articles and not abscond with the cash advance the newspaper had paid him.

What Boas did have was energy. He was a talker, someone with little compunction about contacting people he didn't know or showing up at their offices with a long list of plans for an expedition or a revolutionary hypothesis he was burning to describe. He might lead off with a story about how his facial scars had been sustained in a polar bear attack, leaving his listener to wonder whether he was joking. After visiting Marie upstate, he began compiling the scientific results of the Arctic expedition, sending them off to learned journals and writing short pieces for the German American press. He knew that Washington, D.C., held a particularly strong collection of materials on the

Arctic, located within a new museum that was then being organized not far from Capitol Hill. Leaving Marie once more, he took the train south toward a meeting that he hoped might launch the next phase of his slow-motion career.

THE FEDERAL CITY IN the autumn of 1884 was in the midst of a whirlwind of political and social change. Chester A. Arthur, the sitting Republican president, watched from the White House as his party put forward another man, James G. Blaine, in that year's presidential race. His challenger, Grover Cleveland, was vying to become the first Democrat to claim the presidency since before the Civil War. Cleveland was a proven womanizer who had likely fathered a child out of wedlock. "Ma, Ma, where's my Pa?" became the Republicans' favorite chant at campaign rallies. The suffragette Belva Ann Lockwood made her own bid on the ticket of the Equal Rights Party, even though most women were not allowed to vote. A gigantic white obelisk dedicated to the memory of George Washington was nearly complete on the National Mall, sited midway between the Capitol and the great bend of the Potomac as it flowed past the old plantation at Arlington, Virginia. Once the granite point was placed on the top that December, it would become one of the capital's defining landmarks.

Passengers could see the structure when they stepped off the train from New York at the railway terminus near the western slope of Capitol Hill. From there Boas took the short walk across the Mall to a pair of sandstone and redbrick buildings. Nearly fifty years earlier, James Smithson, an amateur chemist and illegitimate son of an English duke, had bequeathed his considerable estate to the people of the United States for the purposes of scientific research and education. After years of wrangling over the disposition of the bequest, Congress had finally authorized the creation of something called the Smithsonian Institution in 1846.

To house it, architects had designed two bizarre buildings, one a whimsical castle, the other a collision between a European train station and a Coney Island carousel. Inside, the collections included an equally odd range of donations with dubious labels, such as "Head-dress worn by Atahualpa, the last of the Incas" and "One piece of the sycamore tree under which tradition says 'Joseph and Mary sat.'" But in Boas's day, anyone interested in exploration and the practical arts found the institution's twin buildings magnetic. They formed the core of what people were already calling America's National Museum, a name still to be found today carved in stone on the larger of the two structures.

Smithson had decreed that his money was to be used for the "increase and diffusion of knowledge." No country had a more visible symbol of the relationship between education and good government: the United States had decided to place its new museum complex near the republic's major institutions of governance, at the very heart of its capital city. Nor did any country have a more colorful and convincing spokesperson for this effort: the soldier, explorer, and scholar John Wesley Powell—the person Boas had come to see.

With his right sleeve pinned up to hide a missing arm and his ample beard resting on a barrel chest, Powell had crafted a life lifted straight from a children's adventure book. He was nearly a quarter-century Boas's senior, and any ambitious traveler or geographer might have been forgiven for thinking that all the truly great feats of discovery had already been accomplished by people of Powell's generation—if not by Powell himself.

Born in New York State, Powell had grown up on the western frontier at a time when white settlers were still clumped together in what they saw as a wilderness of unfelled forests and unconquered foes. He rambled in and out of college, a backwoods intellectual with a voracious appetite for reading and an ill-defined desire for exploration. He walked across Wisconsin. He rowed alone down the Illinois, Ohio, and Mississippi rivers, all the way to the Gulf of Mexico.

When war came in 1861, Powell enlisted as a private in the Union infantry. He soon raised his own company of artillery, where he could put to use some of the informal studies he had made of cannonball arcs, sightings, and fusillades. In April 1862, by then an officer, he saw action at the gruesome Battle of Shiloh in southwestern Tennessee. When he raised his right arm to give the order to fire, a minié ball tore through his wrist. A surgeon later removed the arm below the elbow. After recuperating, he returned to the field and helped drag his men and their guns to further engagements along the Mississippi and throughout the western theater. Between battles, he collected fossils from the trenches.

At the war's end, Powell barely rested before resuming the travels he had undertaken haphazardly as a younger man, this time with the aim of publicizing them. In 1869, commissioned by the Smithsonian, he made the first recorded float down the Green and Colorado rivers and through the Grand Canyon. He returned to make a similar journey in 1871 and 1872, an expedition that produced some of the first maps, diaries, and photographs of the wonders of the American Southwest.

When Powell published his *Exploration of the Colorado River of the West and Its Tributaries* in 1875—dictated to a scribe, since he was barely able to scrawl a signature with his left hand—he immediately became the best-known explorer in the country. The volume's unexciting title masked the literary decision that sealed Powell's fame: he had written the entire account in the present tense. "The good people of Green River City turn out to see us start," he began, midscene. "We raise our little flag, push the boats from shore, and the swift current carries us down." His you-are-there style gave readers a sense of urgency and uncertainty, as if they, too, were besting the rapids, with the Grand Canyon's chiaroscuro walls towering above their heads. Engravings from the era show Powell manhandling the tiller with one arm, the river spray engulfing his small boat and threatening to send it to the bottom.

By the time Boas arrived in Washington, Powell was the acknowledged leader among the country's naturalists and adventurers. Amateur explorers and former soldiers, bureaucrats and clergymen, the circle around Powell gradually coalesced into a new, untrained, but intellectually curious establishment committed to uncovering the natural wealth of the United States and making it intelligible to government planners. The informal parlor conversations Powell hosted in his home on M Street, N.W., would eventually become the Cosmos Club, a gathering place for the capital's foremost men of learning. His reports and practical advice to Congress on the management of land and water resources in the West gained him many friends and supporters. In 1879 he organized the first U.S. Geological Survey to provide information on physical geography, geology, and hydrography for policy makers.

At the same time, Powell was appointed to direct the government's new Bureau of Ethnology. Just as the Geological Survey was conducting work on the physical wealth of the western territories, the bureau's task was to do the same thing among the peoples who lived there. In later years, much of what Americans thought they knew about their own frontier—its topography and its river systems, its mountain ranges and its prairies, its indigenous inhabitants and their languages—would be shaped by Powell's vigorous research and collecting. By the mid-1880s, the Geological Survey and the Bureau of Ethnology had more staff, more money, and more ambitious projects than any other learned organization in the world, dwarfing anything Boas might have seen in Germany. Its annual reports were thousand-page doorstoppers of original findings, meticulously edited and illustrated, and each one introduced by Powell's summary of that year's discoveries about native peoples and their ways. They were so important that they were entered, every page, into the record of the Smithsonian's direct overseer, the U.S. House of Representatives.

Other countries had royal academies and private museums, but in the United States, basic science now bore the imprimatur of the country's highest representative body—as if the people themselves were surveying the land bestowed on them by Providence. It was all enormously exciting, and for any ambitious young explorer, to be in Powell's orbit was to feel at the very center of something big and wonderful. An entire continent provided raw material for original research, and a national government had appropriated the money and manpower necessary to undertake it. There was no one in the world whom Boas might have more readily wanted to meet—or truth be told, to *be*—than Powell.

But that was also why, for Boas, actually meeting Powell turned out to be such a disappointment. There were no open positions in the Bureau of Ethnology, Powell informed him. Nor was the broader Smithsonian prepared to do any further hiring. Despite the generous budget of both institutions—and plans for their merger into a new museum of natural history—Boas had arrived, it seemed, a few years too late. The staff positions had all been allocated. Plans for further exploration and mapping expeditions had already been put in place. Even as he spoke, the bureau's researchers were completing massive studies of treaty relations with the Cherokee, Navajo chants and ceremonies, customs of the Florida Seminoles, child rearing among the Zuñi, and other topics.

Boas had little to recommend him besides recent field experience, none of it in the United States. Still, Powell agreed to publish some of his Baffin Island work, once it was written up, in the next installment of the bureau's annual report. This was at least something to show for his trip to Washington, but even then Boas worried that the money Powell offered would not be sufficient to cover the project's full cost. Maps would have to be drawn and etchings made. He would also need help with his English. His command of the language might have impressed Weike or Signa, but it did not move his American hosts. He found himself unable to follow the discussion during a meeting of one of Washington's scholarly societies, and a secretary was forced to read Boas's paper aloud while he looked on in silence. He soon returned to New York, depressed and embarrassed. Two lectures that he was invited to give at Columbia College, arranged by Uncle Jacobi, proved yet another linguistic disaster.

Every application for employment in New York and Washington was rejected. No museums or universities seemed to be hiring. He now had little choice. He would have to return to Germany. The news must have thrilled Meier and Sophie, but for Boas it represented defeat. Marie would stay behind, their marriage postponed, until he could acquire the credentials that might put him in a position to land a real job. In March 1885 he set off on the return journey across the Atlantic, not knowing for sure when, or if, he would return.

His only consolation was that his English had improved enough for him to be able to name how he felt. It was a state of mind that he had learned from Marie to call "the blues."

Chapter Three

"ALL IS INDIVIDUALITY"

....

When he arrived here," Sophie Boas wrote from Minden to Abraham Jacobi back in New York, "he was so downhearted and discouraged after all of his failures over there, that my heart bled for him." Boas could not have picked a worse time to leave the United States. The scientific field that he had been circling since his voyage to Baffin Island was on the brink of an explosion, one that he was now well placed to miss.

A version of the word *anthropology* had been around since Aristotle, but in the nineteenth century, it was most likely to refer to the study of the development of human beings as a species: the unearthing of bones and skulls that might shed some light on how a thing called *Homo sapiens* originally came about. Scholars were only beginning to see the subject as worthy of its own separate professional label or university department. One of the first professors appointed with the title of "anthropologist," Edward Burnett Tylor of Oxford University, defined the field simply as "the science of Man." He began his textbook on the subject, in 1881, by inviting his readers to stand with him on the docks of Liverpool or London and mark the myriad varieties of humanity as they paraded past: "the African negro" with "flat nose, wide nostrils, thick protruding lips, and . . . the remarkable projecting jaws" or "the Chinese . . . [with] his jaundice-yellow skin, and coarse, straight black hair." Some of the earliest scholarly bodies to use the term—Britain's Royal Anthropological Institute or the chair in anthropology at the French Musée d'histoire naturelle—likewise conceived of the field as a branch of anatomy or natural history, the study of physical changes in plants and animals over geological time. The word that defined John Wesley Powell's area of interest—*ethnology*—was far newer, coined only in the 1840s. If anthropology was the study of the Greek *anthropos*, or literally a "human" as a kind of being, ethnology was the study of humans in the context of their *ethnos*, the specific societies or communities—nations, ethnic groups, tribes, races—into which they seemed to sort themselves. Such a "science of Culture," as Tylor called it, would reveal how "a stone arrowhead, a carved club, an idol, a grave-mound, . . . a sorcerer's rites, . . . the conjugation of a verb" represented a primitive people's way of life as readily as tables of imports and exports described that of a civilized one. How had these social groups come about? How did they differ from one another in their languages and habits? What worldview animated them, and how did they derive their peculiar ways of thinking about everything from who counted as kin to the proper way of summoning the gods?

In answering these questions, the chief requirements for renown were an academic chair and access to the postal service. Tylor acceded to his post at Oxford in part by sifting through the writings of collectors and adventurers who described how things were supposedly done, said, and believed among a remote and exotic population. One of his contemporaries, the lawyer and Cambridge don James G. Frazer, assembled his own comparative study of classical texts and reported religious practices in a work he called *The Golden Bough* (1890). Frazer surveyed classical written sources for the origins of magic and mythology—or the "primitive religion" of the "Aryan race," as he had it—but he also believed there was evidence to be found just beyond one's own door. "Indeed, the primitive Aryan, in all that regards his mental fiber and texture, is not extinct," he wrote in the opening pages. "He is amongst us to this day" in the "superstitious beliefs and observances of the peasantry." For scholars such as these, the secrets of human societies lay mainly in the texts they produced: sacred literature, inscriptions, hieroglyphics, or epic tales noted down by medieval scribes or modern translators. Oral traditions and the contemporary "religion of the woodman and the farmer," as Frazer said, were valuable to the degree that they shed light on these ancient practices.

The mission of Powell's Bureau of Ethnology, however, was to be more systematic, professional, and data-oriented—to go beyond what was written and ancient into what was observable and alive right now. Its task, buttressed by the full power and budget of the U.S. government, was to delineate and catalog the origins, languages, and customs of the various groups that had inhabited the American landscape before the arrival of Europeans. It was also a route toward making sense of their living remnants—the native women and men whom any traveler could still encounter on a train journey west. This was all the more important since the government was now charged with managing them.

With the passage of the Indian Appropriation Act of 1871, Congress rejected the old system of negotiating with Indian tribes. Washington no longer saw indigenous groups mainly as collectivities, homegrown nations with which it concluded formal treaties, as it did with foreign powers. From this point forward, individual Indians were to be treated as "wards" of the federal government. They were now placed in a legal netherworld between foreigners and full citizens, a status that would only come several decades later. Their tribal identities ceased to be the concern of state officials and became instead the purview of artifact collectors and museum curators.

IT WAS POWELL'S INTELLECTUAL mentor—a businessman and part-time scholar from Rochester, New York—who had provided the philosophical schema that would map out precisely how the bureau's "ethnologists" were supposed to go about their work of describing and explaining Indian societies. Lewis Henry Morgan was, like Powell and Boas, an enthusiast who had stumbled into his vocation. He was born in 1818 into a family of landowners and educated townspeople. Upstate New York was booming, with the rise of local manufacturing and the flood of commercial goods that made their way down the Erie Canal, which opened in 1825. It may have been the sheer pace of change that made upstaters especially eager to look for rootedness. As Morgan was growing up, people all around him seemed obsessed by the idea that America was secretly more ancient than it seemed.

In town after town, people were awakening to hidden realities suddenly revealed by a succession of seers, mystics, and spiritual guides. Near Rochester, a farmer named Joseph Smith claimed to have found metal tablets containing the writings of a long-ago prophet, Mormon, who had described a lost American civilization visited by Jesus Christ. Smith's followers took the name Latter-Day Saints in order to distinguish themselves from those who had inhabited the same hills and forests in a simpler, less corrupt time. Farther to the east, members of the Oneida Community believed that human perfection could come through the recognition that Christ's second coming had already taken place long ago. The recipe for happiness was to resurrect the old ways forsaken by modern society, from free love to communal property.

For Morgan, the recoverable past was embedded in the seeable present. It lay in the scattered indigenous communities that were dotted to the south and east of Lake Ontario. His particular obsession was the former Iroquois Confederacy, the alliance that had once united the Mohawk, Onondaga, Oneida, Cayuga, Seneca, and Tuscarora peoples into a complex political and economic unit. The confederacy had gradually faded after the arrival of French and British settlers, but in the 1840s, Morgan and several associates drew up a quixotic scheme to re-create it. This revived union, they hoped, would reacquaint both Indians and Europeans with a purer, more authentic way of life, resurrecting the prior civilization that had once existed on American soil.

Rituals were devised for the "Inindianation" of white recruits, with new phonetically spelled Iroquois names and divisions into tribes and bands. Space was borrowed from the Freemasons for holding secret meetings. Plans for teaching native languages were drafted. But like many similar schemes during what came to be called the Second Great Awakening—the widespread American spiritual renewal of the mid-nineteenth century—the whole project eventually fell by the wayside. The new confederacy's membership peaked at perhaps four hundred men. Morgan moved on with building his own businesses and starting a family. What survived, however, was his abiding interest in documenting the past and present of his Iroquois neighbors.

As he traveled around New York's Finger Lakes district, he found himself meeting more and more indigenous men and women, even developing genuine friendships with them. He was shocked to see how many families had been swindled in land deals and pushed off their ancestral territories. In 1851 he published everything he had learned as *The League of the Ho-de'-no-sau-nee or Iroquois*. The book was soon regarded as the definitive study of the history, language, and customs of the greatest Indian alliance ever to have existed on the continent, especially notable for its peculiar politics, which placed women in the role of clan leaders and decision makers. "To encourage a kinder feeling towards the Indian, founded upon a truer knowledge of his civil and domestic institutions, and of his capabilities for future elevation, is the motive in which this work originated," wrote Morgan in the preface. The "residue" of these old ways, as he called it, was still there for anyone who might wish to see it; properly understood, it could contribute to the Indians' "reclamation" as full citizens of the United States. He dedicated the book to Ely Parker, a Seneca translator and attorney who had become his primary informant and research partner.

The League of the Ho-de'-no-sau-nee was followed, in 1877, by *Ancient Society*, a broader work in which Morgan attempted to create a global model for how human societies organize themselves and their property, based on his knowledge of the Iroquois but also including cases from Greece, Rome, and around the world. All societies run through the same stages in their evolution, Morgan believed. In ancient times and in our present moment, it was possible to discern the laws that governed the transition from simpler forms of organization—families, brotherhoods, tribes—to modern, complex nation-states. Morgan's work was considered so pathbreaking that other theorists credited him as an authority in understanding social change. Charles Darwin quoted him in *The Descent of Man* (1871) on the development of marriage patterns and kinship systems. Karl Marx took reading notes on *Ancient Society*, especially on what Morgan identified as the three major stages of social evolution, which he termed savagery, barbarism, and civilization. Friedrich Engels cribbed much from Morgan in his own *The Origins of the Family, Private Property, and the State*, published in 1884. John Wesley Powell followed their lead. When he began to imagine how the Bureau of Ethnology should go about its work, he made Morgan's *Ancient Society* required reading for the entire staff.

IN MARCH 1886, Powell rose before a grand meeting of Washington's scientific elite to lay out a vision for the future, one grounded in Morgan's thought. "The course of human events is not an eternal round," he began. We can see progress all around us, not just a succession of the same events over and over again. History had a direction. Anthropology should be the science of change, whether in the physical appearance of humans or in the whole panoply of behaviors, institutions, and customs that defined the *ethnos* that ethnologists took as their object of study.

For Powell, there was a clear road map for how those changes came about. "There are stages of human culture," he stated plainly, channeling Morgan. Human societies naturally move from savagery to barbarism to civilization, each having its particular characteristics in "all the grand classes of activities," the "culture" specific to that stage of development. Individual people might fail to exhibit all the characteristics of the stage in which they were embedded; they might be "degraded," "decayed," or "parasitic" versions of human culture—"like the gypsies," Powell explained. (If he wanted an example—the potential savagery of civilization, say—he could look down at his own missing right arm, lost to the modern-day horrors of Shiloh.) But "the general progress of culture" was toward ever higher achievements.

The stages of progress often blended into one another. "To the scientific man the absolute light and the absolute darkness are never found, but the phenomena of light and darkness cover infinite degrees of chiaroscuro, with absolute light on one hand and absolute darkness on the other, beyond the boundaries of observed phenomena and existent only in statement." The ethnologist was meant to live in this half-light, to study the frontiers between the stages of human progress and to describe how different peoples have traveled from one era of human culture to the next; the development of languages and other specific characteristics that defined each of them; the various institutions— from tribes to states—that enabled them to remain coherent units; and their changing opinions about life and the universe, their "mentations," as Powell had it.

All this sometimes took place at glacial speeds; at other times— for example, when savage communities came into contact with civilized ones, as was happening right at that moment in the American West—it could be very rapid indeed. But the starting point was to understand that people unlike ourselves weren't simply degraded or lesser versions of some obvious ideal. They were at different stages along a common path of human progress, each one having its own traits and inner logic.

"The age of savagery is the age of stone," Powell said; "the age of barbarism is the age of clay; the age of civilization is the age of iron." Savages clung to primary kinship groups, small families of people descended from the same ancestor. Barbarians clustered in bigger units such as the tribe. Civilized peoples had devised the nation-state, with its system of formal government and clear territorial boundaries well defended against attack. Savages could manage only individual words and simple concepts, while barbarians expressed themselves in complex phrases; civilized peoples used languages capable of handling complicated, abstract ideas. Music, too, differed from one stage to the next. Savages might beat out a rhythm on a log or a stone, but barbarians sang a melodic line, while civilization added counterpoint and harmony. The gods of savages were many, often represented as a beast or fowl. Barbarians turned the forces of nature into their gods.

Civilized men had realized, at last, that the divine was a single force, with one name and identity.

The essence of humanity was what Powell called its "humanities," the ability to make language, create institutions, and apply reason to understand the world. His grammatical tautology was in fact a daring bit of philosophy, for he was taking Morgan's schema and turning it into a weapon. It was aimed squarely at those who believed that change in human societies operated according to the same laws that drove the differentiation of species in the natural world. The English biologist Herbert Spencer had recently coined the term "survival of the fittest" to describe the fight for biological superiority outlined by Darwin in his *On the Origin of Species* (1859). For Spencer and other theorists, societies, too, were engaged in a struggle for survival, and nature itself determined which peoples would, through their superior achievements and worldviews, dominate the less providentially endowed. On the contrary, Powell claimed, social evolution was not at all like biological evolution. Change in society was instead a human-centered progression from lower to higher forms of thought, behavior, and institutions. No people was inherently incapable of completing the same transformative journey already taken by others. Ethnology, then, was simply the act of civilized man conversing with those who had yet to travel the same pathway he had once trod.

The response to Powell's speech went unrecorded, but it must have been electrifying. The sponsoring organization, the Anthropological Society of Washington, included the city's foremost curators and professors, and even the separate Women's Anthropological Society had been allowed to attend. Powell had firmly established Morgan's tripartite schema as the boxes into which any society could be immediately placed. He had separated the object of ethnologists' concern— culture—from those things studied by biologists. This reframing opened up an entire world of possibilities for his bureau. One might study the savage Sioux, who wandered in dislocated tribes across the Western Plains, or the merely barbarous Iroquois, whose elaborate confederal politics Morgan himself had eloquently described, or even the civilized Englishmen who had brought industry and commerce to the New World. Instead of an undifferentiated mass of peoples, the world now appeared as a finite set of types, each of them at different way stations along the same human highway.

A few years later, across Washington from Powell's home, construction began on a magnificent new building to house the Library of Congress. When it was completed, in 1897, readers could walk up the grand exterior staircase and come nearly face-to-face with Powell's schematic hierarchy of the human world. A collection of thirty-three granite heads, designed from models in Powell's collections, served as grotesques above the second-story windows. The civilized European peoples were placed near the front door, facing the Capitol. Barbarous Chinese and Arabs wrapped around the sides. Savage Africans and Pacific Islanders hid around back. Even today, by circling the outside walls of the library's main Jefferson Building, visitors can take a visual journey along the path that Morgan and Powell had described.

BOAS HAD ALREADY SENSED that American scholars were working toward a scientific framework that could help organize the disconnected observations he had made on Baffin Island. It took only a few months back in Minden to realize that the decision to return to Germany had been a terrible mistake.

He managed to publish a short book in German on his Baffin Island expedition, which allowed him to secure the coveted higher doctorate that would be required for a professorship. Now he had only to wait until one of the empire's small cadre of professors was kind enough to die and open up a spot. He was offered a few lectures, paid more or less by the hour, and was taken on as a research assistant at the prestigious Royal Ethnological Museum in Berlin. There he worked for a time in the shadow of two of the principal figures in the human sciences in Germany, Rudolf Virchow and Adolf Bastian, both of whom encouraged exactly the kind of fieldwork that Boas had stumbled into organizing on his own. But even then he had little hope of advancement beyond cataloging artifacts. It all seemed enormously dull, and the pull from across the Atlantic was immense. Marie, for one thing, was unlikely to leave her family in Manhattan for an uncertain future in Germany. The decision almost made itself. In July 1886, just over a year after his reluctant homecoming, Boas boarded an ocean liner bound for New York. He wasn't quite sure of it at the time, but he was coming back to stay.

Boas was one of nearly 1.8 million German speakers who settled in the United States between 1880 and 1900, the peak of German immigration. Marie's family, the Krackowizers, as well as Boas's uncle, Abraham Jacobi, were among the professionals and political activists who had fled central Europe in the wake of the failed 1848 revolutions. They had been pioneers of a sort, eager to set themselves apart from the farmers and shopkeepers who crowded the steerage sections of the same ships. But now, to people in Boas's wave—more urban and more skilled than those who had come before, often Protestant and Jewish rather than Catholic, and like Boas, typically male and unmarried—arriving in America was not about starting over in a strange country. New York seemed as much a German city as an American one.

Only two cities in the world at the time, Vienna and Berlin, could count bigger German populations. Had the residents of a single Manhattan neighborhood known as Kleindeutschland, or Dutchtown—more famous in later years as the Lower East Side—been magically transported back to Kaiser Wilhelm's Reich, they would have instantly formed the empire's fifth-largest city. Germans were so successful and so numerous in New York that even outside Kleindeutschland, it was not uncommon to hear your doctor, your college professor, your bookseller, your barkeep, and your piano teacher—playing on a German American Steinway, perhaps—all speaking English with the same foreign accent.

Rising in life meant rising on the map, which is why Boas's first stop when he arrived was not the small shops and artisanal factories of Kleindeutschland, but the Krackowizer home on West 60th Street. The reunion with Marie had to be postponed, since she was again visiting relatives upstate, so in the following weeks, Boas kept himself busy developing a new network of scholarly contacts. He hit up family members and acquaintances in the German community for recommendations and, occasionally, a loan. He had no job and, even with his newly minted *Habilitation* degree, no prospects for one. His English was still so shaky that he passed up an opportunity to read a paper before the prestigious American Association for the Advancement of Science, fearing that his grammatical mistakes would mark him as a rube. But he was more optimistic than he had been in over a year. "I see such a wide and free field of labor before my eyes that the mere thought excites me," he wrote to his parents in August.

Meanwhile he wasted no time in scouting a new field site for the next phase of his research. While working at the museum in Berlin, he had made the acquaintance of a group of Bella Coola, or Nuxalk, Indians visiting from British Columbia. He was fascinated by their language and ritual dances, performed with elaborately carved wooden masks. The indigenous peoples of the Pacific Northwest were known for their large plank-built lodges, their intricately designed monumental poles, and the institution of the potlatch, in which the heads of families competed for who could give away the most food and treasure to the rest of the community, sometimes to the point of personal ruin. The region might provide a good follow-on from his Baffin Island work, Boas reckoned, not least because it afforded him an opportunity to gain some expertise on a North American topic. It might also place him in a better position to find permanent employment in New York or Washington. In the autumn of 1886, with a loan from Uncle Jacobi and the chance to earn more money by collecting a few artifacts to sell to a museum, he set off for the West.

THE NORTHERN PACIFIC RAILWAY had reached the ocean only recently, depositing its passengers at a young port city called Tacoma, Washington. From there, Boas could take a coal-fired steamer on the Salish Sea to the Canadian province of British Columbia. Inlets and fjords defined the ragged coastline, with great stands of Douglas fir and Alaskan cedar wrapped in dense mist, hiding logging camps and fisheries. Farther off, the peaks of the Olympic range stood out snowy against the sky. "Vancouver makes a very strange impression," he wrote.

> It is scarcely a year since the city arose from the wilderness, the moment it became known that the Canadian Pacific would have its terminal here. Where there are no houses, even in the middle of the city, there are burned or burning tree stumps. People from all lands, no one really seeming at home, swarm about the streets, which are covered with wooden planks. The streets are not yet completely finished, and where there are no wooden side streets, as well as other streets not covered with wood, there is nothing but impassable swamp. A white collar is still an event in Vancouver, but all this seems to be disappearing rapidly.

"The stranger coming for the first time to Victoria is startled by the great number of Indians living in this town," Boas reported about the provincial capital. He estimated that the total Indian population in British Columbia stood at thirty-eight thousand people, with most living along the coast and far outnumbering people of European descent. They dressed, he was surprised to see, in the European fashion and worked as stevedores, fishmongers, and washerwomen, their shacks and light tents dotting the suburbs. They spoke a variety of unrelated languages, and their social organization seemed different as well: some tribes, such as the Tlingit, divided themselves into powerful clans, and others, such as the people Boas knew as the Kwakiutl, gave pride of place to a complex system of secret societies much revered, even feared, by ordinary people. What united the Indians, however, was "their highly developed artistic taste," Boas wrote, in particular the stunning wood carvings and paintings of stylized animals that decorated their lodges.

The rain could turn the limited roads into impassable sloughs, but it was at least more bearable than the pack ice and subzero temperatures of Baffin Island. Boas threw himself into his work. "I go about visiting and listening to stories," he wrote to his parents, "then write until my fingers are lame." At the end of each day of conversations and travel, he would rush to get down everything he had heard. Over the next few months, he filled more than three hundred pages of his leather-bound notebooks, keeping a running tab in his dispatches to Meier and Sophie back in Germany.

He decided to concentrate on collecting myths and folktales up and down the coast, focusing mainly on Vancouver Island. He already had a few words of Bella Coola, which he had picked up from the visiting Indians in Berlin, and could make his way in Chinook, a simplified trading language. But he mainly relied on the same technique he had often used back home: buttonholing someone he barely knew, a Christian missionary perhaps, or an English-speaking local, and politely demanding that they accompany him to an urgent meeting. George Hunt, a half-Tlingit, half-English man who had married into Kwakiutl society, served as his guide and point of entry, much as Signa had done on Baffin Island.

Things worked better at some times than others. On one occasion he spent two hours taking down an intricate text, carefully dictated to him by a woman from the coastal village of Comox, only to be told by an interpreter that what she had been saying the entire time was a long, made-up conversation. She had thought he was just looking for language practice.

The problem was how to make sense of it all. An old man and an old woman practically came to blows when trying to answer Boas's questions, he reported from Somenos, a village in the valley of the Cowichan River.

He said a man had lain dead for nine days and she said ten, whereupon he became so angry that I could not get another word out of him. . . . Every five minutes he assures me he is the best among all the men here and knows everything. In the meantime screaming, dirty children run about; sometimes a meal is eaten. Dogs and chickens force their way between the people; the fire smokes so badly one can hardly see. The old man watches to see that I write down every word he says, and, if I fail to do so, he takes it as a personal insult and holds a long speech of which I do not understand a word.

Even then, the myths were sometimes so full of coarseness and ribaldry, he worried he would never be able to publish them. "They always try to bluff strangers," Boas complained. That was a problem for science, but it was also a problem for history. What he didn't manage to collect now might never be collected at all.

Once while wandering near the rocky seashore near Comox, on Vancouver Island, he discovered that the entire area was scattered with human bones. It was all that remained of an old burial site that had been tilled up by a local farmer. The new Canadian Pacific Railway would soon cut through these lands, bringing freight cars of industrial goods and passenger wagons full of white settlers. More of this kind of thing could be expected: plank lodges would be torn down to make way for modern houses, a graveyard would be covered by a new road, old bones would bleach on the pebble beach. The work was a race against time, just as it had been among the Inuit. Whether from diphtheria or steam engines, the old ways, or what was left of them, would soon be gone. He was amazed to find that no one—not the local settlers, nor even the Indians themselves—seemed to think of all this as a tragedy. News of his own arrival and departure—a German doctor carrying out ethnological research on the frontier—was what made headlines. He departed a minor celebrity.

WHEN HE RETURNED TO New York that December, Boas hoped that he would have time to write up his findings and present them to an American publisher. A book in English would surely establish his reputation as a serious scholar. Instead, a month later, an opportunity landed in his lap. A position as an assistant at *Science* magazine had come available, and after one dinner with the editor, Nathaniel D. C.

Hodges, the job was his. He cabled his family that he was formally taking up residence in America. He told Marie they could now make plans for a spring wedding.

Science was a young and struggling journal, founded in 1880 as a "weekly record of scientific progress," as its title page announced. Boas's assignment was to manage the publication of articles in the domain of geography—which was how he still described his primary area of interest—and to prepare maps and unsigned notes on developments in the discipline. But it also provided him with something he had never quite had before: a relatively secure platform from which he could present not only his field observations and geographical descriptions but also some of the broader ideas that he had begun to formulate about the emerging social sciences.

Geographers and ethnologists should give up trying to model themselves after physicists and other students of the natural world, he wrote in one of his first forays in the pages of *Science*, in early 1887. It was impossible to generalize about a thing that depended fundamentally on context, like why a myth about a raven seems to mean one thing in Comox but something else entirely down the Salish coast. By its very nature, ethnology was dependent on a particular time and a particular place. It was animated by the drive to understand "the life of man as far as it depends on the country he lives in."

One place had gotten all this profoundly wrong, he felt: the National Museum in Washington, D.C., and the community of eminent scholars gathered around John Wesley Powell.

Not long after returning from British Columbia, Boas had made a trip to Washington to study the Smithsonian's collections on the peoples of the Northwest Coast. The institution in many ways still bore the hallmarks of its type, a kind of proto-museum known in German as a *Kunstkammer*, an assemblage of curiosities that Renaissance and early modern kings and princes had once dragged together for the delight of themselves and their friends. They were jumbles of oddities: clothing from a distant, perhaps fantastical tribe, the skeleton of a malformed animal, an especially large tumor, or most famously, at Oxford's Ashmolean Museum, the fragmentary remains of a dodo that would later inspire a character in Lewis Carroll's *Alice's Adventures in Wonderland.*

By contrast, modern museums of natural history and ethnology, which had developed gradually over the course of the nineteenth century, were concerned with classification. They were meant not just to astonish or entertain but to instruct the public. Objects had to be placed according to some logical plan, rather than be shoved willy-nilly into cabinets or piled on tables. The new buildings of the British Museum (which opened in the 1850s), Boas's old Royal Ethnological Museum in Berlin (founded in the 1870s), and the Pitt Rivers Museum in Oxford (established in the 1880s) cleaned up what had been a mess of feathers, stone, and wood into a neater array. To walk through their open and airy galleries was to stroll through a rational, comprehensible world, to see the inner logic of nature—flora, fauna, fossil, and footprint—unrolling before your eyes.

It struck Boas that the Smithsonian's National Museum told a similar story. The museum's curator for ethnology, Otis Tufton Mason, was one of Powell's partners and had overseen the transfer of the bureau's collections to the new building, just east of the Smithsonian Castle. He had helped found the Anthropological Society of Washington, where Powell had given his speech on the stages of human development, and he had designed the new museum as the instantiation of these ideas. Since rituals, tools, weapons, styles of dress, and other habits and practices passed through definite stages—as Morgan and Powell insisted—it was appropriate to group together all the bone rattles or all the animal-hide drums, regardless of their geographic origin, in the same place. They were, after all, common expressions of a distinct evolutionary stage. Like individual cars on a train, they were all rolling at more or less the same speed through stations marked "Savagery" and "Barbarism" toward the terminus, "Civilization."

The more Boas made his way around the vitrines, the odder all this seemed. In Vancouver and Victoria, he had seen how messy ethnology was in practice. The reality of fieldwork was a far cry from the clarity presented to museum visitors. The organization of the collections seemed to reflect the *collector's* sense of what an object was for, as opposed to the worldview of the artisan who had originally made it. A viewer had no way of discerning the use that the maker might have intended for it, nor how it was actually employed in its original context.

Once he got back to New York, Boas put some of these thoughts down on paper. In June he wrote to "Major Powell," as the great man was typically called, stating that he had come around to a "fundamental question" for ethnology toward which he wanted to direct his own research: "How far does an influence of the surroundings exist?" he wrote. It was the first clear statement—even in his still imperfect English—of the question that had been animating Boas since he set off for Baffin Island. "The longer I studied the more I became convinced that the phenomena such as customs, traditions, and migrations are far too complex in their origin . . . to enable us to study their psychological causes without a thorough knowledge of their history." He had been able to come to no clear conclusions about how geography shaped the migration patterns of "his Eskimos." Likewise, on the Northwest Coast, he had found that songs, stories, and myths seemed to follow no obvious pattern, even among peoples living in close proximity. He wondered, therefore, whether "historical facts are of greater influence than the surroundings." The next issue of *Science*, he said, would contain some thoughts along these lines—as well as a full-bore critique of one of Powell's colleagues, the venerable Smithsonian curator Otis Tufton Mason.

"We cannot agree with the leading principles of Professor Mason's ethnological researches," he wrote plainly in the magazine that May. In his own writings and in the organization of the museum, Mason had overlooked an obvious possibility. It might be the case that like conditions produced like effects, but there were numerous instances in which like conditions produced very different ones. On the Northwest Coast, Boas had found both wide variety and striking similarities among indigenous communities, with nothing to suggest that the Bella Coola and Salish, for example, were all at the same stage of development. The same environment—pine forests and fishing, rainy winters and the churning surf—had produced a wealth of overlapping, shared, or utterly distinct practices and artifacts. In the National Museum, though, a visitor could traipse through all the galleries and never realize this basic fact. On the contrary, artifacts taken from the Northwest were scattered throughout the exhibitions, grouped not with one another but with allegedly similar items from entirely different places, those that were thought to represent the same phase of cultural evolution. "By regarding a single implement outside of its surroundings," Boas wrote, "outside of other inventions of the people to whom it belongs, and outside of other phenomena affecting that people and its productions, we cannot understand its meaning." To do otherwise was like organizing an attic, with the big items here, the little items there, the Christmas decorations fighting for space with old shoes and a dusty steamer trunk. It certainly wasn't science.

Mason replied in the pages of the journal later that summer. "I think it is a growing conviction," he wrote, "that both customs and things spring from prior inventions, just as life springs from life, and that the sooner we recognize the fact that in the study of arts, institutions, language, knowledge, customs, religion, and races of men, we must always apply the methods and instrumentalities of the biologist, the sooner will our beloved science stand upon an immovable foundation." Classification was the first step toward true scientific understanding, Mason claimed. In rejecting the obvious fact that similar traits must spring from similar causes, Boas seemed to render comparison impossible. "The explorer who goes among a people to study their entire creed and activity will do his work better by having in his mind the determination to bring each industry into comparison with the same activities in other times and places."

Boas continued the conversation in June, winding up to what he clearly considered to be a grand and overarching statement. He was making a particular criticism of Mason, he wrote, because of the esteemed ethnologist's important role in the field and the necessarily far-reaching effects of the museum whose collections he superintended. That was why Mason's faulty arrangement of objects was such a critical mistake. He had effectively claimed that the peoples whose objects were on display lived in a kind of eternal present, their handiwork allegedly frozen in time. But these people had a history. They migrated. They came under the influence of different peoples and ideas. Boas had seen it himself on Baffin Island, as he pieced together the life story of his guide, Signa. He had seen it in British Columbia, where people speaking very different languages nevertheless told the same stories and repeated the same myths.

The only way to get at these issues was through what Boas knew as the inductive method—that is, by examining a range of groups in depth and suspending one's theorizing until data had been collected from as many sources as possible. The alternative, to reason in the deductive fashion, involved beginning with a set of general principles and then applying them to the case at hand. But that was simply fishing around until you found some evidence to confirm your prejudices, Boas felt. Science demanded that researchers leave their preconceived notions back in the laboratory. They should allow their theories about human society to emerge gradually from studying the surroundings in which people lived. There might be laws to social evolution, but discovering them would require a researcher to spend some time contending with his own ignorance. "All that stuff is beginning to make me feel very stupid," Boas had written from the Northwest Coast. Now, however, he was beginning to twist that feeling—the sense of being disoriented inside a cyclone of data—into a scientific method.

"In ethnology all is individuality," he concluded somewhat cryptically. "It is my opinion that the main object of ethnological collections should be the dissemination of the fact that civilization is not something absolute, but that it is relative, and that our ideas and conceptions are true only so far as our civilization goes." That was the conclusion toward which he had been working ever since he wrote to Marie with his revelations from Baffin Island. The only people who could really say whether something that looked like a bow was a weapon, a child's toy, or an instrument for making fire were the true experts—that is, those who actually used it, in a given place, at a given time. This bone rattle might make music. That one might drive away evil spirits. Yet another might distract a wailing child. It all depended on *where* you were in the world, not *when* you happened to be on some linear path of social evolution. The way to set up a museum was not to follow Morgan and Powell's formula of savagery, barbarism, and civilization. It was rather to cluster the objects on display so that they corresponded to the peoples who had created them.

Boas might have justifiably felt he had won the day—until the editorial offices of *Science* received a long letter from Major Powell himself. It was printed in the next issue. Powell dismissed Boas's proposals as being practically unworkable and scientifically suspect. Boas clearly had no conception of the multiple functions of a museum, Powell suggested, and his desire to group items by the societies that had produced them would offer neither instruction to the masses nor enlightenment to scholars. It was much better to stick with the universal "human activities which characterize mankind," Powell concluded—"arts, institutions, languages, and opinions or philosophies"—and any museum worthy of the name should be laid out along similarly obvious lines.

Boas could do little but reply sheepishly in a short note that he and Powell agreed on many fundamental points. The entire affair, he wrote to his parents, had given him a headache. He had taken on two of the most important figures in the field, from his insecure perch as an editorial assistant, and the weight of opinion seemed to be that he had lost. His contract with *Science* was ending, and he now found himself in the same position he had been in two years earlier, albeit with more standing than he had enjoyed before. He had been elected a fellow of the American Association for the Advancement of Science and had even begun to make spoken presentations in extemporaneous English. His longest publication yet in his second language—*The Central Eskimo,* the result of his Baffin Island research—was due to appear in the annual reports of the Bureau of Ethnology. Still, the timing could hardly have been worse. He and Marie had welcomed their first baby, Helene, in the autumn of 1888, and here he was once again an itinerant scholar.

Chapter Four

SCIENCE AND CIRCUSES

....

B oas's move to the United States coincided with the emerging age of the anthropologist—a term that more and more people were beginning to use for the combination of travel, artifact collecting, language learning, and bone hunting that Boas had done on Baffin Island and in the Pacific Northwest. To call yourself by that label was to feel that you were on a frontier. Unexplored realms lay before you. You could stare back through time at the origins of humanity itself. Lost ancestors emerged out of the dust at the stroke of your trowel. Primitive man spoke to you in his confused tongue, one that, with great persistence, you had managed to decipher. To do it well took a lust for travel, a willingness to risk dysentery, and supreme confidence that what you were building, bit by bit, was a master science of humankind.

On a train ride toward a conference in Cleveland, Boas happened to fall into conversation with someone who understood these ambitions better than nearly anyone he had ever encountered: an academic impresario named Granville Stanley Hall. As a student at Harvard, Hall had earned America's first doctorate in the new field of psychology. He had gone on to set up the first genuinely experimental laboratory in the discipline at the new Johns Hopkins University in Baltimore. The study of the human mind ought to be approached as a science, Hall believed, not as a branch of philosophy, as it had normally been seen in the past. It should give up flights of speculative fancy and focus on the careful testing of hypotheses in controlled conditions. He saw himself not only as an experimentalist par excellence but as a booster for truth in an age when everyone knew that science, properly understood, would help make life healthier, richer, and longer.

As a psychologist, he understood something of human desires and foibles. It was perhaps this talent that made him particularly adept at persuading people to sign on to his grand academic schemes. In 1887 he founded the *American Journal of Psychology* at a time when there was barely a discipline to fill its pages. He established the American Psychological Association at a time when the entire population of psychologists could fit comfortably in a large seminar room—which was, in fact, what the association's first meeting looked like. Hall collected people the way ethnologists collected folktales. With his striped neckties and easy conversation, he was a charismatic presence, the kind of person who always seemed to have a crowd of eager young people around him at the end of a public lecture. He became famous as a debunker of mediums and soothsayers, a controversial authority on adolescent sexuality, and the author of popular books with head-scratching titles such as *Senescence: The Last Half of Life*, *A Study of Dolls*, and *Jesus, the Christ, in the Light of Psychology*, in two volumes.

Just as Boas's contract at *Science* was coming to an end, he received an unexpected message from the confident scholar he had met on the train. Would Boas be interested in a position lecturing at Clark University, a new institution in Massachusetts that Hall was in the process of establishing? He would be the first person in any American university to be hired specifically to teach a still inchoate subject called anthropology. It promised to be one step closer toward the fulfillment of Boas's dream of eventually bearing the title of professor. He accepted without hesitation. In the fall of 1889, he moved the family to suburban Worcester and set about writing his course of lectures, still worried about his shaky English.

Clark was marketed to incoming faculty and prospective students as a leap forward in scientific education. Its principal funder, Jonas Gilman Clark, a successful hardware merchant, had hoped to follow the lead of other industrialists who were applying their fortunes—and their names—to institutions of higher learning. Ezra Cornell, an early investor in the national telegraph system, had devoted his later years to setting up a university in Ithaca, New York, which opened its doors in 1865. Cornelius Vanderbilt, the shipper and railroad tycoon, founded his own version in Nashville, Tennessee, in 1873. The oilman John D. Rockefeller provided the initial endowment for what would become, by 1890, the University of Chicago, while the gold rush wholesaler Leland Stanford did the same thing a year later at a site in Palo Alto, California.

Clark University was to have a special twist, however. It would offer only graduate-level degrees. The plan was to combine advanced teaching with a faculty whose duties would include less lecturing and marking of exams and more original research in their fields of specialization. Few places besides Johns Hopkins had quite managed to embody this new ideal of a "research university." Graduate education was expensive, since doctoral students expected fellowships and free tuition if they were to devote their lives to purely academic pursuits rather than law or business, and universities competed aggressively for the limited faculty talent to be had. People with degrees from research-focused universities abroad—like Boas—were particularly desirable, and Clark was committed to using its resources to create a new community dedicated to the advancement of original knowledge. When Boas stepped onto the Clark campus, with its two spacious buildings surrounded by the riotous color of a New England autumn, the institution seemed full of promise. Its endowment, at some $700,000, put it on par with those of Stanford, Cornell, and Chicago.

The university was Hall's personal project. As the president he oversaw every class and faculty appointment. It didn't take Boas long to realize that things weren't going well, however. At his first lecture, in early November, only eight students sat in the classroom, which was so dark that Boas could barely make out his own notes. Hall had a habit of promising too much and delivering too little. Expenses in the first year outstripped the payout from the endowment, and one tragedy after another seemed to hit Hall himself: a bout of diphtheria that rendered him speechless and then the asphyxiation of his wife and child in a gas leak.

The faculty was soon in quiet revolt. Every year administrators from the University of Chicago arrived on a raiding expedition, driving away from Worcester with cartloads of tweed-clad lecturers, their salaries now doubled. Boas felt unable to join them. He had promised Marie that they would settle down for a while, especially after the arrival of a son, Ernst, during a cold Massachusetts February in 1891. "I only wish that I could have greater faith in the university," he wrote to his parents.

Boas continued to work on writing up his British Columbia material, including the results of further summers of collecting. Clark University's one advantage was that it had managed to pull together a group of talented—if perpetually discontented—scholars from a range of different fields. Boas found himself profoundly influenced by working closely with trained researchers, people guided by their own curiosity toward resolving some of the greatest questions science had to offer. His first doctoral student, A. F. Chamberlain, completed his degree in 1892, the first one awarded in the entire country in the field of anthropology. But it was hard going. Hall, who had seemed a visionary earlier on, now became a recalcitrant and occasionally vindictive administrator. He depended entirely on Clark, the school's founder, for resources, and the donor proved to be as erratic as he was interfering.

The summers in British Columbia were an escape for Boas, but then came the fall and the return to the mix of drudgery and intrigue in Worcester. By 1892, faculty discontent was the subject of daily conversations in the hallways and around lunch tables. At the end of that academic year, two-thirds of the Clark faculty resigned en masse—an event that Hall called "the hegira," after Muhammad's flight to Mecca. It was a devastating blow from which the university would never fully recover. Most went to the University of Chicago, the traditional destination for people who got fed up with Hall's deficiencies.

Boas was soon bound in the same direction, although not to the university. In November he packed up the Worcester house and moved with Marie and the two children, Helene and baby Ernst, to Englewood, on Chicago's South Side. From there it was an easy commute to the swampy barrens along Lake Michigan, which would soon be teeming with activity. The city was preparing for the greatest public exhibition of science, technology, and the arts that the world had ever seen. Boas had recently become an American citizen, and he was eager to play his own small part in showcasing the wonders of his adopted country: working inside a building that—for the first time ever in the United States—would have ANTHROPOLOGY carved over its entrance.

BOAS HAD DREAMED OF being taken onto the staff of the Chicago world's fair—officially the World's Columbian Exposition—set to open on May Day 1893. As with his move to Clark, this latest turn in his career came about through another of the established academics he had spent his short time in the United States eagerly courting—in this case, through the curator of Harvard's Peabody Museum of Archaeology and Ethnology, Frederic Ward Putnam.

A prominent archaeologist of American Indian sites, Putnam had a scholarly lineage that went back to his mentor, the great Harvard naturalist Louis Agassiz. In the run-up to the Chicago fair, he had audaciously crafted a detailed proposal for "a collection of the habitations of the dwellers in the three Americas from Primitive savages up to the present time," which he published in the *Chicago Tribune*. The fair's organizers took note and offered a generous budget of $300,000 for a department of ethnology and archaeology, known as Department M. Putnam immediately set about acquiring assistants to assemble collections, design public galleries, and collate the mass of original material called for in the exposition's planning documents.

The world's fair was a celebration of the four-hundredth anniversary of Columbus's voyage to the New World and an opportunity for Chicago boosters to showcase the city's renewal after the devastating fire of 1871. But as Putnam knew, it was also a rare opportunity for anthropology to define itself as a coherent field of knowledge. The first journal to use the term in its title, *American Anthropologist*, had been launched only in 1888 by the circle of scholars around Powell in

Washington. Its first issue had contained a grab bag of subjects: the evolutionary development of the human hand, the nature of timekeeping in ancient Greece and Rome, metallurgy among the Algonquian Indians, games played by children in the nation's capital, and even the text of Powell's speech "From Savagery to Civilization," which he had delivered two years earlier. Putnam's plans called for Department M to corral this unruly discipline and place it, metaphorically, under one roof. It would feature items dug up from Indian mounds by archaeologists, native clothing and ritual objects brought back by ethnologists, songs and chants assembled by linguists, and even real people from indigenous communities who would create living dioramas to instruct and astonish visitors.

Putnam knew he had several competitors. Otis Tufton Mason and other curators in Washington were already packing up some of the riches of the Smithsonian for shipment to Chicago. The old Bureau of Ethnology was to have its own gallery inside the United States pavilion, in the heart of the fairgrounds. Nearby was another attraction called the Midway Plaisance, where peoples of the world would be on parade, with dancers, acrobats, and food purveyors offering delights from around the globe. Department M had to offer something different, which was perhaps why Putnam tapped Boas for a special assignment: to create a display on the one area where anthropology looked most like real science, a discipline of numbers, precision, and careful measurement, especially of the various proportions of the human body. It was a rarefied area of study known as anthropometry.

From the late eighteenth century forward, students of natural history had cataloged human differences by assembling ad hoc collections of human skulls and entire skeletons. Boas himself had done the same thing in British Columbia, carting away bones from ruined burial sites that he found around Vancouver Island. But why measure living people? In the 1890s, the answer was obvious, and it came directly from the evolutionary view of social development that had been championed by Morgan, Powell, and others.

Just as individual humans change physically over time from childhood forward—growing taller, with stronger bones and bigger heads, then retreating as their bones grow brittle and their spines bend into old age—human society, it was believed, was likely to show evidence of patterned change as well. Humans had clearly evolved from earlier versions of themselves, and merely by looking around the world, at savage and barbarian societies, one might well obtain clues as to how civilized man appeared in an earlier stage of development. Moreover, physical features were obviously clustered according to geography. People of dark skin tones, for instance, lived in some regions; those with lighter skin lived elsewhere. Science demanded moving from such surface-level observations to the careful recording of measurable physical distinctions, from head shape to height, weight, and femur length, with the goal being to categorize people according to the physical features that distinguished them.

Calipers and measuring tapes could be applied just as easily to living people as to bones from old graves. Researchers in Europe were showing the way. In Britain, Francis Galton, a cousin of Charles Darwin's and one of the pioneers of modern statistical methods, constructed a map of the British Isles based on what he believed to be the objective, calculable beauty of its inhabitants. Paul Broca, professor of surgery and founder of the Anthropological Society of Paris, collected the brains of both wild animals and eminent humans, to compare their sizes and account for their different mental faculties. Any gathering of anthropometrists was alive with the latest findings reported in indices, averages, and Greek vocabulary. Dolichocephalic individuals, with their relatively long heads, were said to be found among many peoples of Africa and the Mediterranean. The brachycephalic, or short-headed, were located mainly in Central Asia. The mesaticephalic, or medium-headed, were dotted throughout Europe and North and South America. The allure of quantification was irresistible. It was the surest route toward respectability for this youngest of the human sciences.

None of this was confined simply to descriptive data collection, however. The general theory underlying work in anthropometry was the belief that physical differences might provide hints about other puzzles of current interest, from public health to intelligence. Only a few decades earlier, the Swedish anatomist Anders Retzius had developed a calculation known as the cephalic index: the maximum width of the skull divided by its maximum length, then multiplied by 100. The numbers generated by Retzius's formula became the principal figures that concerned anthropometrists. With a little bit of arithmetic, a researcher could produce a number that could be used to compare one individual's head with that of another. But the real value lay in the comparison of average cephalic indexes across entire populations. If you calculated the average figure for a broad swath of people, then placed those numbers on a map, you might have a picture of how human beings had evolved and migrated over time, differentiating themselves from some earlier type and fanning out into the many varieties of humans that exist on the planet today. It was a way of looking back through time, charting essential human differences in the way one might fill in the boundaries of lost empires and kingdoms, or the invisible temperature gradients that ran from deserts to mountain peaks—nature's ur-types revealed in the clustering of contemporary humans by head shape and cranial capacity.

And since the head also contained the brain, the cephalic index and other cranial features might well provide keys to understanding behavior. A few years before Boas moved to Chicago, a French police clerk, Alphonse Bertillon, had proposed the systematic use of photography to study criminals. Police stations could be outfitted with cameras and officers trained in the collection of visual data on the suspects they arrested. Bertillon suggested that suspects be photographed in two poses, one showing a front-on view and another in profile. The point was not simply ease of identification, since the suspect was, after all, already in custody. Rather, Bertillon's idea was to provide an image that could be used for research purposes to correlate key facial features with the traits of known criminals—from the shape of the forehead and chin to the volume of the skull. It might then be easier to determine not just who *was* a criminal but also who *might be* at some point in the future. Perhaps crime ran in families, or in particular types of human beings; perhaps it was visible in the brow or the jaw, if you knew what to look for. The system that evolved into the iconic police mug shot was anthropometry in action: an entire theory of human normalcy and deviance standardized in a photographic pose, which could then be correlated with a single number, the cephalic index.

For Putnam and most other scientists of the day, psychology, ethnology, and anthropometry were all aiming at the same thing: using systematic observation of the outward traits of individuals to arrive at conclusions about the apparent differences across social groups. Boas was to be the person to head up Department M's effort to link these fields of study. He had trained in mathematics and statistics as part of his doctoral studies in Germany, a rarity among the geographers and amateur explorers who made up the bulk of America's small community of ethnologists. He already had significant field experience in multiple locations, from Baffin Island to British Columbia. He had the imprimatur of Hall, one of the founders of American psychology, and while at Clark University, he had made a few tentative forays as a practicing anthropometrist. In 1891 he had formulated a large-scale plan for measuring children in Worcester public schools, a research project that was approved by the school board as a way of studying growth, nutrition, and mental development. It was eventually denounced by a local newspaper, however. The idea of an accented German, "his scalp scarred with saber cuts, and slashes over his eye, on his nose, and on one cheek," asking children "to have their anatomies felt" was too much for Massachusetts parents.

The controversy over the project—and Hall's faint public defense of it—was one of the reasons Boas had been eager to leave the struggling university. But this early research did provide him with the bona fides that would eventually attract the interest of Putnam. Now each morning he left Marie and the children in Englewood and made his way toward the sound of hammers and handsaws on the lakeshore.

BY THE TIME BOAS reported for duty at the fairgrounds, things were already behind schedule. The building that was to house Putnam's exhibits was little more than a blueprint. Collections had yet to be assembled, much less set out for public display. In addition to designing the anthropometry laboratory, Boas lent a hand with the other ethnological exhibits. He coordinated his own team of more than seventy fieldworkers, each assigned to collect artifacts from among the Northwest Coast tribes. He mobilized the contacts he had made since his first visit to British Columbia and, through a series of local agents, hunted down ceremonial artifacts, masks, canoes, totem poles, and other items for dispatch to Chicago. Other assistants made similar entreaties to their agents in Mexico and South America, all for the purpose of filling the large two-story hall that Putnam was busy building.

The fair opened to enormous acclaim on May 1. A "Great White City," laid out by the landscape architect Frederick Law Olmsted, spread across nearly seven hundred acres along the old swampy shoreline. More than two hundred temporary pavilions, illuminated by electrical lighting, showcased the march of science and technology in every imaginable domain. The monstrous Manufacturing and Liberal Arts Building, a wooden structure covering some forty acres, wrapped in simulated marble and Corinthian columns, was at the time the largest covered space on the planet. The Midway Plaisance featured exhibits on the peculiar ways of the world's peoples, from a Bedouin encampment to a Viennese café, most of them thin disguises for hawkers of merchandise and cheap entertainment. An entire building was devoted solely to the lives and progress of women, while others highlighted advances in agriculture, electrification, and the plastic arts. A new fastener called a zipper made its debut over the six months of the fair's operation, as did a chewable gum labeled Juicy Fruit, a tall circular ride presented by a Mr. Ferris, a prize-winning beer offered by the Pabst family, and a breakfast dish with the rather confusing name Cream of Wheat.

From the agricultural complex, visitors walked across a bridge over the South Pond and boarded an elevated railway that conveyed them to the ethnological area. A replica of Mayan ruins from the Yucatán Peninsula stood next to the birch-bark wigwams of Penobscot Indians, which in turn gave way to six carved totem poles, one of them a two-story bear leaping out at spectators. Two full-scale long-houses were inhabited by seventeen Kwakiutl, including two children, who had been brought to Chicago by Boas's field agents. Right next to a huge replica of a southwestern cliff dwelling was the Anthropology Building itself, which finally opened to visitors just in time for the July Fourth holiday.

It was as though a planet-wide high school science fair had run full-tilt into a circus sideshow. The building was stuffed to the rafters with items that Putnam's assistants had amassed, nominally grouped together by country or people—just as Boas had urged the Smithsonian to do years earlier. The building's two floors took visitors through the history of human evolution, highlighted the wide variety of practice, dress, and belief in regions around the world, and then ushered guests into more contemporary displays on hygiene, public charities, and prisons—a reminder that the science of humankind was also a route toward making individual human beings cleaner, safer, and nicer. Rush mats were piled next to birch baskets and pieces of twine. Ankle ornaments shared vitrines with hide tambourines, human-hair skirts, and monkey-teeth amulets. Mannequins wearing handwoven clothing stood beside a scale model of a Haida village before a painted backdrop of misty pines. A garden of Greek statuary led on to displays of fishing nets, grass baskets, and buckskin tunics, along with thousands and thousands of printed placards, labels, charts, and maps, many of them hand-corrected by Boas himself.

Along the north gallery of the Anthropology Building were the eight rooms housing Boas's anthropometry section. The rooms were dedicated to three main fields of study: a display on the physical features of American Indians and "half-bloods"; material on the growth and development of children; and a working laboratory that would conduct real-time research—including using visitors themselves as subjects—in the domains of psychology, neurology, and craniology, the study of human head shapes. Nothing quite like it had ever been created: a large-scale experiment in public science that aimed to be both an exhibit and a research center. Patrons could see the full skeletons of a gorilla, an Australian, a Hottentot, two Peruvians, and a European, plus a skull collected in Athens and said to be that of Sophocles. Fairgoers could have their physical measurements taken on the spot with some of the latest instruments for acquiring and processing human data: calipers for measuring length, goniometers for taking facial angles, mechanical comptometers used for adding up large figures, an instrument known as Zambelli's tachycraniograph for drawing cross sections of the skull, and even, as Boas wrote in an entry in the fair's official program, "the Vertical Head-Spanner of the Cambridge Scientific Company . . . a large instrument intended for an accurate measurement of the height of the vertex over a plane passing through the lower rim of the orbit and the entrance of the ear." A series of diagrams and posters illustrated the latest findings in the field of anthropometry.

Yet to anyone who ventured through the eight rooms of Boas's Chicago exhibit, the conclusions of all this quantifying and calculating were probably rather confusing. If science was about certainty, there seemed little on display here. Measurements of North American mulattoes showed them to be roughly the same height as white people. An exhibit on the fingerprints of North American Indians informed visitors that they were all unique to each individual, with no real patterning from group to group. The distribution of people by stature in the city of Paris varied widely, just as it did for a study of Civil War veterans (although it was found that those from western states were in general taller than the easterners). An attempt to show the heights of Italians ended up finding no obvious pattern from northern Italy to the south. The head shapes of Tyroleans and Bavarians were shown to be highly variable—more so, in fact, than among the many white Americans, of varied extractions, who had been subjected to review. The peoples of "Old Europe" were, perhaps surprisingly, shown to be even more physically mixed than the population of the avowedly immigrant United States.

Boas was developing a distaste for theory unsupported by evidence, and when given a choice between presenting data and draw-ing grand lessons from it, he tended to prefer the former. It was what had prompted his initial controversy with Mason and Powell, and it guided the creation of his laboratory in Chicago. Already in 1889 he had published a short essay on the ways researchers could get things monumentally wrong. The piece concerned what Boas called "sound blindness," that is, the inability of listeners to perceive distinctions in the pronunciation of certain words, much the way color-blind individ-uals have difficulty perceiving certain distinctions in color. The domi-nant view among scholars was that different societies demonstrated a greater or lesser propensity to sound-blindness, based in large part on their level of development. The languages of primitive peoples tended to allow a great degree of speech variation, with pronunciations that remained wavering and unfixed. More advanced peoples tended to solidify their pronunciation, not least because of the advent of writ-ing and spelling rules. They could readily perceive—and correct—mispronunciations among their compatriots, which was something Boas himself had experienced in trying to wrap his tongue around English.

But Boas reckoned that this view of language rested not only on bad data but also on bad theory. In his travels among the Inuit and Kwakiutl, indigenous people showed no more propensity to unmoor their pronunciation than did the ethnologists observing them. If any-thing, sound-blindness seemed to be at work more frequently among the observers themselves. Boas compared the vocabularies of native languages compiled by European and American explorers and found that the same researcher recorded the spelling of native words in mul-tiple ways. Looking back at his own leather notebooks, Boas realized he had made the same mistake himself.

Researchers were seeing the world not in terms of its objective reality but, he was beginning to realize, in terms of the speech system that they knew best: the sounds produced by their own tongues, teeth, throats, and noses in everyday conversation in their own language. "It is found that the vocabularies of collectors, although they may apply diacritical marks or special alphabets, bear evidence of the phonetics of their own languages," Boas wrote. "This can be explained by the fact that each apperceives the unknown sounds by the means of the sounds of his own language." The conclusion could only be that sound-blindness was not somehow restricted to primitive peoples. It was a general feature of humans' understanding of the world, or "apperception," as Boas had it: the universal tendency to interpret new experiences in light of the experiences with which we are most familiar.

What counted as social scientific data—the specific observations that researchers jotted down in their field notes—was relative to the worldview, skill sets, and preexisting categories of the researchers themselves. All science is provisional, Boas was coming to believe. Theories were neither true nor false. They might better be described as successful or unsuccessful: they either fit the observable data or they didn't. When observation bumped up against the walls of an existing theory, the theory was the thing that had to be changed. The first step was to get good data and then let the theory follow, which was the entire point of all those confusing tables and graphs in his Chicago anthropometry lab.

Since the Anthropology Building was sited on the margins of the fairgrounds, it was "liable to be overlooked by the ordinary visitor," one guidebook warned. Despite the sizable initial budget, Putnam's actual expenditures had been just over $83,000, or less than a quarter of one percent of the fair's cost, and the relatively small outlay showed in attendance. More than twenty-five million visitors walked through the fair's front gates, but to Putnam's great disappointment, few of them seemed to make it to the anthropology exhibit. People seemed more drawn to the Dairy Building next door, with its cows and cheeses, or the Leather and Shoe Trades Building, which formed an incongruous backdrop for the Kwakiutl dancers. The rival ethnological collection organized by the Smithsonian also drew attention away from the work of Putnam's team, as did the tepees of Buffalo Bill's Wild West show, located just outside the official fairgrounds. Even a hastily arranged "congress of anthropology" attracted only a trickle of professors.

The Chicago fair had been a chance for Boas to help design a museum space according to the principles he had laid out in his debate with Mason and Powell a few years earlier—one that presented raw data and the latest field research, not preconceived theories, to a public audience. It by and large flopped. The fair's director, Harlow N. Higginbotham, never even bothered to visit the ethnological area. Even the Kwakiutl attracted only modest numbers of spectators. Those who did wander over were sometimes scandalized by what they saw. When the Kwakiutl simulated bloodletting during a ritual known as the "cannibal dance," one fairgoer interrupted the performance by screaming, "Stop it! Stop it! This is a Christian country!" "Scientifically, the summer has been extremely unsuccessful," Boas wrote to Meier and Sophie as the fair was winding down. He promised himself "never again to play circus impresario."

He could only feel that it had all been waste and chaos, for himself and for Chicago. A smallpox epidemic spread throughout the city, followed by a round of influenza. Chicago's popular mayor, Carter Harrison, fell to an assassin's bullet just before the fair's closing ceremonies, and a fire set by unemployed workers would later destroy most of the exhibition buildings. The home Boas had rented in Englewood turned out to be only a few blocks from the boardinghouse of H. H. Holmes, a serial killer who, newspaper reports revealed, had rigged its rooms with special piping to asphyxiate his unwitting guests. Another tragedy hit closer still. In the Boas household, a new daughter, Hedwig, had arrived in March 1893 just as Boas was scrambling to open the anthropometry lab. She died not long after the fair closed.

Boas was taken on temporarily to help transfer the anthropological materials to a more permanent location, the site that would eventually become Chicago's Field Museum. But with no need for the large staff that had been assembled for the fair, he was soon let go—a move that he learned about only secondhand. It was "an unsurpassed insult," he wrote to his superiors in a fit of pique. Overeducated and with no explanation for his predicament beyond there being simply no position for which he was thought best qualified, he was once again jobless.

His personality didn't help. Irascible, stubborn, impatient, and not given to compromise, he had created not a little bad blood with some of his more senior colleagues. He was developing a habit of leaving one position after another with a feeling of having been wronged—and a growing sense among his former associates that it was just as well to let him go. Boas was left to return to New York and eke out what income he could by doing contract work for museums, while making a continual round of office calls to universities. He continued to collect on the side, carting back masks or other artifacts from his expeditions to the Northwest Coast. To assist the Smithsonian with a new exhibit, he posed for a series of photographs—ridiculously, in a wool suit and even in his undergarments—to illustrate the ritual dance characteristic of a Kwakiutl secret society, something he had probably first seen at the Chicago fair. When the exhibit opened in 1895, few visitors would have realized that they were viewing not a display drawn from real life but rather a model of a model, based on an anthropologist cavorting in his long johns. "What good is the consciousness that I am among the best in my field here in America," he wrote to Marie from another expedition to the West, "if I cannot use my ability, but am forced to work, here and there, to earn our living."

The Chicago experience did have several benefits, however. Boas had been able to showcase the work he had done among the peoples of the Northwest Coast. He had gained experience in managing a large scholarly enterprise focused on a cutting-edge field of research: the physical measurements of anthropological types and the categorizing of differences in head shape, nose form, and other features of distinct human groups. Those skills—and his connection with Putnam—would eventually pay off. Putnam had been taken on as curator of the American Museum of Natural History in New York, a moribund institution that had recently been infused with new life by Morris K. Jesup, a railwayman and financier who had turned his business success toward philanthropy. Boas was invited to join the new enterprise in 1896. Leaving Chicago, the Boas family settled into a three-story brownstone on West 82nd Street, not far from the museum's unmistakable pinkish building on the edge of Central Park.

ESTABLISHED IN 1869, the American Museum of Natural History had originally been cobbled together from the private collections of European nobles, naturalists, and taxidermists, all piled inside an old arsenal in Central Park. On June 20, 1874, President Ulysses S. Grant laid the cornerstone for a new building in the dusty, treeless wasteland north of West 77th Street. Three years later the neo-Romanesque building of granite and pink brownstone, stretching all the way from the park to Columbus Avenue, finally opened its doors to visitors. Not until the 1930s would the building be reoriented, with a grander, columned entrance on Central Park West, guarded by an equestrian statue of Theodore Roosevelt. But even at the time Boas arrived, the addition of several buildings to the original eighteen-acre site had already made it one of the largest museum complexes in the world.

The naming of Putnam as anthropology curator ensured that the work would proceed in good order, with some of the energy that he had brought to the Chicago fair now applied to the creation of a new, permanent collection in New York. Under Putnam's direction, Boas set to work assembling material for a new hall on Northwest Coast peoples, where his own expeditions and field contacts were crucial. A sixty-three-foot-long painted canoe, outfitted with mannequin rowers and a masked shaman, dominated the exhibition. With support from Jesup, the museum's president, Boas helped organize a team of researchers to undertake major expeditions across the North Pacific in order to explore the relationship between the indigenous peoples of Asia and the Americas. Another program focused on documenting the vanishing tribal groups of the American West. Both projects would swell the museum's collections and produce a mountain of reports and publications. Boas's tiny handwriting snaked through volume after volume of accession catalogs, with his meticulous annotations on the provenance of baskets, boats, totems, and bones. The Boas family was expanding as well. A new daughter, Gertrude, arrived in the spring after he and Marie moved back east. Another boy, Henry, came two years later. Another daughter, Marie Franziska, was born at the beginning of 1902, making five living children in all. The return to New York also brought a change of fortune that Boas could not have imagined during the dark winter after the closing of the Chicago fair: he gained an academic position and professorial title in a stable and ambitious institution. At the beginning of 1897, he was appointed to a professorship at Columbia University. It had taken him until his forties, but he had finally realized the goal he had set for himself when he first embarked on the *Germania* toward Baffin Island. He suspected, but couldn't fully confirm, that it had only come through the marshaling of family connections. Uncle Jacobi had secretly interceded with the administration and offered to underwrite his salary. The job was only part-time, however, and would be linked to his continuing responsibilities collecting, curating, and cataloging at the museum.

Founded as King's College in 1754, Columbia had adopted its more patriotic name following the American Revolution. Under its boosterish president, the Brooklyn politician and progressive Republican Seth Low, it had redefined itself as a university, offering graduate degrees and a fully revised curriculum, including a new emphasis on the social sciences. The same year that Boas joined the faculty of philosophy as a professor of anthropology, Low had engineered Columbia's move from midtown to new quarters in upper Manhattan, a few dozen blocks north of the Natural History Museum. Boas could divide his time between the two institutions—the Ninth Avenue elevated train, flanking the museum's western facade, shuttled him right up to the growing campus in Morningside Heights.

Boas was now in a more secure position than he had ever enjoyed. He threw himself into the academic work. In the spring of 1899, he oversaw the launch of a new series of Powell's old *American Anthropol-*

ogist, with a new editorial board and ambitions of becoming a national journal rather than the in-house publication of the small Anthropological Society of Washington. Boas urged his own colleagues to contribute to the new publication, and as his reputation at Columbia grew, he could draw on the research of a small coterie of graduate students to fill the pages with field reports and new findings. The next year Boas was informed of his election to the National Academy of Sciences, a signal honor. With the rise of a younger generation of scholars attached to the Museum of Natural History and the hands-on attention and financing of President Jesup, the center of gravity in anthropological research was gradually shifting from Washington to New York. For all the years Boas had been in the United States, the estimable John Wesley Powell had remained director of the Bureau of Ethnology, but his death in 1902 was a symbolic passing of this earlier cohort of explorers. The future seemed to belong to people of Boas's generation. The year of Powell's death, Boas helped organize the revival of an older scholarly society and rename it the American Anthropological Association, the first national academic body with that label. *American Anthropologist* became its official publication.

Boas appeared in the first issue of the reworked journal with a critique of the convictions that he believed had defined his disciplinary forefathers. No one should be creating broad theories of human difference, he argued, until more data had been collected. But he defended the idea that measuring bodily forms—from calculating the cephalic index to noting down differences of height or nose shape—could eventually lead to a clear definition of the natural varieties of humankind. "These facts are very strong arguments for the assumption of a great permanence of human types," Boas wrote. "It is necessary that the analysis of distributions of measurements be carried much farther than it has proceeded up to the present time; this is done, and I believe we shall obtain a means of determining with considerable accuracy the blood relationships of the geographical varieties of man."

However, there were limits to all this, Boas felt. Anthropology required approaching problems from several different angles, each with its own data, theories, and explanations. Physical differences cataloged by anthropometrists might show something important about the mixing of distinct human populations over time. Ethnologists might reveal how rituals, songs, and myths moved across space. Linguists might understand how languages spread and changed. Each of these might describe a unique "type" of human community, but none on its own was sufficient to describe the scope of difference that one observed in the world. That was especially the case when it came to a word that Boas had danced around in various ways since his first foray on board the *Germania* nearly two decades earlier—*culture*.

In an article in *Science* published just as he joined the Museum of Natural History, Boas had toggled back and forth between using the word in the singular and in the plural. At times he applied it to the entirety of universal human thought and practice; at other times he seemed to mean a way of being and doing specific to a given village or region. Anthropology in general, he wrote, "will not become fruitful until we renounce the vain endeavor to construct a uniform systematic history of the evolution of culture." The discovery of "universal ideas" that animate all human societies was only the starting point. The next step was to "answer two questions in regard to them: First, what is their origin? and second, how do they assert themselves in various cultures?" Humans might organize their social worlds in ways that are common across time and space; there might well be universal laws that govern social behavior. But from his own studies as both an ethnologist and an anthropometrist, Boas had realized that these laws—if they existed—seemed to express themselves in many different ways. The common *culture* of humanity could only be approached through the *cultures* we can actually observe.

That plural made all the difference. Over the next decade, Boas would come to argue the exact opposite of what he had claimed in the *American Anthropologist*, namely, that each person is an expression of one of the unchanging biological types into which humanity is naturally divided. On the contrary, he would argue, the preponderance of the evidence confirms the plural, fluid, and endlessly adaptable nature of both human bodies and the societies they make. It was one of the great shifts of opinion in the history of science, and it derived largely from Boas's basic method: to reason inductively and follow the data. The resulting path led straight toward a collision with his adopted country's most time-honored way of understanding itself, a cultural obsession that Europeans and Americans had learned to call race.

Chapter Five

HEADHUNTERS

....

Like any anthropologist of his day, Boas took for granted that human beings came in a set of natural categories. One goal of the discipline was to name and understand these building blocks of human society. The color, shape, size, and texture of external body parts were thought to provide the raw data according to which these classifications could be made. The function of Boas's laboratory at Clark and his anthropometry exhibition at the Chicago fair had been to collect enough data that one could be reasonably sure that the types into which one sorted human bodies were the truest representation of a deeper biological reality.

The concept of race was central to the field. To virtually any observer, type and race—or "color," as the U.S. census had it, starting in 1790—were virtually synonymous. Human communities might dress or sing differently, in polyphonic choruses or rude grunts; they might live in deserts, plains, or swamplands, in adobe huts or shingled Cape Cods. But underlying this chaos of behaviors was an unshakable natural order. Humans had races in the same way that other animals had stocks or pedigrees: smooth-haired or wiry, greater or lesser, horned or polled. You had only to open your eyes—to have a look, say, at someone's lips, hair texture, nose shape, and skin tone—to confirm this fact.

More than a century earlier, the German anatomist Johann Blumenbach had created the fivefold classification that would serve as the basis for racial delineation. In his treatise *On the Natural Variety of Humankind*, published in 1775, Blumenbach sorted human beings into boxes based on their geographic location as well as the visible characteristics that seemed to define them. There were the peoples of Africa, whom he called "Ethiopians"; those native to the Americas and the Arctic, whom he called "Americans"; those residing in Asia, whom he called "Mongolians"; the peoples of the Pacific, whom he grouped as "Malay"; and a final category that encompassed the nations of Europe and their diasporas overseas, to which he gave the name "Caucasians."

The first four categories were already in wide use, a list that went back, in slightly different form, to at least Carl Linnaeus (1707–78), the great Swedish naturalist and creator of the modern system of classification by species. The last label was Blumenbach's own invention. He had created his list based on a private collection of human skulls, the same kind of data source that Boas and other anthropometrists were still using a hundred years later. One skull in particular had caught his eye: the remains of a young girl from Georgia, in the Caucasus Mountains at the southern edge of the Russian Empire.

Blumenbach reckoned that her skull, with its graceful lines and modest proportions, was especially beautiful—the kind of head that must have been created in the image of God, as the earliest human beings had been. He proposed the label *Caucasian* not only because the girl was from the Caucasus but also because the mountain range was located near where some mapmakers had placed the biblical Garden of Eden. God had created perfection—this Georgian girl proved it—but over time the pressures of the environment and the vicissitudes of life had taken their toll: the fine hair became coarse, the white skin darkened to brown, the narrow nose flattened and flared. For Blumenbach, Caucasians were the ur-source from which all subsequent varieties of humans had devolved.

This schema had remarkable staying power. A Blumenbachian understanding of human difference wended its way into virtually every sphere of intellectual endeavor, from the natural sciences to history writing and the arts. Geography textbooks repeated it. Medical journals took it for granted. Museum displays explained it to public audiences. In the late 1890s, Powell's Bureau of Ethnology changed its name to the Bureau of *American* Ethnology, a recognition not of its geographical remit but of its racial vocation: to study the native peoples of the United States, that is, Blumenbach's "Americans." In Boas's day, even children were unconsciously intoning Blumenbach's framework. "Red, brown, yellow / Black and white," they sang, in the lyrics of a popular late-nineteenth-century Sunday school hymn. "They are precious in His sight / Jesus loves the little children of the world."

Race was never just a matter of classifying people by appearance, however. It had long been associated with other traits such as physical ability, intelligence, language, and level of civilization. Every race seemed to come prepackaged with its own ways of speaking, eating, dancing, and dressing. All these were thought to cluster together, much the way a bird's plumage, its distinctive warble, its flight pattern, and its instincts for nesting and migration might define a species. "The *permanence* of existing physical types will not be questioned by any Archaeologist or Naturalist of the present day. Nor, by such competent arbitrators, can the consequent permanence of moral and intellectual peculiarities of types be denied," declared the most important American textbook on geography and human biology, *Types of Mankind*, published in multiple editions after 1854. "The intellectual man is inseparable from the physical man; and the nature of the one cannot be altered without a corresponding change in the other."

The mystery, to any well-informed observer, was not whether such things naturally aligned; history had clearly shown that races came in more able and less able varieties—the complex, world-conquering peoples of Europe, for example, versus the simpler, benighted peoples of Africa. Beauty "predominates in the white races, mainly by reason of the relatively great individual variation among them," concluded the Smithsonian's first curator of physical anthropology—as the field of anthropometry was coming to be called—the Czech-born Aleš Hrdlička, in 1906. "It is less apparent among the yellow-brown peoples, and least so among pure blacks, where physical individualization, also, is most limited." Few anthropologists of the time would have disagreed. Daniel G. Brinton, a noted ethnologist and president of the American Association for the Advancement of Science, had used his leadership positions in several learned societies to affirm the view that "the black, the brown and the red races differ anatomically so much from the white . . . that even with equal cerebral capacity, they could never rival its results by equal efforts." The deep inequality of potential and achievement across the races was taken for granted. The real issue of concern to scientists was how these gradations of human-kind had come about in the first place. On this point, scientific opinion diverged into two rival camps, each launching barbs at the other as the twentieth century began.

So-called monogenists stressed that all human beings were vari-eties of the same basic type. Christian scholars defended this view on the basis of biblical evidence, pronouncing all humans to be descended from a single created pair, the Edenic Adam and Eve. More empiri-cally minded writers shared the same opinion but for different reasons. Social habits or external influences, such as patterns of reproduction or the environment, had created the varieties that went by the label of races. For Blumenbach and his monogenist followers, modern racial variety was simply evidence of how far human beings had fallen since being ejected from Paradise.

Even white Europeans, with their squalid cities and disease-wracked bodies, were surely a poor representation of the older, purer creations that had existed in epochs past. "It is not against experience to suppose that different species of the same genus, or varieties of the same species, may possess different qualifications," wrote Thomas Jefferson in his *Notes on the State of Virginia* (1785). "Will not a lover of natural history then, one who views the gradations in all the races of animals with the eye of philosophy, excuse an effort to keep those in the department of man as distinct as Nature has formed them?" Man-kind was a single entity, Jefferson suggested, but nevertheless one that had its own natural "departments," with characteristics as distinct as those marking off a Thoroughbred from a plow horse.

By contrast, polygenists believed that modern races had emerged either through separate acts of divine fiat or from distinct ancient progenitors. That view seemed to contradict the biblical story, of course, but many naturalists felt that the civilizational inequalities and physical differences among races could be explained in no other way. During the Enlightenment, polygenism had a stellar cast of sustainers, from Linnaeus to Voltaire and David Hume. By the nineteenth century, polygenist thought had been buttressed through exactly the same kinds of anthropometric techniques that Boas had been employing since his days at Clark. Amateur researchers such as the Philadelphia surgeon Samuel Morton and the Alabama physician Josiah Nott, as well as the zoologist Louis Agassiz—Putnam's old mentor at Harvard—published widely read studies showing the radical and inherent differences across the races. Science itself seemed to explain the natural sense of revulsion when this racial order was transgressed. "In seeing their black faces with their thick lips and grimacing teeth, the wool on their head, their bent knees, their elongated hands, their large curved nails, and especially the livid color of the palm of their hands," Agassiz wrote to his mother on first seeing black people in Philadelphia, "I could not take my eyes off their face in order to tell them to stay away."

By the time Boas was born, however, monogenists seemed to have won the argument, at least in scientific circles. In 1859 Charles Darwin's *On the Origin of Species* famously showed how distinctions in the physical appearance of living organisms could arise from small random changes over time. All forms of life were connected through the process of differentiation from previous forms. Separate species were the outcome of natural selection over very long periods of time. When Darwin turned his attention from finches to humans, in his *Descent of Man* (1871), he took aim squarely at the concept of race itself. No one could even agree on how many races there were, he wrote, subtly mocking his scholarly rivals:

> Man has been studied more carefully than any other animal, and yet there is the greatest possible diversity among capable judges whether he should be classed as a single species or race, or as two (Virey), as three (Jacquinot), as four (Kant), five (Blu-

menbach), six (Buffon), seven (Hunter), eight (Agassiz), eleven (Pickering), fifteen (Bory St. Vincent), sixteen (Desmoulins), twenty-two (Morton), sixty (Crawfurd), or as sixty-three, according to Burke.

The conclusion was clear. "Those naturalists . . . who admit the principle of evolution, and this is now admitted by the majority of rising men, will feel no doubt that all the races of man are descended from a single primitive stock." Human beings came in backward varieties and more advanced ones, Darwin believed, but these were largely a result of environment and habit rather than of innate biological distinctions derived from separate paths of evolutionary development.

Yet even after Darwin, polygenist ideas never really faded from scientific research or public discourse. Late in the century, they made an energetic comeback. In the United States, the end of the Civil War produced not so much a dismantling of the Old South as a transfer of many of its core traits to the national level. Pardons of former Confederate generals and officeholders allowed many to return to Congress or occupy appointed posts in the federal government. With the formal end of Reconstruction, these leaders launched a new wave of race-oriented legislation. Legally enforced segregation, prohibitions on interracial marriage, voting restrictions, and other policies introduced from the 1890s forward created a race-based system of politics and social relations—the authoritarian apartheid scheme eventually known as Jim Crow. The U.S. court system similarly developed an expansive body of case law that made whiteness into a clear legal category. Attorneys called on the expertise of historians, ethnologists, and other specialists to confirm the scientific validity of the country's bedrock schema for coding human beings. In 1878 a precedent-setting opinion affirmed that Chinese were not white. Similar decisions determined the nonwhite status of Hawaiians in 1889, Burmese and Japanese in 1894, Native Americans in 1900, Filipinos in 1916, and Koreans in 1921, while judges ruled Mexicans, Armenians, "Asian Indians," and Syrians to be biological "Caucasians" in 1897, 1909, and 1910, respectively. The consequences of these cases were immediate and practical. They determined one's ability to buy property in a race-restricted neighborhood, give birth in a race-restricted hospital, enroll a child in a race-restricted school, or be buried in a race-restricted cemetery. Rather than an inheritance from the era of slavery, Jim Crow and racial case law were new, national, and allegedly natural, based on the latest findings of racial science.

Things worked similarly on a global scale. In the late 1870s, the scramble for Africa among European colonial powers created a new interest in native peoples and the best ways of administering—or exploiting—them. From the rubber plantations of the Belgian Congo to the gold mines of South Africa, a new system of effective enslavement spread out across the continent. It was not so much that ideas about race caused European imperialists and American legislators to enact race-conscious policies. Rather, the assertion of power by people of European descent—whether the colonizers of Africa or the emboldened white majority in the post-Reconstruction United States—called out for justification. Racial theorists of all stripes were eager to provide it.

Race as a principle of political power energized the study of race as a scientific one. Popularizers abounded, and in a global scientific network of the confidently race-obsessed, they all read one another. Nott read Arthur de Gobineau, the French theorist whose thousand page *Essay on the Inequality of Human Races* (1853–55) posited an ancient "Aryan" population from which modern white people were descended and decried its spoliation through inbreeding with lesser types. Gobineau, in turn, had read Morton, whose study of mummified Egyptians had convinced him that the builders of the pyramids must have been white Europeans. Everyone read Agassiz, who, as director of the Harvard Museum of Comparative Zoology until his death in 1873, figured into legal debates, legislation, and public policy on everything from the naturalness of slavery to the prohibition on interracial marriage. *Types of Mankind*, the widely used textbook co-edited by Nott, made clear the practical uses of race-based science:

There are reasons why Ethnology should be eminently a science for American culture. Here, three of the five races, into which Blumenbach divided mankind, are brought together to determine the problem of their destiny as they best may, while Chinese immigration to California and the proposed importation of Coolie laborers threaten to bring us into equally intimate contact with a fourth. It is manifest that our relation to and management of these people must depend, in a great measure, upon their intrinsic race-character. . . . To the American statesman and the philanthropist, as well as to the naturalist, the study thus becomes one of exceeding interest.

Yet among the pantheon of writers, thinkers, and public lecturers on this topic, no one was more important than a person named Madison Grant. His particular gift was a facility for translating arcane data on human crania into practical suggestions for how Americans ought to live. Grant, it turned out, grasped one fact about his own country better than anyone else. The real utility of racial science lay not in determining who fit into which of Blumenbach's categories—this was as easy as glancing at a patch of skin or stroking a wisp of hair. The real trick was to delineate the better and worse brands of white people.

HANDSOME, WELL SPOKEN, AND patrician, with an ample mustache waxed to twin downward points, Madison Grant bore an unimpeachably American pedigree. His forefathers had been among some of the earliest Puritan and Dutch colonists in the New World, fighting in all of America's wars and signing its major documents of governance. A born New Yorker, Grant had taken degrees from Yale and Columbia before embarking on a life of public service, using his energy, ambition, and family wealth for projects that benefited society at large. Like his close friend and fellow man of action Theodore Roosevelt, he embodied progressive ideals: that government should make life better for the governed, that people of ability should turn their talents toward improving the commonweal, and that the latest advances in science would help show the way. By the age of forty, he had explored the American West, made original studies of moose and caribou, urged the creation of a system of national parks, and helped found the Bronx Zoo, which opened in 1899.

The zoo became one of Grant's beloved projects. It was incumbent on human society, he believed, to conserve the riches of the natural world in their most unadulterated forms. Like Roosevelt, he had been an avid big game hunter, and close interaction with the magnificent species to be found in the Rockies and on the Great Plains had convinced him that the well-planned management of wildlife would both ensure the preservation of America's distinctive fauna and prevent environmental tragedies. Through public awareness campaigns and relentless lobbying of Congress, Grant secured refuges in the Dakotas and Montana for the endangered American bison. In fact, had it not been for Grant, the animal would likely no longer exist.

You didn't need to care about *every* bison, Grant believed, but you did need to have some regard for the type. That was the whole point of a protected wilderness or a zoo. They were places of purity, preservation, and public education. Each specific animal was a representative of its kind, with all the traits one might expect to see in every other member of that same species. It was impossible to see all the lions or hippopotamuses in the world, of course, but by visiting a zoo, you might convince yourself that you had. Each individual was nothing less or more than a perfect embodiment of its category.

Left to its own devices, nature would yield its own grandeur—a bison bull with a towering neck hump; a moose cow that might face down a wolf pack to save her calf. But in his fieldwork, Grant had seen how noble species could decline. Entire populations disappeared when their most able-bodied representatives fell prey to irresponsible hunters. Habitats were transformed through the introduction of non-native animals. Majestic creatures could fade away under the stress of stealthy invaders.

Back home in New York, Grant became convinced that the same processes were at work in the squares and canyons of lower Manhattan. As he wrote to President William Howard Taft in the autumn of

1910, anyone who had occasion to "walk down Fifth Avenue during the noon hour, as far as Washington Square," could make up his own mind about the effects of invasive species. It was impossible to miss the immigrant Jews going about in caftans and untrimmed beards, the interrupting Italians and the bothersome Slovaks, the insistent hawkers just arrived from some foreign port, the babel of unintelligible languages. The whole city was swollen with newly deposited human types ignorant of how to keep out of the street or walk properly on the right side of the pavement. Around that time, with the Bronx Zoo operating to record crowds and other conservation efforts well on their way to success, Grant decided to turn his expertise to a new area of study and activism: the preservation of his own race against an onslaught of immigration.

There was no shortage of literature to read on the subject. A bibliography compiled in 1899 ran to some two thousand titles. The works of Nott, Gobineau, Agassiz, and other polygenists were readily available in any well-stocked library. In the first decade of the twentieth century, there was a forest of recent research on the relationship between human racial types and the fitness and ability—even survivability—of the world's most powerful people, white Europeans and their overseas descendants. The latest findings used anthropometric observation to define in clear, scientific terms the precise lines of racial membership. The statistician Frederick L. Hoffman showed that the heel length of the Negro—0.82 inches on average—bore a marked contrast to that of the Caucasian, at 0.48 inches. The German sociologist Otto Ammon, through genealogical investigations and head measurements, demonstrated that dolichocephalics tended to cluster in urban centers, and that the upper classes in cities tended to be longer-headed than the rest. "Dolichocephalic Nordics were dominating, enterprising, and Protestant," as one summary put it, while "brachycephalic Alpines were plodding, conservative, and Catholic."

A Harvard sociologist, William Z. Ripley—whom Grant probably heard at a lecture in 1908—synthesized these studies into a sweeping account of the relative contributions to human history of long-heads, broad-heads, and other types. Ripley's *The Races of*

Europe (1899) divided European peoples into "Teutonic," "Alpine," and "Mediterranean" types, the first of which were largely responsible for the achievements of world civilization. European history was one great racial pageant, as people entered and exited the stage, either adding lines to the script or fouling the narrative with their foreign ways. Modern Europe was a record of racial migrations, given the patchwork of types that now defined the continent. Long-headed Teutons had been chased into their redoubts in northern and western Europe, the high-water marks of previous floods of short-headed peoples from the south and east. As Ripley informed his readers, "Beyond the Pyrenees begins Africa."

For Grant, these works must have been revelations. He soon realized that he was witnessing, in real time, the waves of race migration that Ripley had described with such erudition in his treatise. He learned, too, that there was now a word to describe the publicly minded concern with racial fitness and the erosion of the human landscape. It was a term coined in the early 1880s by Francis Galton, the British naturalist and statistician who had also laid the foundations for anthropometry. The field of study and activism that Galton called "eugenics" took as its aim the betterment of humankind through the purposeful perpetuation of good qualities over bad ones. Derived from the literal Greek words for a "good type" or someone "well born," eugenics sought to apply to human beings the same scientific principles that Grant had already put to such good use in bison refuges and lion enclosures. If humans came in natural races, then the surest way to improve humanity was to encourage those racial qualities that Ripley and others had documented so brilliantly in the long arc of European history: the energetic, innovative, adventurous, and intelligent traits of the very best kind of white people.

Grant was no historian or anthropologist; he had never done original research on these themes, nor had he ever taken calipers in hand to calculate a cephalic index, as Boas had done to sparse crowds in Chicago. But his ability to summarize a vast amount of scholarship was nothing less than breathtaking. To this he added the steely assurance of a New York patrician with something to say. In the spring of

1916, he shared with friends the first draft of a manifesto on race and human history, which they encouraged him to send to a publisher. That autumn Charles Scribner's Sons—whose muscular author list already included Theodore Roosevelt and Rudyard Kipling—brought out Grant's text as *The Passing of the Great Race*. Bookstores shelved it not as a study in European history, although that was its primary theme, but rather as a work of science.

The book began with a discussion of race and democracy. "In America we have nearly succeeded in destroying the privilege of birth," Grant wrote, "that is, the intellectual and moral advantage a man of good stock brings into the world with him." Universal suffrage had created a "rule of the average" in American society. Claims for government to speak on behalf of the people had become "an unending wail for rights." History had shown, however, that "mankind emerged from savagery and barbarism under the leadership of selected individuals whose personal prowess, capacity, or wisdom gave them the right to lead and the power to compel obedience." And those people should be selected, Grant concluded, through the insights provided by the new sciences of race and eugenics.

Science had long discarded the "Adamic theory" that the origins of humankind lay in some original pair, he said, repeating the standard polygenist critique. Rather, each person was a summation of the traits of his race, a library of past couplings and admixtures. Bodies themselves offered the evidence. The human nose, he said, was of "the greatest value." The original human nose was broad and bridgeless, as is shown in infants, who recapitulate in their own facial characters the earliest forms of humankind. Long, narrow aquiline noses were associated with the more advanced races and civilizations. Lips, too, merited careful study. "Thick, protruding, everted lips are very ancient traits and are characteristic of primitive races," he wrote.

In all this, Grant was merely repeating what many anthropometrists had long maintained. But he took things two steps further. First, races themselves could be divided on the basis of discernible physical differences. Even white people, he said, came in "subspecies." Second, race characteristics were largely immutable. Both physical features and traits of behavior derived from deep differences among races and their subtypes, which science, properly focused, could help elucidate. Just as wearing a toga could not make a Syrian into a Roman, "it has taken us fifty years to learn that speaking English, wearing good clothes, and going to school and to church . . . [do] not transform a negro into a white man." Human faces and bodies were "an intricate mass of hieroglyphs" that scientists were still straining to read. Once they were able to do so, it would at last be possible not just to classify human beings properly but to select those traits for onward transmission that would congeal into genuinely better populations. "One of the greatest difficulties in classifying man," he wrote, "is his perverse predisposition to mismate." Scientific study could provide ways of rectifying that. Since primitive races were leftovers from older versions of human beings—"primitive" because they were reversions to some "primary" form of humankind—their admixture with advanced races tended to produce a reversion to this lower, more ancient type. "The cross between a white man and an Indian is an Indian; the cross between a white man and a negro is a negro; the cross between a white man and a Hindu is a Hindu; and the cross between any of the three European races and a Jew is a Jew."

Like Ripley—whom he singled out as a model in the acknowledgments—Grant then provided a broad-brush treatment of European history from Paleolithic times, through the ancients and the barbarian invasions, to the modern era, all recounted through the prism of contests among European physical subspecies. "As soon as the true bearing and import of the facts are appreciated by lawmakers, a complete change in our political structure will inevitably occur," Grant concluded, "and our present reliance on the influences of education will be superseded by a readjustment based on racial values." What this meant in practice, he said, was that the "altruistic values" and "maudlin sentimentalism" that let in millions of lower-rank Europeans were "sweeping the nation toward a racial abyss." No longer could the country remain an "asylum for the oppressed." Otherwise, America would surely follow in the path of Athens and Rome, pushed off the stage of world history by an invasion of inferiors.

White Nordic Americans were the great race whose passing he had been chronicling all along. If you needed a visual representation, you could simply turn to the back of the volume, where foldout maps, in bold colors, showed the waxing and waning of physical types across the European landscape, a time-lapse history lesson in the transience of races that failed to heed their own fragility.

The Passing of the Great Race was hailed as a milestone in the application of scientific ideas to history and public policy. It inspired an entire generation of acolytes who would go on to write their own treatises, advise policy makers, and push through new legislation. Three-quarters of American universities, from Harvard to the University of California, introduced courses on eugenics, many of them using Grant as a primary text. Lothrop Stoddard—a young, well-educated New Englander who was frequently grouped with Grant among America's most reliable racial scientists—went on to write the best-selling *The Rising Tide of Color* (1920), which warned of racial inundation by the dark-skinned, and *The New World of Islam* (1921), which surveyed the threat to the West of a "Mohameddan revival" among Arabs, Turks, and Persians. "Well, these books are all scientific," says Tom Buchanan confidently in F. Scott Fitzgerald's *The Great Gatsby*, referring to Grant and Stoddard. "It's up to us who are the dominant race to watch out or these other races will have control of things."

By 1910 the foreign-born population in the United States had swelled to some 13.5 million, the result of a large wave of migration over the two decades spanning the turn of the century. They accounted for 14.7 percent of the entire U.S. population, only slightly less than the highest-ever peak, at 14.8 percent, in 1890. The rate of increase was staggering. Nearly a third more people were foreign-born in 1910 than in 1900. (It would take another century, into the 2010s, before immigration figures would ever again approach similar levels. At the time Donald J. Trump announced his campaign for president by denouncing Mexican "rapists," for example, the foreign-born figure was within a little more than a percentage point of the 1910 level.)

Most of these newcomers lived in dense urban areas, which is why intellectuals and politicians were so concerned with them. The new-comers were on the very doorstep of older, wealthier American families such as Grant's. The Chinese Exclusion Act of 1882 had halted the legal arrival of Chinese laborers, but from the 1890s onward, the country's doors were flung open to millions of Europeans, especially from the continent's east and south. Indeed, by the turn of the century, close to 90 percent of the foreign-born population listed their place of birth as somewhere in Europe. New York City's orderly old Kleindeutschland was now brimming with Jews, Poles, Italians, and Slovaks. That is why, for Grant and other theorists of the era, the problem of race was not about delineating Caucasians from Asians or Negroes. Such distinctions were plainly evident to any educated person. The deeper concern was how to distinguish advanced, healthy, and vigorous northern Europeans from the lesser subraces now stumbling over one another on the streets and alleyways of the Lower East Side.

But Grant did not take up his pen just to make an academic point. In the earliest pages of *The Passing of the Great Race*, he made specific reference to a recent government-funded study whose results—if taken seriously—could serve as the death knell of America's most able race. According to Grant:

> Recent attempts have been made in the interest of inferior races among our immigrants to show that the shape of the skull does change, not merely in a century, but in a single generation. In 1910, the report of the anthropological expert of the Congressional Immigration Commission, gravely declared that a round skull Jew on his way across the Atlantic might and did have a round skull child, but that a few years later, in response to the subtle elixir of American institutions, as exemplified in an East Side tenement, might and did have a child whose skull was appreciably longer; and that a long skull south Italian, breeding freely, would have precisely the same experience the reverse direction. In other words, the Melting Pot was acting instantly under the influence of a changed environment.

This was all nonsense, Grant declared, and his book had shown why. His reference to an obscure government report was not accidental. It was in fact one of Grant's primary targets—as was its author, the unnamed "anthropological expert." For in the years that Grant had been reading Ripley and Galton, Boas had been quietly busy on his own work. It involved actually visiting the neighborhoods of lower Manhattan that Grant had been theorizing about uptown.

AFTER HIS APPOINTMENT AT Columbia, Boas's connections with the American Museum of Natural History began to fade. He had a habit of making himself more respected than liked. His time at the museum had produced new research and exhibitions but also disappointments, professional disagreements, and hurt feelings among his colleagues, who found him confident to a fault, officious, and given to pique. When he formally resigned his curatorship in 1905, no one begged him to stay.

The move to full-time work at the university gave Boas the opportunity to build his own team of researchers. "Neither Berlin with its five anthropological professorships, nor Paris with its anthropological school, nor Holland with its colonial school, could give a proper training to the observers whom we need," he wrote to a colleague in 1901. He reorganized the department's coursework to include training in linguistics and ethnology, not just the traditional anthropometry. "With archaeology represented," he told the university's president, Nicholas Murray Butler, "we should be able to train anthropologists in all directions."

Boas had decamped with Marie and the children to a rambling house across the Hudson River in Grantwood, New Jersey. It soon became an informal gathering place for a growing coterie of graduate students. Many were already making names for themselves as well-rounded scholars with knowledge of ethnology, linguistics, archaeology, and physical anthropology, the four distinct fields that Boas had come to see as the foundation of a proper discipline of anthropology. The first of these to complete the doctorate at Columbia, in 1901, was

Alfred Kroeber, another member of New York's German immigrant community. He was soon on his way to California, where he set up the new anthropology department at Berkeley. Robert Lowie, an Austrian émigré and budding expert on the Plains Indians, graduated in 1908 and later joined Kroeber on the West Coast. Edward Sapir, a Jewish immigrant from the Russian Empire, finished his degree under Boas's direction in 1909 with a dissertation on the languages of the Pacific Northwest. He soon moved to Ottawa to head up the Canadian government's geological survey. Alexander Goldenweiser and Paul Radin, Jewish immigrants from Kiev and Łódź, finished in 1910 and 1911, with work on anthropological theory and Native American ethnology. "It is gratifying to note that the demand for graduates of the Anthropological Department of Columbia University has always been such that practically all the young men in anthropological museums and colleges are those who have either graduated here or studied a considerable number of years in this Department," Boas bragged to President Butler.

Within only a few years, however, that early momentum seemed to stall. Butler frowned on teachers' spending so much time on research rather than in the lecture hall. He informed Boas that no increases in appropriations for anthropology would be made. There was no money for teaching materials. There were too few lecturers to cover all the fields of study. Things were in "a pitiable condition," Boas wrote to Kroeber at the beginning of 1908, "and . . . for the time being all our former hopes and aspirations have gone to pieces." The only solution was to try to find new sources of income, even "a complete change of interests," he added, which might provide a more stable financial footing for the fieldwork that he hoped to continue.

Boas began sending out letters to virtually any source he could think of, proposing grand research projects that might somehow attract new funding. He contacted his old colleagues at the Bureau of American Ethnology with the idea of creating a handbook of American Indian languages, which he hoped would provide additional travel money for his students and co-workers. In the 1907–1908 academic year, he broadened the course offerings, including a new class on "The Negro Problem." "I am endeavoring to organize certain scientific work on the Negro race which I believe will be of great practical value in modifying the views of our people in regard to the Negro problem," he told Booker T. Washington. Aware that more bodies in the classroom meant more reason for President Butler to increase the department's budget, he also pushed to open classes for undergraduates. Then in the spring of 1908, a special new opportunity came Boas's way that promised to resolve a host of difficulties at once.

A year earlier the U.S. Congress had established a special commission to study the rise in immigration and its practical effects on the United States. Rumors had circulated that foreign governments were willfully sending over criminals and the infirm as a way of ridding themselves of undesirables and, in the process, weakening American society. Chaired by Senator William P. Dillingham, a Vermont Republican, the commissioners eventually included such luminaries as Henry Cabot Lodge, a Massachusetts Republican and immigration opponent, and LeRoy Percy, a Mississippi Democrat and prominent Delta planter. Decked out in straw boaters and linen suits, this distinguished group of commissioners set out on a steamship journey to Naples, Marseilles, and Hamburg, among other European ports. There they found squalid detention camps full of Italians, Greeks, and Syrians, all willing to pay unscrupulous captains whatever they might charge for passage across the Atlantic. They uncovered no evidence of a conspiracy to dilute the "great race," as Madison Grant would soon term it. Still, when they returned, they decided to organize a series of working groups to study the overall problem of immigration, assemble statistical data, and issue detailed recommendations toward creating a more rational policy for dealing with the waves of foreigners now crashing on American shores.

In March 1908 the commission contacted Boas with the idea of preparing a report on "the immigration of different races into this country" and asked what thoughts he might have on how it could be carried out. Boas wasted no time in responding. He proposed to examine physical changes among immigrants who had recently arrived in the United States. After all, if immigration was in fact having an effect on American society, its clearest results were likely to be seen in the bodies of the newest Americans: the immigrants' children. Were they assimilating to some common American type? Or were the hereditary traits common to the several races of Europe so powerful that they would survive across time and distance, to be passed on to children who were the products of marriage across racial or ethnic lines? Might those conserved traits, the vestiges of ancient races and subraces, throw up natural barriers to what was being called America's "melting pot" ideal?

"The importance of this question can hardly be overestimated," Boas wrote to the commission staff, "and the development of modern anthropological methods makes it perfectly feasible to give a definite answer to the problem that presents itself to us." He proposed a budget of nearly $20,000, which would pay for a team of observers to measure heads, take family histories, and compile the gargantuan statistical data set that would be required to answer the questions he had posed. "I believe I can assure you that the practical results of this investigation will be important in so far as they will settle once and for all the question of whether the immigrants from southern Europe and from eastern Europe are and can be assimilated by our people." The commission balked at the price tag but agreed to fund a preliminary study. That fall the government agreed to expand the work into a full-scale research project.

Boas's graduate students, Columbia colleagues, and hired assistants soon fanned out across the city. They lugged along many of the same measuring devices Boas had used at the Chicago world's fair, plus a set of glass marbles specially crafted by a New York optician for comparing eye color. They measured the heads of students in Jewish schools on the Lower East Side. They distributed questionnaires to Italian families in Chatham Square and Yonkers. They queried Bohemians in their neighborhoods on the East Side, between Third and First avenues and East 70th and 84th streets. They chased down Hungarians, Poles, and Slovaks in Brooklyn. They stood on the docks at Ellis Island, calipers and eye color meters in hand, as people waited for medical inspections. At reform schools and juvenile asylums, at parochial and private schools, at the Young Men's Hebrew Association and the YMCA, some 17,821 people subjected themselves to Boas's scales and measuring tapes. Nothing like it had ever been attempted before, certainly not under the auspices of an official government commission whose charge was to understand precisely how immigrants were affecting the literal body politic of their new country. In the spring of 1910, Boas wrote to colleagues at the Bureau of American Ethnology to tell them that his work was producing "entirely unexpected results, and [makes] the whole problem appear in an entirely new light."

After countless hours of data collection, analysis, and write-up, the conclusions were finally published in 1911 as *Changes in Bodily Form of Descendants of Immigrants*, part of the Dillingham Commission's official record. Boas expressed his main conclusion in a simple sentence on the second page: "The adaptability of the immigrant seems to be very much greater than we had a right to suppose before our investigations were instituted." Children born in the United States had more in common with other U.S.-born children than with the national group—or race, as Grant would have termed it—represented by their parents. Round-headed Jews became long-headed ones. The long heads of Sicilians compressed into shorter heads. The wide faces of Neapolitans narrowed to match those of the immigrants by whom they were surrounded, not those of their racial brethren in the old country. There was, in other words, no such thing—in purely physical terms—as a "Jew," a "Pole," or a "Slovak," if one judged by the bodies of the children of first-generation immigrants. The conditions of life, from diet to environment, were having a quick and measurable effect on head forms that were thought to be fixed, inheritable, and indicative of one's essential type.

Races were unstable, Boas concluded. And if they didn't exist as physical realities in our present moment, then neither could they have existed in the past—which meant in turn that any history of humanity that presented itself as a battle royale of races was essentially false. If there was no physical permanence to the concept of race, at least as it had been popularly defined, then there could be no clustering of other traits around it, such as intelligence, physical ability, collective fitness, or aptitude for civilizational advancement. "These results are so definite that, while heretofore we had the right to assume that human types are stable," he wrote, "all the evidence is now in favor of a great plasticity of human types, and the permanence of types in new surroundings appears rather as the exception than as the rule."

Boas had been working up to this conclusion since his days on Baffin Island, but he now had more than simple intuition to back up his claims. He had data, masses of it, all pointing toward a revolutionary—and to many, discomfiting—conclusion: that the "peoples" he had been helping to document in museums and exhibitions since his own immigration to the United States were not natural varieties of humankind. There was no reason to believe that a person of one racial or national category was more of a drain on society, more prone to criminality, or more difficult to assimilate than any other. What people *did*, rather than who they *were*, ought to be the starting point for a legitimate science of society and, by extension, the basis for government policy on immigration.

In the same year that the Dillingham Commission report was published, Boas elaborated on these ideas in his first book for a popular audience, *The Mind of Primitive Man*. For someone who had wanted a public voice since his journalistic dispatches from the Arctic, it was a long-awaited step—in fact, more of a plunge—into the churning debates about race, science, and power. It was also his first attempt to form the enormous mounds of empirical data—built up, layer by layer, from his work at the Chicago world's fair, the American Museum of Natural History, and the seminar room at Columbia—into something that might be called a worldview.

Europeans and their descendants have made forests into productive fields, Boas began, dug up mineral treasures hidden deep inside stony mountains, and crafted machines that magically do their bidding. Primitive peoples, succumbing to the elements rather than subduing them, have none of this, and it is natural for civilized people to look on them with "a pitying smile." But behind the smile, he argued, lay an unproven assumption: that the successes of one's own society today were due to some inherent superiority on the part of the people typically called civilized, especially "the Northern European type," over lesser-achieving primitives.

That assumption, Boas wrote, had no basis in fact. Chance and time might be equally good explanations for disparities in achievement, since comparatively "high" civilizations had developed in the New World at a time when the Old World remained in its own civilizational infancy. The spread of Europeans overseas during the age of exploration and then the establishment of empires across the lands they conquered only cut short whatever material and cultural development had been in process there. "In short," he concluded, "historical events appear to have been much more potent in leading races to civilization than their faculty, and it follows that achievements of races do not warrant us in assuming that one race is more highly gifted than the other."

Physical traits, too, were a poor guide to distinguishing advanced peoples from more backward ones, Boas wrote. People had the habit of referring to "higher races," implying that there was a linear pathway that led from animals toward high-achieving Europeans, with so-called lower races retaining some of the physical traits of the animals from which all humans had descended. In the footrace of civilization, those who lagged behind were said to be those whose bodies were as brutish as their customs. But a moment's reflection revealed this to be nonsense, Boas pointed out. The most truly apelike creatures among human beings—from an anthropometric point of view—were not the "lower" races but rather certain Europeans, those who tended to be thin-lipped and short-legged, with loads of back hair.

Boas next turned to the problem of human types, which involved what he called "the indefiniteness of distinctions." It was possible, of course, to find two people, one from sub-Saharan Africa, say, and another from northern Europe, with physical distinctions that were marked and easily observable: significant differences of skin color, nose shape, hair texture, and so forth. But to believe that these things necessarily clustered together in all cases flew in the face of scientific observation. Physical differences were about minute gradations, about the mixing of physical traits from population to population, not about clear dividing lines separating one physical type from another. Hair and skin color, femur length and head shape, actually differed widely *within* the human populations that were routinely classed as belonging to the same type, if one only took a moment to look—or, as Boas had done, to do the numerical measurements that had consumed him in Chicago and, more recently, on the Lower East Side. To believe otherwise was to put theory before empirical observation, to reason deductively rather than inductively. And that, Boas believed, was not science at all. "When . . . we compare all the races and types of man, we find that innumerable transitions exist, which would make it difficult to state that any one particular feature belongs to all the individuals of one type, to the exclusion of all others." Moreover, given that many of these traits change from generation to generation or even over the lifespan of a single human being, "man cannot be assumed to have a stable form."

Without homogeneous, easily identifiable "races," the entire edifice of racial hierarchy crumbled. "The differences between different types of man are, on the whole, small as compared to the range of variation in each type," Boas concluded. Not only was there no bright line dividing one race from another, but the immense variation within racial categories called into question the utility of the concept itself. Once you really tried to define what a race was, much less quantify it with calipers or measuring tapes, you found that you were holding ashes in your hands.

The Mind of Primitive Man represented a summation of Boas's anthropometric research. It was also a foray into defining a way of seeing not just race and physical difference but the world at large. Even though he spent the first half of the book dismantling the idea of racial hierarchy and, indeed, of race itself, he intended the book to be about the *mind* of primitive peoples. It turned out that the "activities of the human mind exhibit an infinite variety of form among the peoples of the world" that was no less pronounced than their physical differences.

"It is a common observation that we desire or act first," Boas wrote, "and then try to justify our desires and our actions." He was identifying a mechanism that he labeled the "secondary interpretation of customary actions": the tendency to rationalize our cultural practices according to some other—usually nonsensical—set of explanations. For example, it was often said that civilized societies developed forks because of the danger of cutting one's mouth when eating with a knife, as barbarous peoples might do. Yet this was clearly ludicrous. It was just as easy to damage one's mouth with a fork as with a knife. All societies had the tendency to treat their own customs, especially those wrapped up in a great deal of emotion—for instance, table manners among high-society Americans—as the product of some prior rational development. But it was far more reasonable to believe that these customs had come about for any number of reasons, from historical borrowing to pure chance, than to seek their origins in some universal logic. If you found yourself upset at some other society's customs, Boas argued, the truly scientific thing to do was to analyze your own reaction. It was probably a good clue to the things that your own culture held dear. The best data generator was your own sense of disgust.

Here, Boas believed, method was everything. If you really wanted to understand what was happening in a Kwakiutl village or an Inuit camp, you had to try as hard as possible to divest yourself of the opinions common to the environment in which you were born. You had to struggle to follow new trains of thought and new logic, to grab on to new emotions. It took work to feel a fearful tug in your gut, a rising anger, a deep sadness—all for reasons that might seem strange and unfamiliar—and then take yourself to the point of acting in accordance with those feelings: the twitch of a foot ready to take flight or the tremble of a hand about to strike out. Otherwise you couldn't claim to understand anything at all. You were simply staring at your own biases, reflected back at you in the mirror of someone else's culture.

If you applied this method to what travelers, journalists, and even people who called themselves anthropologists typically said about primitive people, Boas wrote, you would see that most of their commentary was nonsense. Tribal people were often said to be indolent, but what if they were only lazy when it came to things that they didn't happen to care about? Why should we expect that every people everywhere would necessarily attend to the same things with equal zeal or approach the same projects with diligence and commitment? Primitive people were sometimes said to be quick to anger and to lash out wildly according to their emotions. To be civilized, after all, was to be coolheaded and rational. But didn't it take coolheadedness and logical thought to follow a seal pod across a featureless ice floe, or to track a whale in an oared canoe to the point of its, and your own, exhaustion? "The proper way to compare the fickleness of the savage and that of the white," he wrote, "is to compare their behavior in undertakings which are equally important to each."

Throughout *The Mind of Primitive Man*, Boas was elaborating not only a method and a set of first principles for understanding human societies. He was also working out what would become his signature style of argumentation. In chapter after chapter, his literary approach was the same. He stated a common idea and admitted that it had certain attractions as a way of seeing the world. He showed how it accorded with our normal experience, how it explained different phenomena, how it made sense of a wide variety of observations. But then came the kicker: What if our experiences and observations are themselves the problem? What if we are gazing at the world through spectacles of our own making, inherently hemmed in by our own experience? If we really want to test our theories of human development and social organization, we first need to open our eyes.

It is somewhat difficult for us to recognize that the value which we attribute to our own civilization is due to the fact that we participate in this civilization, and that it has been controlling all our actions since the time of our birth; but it is certainly conceivable that there may be other civilizations, based perhaps on different traditions and on a different equilibrium of emotion and reason, which are of no less value than ours, although it may be impossible for us to appreciate their values without having grown up under their influence. The general theory of valuation of human activities, as developed by anthropological research, teaches us a higher tolerance than the one which we now profess.

Boas was coming to see his profession not just as a science but also as a state of mind, even a prescription for a good life. Properly practiced, it could cultivate a disposition that pointed toward "a higher tolerance"—one that would leave even the pitying smile behind. It was a blueprint for how anthropology might turn itself into the most hopeful of sciences, one whose job was not just to catalog the many different ways of being human but also, in a way, to love them.

Chapter Six

AMERICAN EMPIRE

....

The year 1911 had been a triumph for Boas. His letter writing and networking had put the anthropology department on firmer financial footing. The Dillingham Commission had enabled the largest statistical project he had ever completed. He published the first volume of the *Handbook of American Indian Languages*, sponsored by the Smithsonian, which promised to be a continuing source of research funds. And *The Mind of Primitive Man*, although not much of a commercial success, had marked his first major foray beyond the academy.

By the summer of his fifty-third birthday, he was at last the public intellectual he had longed to be since his journey to Baffin Island. "We recognize thus that every classification of mankind must be more or less artificial, according to the point of view selected," he wrote in the introduction to the first volume of the *Handbook*. He was now considered an expert on the very classifications he had been working to unweave. Invitations flowed in to deliver scientific papers and speak at gatherings on the race problem.

Years earlier he had given a stirring graduation speech, at the invitation of W. E. B. Du Bois, at Atlanta University, where he called on Americans to reject old ideas of racial hierarchy. Now he and Du Bois again appeared on the same stage in London at the First Universal Races Congress, a global assembly of notable authorities on everything from "inter-racial economics" to "positive suggestions for promoting inter-racial friendliness." "The assumption of an absolute stability of human types is not plausible," Boas said plainly in his speech, repeating the findings of his Dillingham Commission report—something he would do whenever he had the chance, in public lectures and popular articles. Our ideas about race are themselves products of history, Boas implied, a rationalization for something a group of people desperately want to believe: that they are higher, better, and more advanced than some other group. Race was how Europeans explained to themselves their own sense of privilege and achievement. Insofar as races existed, at least as Europeans typically understood them, it was through an act of cultural conjuring, not biological destiny.

All around him, however, Boas's own country seemed to be moving in the opposite direction from the one his scientific conclusions dictated. The Dillingham Commission spent nearly a million dollars on the forty-one volumes that formed its final report—and largely ignored everything Boas had said in his contribution to the effort. Dillingham, Lodge, Percy, and their congressional colleagues, most of them inveterate opponents of immigration, reasserted their convictions. The commission's conclusions reaffirmed the power and meaning of racial distinctions. In thinking about immigrants, the summary report read, the commission "deemed it reasonable to follow the classification employed by Blumenbach, which school geographies have made most familiar to Americans, viz, . . . the white, yellow, black, brown, and red races." People who had arrived since the 1880s were mainly from the first of these racial groups but, unfortunately, from the "less progressive and advanced countries of Europe." Their propensity to assimilate had been "slow as compared to that of the earlier non-English-speaking races." They were "as a class far less intelligent than the old" and "essentially unlike" the earlier arrivals from the British Isles and the German lands. Having come mainly to profit from the advantages that America provided, not to contribute to the common good, they would forever have one foot out the door, with dubious loyalty to their new country and a trailing sense of affinity for their benighted homelands.

Boas was an immigrant, too, of course, but at least according to the Dillingham Commission, his own community was as close as one could imagine to a model minority: the successful and well-integrated German speakers whom the commission took pains to point out were very different from the more recent Italians, Poles, and Jews. Despite the upsurge in immigrants from eastern and southern Europe, people from the German lands were still the largest non-Anglo-Saxon group in the United States overall and the largest in just under half the forty-eight states. Over the previous decades, German Americans had emerged as leaders in virtually every aspect of the country's public life. They populated the professoriate and state bar associations. They edited newspapers, tilled farmland from Pennsylvania to the Dakotas, taught in elite academies and one-room schoolhouses, and preached from pulpits before congregations of Lutherans, Evangelicals, and Roman Catholics alike. Even German-speaking Jews, at least those who remained religiously observant, attended synagogues whose architecture and decor—pews, chancels, stained glass—emphasized their connections with their Christian neighbors.

That was why it came as such a shock when, only a few years after the Dillingham Commission's report was submitted to Congress, Boas found himself in a position he never could have predicted—as a member of one of the most feared, even hated, minorities in the United States. Boas had come into the world amid the reassertion of autocratic rule across Europe in the wake of the failed 1848 revolutions. Now, in middle age, he could feel a similar shift in his adopted country—not because he was Jewish but because he was German. With the outbreak of the First World War, the two largest European immigrant communities in the United States—those with ancestral ties to the British Isles and those with connections to Germany—increasingly found themselves on opposite sides of an international struggle.

Germany's brutal attack on Belgium in August 1914 prompted strong condemnation from supporters of the Allied powers. In turn, German Americans called for calm and a fair hearing for all sides in the conflict. Over the next year, as the German navy increased submarine activity in the Atlantic—culminating in the infamous sinking of the *Lusitania* in May 1915, with the loss of nearly twelve hundred passengers, including Americans—public commentary shifted toward the idea that ethnic Germans were a direct security threat to the United States. German businesses faced informal boycotts. Beethoven and Wagner were removed from the repertoires of major orchestras. Monuments to Goethe and Schiller were splashed with paint. Cartoons in major newspapers and magazines cast Germans as conspirators and closet barbarians, waiting for their chance to wreck a factory or poison a reservoir. No longer was U.S. citizenship any guarantee of loyalty, warned President Woodrow Wilson in his December 1915 State of the Union address. Spies and saboteurs "born under other flags but welcomed under our generous naturalization laws" were likely to use it to disguise their terrorist schemes.

The next summer secret agents working for Germany exploded the huge Black Tom munitions dump in Jersey City, New Jersey. Buildings were leveled for a mile around. Windows broke as far away as Manhattan, and the Statue of Liberty was pocked with shrapnel. Some six hundred thousand German noncitizens were required to register with the federal government and were barred from visiting wharves, traveling by train, or residing in the District of Columbia. The Justice Department urged Americans to remain vigilant and to report suspicious activity, especially if it involved people fitting the cultural profile of an enemy sympathizer or agent—someone who looked German, sounded German, or expressed pro-German opinions. Louisiana, Kentucky, South Dakota, and Iowa prohibited the use of the German language in public gatherings or over the telephone. Nearly half of all states placed a full or partial ban on teaching it in schools (legislation that it would eventually take a Supreme Court decision to undo). The public reaction to these shifts in policy and political rhetoric was predictable. Murders, floggings by impromptu "citizens' committees," lynchings, tarrings-and-featherings, and widespread vandalism were reported from Wisconsin to Florida. Families stopped speaking German, even at home, or swept away suspicious *k*'s and *sch*'s from their surnames.

Boas and Marie had found a sizable and welcoming community

of Germans in New York, with their own restaurants, religious institutions, and cultural centers, from Kleindeutschland to the Upper
West Side and the New Jersey suburbs. But the U.S. government, and
American society at large, seemed to turn rapidly against this overwhelmingly assimilated group. For the first time, Boas was no longer the confident immigrant, making his life in a new country on the
assumption that it was part of the same civilizational space as in his
native Germany. He was now an outsider. Soon the *New York Herald* began regularly publishing the names and addresses of people
thought to be German or Austro-Hungarian nationals. Boas's U.S.
citizenship, which he had acquired in 1892, seemed scant protection.

It didn't help that Boas had also became one of the war's most public critics. In 1915 he announced his sympathy for the German cause in
a letter to the *New York Times*, arguing that this personal point of view
should in no way be a reason to condemn a fellow citizen. If things
continued as they were, Germany might have good reason to declare
a state of war with the United States. "No matter what the letter of
the law may be," he wrote, "the mind of the man in the street who
has German sympathies will utterly fail to understand why one man
who sends provisions to a German man-of-war should be prosecuted
by our Government and the severest punishment within reach of the
law meted out to him, while others who send ammunition worth millions of dollars to the armies of the other side should be protected and
coddled by our Administration." Were the United States in the same
position as Germany or Austria—surrounded by unstable neighbors,
ruled by a small clique, provoked by the ambitions of other imperial
powers—it would likely react in the same way Germany had. In fact,
the United States had done so little more than a decade earlier, during
the Spanish-American War, when it was the Americans who were the
threat to international peace and Europeans the ones calling for calm.

Boas reiterated his position early the next year, arguing in another
lengthy letter to the *Times* that the United States was now setting itself
up not just as a partisan in the European conflict but also as a potential
"arbiter of the world." The letter was a kind of intellectual biography.

He had come to the United States full of optimism that the nationalist conflicts he had known in Europe would be foreign in this melting-pot nation. But in 1898, he had had a "rude awakening" and a period of "profound disappointment." America had embarked on its own imperialist expansion in the war with Spain and in its brutal colonial administration of the Philippines. His political faith had always been based on the conviction that self-restraint should define American foreign policy. Americans' ignorance of the lifeways of others demanded it. "I have always been of the opinion that we have no right to impose our ideals upon other nations," he wrote, "no matter how strange it may seem to us that they enjoy the kind of life they lead, how slow they may be in utilizing the resources of their countries, or how much opposed their ideals may be to our own."

In early 1917, Boas denounced the slide toward U.S. involvement in the European war and blamed President Wilson for the growing hostility toward Germany. In April, when the United States finally entered the conflict, Boas's views were not merely suspect but, in a time of war fever, plainly unpatriotic. "What had been tolerated before became intolerable now," Columbia's President Butler declared at that summer's commencement, seemingly targeting radical professors such as Boas. "What had been folly was treason." Another university colleague wrote to the *Times* to condemn Boas's views as "un-American" and certainly not shared by the majority of "Columbia men."

Boas's bosses at the university urged him to limit his public pronouncements. When this failed, the trustees cut his salary, denied him access to research funds, and openly criticized his propensity for teaching "anthropology, as construed from the German viewpoint," as one board member put it. As bills piled up and research costs continued to accrue, at times all that kept him afloat financially was a fund collected by academic friends and sympathetic patrons.

Boas was not for reining in, however. He continued to blast off articles and letters to the editor. He railed against politicians from President Wilson on down and picked fights with some of America's foremost public figures. When asked to review Madison Grant's *Passing of the Great Race*, he seized the opportunity. Grant had produced "a Cassandric prophecy of all the ills that will befall us on account of the increase of dark-eyed types," Boas wrote in *The New Republic*. In fact, he said, there was little evidence to support these claims; they were little more than "dogmatic assumptions," most of which turned out to be plainly wrong. The categories Americans called "races" had no hereditary basis at all. When you actually measured the bodies of people belonging to any one race, what you found was not clusters of physical features—much less intellectual or moral ones—but rather an immense diversity of types. "To speak of hereditary characteristics of a human race as a whole has no meaning."

Grant had also committed a deeper sin, Boas felt. Racism wasn't only the idea that some races were higher or lower than others. Racism was at base the belief in the inheritable reality of race itself—an idea trussed up in the language of science and, as such, every bit as much a product of Western culture as, say, a painted mask was the product of the Kwakiutl. When there was no evidence for a theory, Boas had suggested in *The Mind of Primitive Man*, you had to let it go—especially if that theory just happened to place people like you at the center of the universe. Otherwise, what you called science was nothing more than nonsense on stilts.

Boas was making a point that required readers to make a difficult conceptual leap: he was asking Americans and western Europeans to suspend their belief in their own greatness. Grant, for his part, had something simpler and more powerful on his side: the deep self-confidence of Western society founded upon the observable reality of Anglo-Saxon dominance around the globe. According to Grant, Germany's wrongheaded alliance with the Ottomans and the Japanese only proved what could happen when the race-privileged lashed their fate to the race-backward. By contrast, all Boas had was some arcane head measurements and a scientific theory that flew in the face of accepted wisdom. Predictably, Grant's *Passing of the Great Race* continued its brisk sales. The book soon went into a new edition, this time with references to "Teutons"—whom American doughboys were now fighting in the trenches—replaced with the more politically acceptable "Nordics."

AFTER THE WAR ENDED, Boas's professional problems only got worse. Science was a siren call, he felt. Improperly used, it would always draw policy makers into dangerous waters. He published an essay in *The Nation* calling out, although not naming, scholars he alleged had conducted espionage abroad under the guise of fieldwork and denouncing the use of anthropological research for any governmental purposes at all. The American Anthropological Association—a body he had helped found—responded by censuring him for politicizing scholarly research and by removing him from its governing council. Leading scholars wrote to the Smithsonian calling for the institution to sever ties with him altogether for, among other things, "impugn[ing] the veracity of the President of the United States." The Smithsonian's secretary, Charles D. Walcott, had already decided to fire Boas from his position as honorary philologist with the Bureau of American Ethnology, a post he had held since beginning work on the *Handbook of American Indian Languages*. Beyond that, Walcott urged President Wilson to have the Justice Department investigate Boas for radicalism. Attorney General A. Mitchell Palmer—who would soon launch the infamous "Palmer Raids" against leftists and other alleged dissidents—opened a file on him.

Boas "now occupies a comparatively obscure and uninfluential position," wrote Henry Fairfield Osborn, president of the American Museum of Natural History, to Walcott. Osborn had succeeded Jesup as head of the museum and had long seen Boas as something of a crank. He had even written a laudatory preface to the revised edition of Grant's *Passing of the Great Race* and was busy recasting the museum's exhibits to illustrate Grant's philosophy of racial superiority. He was hardly sorry to see Boas get his comeuppance.

Boas's difficulties were also personal ones. Close family members were still in Germany, and Boas, like many German Americans, had been trapped between loyalties to home and to homeland. After the signing of the Versailles treaty, his family was caught up in the financial crisis and social turmoil that followed. His oldest sister, Toni, managed to move to the United States, but as a German citizen, and therefore a former enemy alien, she had her assets confiscated by the U.S. government. She settled into the house in Grantwood under Boas's care.

Toni had skirted into the country just before a sea change in U.S. immigration policy, the fruit of the Dillingham Commission's efforts. Under the Johnson-Reed Act of 1924, the U.S. Congress allowed in newcomers only as a proportion of the people of their national origin in the country in 1890. This rather arcane framing was meant to tilt the country's demographic makeup back to what it had been before the mass migrations around the turn of the century. Immigration from much of Asia—a source of cheap workers and, as such, a worry both to nationalist politicians and to labor unions—was effectively banned altogether, although no limits were placed on arrivals from Latin America, from which the flow of people had been small. The act was explicitly designed to reduce the future populations of those people whom Boas knew so well from the Lower East Side— Jews, Italians, Poles, Slovaks, and others whose communities had ballooned—and to prevent the influx of people deemed dangerous or culturally inappropriate. The policy would remain the centerpiece of America's immigration system for more than four decades, until its reversal in 1965.

Further restrictions soon created a bulwark against aliens. The U.S. Department of State introduced a new bureaucratic tool—the visa—to monitor entrants to the country. It offered visas only to eligible travelers and only for a mandatory fee. Consular officers encouraged family reunification—today sometimes denigrated as "chain migration"—but for a very specific reason: since the Johnson-Reed act privileged immigrants who were classed as white, allowing U.S. citizens to bring in family members from abroad was a way of increasing the white share of the overall population. Other legislation explicitly blocked families who were deemed to be wrongly structured. The

1922 Married Women's Act, for example, revoked the citizenship of American females who married a foreign male who was ineligible for citizenship because of his race or national origin—in other words, it stripped citizenship rights from many women who married nonwhite foreign men. That same year the Supreme Court affirmed the constitutionality of the entire system in *Ozawa v. United States*, one of a string of court cases that delineated the boundaries of whiteness, in this instance denying Japanese people eligibility for naturalization because of their race.

"We have closed the doors just in time to prevent our Nordic population being overrun by the lower races," said Madison Grant at the time. The new origins-based system adopted by Congress was, he wrote, "one of the greatest steps in the history of this country." His own lobbying had been critical to the passage of the series of immigration restrictions that culminated in the 1924 legislation. Scribner's issued two more editions of *The Passing of the Great Race*, now nearly doubled in size and accompanied by a substantial bibliographic appendix. Even Boas's employer, Columbia University, began to limit the race-alien and foreign-born, as did most of the country's premier colleges. Application forms now required a student to list his family's religion and parents' place of birth. New scholarships were created for people "of either the Anglo-Saxon, the Germanic, the Scandinavian or the Latin Race." With each freshman class, it became easier to "pronounce every name without tying a double knot in your tongue," as the undergraduate dean, Herbert Hawkes, noted approvingly.

In 1925 *The Passing of the Great Race* appeared in German translation. That same year an Austrian radical, just out of prison, wrote a letter to Grant praising the work as "my Bible." Not long afterward, when he published his own treatise on history and world affairs, he followed Grant in arguing that European states had fallen victim to mongrel populations now laying false claim to being British, French, or German. There was one country, however, "in which at least the weak beginnings toward a better conception are noticeable." By expressly excluding the race-alien, Adolf Hitler wrote in *Mein Kampf*, the United States was showing the way toward a brighter, more scientific way of building a political community. "A state which in this age of racial poisoning dedicates itself to the care of its best racial elements must someday become lord of the earth."

FRANZ BOAS EMERGED FROM the war years profoundly changed. His son Ernst had volunteered for the U.S. military, contrary to Boas's wishes, and until Ernst returned home safely from France, the worry would prove nearly unbearable. In the spring of 1915, a tumor had appeared on one of Boas's salivary glands. He saw it as a kind of death sentence, which was also perhaps why he felt so confident in his blistering critiques of the war: a dying man had nothing to lose. The growth was removed, but the operation severed a nerve. His left eye and cheek now drooped, his vision was blurred, and his face felt "like a board," as he put it. His accented speech became thicker. He neglected his teeth for fear that dental work would somehow reactivate the cancer. When he later submitted himself to an anthropometrist colleague's calipers and tape measures, the cumulative effects were recorded in stark detail: hair two-thirds gray, "face crippled."

"The disappointment of my life," he told Ernst, was that Americans had succumbed to nationalism. His adopted country had come to look more and more like Germany or any other European nation-state: obsessed by its own purity, wary of outsiders, and more concerned with being great than doing good. Americans turned out to be less exceptional than anyone, himself included, had supposed.

"Whether that be family life, local patriotism, college spirit, nationalism, religious intolerance—it is always the same," he said. "Must one always kick the other fellow just because one likes one's own way of life?" He felt more distant, more on the margins of things, than at any point since first becoming an immigrant. His department, downsized by President Butler, now consisted of three rooms, up seven flights of stairs, in the Journalism Building: one for Boas, one for his secretary, and the third one empty. He doubted he had the power to do much about any of it. In a kind of internal exile at Columbia, he was dependent on the kindness of a few wealthy friends for research funds and, occasionally, a salary.

News came from Germany that his old traveling companion, Wilhelm Weike, had died. "It is very painful when one's whole youth begins to die off on all sides," Boas wrote to Ernst. Had this whole foray into public scholarship been a mistake? He was a scientist, after all, not a polemicist, no matter how virtuous the message. "I do not command modes of expression that enable me to talk effectively . . . ," he told Ernst. "It goes contrary to my innermost feelings to achieve something by external form that I cannot compel thru its content. . . . This naturally prevents one from taking active leadership in a large movement. Indeed one is also excluded from playing a significant role in lesser activities. What one can do is to work quietly in one's own field, where things depend on knowledge and control of facts, where emotional factors play a relatively small role."

What he did command was the classroom. The undergraduate program in anthropology had been phased out at Columbia during the war, another way President Butler had devised for inoculating "Columbia men" from Boas's radical influence. What remained was the graduate program and a series of popular introductory lectures, "vaudeville courses," as he called them. His most enthusiastic audiences seemed to be drawn from the population of Columbia students segregated a short walk across Broadway: the women.

LIKE MOST UNIVERSITIES AT the time, Columbia was built for the education of young men. But in the early 1880s, the board and deans instituted a special program that allowed women to sit examinations for undergraduate degrees—even though they were not permitted to attend lectures to prepare for them.

One of the program's early graduates was a woman named Annie Nathan Meyer. She was a descendant of one of New York's oldest Sephardic Jewish families, whose many-branched tree included the poet

Emma Lazarus and the jurist Benjamin Cardozo. A minority within a minority, the Sephardim had roots stretching back to the Spanish-speaking Jews expelled by Spain's Catholic monarchy in the fifteenth century. Meyer's American credentials, though, were as impeccable as Madison Grant's. Her great-grandfather, Rabbi Gershom Seixas, had presided over a prominent synagogue in colonial-era New York. When he refused to pray for King George III, the British authorities closed it down. He later assisted at the inauguration of George Washington.

Married to Alfred Meyer, a respected Jewish physician, Annie Nathan Meyer turned her considerable connections—and her status as a de facto Columbia alumna—into a movement to create a brick-and-mortar college for women. The idea was for the college to be formally part of the university but safely across the street, to shield the main campus from co-eds. "I had a shrewd theory that to put any radical scheme across, it must be done in the most conservative manner possible," she recalled. Once the college opened, in 1889, Meyer became its patron saint and guiding hand. Had times been different, the college might also have been her namesake. But her canniness, if not her name, was fully on display. It was her idea to call it after Frederick A. P. Barnard, a beloved former university president. That suggestion seemed to convince Columbia's trustees that women might not ruin the institution after all. Until 1983, when the university at last dropped its men-only policy, Barnard College remained the main route into Columbia for female applicants.

For all her progressive views on education, Meyer was an outspoken antisuffragist. She believed in improvement first and political voice second if at all. But that was not the kind of student—or professor—that Barnard tended to attract. After the First World War, instruction in the social sciences—psychology, government, applied statistics, and anthropology—was at least as good at Barnard as at the main university and often better. Virginia Gildersleeve, Barnard's visionary and long-serving dean, placed a premium on hiring the best professors from Columbia for additional lectures west of Broadway.

She had approached Boas in particular about providing instruction to Barnard students, ensuring that, even when his relationship with President Butler was strained, he remained in the classroom.

Boas's teaching style involved starting at the deep end of things, with students doing advanced, independent research early on and then filling in the blanks with general theories as needed. He never used textbooks and instead encouraged students to share notes on lectures and specialized readings. If someone needed instruction in statistical methods or calculus in order to understand the basics in an anthropometry course, he might quickly fill up chalkboards with equations and formulas, expecting students to pick it all up on the fly. Getting your hands dirty in empirical data and building hypotheses out of what you could actually observe—that was the way to do real science, he taught. Everything else produced the likes of Madison Grant or Lothrop Stoddard.

Boas proceeded in much the same way in his graduate classes east of Broadway on Columbia's main campus. Tardy with grades and light on concrete feedback, he was convinced that working hard was more important for students than meeting formal requirements. They would learn what they needed once they got into the field. He also wore his political views on his sleeve, which alienated some students. When Ralph Linton, a recently demobilized war veteran, showed up for his doctoral studies dressed in his military uniform, Boas berated him so strongly that Linton soon transferred to a rival program at Harvard. He would later complain that the "Jewish Ring" at Columbia had conspired to keep him down. But especially for someone whose demeanor swung from absent-minded to vinegary, Boas could also be surprisingly warm. For more than a decade, he had been working to bring more women into the graduate program, which had no gender restrictions. A science that had access to only half the available data—the practices, stories, and rituals of men—wasn't worthy of the name, he believed.

To a tall, round-faced young woman who appeared in Boas's classroom in 1921, this outlook seemed nothing short of thrilling. She had little experience with the world of ideas, other than teaching school and being a housewife to her academic husband, much less with the adventure travel she began to discover in the learned anthropology papers Boas assigned as required reading. She had not taken any lower-level classes in history, philosophy, or anthropology at Barnard, but on her own she had been making her way through Mary Wollstonecraft and Nietzsche, and she had taken some free social science seminars downtown. "I don't have children," she told a friend, "so I might as well have Hottentots."

Before long, Ruth Benedict would find herself in the middle of a wholesale population change in the anthropology department. "I have had a curious experience in graduate work during the last few years," Boas wrote to a colleague. "All my best students are women."

RUTH FULTON, AS SHE was born, would later say that her life really began with the death of her father, who succumbed to an infection when she was only twenty-one months old. The loss devastated her mother. During the wake she took her daughter into the room where her father's body lay in its coffin and, weeping wildly, implored her to remember. Every March, on the anniversary of his death, her mother would repeat the scene, crying loudly, making out of her husband's death "a cult of grief." From childhood forward, Ruth learned to live in two worlds: one of death, which was serene and beautiful; and another of life, which was confused, explosive, and full of worry. She imagined that there might at last be some peace if she could make it to age fifty—past the tortures of early adulthood, of figuring out her life's work, of finding a husband—which somehow seemed unlikely. Until then, she had no choice but to deal with the darkness, a presence as palpable as the rush of hot wind from an approaching subway train.

She had been born in New York City, on June 5, 1887, but moved with her mother to the family farm upstate just before her father's death. She took a degree from Vassar in 1909 and soon married Stanley Benedict, a biochemist at Cornell Medical College. The couple moved back to the city, but Ruth was adrift. The home became the focus of her activities: cooking, cleaning, and staying quiet so Stanley could indulge his hobbies of engine repair and photographic processing. "All he asks," she told herself, "is to keep an even tenor." She took comfort in routine, which she later said was her technique "to keep suicide from becoming too strong for me in an unguarded moment."

When Stanley sought the calmness of the suburbs, Ruth agreed to move but kept a room in the city. It was the first time in their marriage that she had managed to carve out her own space. She wrote poetry, began a journal, and eventually signed up for classes at the Free School, an experimental grade-free institution operating out of town houses in the West Twenties, later to become the New School for Social Research. There she entered a graduate class taught by Elsie Clews Parsons, a Barnard graduate and an emerging authority on Native Americans of the Southwest.

Adventuresome, brilliant, and born with a Wall Street inheritance, Parsons was magnetic. She delighted in upturning convention and had the financial security and social confidence to do so. After Barnard, she had earned a doctorate in sociology at Columbia and became the key patron bankrolling the anthropology department during Boas's wartime troubles. One of her early books, *Fear and Conventionality* (1914), had been a popularizing gloss on Boas's *Mind of Primitive Man*. Give up your old ways of thinking, she had urged her readers, and imagine a world in which everything you think of as normal becomes strange and unfamiliar. "Fear of change is a part of the state of fear man has ever lived in but out of which he has begun to escape. . . . What he now calls conventionality is that part of his system of protection against change he has begun to examine and, his fear lessening, even to forego."

We are all prisoners of the classifications we inherit, Parsons believed. The things that seemingly unite us into nameable units— our existing families, tribes, or nations—are in fact barriers to "a perfectly fearless love" of other people and societies. They are also the things that cause individuals to feel out of sorts in their homelands (or even their homes), to suffer from never quite fitting into the premade categories that society insists should shape their lives. The beginning of social science, then, was to learn to recognize the square pegs and the round holes—the disconnect between individuals and their expected social behaviors—in distant, exotic societies as well as in our own. Otherwise, our natural "predisposition to classify . . . may be the source of disastrous failures as well as of great achievements." The editors of the Social Register proved her right. After a string of books that extolled the virtues of free love, divorce, and contraception, Parsons's name was removed from the official list of New York's best families.

All this was a revelation to Ruth Benedict. She was enchanted by the atmosphere that Parsons and others had created at the Free School. In her written coursework, she tried on some of Parsons's ideas for size. A society that advocated free love, she wrote in a term paper, was clearly more advanced in human freedom than one that restricted women's sexual lives to the categories of maiden, wife, and prostitute. The world was a collection of potentialities, not givens, and social science was the process by which one sharpened one's understanding of the possible. Parsons invited readers to alienate themselves from their surroundings and begin to see their own customs as bizarre. But Benedict didn't really need to practice what had seemed natural to her from childhood: to see the world as inherently off-kilter—a "bewilderment of soul," as she called it, which could produce terror but also adventure and insight. Her every conversation, in fact, was an exercise in translation. Childhood measles had left her partially deaf, and she strained to make sense of words and phrases that seemed crystalline to everyone else. The world came with fuzzy edges, not the bright lines that seemed so obvious to her husband.

Another of Benedict's professors, Alexander Goldenweiser—one of Boas's students—encouraged her to explore her interests further by enrolling in the doctoral program uptown at Columbia. The department was only now recovering from Boas's effective banishment, with Parsons and other philanthropists paying for new fieldwork expeditions, publications, and even the department secretary. The older generation of students—Kroeber and Lowie at Berkeley, Goldenweiser at the Free School, Sapir in Canada—had given way to new arrivals: Gladys Reichard, a recent Swarthmore graduate, working on the

Navajo; Melville Herskovits, an army veteran and University of Chicago alumnus, with an interest in African American culture; and soon Benedict, too—painfully shy, on the outside of most conversations, and much older, at thirty-four, than many of her fellow students. She spent her days poring over books and field reports in a mad rush to write a dissertation.

Most doctoral theses were more performance art than original research, an exercise to convince examiners that a student had mastered some body of technical knowledge. But Benedict was genuinely inspired. From what she had gleaned in the library, she felt that the old ways of carving up religious experience were inadequate. Scholars divided primitive beliefs into neat boxes—animism, magic, and mysticism. As she delved into learned articles and field reports, though, it took only a quick look to see a messy richness, for example, in the practices of tribal groups on the Great Plains. "All known classifications of religion . . . jostle each other in this one area," she wrote in her first published paper, in 1922. "Is it not our first task to inquire as carefully as may be in definite areas to what things the religious experience attaches itself, and to estimate their heterogeneity and their indefinite multiplicity?"

It was a budding scholar's ham-handed way of saying precisely the thing she had been learning from Boas: that our categories for human experience ought to begin with the experience itself, not with the mental frames imported by an observer. She was also on to something deeper, however. Religion as it was actually practiced in the American West—ecstatic visions, torturous ordeals, the descent of a guardian spirit that could be as real as the milkman—involved an array of "psychological attitudes of the utmost diversity." She now had a scientific way of saying a thing she had known intimately from childhood. The mind, too, resists easy pigeonholing.

Benedict spent the summer of 1922 in California, working with Kroeber on an Indian reservation. That fall Boas asked her to become his teaching assistant at Barnard, overseeing seminars, holding office hours, and taking students on field trips to the American Museum of Natural History. It was her first experience in being a real academic, if one with neither title nor position. She had few other options at the time. It took her only three semesters to produce a long manuscript that she called "The Concept of the Guardian Spirit in North America," enough to earn the doctorate in anthropology, in 1923, one of only forty in the country to be awarded to women that year in all the social sciences. But her proposals for research support were, one by one, rejected. Anyone not fully established with a university post by the age of thirty-five, replied the National Research Council, a federal funding body, "is not very promising material for development."

By the summer of 1924, however, through a combination of part-time work, Boas's goodwill, and the continuing good graces of Parsons, the department's steadfast backer, Benedict had enough money to set off on an expedition of her own, to one of Parsons's old field sites. She was soon on a train to Gallup, New Mexico.

FOUR CENTURIES EARLIER the peoples of the American Southwest had been among the first indigenous populations to live in settlements that early Spanish explorers recognized as cities, or pueblos, stretching out across the river lands and desert from Texas to Nevada.

At Zuñi, south of Gallup, layers of square-built apartments, fashioned from adobe and timber, clustered on a valley floor. They housed a small community speaking a language unlike any around it. Neighboring Navajo and Apache raiders had traditionally descended on the irrigated maize fields and livestock herds. A towering red-banded mesa called Dowa Yalanne, or Corn Mountain, loomed in the distance, a reminder of the times when the people of Zuñi would repair to it as a last-chance fortress. One of the Smithsonian's ethnologists, Frank Hamilton Cushing, described his first encounter with the stunning scenery in 1879. "Down behind the hill the sun was sinking," he wrote breathlessly, "transforming it into a jagged pyramid of silhouette, crowned with a brilliant halo, whence a seeming midnight aurora burst forth through broken clouds, bordering each misty blue island with crimson and gold, then blazing upward in widening lines of light, as if to repeat in the high heavens its earthly splendor."

Parsons had warned Benedict that getting inside Zuñi was like trying to breach "a spiked fence." Locals had been wary of researchers since Cushing, half a century earlier, published sacred ceremonies and religious secrets as part of the Bureau of Ethnology's reports. He had left behind him bad feelings and a deep suspicion of outsiders. But together with Ruth Bunzel, another Boas student and a traveling companion on the journey, Benedict found informants who were willing to subject themselves to long interviews, sometimes for cash. She sat up into the night transcribing folktales and trying to make sense of her notes drawn from hours of conversation. Even when everyone was speaking English, she strained to understand what was being said. Puebloans sometimes wondered why "a deaf," as one called her, was so desperate to collect old stories she could barely hear. But Benedict couldn't help but be enthralled by what she found. The men of the household worked for the women, who held exclusive property rights. Mothers passed down their wealth to daughters, who repeated the female-dominant order. The society privileged the matrilineal line of descent, meaning that they reckoned their main ancestors along their mother's family line, not their father's. People could name their great-grandmothers' ancestral trees in the same way that old New Yorkers knew which of their Dutch forebears had first sailed for New Amsterdam.

The people of Zuñi, like other western tribal groups, also had a well-established tradition of gender-crossing. French explorers had given it the name *berdache*. Biological men could assume the role of social women, donning women's clothing, performing work tasks typically assigned to women, and even forming relationships with non-*berdache* men. That these people were routinely described in English as "men-women"—or with the imported French word, which was itself weirdly derived from an Arabic term for a boy sex slave, something the *berdaches* plainly were not—was simply evidence of how difficult it was to translate Zuñi realities into the language of American normalcy. A woman could have a penis; a man could wear a wedding dress. Benedict had little trouble seeing why all this had been so intriguing to Parsons.

Zuñi was by now well-plowed territory, though. Even Boas had visited briefly. Benedict couldn't really hope to contribute much new. But on hot afternoons, with only the shadow of an adobe wall for shade, she was beginning to glimpse the idea that ritual, story, and personality might form some kind of system. From Boas, she had learned that cultures had to be understood on their own terms. She knew from her dissertation research that minds had a shape that might resemble the society in which they were formed. Now she had some experience with gathering evidence for herself, however imperfect and secondhand. She was sitting in a place in which it was normal for wealth and identity to follow the female family lineage rather than the male one. Back home, Stanley Benedict would have laughed at the idea of becoming Stanley Fulton.

"One of the most striking facts that emerge for a study of widely varying cultures," she later wrote in an essay called "Anthropology and the Abnormal," "is the ease with which our abnormals function in other cultures." For nearly any deviants or miscreants you could name, it was possible to identify a society where their afflictions produced not just acceptable lives but easy, even honorable ones, too. The strangest people might find places where they could be something other than bizarre. Trance seekers and cataleptics, neurotics and the possessed, schizophrenics and the chronically depressed were categories impossible to define outside the local contexts in which these conditions manifested themselves.

Homosexuality was another good example, Benedict wrote. In societies such as Zuñi, where the social structure made a seemingly aberrant behavior "available," as she put it, homosexuals were "socially placed." That is, they had a specific role that both set them apart from the standard structure of their society and still wrapped them safely inside it. *Berdaches* were not outcasts. Rather, they were a type of person that everyone recognized as understandable if unusual. "Normality, in short, within a very wide range, is culturally defined. It is primarily a term for the socially elaborated segment of human behavior in any culture; and abnormality, a term for the segment that that particular civilization does not use."

Deviance of any type, she argued, was no more than a mismatch between an individual's way of navigating through life and the catalog of behaviors and emotions that her society tended to prefer and value. Normalcy in any society was only an edited version of the grand text of all possible human behaviors; there was no reason to expect that every society would do the editing in precisely the same way. Ways of being in the world were abnormal only in the sense that the local context created "the psychic dilemmas of the socially unavailable." The phrase was conjured straight from her own experience. The long hours in the library studying vision quests among the Plains Indians and the field interviews in the pueblos had taught her to make sense of her own stammering deafness, her dark moods, her shyness—to see these things not as innate inadequacies but rather as the product of invisible forces that made the culture she knew best deeply unsuited to people like her.

After concluding her fieldwork, she returned to New York and started a new cycle of mailing out résumés and applications for research funding. As in the past, no academic jobs were forthcoming, despite Boas's support. Her marriage to Stanley had reached a point of comfortable stasis, the two essentially living apart but not moving toward a formal divorce. Her diary entries were filled with records of work and meetings, occasional dinners with Boas, mornings spent in the library, entire days marking student papers. But quietly, in fits and starts, her life was taking a turn, wholly unexpected but somehow unspeakably right.

After her experience in the Southwest, she seemed at last to be shedding the binding conventions she had inherited from her own society's folktales, faux science, and religious dogma. The immediate cause was someone she had been looking after in Boas's introductory courses at Barnard, a slight, square-shouldered undergraduate named Margaret.

Chapter Seven

"A GIRL AS FRAIL
AS MARGARET"

....

If Margaret Mead had an interest in rituals and rules, it was because she was the kind of child who often made them. She could marshal her girlfriends into a club that required everyone to write down all the interesting things that happened at home or school. She recorded the mental development of her siblings in a notebook, along with comments on whether their actions were cunning or merely babyish. She made lists, as many children do, and gave them titles such as "What Studdies I Like Best" and "The Years We Had Contageous Deseases."

She was born on December 16, 1901, the first child to appear in the new maternity ward of Philadelphia's West Park Hospital. Freedom to experiment, the possibility of perfection, and the urgency of reform—in politics, social life, and one's own behavior—were part of the family inheritance passed down to all four of Edward and Emily Mead's children who survived infancy. Emily had studied sociology at the University of Chicago, where she met Edward, and eventually started a doctorate on the hard lives of Italian immigrants in the New Jersey Pinelands. The first wedding young Margaret attended, at age six, was of two recently arrived Italians whom Emily had come to know in her work. Afterward she asked Margaret to report carefully on the unfamiliar food and customs she had just seen. Edward, a professor of finance at the University of Pennsylvania's Wharton School, might spend an afternoon on the family porch, in a bowler hat, reading a volume of Thorstein Veblen. According to family lore, Margaret learned to pronounce the words *sociology* and *economics* before even knowing what they meant.

The Meads moved frequently, but their most stable homes were in the dells and ridgeways of Bucks County, Pennsylvania. The children spent summers putting on original plays at Longland, the family farm near the small community of Holicong, the first address that Mead would ever have printed on her personal stationery. Mead's paternal grandmother, Martha, was intent on molding her into a well-read, confident young woman, someone who knew the thin, bright line between wit and silliness. Mead's youth became a shining example of how rectitude could be its own form of rebellion. At age eleven she informed her father, a born Methodist but practical atheist, that she had decided to be baptized in the Episcopal Church.

In 1919 Mead entered DePauw University, Edward's undergraduate alma mater. She authored earnest, prize-winning allegories for campus pageants. She decorated her dorm room with custom-made curtains but also hung up photographs of Rabindranath Tagore, the Bengali philosopher, and Catherine Breshkovsky, a Russian revolutionary. For sorority rush week, she designed her own dress, meant to invoke the local wheat fields dotted with poppies. The Kappa Kappa Gammas politely passed her over. No right-thinking girl should want to look like Indiana.

It was not a devastating rejection, but it did contribute to Mead's sense of being in a kind of exile. It was the first time in her life that she was made to feel wholly unacceptable to her peers. The things in which she had previously taken pride—her fashion sense, her Episcopalianism, her studied Mid-Atlantic pronunciation—were suddenly foreign and vaguely suspect. The East Coast seemed a world away from Greencastle, where the semester revolved around the predictable poles of a midwestern college: "fraternity life, . . . football games, and . . . establishing the kind of rapport with other people that would make them good Rotarians in later life and their wives good members of the garden club," as she recalled. Mead herself was already engaged to Luther Cressman, a country doctor's son who had entered the General Theological Seminary in Manhattan. After a year of coursework at DePauw, with diligent note-taking if indifferent grades, she persuaded her father to allow her to transfer closer to him and to home. In the autumn of 1920, she enrolled as a sophomore at Barnard College. "For the first time, I felt that I had found something really better than myself, and was happy," Mead later remembered. At Barnard she had friends by choice rather than by chance, a circle of ten or so young women who included the future U.S. poet laureate Léonie Adams. Each year they would adopt a derogatory name as a badge of honor, perhaps something hurled at them by West Side townies or by a professor outraged at some boneheaded behavior or radical political pose. The one that really stuck was the Ash Can Cats, a good label for a group of freethinking, adventurous women, disheveled but intellectually fashionable, half of them Jewish, and all equally acquainted with Bolshevism and the poetry of Edna St. Vincent Millay—bluestockings with bobs. The group apartment on West 116th Street was abuzz with impromptu aphorisms, the tinkle of overturned gin bottles, and campus gossip about affairs with older men and, sometimes, older women. By the summer of 1921, Mead informed the Philadelphia Daily Vacation Bible School that she would no longer be able to serve as director for Bible studies during the long vacation.

Mead had gone from a predictable future as a minister's wife into a world of poetry, emotion, and what she called the "various little lesbian friends" who surrounded the core group of Ash Can Cats. She was a political radical, like everyone in her circle, but never to a degree that placed her beyond the bounds of propriety—just "reddish," as one colleague called her. New York was energy and action: marches in support of Sacco and Vanzetti, challenging classes in mathematics and sociology, the opening night of Isadora Duncan and John Barrymore in *Hamlet*, outings with Luther for dinner at the Jolly Friar's Inn in Greenwich Village, dance cards filled with other young men's names, except for the fox-trots and waltzes, which she marked out with a definite pencil-stub X. It all made up for the fact that, small and often in ill health—debilitating neuritis in her arms, scarlet fever one Christmas—she was required by Barnard to enroll in a class called "remedial gym."

Mead's grades improved, too, especially during the 1922–23 academic year, when she began taking higher-level classes in anthropology and psychology. She turned out pages and pages of notes on the required readings and lectures, in tiny, rapid handwriting, as if trying to capture every word that spilled from her professors' mouths. She drew detailed pictures of basket patterns to remind herself of the distinctive motifs of specific tribal groups, and she wrote up the results of psychological experiments and short opinion surveys that she administered to her circle of friends. She had entered Barnard as a middling student, with mainly C's and B's. By her senior year, she had made the honor roll without being "in the least 'a grind,'" she assured her father. She had done well enough in an anthropology class that Professor Boas and his assistant, Mrs. Benedict, had excused her from taking the final exam.

IN THE MIDDLE OF all this, the suicide came as a terrible blow.

In early February 1923, a classmate, Marie Bloomfield, drank a lethal dose of cyanide taken from a Barnard science lab. Mead, along with several friends, found Marie's body in the dorm room in Brooks Hall. The New York Times was succinct on the root causes: "It appeared that she had become sick in mind, and had persuaded herself through something she had read that death was something to go to in ecstasy and exultation."

Mead blamed herself. Marie had been recovering from the measles, and instead of attending to her, Mead had gone to visit another girl—someone, she suggested, for whom she had more "physical affection" than for the demanding and clingy Marie. Mead had given her a poetry anthology the previous Christmas, and Marie had marked it up with passages that seemed to extol a well-chosen death—the text that the Times said had contributed to her suicidal imagination. The ideas that you introduced into the world could have devastating consequences if you weren't paying attention, Mead felt. She should have seen it all coming. "I was the best friend she had in college, and I never loved her enough," she wrote to Emily Mead shortly afterward.

On hearing of the tragedy, Benedict quickly sent a note. "My dear Margaret," she wrote on February 8.

> You will be needed by the other girls to the limit of your strength, and if there is anything in the world I can do to leave you freer, send me word at the seminar room. Or if you can get away, come yourself. I've nothing all day that can't be put off. I shall be thinking of you today, and wishing people could be of more use to each other in difficult times.

Mead kept the piece of paper until she died. It is the first surviving correspondence between the two of them, a Barnard senior and her Columbia teaching assistant.

They had been acquainted since the previous autumn. Among the small community of women at Barnard, students and teachers knew each other well. Crushes, or "smashes," as Barnard girls called them—chaste ones as well as real flings—were common enough, although perhaps not so common as the talk of them. But the stress of that spring marked a shift. There was now a growing sense of closeness, a new connection between the two women. It would be some time before Mead stopped referring to "Mrs. Benedict" and moved on to "Ruth," but Benedict could feel that something had changed, at least in her own way of seeing things. "She rests me like a padded chair and a fireplace," Benedict jotted in her diary.

A month later, in March, Benedict suggested to Mead that she consider Columbia's graduate programs in the social sciences, of which the anthropology department was a part. "Professor Boas and I have nothing to offer but an opportunity to do work that matters," she said. When Mead received her bachelor's degree that spring, with a Phi Beta Kappa pin on her gown that made even her stoic father proud, Benedict gave her a present of $300. Benedict called it a "No-Red-Tape Fellowship" that could be put toward graduate school. Mead wrote back to thank her "fairy godmother," along with a flirtatious postscript: "I'm afraid this is not a 'no red-tape' reply."

With her undergraduate studies completed, Mead and Cressman

finally brought their long engagement to a close. They married in September 1923 in a small Episcopal church near the Meads' country house in Pennsylvania. They had a short honeymoon at a New Hampshire cottage owned by Benedict and Stanley—with separate bedrooms, since Mead had a research paper and a book report to complete before they returned to New York. Then it was back to school.

Mead had no long-held ambitions to become a social scientist, although she was in some ways now embarking on the graduate career her mother had abandoned some years earlier. She slipped into it easily—the research seminars, the collegial arguments, the sense of broadening one's understanding of the social world. She felt like an initiate into a closed and secretive circle. Every class was a new horizon. She signed up for Benedict's course in anthropometry, which was taught in a rather unconventional way—not with the elaboration of cranial indices and racial hierarchies, as in the past, but rather by treating statistics as open to many interpretations. Scaling up from individual physical measurements to the behavior of groups was a gigantic leap, Benedict taught, and an invitation to fallacious reasoning. Things that looked like social regularities could in fact be fictions created by one's own statistical categories. "Take the problem of determining the difference between Swed[e]s, Bavarians and Negroes," she wrote in her notes on Benedict's introductory lecture. "Naively we say that Swedes differ more from Negroes than they do from Bavarians. But it is another matter to attempt the definition of this difference." Social science meant going beyond the things that seemed obvious, learning to question the precooked verities that society seemed to provide.

She had already picked up some key ideas from Boas and Benedict: get rid of your preconceptions, ask a good question, do the hard work of actually collecting data. Anthropology, she was sensing, seemed to be a kind of master science, one whose method was more genuinely rigorous than what she had been learning in her other courses. She soon proposed a doctoral dissertation on one of Boas's favorite themes.

FOR DECADES BOAS HAD been at the center of the debate over how to explain the differentiation of cultural forms. Even in the same geographic area, practices such as basket weaving, tattooing, and canoe building might be conducted very differently, with different designs, techniques, or ritual associations, depending on the society. Scholars were divided into two schools of thought on the reasons for this variation. One group imagined that evolution held the key. Societies developed some set of behaviors that fit the circumstances in which they found themselves. As human ingenuity and know-how increased, people would devise better and more efficient solutions to the problems that had stymied their forebears. That process worked itself out over great spans of time, which was why modern society was more technologically advanced than, say, that of the ancient Egyptians. But it was also likely to explain differences in ritual, kinship systems, religion, and the decorative arts between civilized societies and present-day primitives. Differentiation was simply the process by which some advanced and ingenious societies moved forward, with occasional "survivals" from earlier periods in their development—a belief in leprechauns in modern-day Ireland, for example—still littering the landscape, like potsherds exposed after a rain.

Boas had a different idea. From what he had seen already on the Northwest Coast, cultural forms were often borrowed among groups, sometimes across great geographic expanses. They changed with no particular regularity and according to no discernible law. The evolutionists' theory ought to have predicted a more or less uniform distribution of cultural practices in a given geographic space, where the opportunities and constraints were presumably also uniform. But what one found in reality was substantial differentiation according to a process that Boas called "diffusion." Tattoos might be the same in settlements located very far apart, just as they might be noticeably different among tribal groups living in close proximity. House-building techniques in one area might appear to be a simple borrowing from a group upriver, but on closer examination, joinery, decoration, and rooflines could turn out to be a complicated mix. Local groups seemed to repurpose techniques from multiple, geographically distant places, so that tracking down the ultimate origin of a practice, story, or ritual could prove futile.

As Boas wrote in the summer of 1924, just as Mead was finishing her first year as a graduate student, "all special cultural forms are the products of historical growth." Human practices and habits did not diverge from some single ancient norm; rather, from the earliest times, people living in different places had done things differently, sharing and modifying their habits as they came into contact with unfamiliar individuals and groups. Chance and personal ingenuity, too, played roles. "We know of cases in which a single individual has introduced a whole set of important myths," Boas wrote.

Any society had to be understood with reference to the past: its legacy of isolation, contact, or migration. Modern societies might be literate and history-conscious, reveling in their own complexity, but that did not imply that premodern ones were therefore simpler and change-free. Primitive societies had histories, too. They did not exist in a timeless state of nature, like a stuck wristwatch, awaiting the arrival of civilized people to tap them into life. Researchers should not go into the field with the assumption that they were looking at a society more or less unchanged since the dawn of time. Rather, fieldworkers were looking at only one contemporary slice of a long story of differentiation, diffusion, and intermingling. Instability and movement, borrowing and fashion, were as common in primitive societies as they were on Broadway, if one only knew what to look for.

Mead had heard all this delivered in Boas's lectures and then reinforced in Benedict's seminars. For her doctoral dissertation, she decided to focus on the diffusion problem in Polynesia. It was a particularly good place to test some of Boas's ideas. After all, if one could find evidence of diffusion in a region where cultural groups were separated by extreme distances and the formidable ocean, it would demonstrate that borrowing and mutual influence were at work regardless of geographical space. Those processes might be even more likely in places where travel and contact were easier.

She devoured everything she could find, every ethnological study and drawing, every assessment of tattooing and canoe building. She submitted the dissertation in May 1925. She had already presented some of her findings at a conference in Toronto and found the response encouraging. The conference organizer, Edward Sapir, was one of Boas's former students and a leader among the next generation of anthropologists. He seemed to take a special interest in her work. She was on her way to becoming a real social scientist, or at least feeling like one. What she needed now was a project that would allow her to spread her wings as an independent scholar, collecting data rather than just reinterpreting the work of others—the same impetus that had sent Benedict to the pueblos. On Boas's suggestion, she turned to a question that cut to the heart of the debate over evolution and diffusion.

Anyone who raised children knew that, around age twelve, something magical seemed to happen to their sweet and compliant offspring. Some unseen force twisted them into new, unrecognizable creatures—perpetually petulant, angry in an instant, ashamed of the very people who had fed and clothed them since infancy. G. Stanley Hall, Boas's former boss at Clark University, had made a study of the phenomenon in his two-volume *Adolescence: Its Psychology and Its Relations to Physiology, Anthropology, Sociology, Sex, Crime, Religion, and Education* (1904), which became a standard reference work. For Hall, the problem was rooted in the deepest recesses of one's organism and, likewise, in the evolution of one's race. Just as racial types passed through phases of development—from savagery to civilization—so too did human beings pass from the primitivism of childhood to the refined rationalism of adult life. The unique struggles of "teeners," as writers of Hall's generation started to call them, were no less than the growing pains of modernity itself.

But what if all this were a product of a particular culture at a particular time? Mead wondered. If even something as seemingly ingrained as adolescent rebellion turned out to be a matter of social learning and not surging hormones (a chemical that had only been named during Mead's lifetime), then Papa Franz would have struck yet another blow against the evolutionists. The subject was also in part personal. Mead herself had only recently stopped being a "teener." She had more or less given up on adolescent dreams of "a huge country parish, and a walled house full of children, where everyone for miles around came for every kind of help." Her way of life at Barnard and Columbia would have seemed a shocking mutiny to the sorority pledge she had been at DePauw. If anthropologists had often gone into the field looking for earlier versions of humanity, Mead was, in a way, looking for an earlier version of herself.

Boas suggested that she consider American Samoa. There she would have the advantage of being an American citizen in a U.S. territory, and the islands had reasonably good health facilities, he pointed out. Mead's neuritis flared up with frequency, making it hard for her to lift her arms. And in her first year in graduate school, she had chased her hat across Broadway on a windy night and run straight into the pathway of a taxi. The broken ankle that resulted had never properly healed. Since she had already done the required background work on Polynesia in her dissertation, she could now create her own field site and begin to assemble original evidence.

Mead had other, more immediate reasons for wanting to get away. Her life was far more complicated than Boas knew. She and Luther, both in the middle of building careers, were drifting apart. She had developed a deep infatuation with Benedict. And Edward Sapir—the urbane scholar who had complimented her conference paper in Canada—had already become her lover.

WHEN MEAD MET SAPIR in Toronto, it was like fireworks, she later recalled. His wife, Florence, had died the previous spring after a long, debilitating illness, and he was only now pulling himself out of the numbing darkness. He remembered thinking Mead had "a brilliant mind," and they soon found themselves completing each other's sentences. In the spring of 1925, only a few months before she was due to leave for the South Seas, they began an affair during one of Sapir's periodic visits to New York, checking into the Hotel Pennsylvania under false names.

Tall and treelike, Sapir was nearly two decades older than Mead but appeared eternally boyish, an intellectual version of the silent film star Harold Lloyd, with round glasses and protruding ears. But he was also a virtuosic writer and speaker, the person among Boas's students whom friends and colleagues most readily labeled a genius—"the most satisfactory mind I ever met," as Mead would remember him. He had a particular gift for divining forests where Boas had mapped the trees. He had invented a classification scheme for Native American languages that would become the standard among professional linguists. He had written eloquently on the nature of language in general, urging his fellow anthropologists to pay attention to the spoken word as an archival record of a distinct way of life. By the time Mead first saw him, he had already begun to systematize the major element of Boas's thought that had so far remained frustratingly vague: the grab bag of ideas, practices, customs, and artifacts that anthropologists routinely lumped together under the label *culture*.

Like Boas, Sapir was an immigrant who had refashioned himself into a native. His homeland, Pomerania, had been passed back and forth among Sweden, Germany, and Poland. On market days, a swirl of languages, Polish, Yiddish, and dialects of German, filled the streets of the small towns and port cities along the Baltic Sea. By 1890 the Sapir family had resettled in New York, part of the same wave of Jewish immigrants to the Lower East Side that enraged observers such as Madison Grant. The family income was supplied mainly by Sapir's mother, a shopkeeper. The ambitions of his father—who had stumbled into a post as a synagogue cantor, with fantasies of becoming an opera star—helped push him toward university.

Sapir entered Columbia on a scholarship, sliding in just before new anti-Jewish admissions policies were put in place to prevent the campus from being overrun by capable immigrants. He stayed around for graduate work in linguistics, building on the Talmudic readings and Hebrew translations that his father had regularly set before him at home. By 1910, when he was appointed chief anthropologist to the Geological Survey of Canada, he had become one of the most prominent members of his profession in North America.

Boas had trained Sapir as an empiricist who could gather ethnological evidence, evaluate it carefully, systematize it, and then leave the grand theorizing to someone else. But linguistics necessarily drew Sapir into the realm of the universal. Cataloging the swooshes, smacks, and pops of language—the sounds that children learned to make by copycatting family members and playmates, placing the tongue, teeth, throat, and palate just so—could never do justice to the intricate web of meaning that these sounds managed to evoke. Boas's *Handbook of American Indian Languages* was already being hailed as an exercise in linguistic salvaging par excellence, with its descriptive grammars and extensive vocabularies of dying indigenous speech. But *language* was more than just *languages*, Sapir felt. All societies communicated. Regardless of what specific sounds or symbols they chose, they seemed equally capable of expressing complex ideas—describing the route to a newly discovered spring in straightforward prose, for example, or memorializing the heartrending loss of a partner inside the strict conventions of a rhymed poem.

Language was both general and diverse, he believed, and languages were both voluntary and accidental. We choose to make a sound or jot down a symbol on a sheet of paper. The choice is an expression of our freedom and individuality. But we do so according to rules we have learned—rules that turn out to be inherently arbitrary. The letter *b* could just as easily represent a sound that we normally symbolize in English with the letter *k*. It is history and convention that tell us to write one and not the other. In speaking and writing, we are engaged at the same time in the most universal of human activities and the one that most tightly binds us to a specific community. For all these reasons, language, perhaps more than any other human behavior, has to be understood in the context of the culture that uses it.

But what, in fact, is culture? Sapir published some of his thoughts on the subject in January 1924, while Mead was still a graduate student. *Culture* was a word that seemed to be used in three major ways, Sapir said. To the ethnologist, it typically meant "any socially inherited element in the life of man, material and spiritual." To others it might mean a certain sense of refinement, like the way a well-planned dinner party might be said to be the work of a "cultured" person. But there is yet a third meaning, he wrote. A culture might be thought of as the specific "spirit" or "genius" of some large social group, the traits thought to be "symptomatic" of the group's "national civilization."

Here Sapir was channeling Johann Gottfried von Herder, the nineteenth-century German philosopher who had been part of Boas's reading list during his university days. Herder had argued that each people, or *Volk,* possesses its own specific *Kultur.* The world sparkled with the plural geniuses of many peoples, each displaying a core set of traits, beliefs, customs, and worldviews that defined them. But Sapir was taking his argument in a direction somewhat different from this well-established line of thought. Cultures could come in "genuine" and "spurious" forms, he said. The entities that most properly deserved to be named cultures were arrays of beliefs and practices that displayed an internal cohesion. Cultures had to make sense to themselves.

"The genuine culture is not of necessity either high or low," he wrote, echoing a tenet of Boas's own thought.

> It is merely inherently harmonious, balanced, self-satisfactory. It is the expression of a richly varied and yet somehow unified and consistent attitude toward life, an attitude which sees the significance of any one element of civilization in its relation to all others. It is, ideally speaking, a culture in which nothing is spiritually meaningless, in which no important part of the general functioning brings with it a sense of frustration, of misdirected or unsympathetic effort.

Boas had long pointed out that we should refrain from judging the worth of any shared social behavior; indeed, we should try to understand it as a product of both history and borrowing across space and time. Sapir, though, was pushing the argument further. Cultures might look like things, solid and tangible, but they were more like systems: the way particular ideas and habits fit together. They were best identified not by how advanced, sophisticated, or modern they might be. Rather, you knew you were looking at a culture when its practitioners seemed to have worked out a sensible and minimally frustrating place for themselves inside it. "A reading of the facts of ethnology and culture history proves plainly that maxima of culture have frequently been reached in low levels of sophistication; that minima of culture have been plumbed in some of the highest. Civilization, as a whole, moves on; culture comes and goes."

A village might have a culture. A neighborhood or a tribe might have one, too. America as a whole—with its frustrated factory workers, its failing marriages, its trainloads of commuting company men—probably didn't, he thought. It was common to see mainly nation-states as the vessels of culture, in the way that we might put French art in one wing of a museum and Dutch art in another. But culture could be anywhere, and in no sense was it fixed and stable. A culture could shift with the times, with new technologies, with new ways of thinking and doing. Knowing when you came up against one was a matter of recognizing when you were seeing a system of thought and practice that allowed individuals to feel at home in their social world.

There was no better way of framing the question that Mead was hoping to answer in the South Seas. Was there a more "genuine" way of being an adolescent than the one that Americans had worked out, some road map for making it through the biological reality of adolescence in ways that avoided social turmoil? And more to the point, did Mead's own society—with its strict gender roles, its sexual frustrations, its Barnard "smashes" that had to be kept secret—even deserve the name "culture" if it couldn't easily accommodate someone like her? She worried that she wasn't meant for romantic love, at least in the form that most people seemed to understand it—in a pairing, as with oxen, say, or socks. Love and sex, marriage and reproduction, households and partners: none of these things had to go together, she thought, nor did they necessarily involve two and only two people.

Whatever the right or wrong of it, she knew the data: her own feelings, her own overlapping relationships. What she lacked was a theory capacious enough to make sense of them.

Later that summer Sapir sent Mead his former wife's wedding ring as a token of his love. He hoped that it might symbolize their future union as husband and wife. For her part Mead had started describing her own notion of an ideal relationship rather differently, using a term she had picked up from her anthropology classes: *polygamy*.

PLANNING FOR THE JOURNEY consumed Mead for more than a year. She persuaded her father to pay for the passage, and she secured a grant from the National Research Council to cover some of the living expenses. In return, she would owe the council a full report with some actual findings, an obligation that would hang over her like a gray cloud. She gathered the train and steamer schedules and plotted her route to the West Coast, then to Hawaii, and finally to American Samoa. Since Benedict was due to conduct field research in Zuñi that summer, the two decided to make part of the cross-country leg together.

It was hard to contemplate the better part of a year away from New York, but Mead and Cressman probably needed the separation. Mead felt closeted by what she would later call, much to Cressman's annoyance, her "student marriage." People came and went through their apartment, which had never really been a haven for the two of them; Mead would occasionally let it out to friends, who might carelessly leave behind a used condom. Cressman was going through his own crisis, both of faith and of career. After seminary, he had been ordained as an Episcopal priest, and he said his first mass on an Easter morning at St. Clement's, a church in Hell's Kitchen. Not long afterward, one of his parishioners died in childbirth, leaving behind twin babies. A God that allowed such a thing didn't deserve his service. He went to his bishop to request that his name be stricken from the church rolls. He soon entered Columbia's doctoral program in sociology and laid out his own project for a year in Europe studying progressive approaches to birth control—the very thing that might have prevented his parishioner's death.

And then there was Sapir. He wanted a wife, a real one, who would help look after the three children left behind by the death of Florence. Mead should divorce Cressman, he pleaded, marry him, then settle down to do serious work in support of his own flourishing career. A chair was being held for him at the University of Chicago. He talked with Boas and Benedict, urging them to intervene to prevent Mead's trip. She was psychologically unbalanced, he said. Her physical ailments were surely a manifestation of latent neuroses. "I am worried about her—distinctly so," he wrote to Benedict. "What is she going to Samoa for? She herself admits it is a flight from a difficult and tangled situation. . . . Are you inclined to think we ought to do something to stop the whole infernal business at the eleventh hour?" Someone would have to take her in hand, carting her off to a psychoanalyst if necessary. "What's all this nonsense about her career? Samoa? Isn't it maddening? How can we all be so blind?" he scribbled across anthropology department stationery. "The girl is going crazy."

Sapir and Benedict had corresponded even before he met Mead, and they had developed their own intense friendship, perhaps even a platonic romance. They had shared poetry and gossiped about Boas's other students. Mead increasingly took pride of place among their subjects of common interest. "Now the theory of polygamy that Margaret evolved (she uses the term herself) is a mere rationalization," Sapir complained. "Having made of her erotic life a mere tentacle of the ego, she could not possibly allow herself to pay the price of love. It had to be a 'quicksilver' love, a modernly beautiful and . . . unfaithful, 'free' love to be truly love!" In scores of letters between them, however, Benedict never hinted at her own growing fixation on Mead, a feeling that was by this stage intensely mutual. She would later tell Mead that the worst day of her life was the day she found out that Sapir and Mead were in love.

The stage was now set for a long drama in the relationship between Mead and Benedict, with different players but the same script. If Boas was the intellectual center of this troubled group, distant and august,

Benedict was its emotional one—an anchor during fieldwork, a font of ideas, an inspiration. Mead had even developed a private code she shared only with Benedict. It would be useful for cutting down on the cost of radio telegrams and even better for sharing confidences. Once she got abroad, she told Benedict, *a* would stand for Papa Franz, *b* for Edward, *h* for being well and happy, *s* for Luther, and *u* for "Your love"—that is, Benedict's—"is keeping me alive." Depressive and long-suffering, "dearest" in letters from Sapir and Cressman, "darling" in letters from Mead, holder of the private telegraph code, and custodian of bank accounts and insurance policies, Benedict had become the village common on which every bilateral grievance would be endlessly aired.

In July 1925, Mead said goodbye to her family and set off with Benedict for the West. The journey took them through Ohio to Illinois, across the prairie, then south toward the deserts that Benedict knew from her fieldwork among the pueblos. It was the longest the two of them had ever spent together, certainly the longest without either husband in tow. Mead wept in Benedict's arms, letting go of the past and embracing this new love. Benedict remembered kissing her eyes and lips.

When Benedict finally stepped down from the train near the Grand Canyon, Mead stayed on board for the journey to California. Benedict stood on the platform looking back at her. At one point, another train passed behind Benedict on an adjacent track, making her hair lift gently in the breeze. The illusion was magical. "Against that background, you and I were both moving, both moving fast—and as my train seemed rushing thru space you were always just opposite my window, a lovely wind blown figure," Mead wrote in a letter just after they parted. "And that picture is the one I shall take with me, darling, and it will hold much of comfort." Benedict would later lie awake dreaming of those moments on the train spent making love, kissing each finger, one and one and one, trailing her lips across the palm of Margaret's hand.

En route to the port of San Francisco, Mead looked back on the entire train ride as a mythical, electrifying, ridiculous leave-taking. It was an unforced separation from the person who had come to mean more to her than anyone in the world. "You are taking notes in Zuñi— and I am going to take notes in Polynesia, and there was never less point to such an arrangement." She had long signed her notes and letters to Benedict with "love," as one might to an older sister or, as she had called Benedict a few years earlier, her fairy godmother. But now, for the first time, she could say it all plainly, outright. "And always I love you."

Mead had given herself a year to untangle the romantic mess she had left behind. But in just the past two weeks, things had already become clearer than she could have imagined. She took the time alone on the train to write a kind of confession to Cressman about her ambivalence to the marriage and her desire for openness and freedom. She devised a plan for dealing with Sapir, letting him down gently by portraying herself as a flighty "Ariel," a creature of the air, whose love could never be bound to only one person or channeled in just one direction. (*J* in her secret telegraph code stood for "It is impossible to [go] on writing Edward. I am going to put my decision into effect. Say the proper things, and comfort him.") And somewhere east of the Grand Canyon, Benedict had become, at last, hers—openly and fully, confessedly.

In San Francisco, Mead climbed up the gangplank of the *Matsonia*, an old troop transport that now serviced the route to Hawaii. She found herself feeling more at liberty and happier than ever before— but also more worried. She had no idea what she would find in Samoa, or whether there was really anything to find at all. She had a vague research question, an unpublished doctoral dissertation derived from other people's work, and a debt to repay to her funders. "I feel dishonest in even attempting the problem for the Research Council," she wrote to Benedict once she arrived in Honolulu. "For the first time in my life, I expect defeat."

POLYNESIA, AS MEAD KNEW, was not so much a place as an idea. Its name, a simple concoction from the Greek for "many islands," had been coined by a French naturalist in the mid-eighteenth century. The people who lived in the huge expanse of the Central and South Pacific used no such all-encompassing label.

The landmasses were diverse, with some islands built up by volcanic eruptions and others formed by mountaintops that peeked up through the surface of the ocean. Their populations shared certain commonalities of language, but it was one of the great marvels of human settlement and migration that they shared much at all. By the time ancient travelers had maneuvered their oar- and wind-powered boats around the triangle of island groups that defined Polynesia— Hawaii in the north, New Zealand in the south, and Easter Island in the east—they had gone the equivalent of three-quarters of the way around the earth.

Reaching to comprehend such vastness, like sailing it, was an invitation to failure. The most famous person to try had died in the attempt. In the 1760s, the English explorer James Cook had launched the first of three expeditions around the Pacific. In many instances, the appearance of Cook's tall ship was the first recorded contact between Europeans and Pacific Islanders. His cartographers were often the first to draw modern sea charts showing the extreme distances between landfalls. Tensions with local populations were inevitable. In February 1779, Cook's crew tried to abduct the Hawaiian king Kaleiopuu, a botched attempt to secure a ransom in exchange for what the Europeans believed was a stolen boat. The crew were soon set upon by the king's supporters, and Cook was clubbed to death in the churning surf.

Cook's journals, published after his first voyage, were an immediate and lasting success. They contained a wealth of knowledge on natural history and geography. Among other things, they introduced English speakers to words such as *tattoo* and *taboo*, the latter referring to the elaborate system of forbidden behaviors, known as *tapu* or *kapu* in local languages, that undergirded many Polynesian societies. Despite the later news of Cook's grisly death, the journals also contributed to a growing belief in the Pacific as a kind of earthly paradise. Writers, artists, and travelers from Robert Louis Stevenson to

Paul Gauguin added to the stock images of blooming lotuses, exotic food falling from trees, and welcoming, even licentious natives. The expansion of European overseas colonialism in the nineteenth century sparked land grabs and imperial rivalries, until a series of agreements in the 1890s forged a clear division among the great powers. Independent Pacific states, such as Japan and China, were expressly excluded from these treaties, as were the small but ancient kingdoms, such as Tonga and Hawaii, that had gradually succumbed to outside influence. After the First World War, there were few inhabited places in the Central and South Pacific unclaimed by some country around the Atlantic—a new transoceanic imperialism vaster even than the scramble for Africa a few decades earlier.

Just before Mead began graduate school, the study of the Pacific had been energized by the work of a Polish émigré living in London. Unlike Mead, his on-the-ground note taking had been furthered not by a research grant but by global politics. In 1914 Bronislaw Malinowski, a young academic at the London School of Economics, had traveled to the southwestern Pacific to begin ethnological research among the peoples of Melanesia—the "dark islands," in literal translation, which included New Guinea, the Solomon Islands, and Fiji, among others. But with the outbreak of the First World War, Malinowski found himself stranded in Australia, the natural jumping-off point for expeditions in the region. As a subject of Austria-Hungary—he had been born in the Polish city of Kraków, then under Austrian crown rule—he was formally an enemy alien and was therefore barred from reentry to Great Britain. He worried that he might even face arrest.

Being a castaway, however, turned out to be the making of his career. His Australian hosts allowed him to continue his plans and relocate to the Trobriand Islands, a set of coral atolls east of what is today Papua New Guinea. If outsiders perceived Polynesians as the barbarian aristocracy of the Pacific, in Lewis Henry Morgan's old schema—with their chiefs and feather robes, their elaborate taboos and social hierarchies—they often saw Melanesians as their savage counterpart. The term itself, like *Polynesia,* was of European origin, coined in the 1830s by the French explorer Jules-Sébastien-César

Dumont d'Urville, who proposed a fourfold division of the wider Pacific and its peoples. Alongside Polynesia, Dumont d'Urville added labels for Micronesia (the "little islands"), Malaysia (the place of the Malay people), and Melanesia, a name that explicitly referenced the darker skin and curlier hair of many inhabitants of the southwestern Pacific, from New Guineans to Australian Aborigines. From Dumont d'Urville forward, when European travelers and scientists looked at the Pacific Ocean, they saw a premade racial order, one that placed Melanesians lower on the developmental scale than the generally lighter-skinned peoples of Polynesia. These "Oceanic Negroes," as they were sometimes called, fit easily into a taxonomy that simply imported the prejudices of the Atlantic into the Pacific, with Melanesians playing the role of sub-Saharan Africans.

Malinowski, however, found a remarkably complex and differentiated society on the Trobriand Islands. Trobrianders traveled unimaginable distances in handmade canoes. They engaged in elaborate gift exchanges from island to island, an economic system that knitted together remote communities perched on small outcroppings in the expansive sea. Practices that might appear to be irrational— risking life and limb to give and receive decorated shells or disk beads, for example—were in fact part of a well-defined network of political authority, obligation, trust, and partnership. *Kula,* as this system was known, might look odd to a European visitor, but on a moment's reflection, it was no stranger than European monarchs giving up their daughters to secure strategic alliances or empires offering annuities to placate a rebellious client state.

After spending the war years in the region, Malinowski wrote up his experiences as *Argonauts of the Western Pacific,* which was published in 1922, just as Mead was entering her senior year at Barnard. It was in some ways an exercise in standard ethnology. Malinowski's aim was a comprehensive treatment of Trobriander society, especially the astonishing voyages that atoll dwellers were able to make across the open sea. (Hence the allusion to ancient Greek mythology in his book's romantic title.) But what was truly novel was Malinowski's method. Rather than observing native peoples from a distance, noting down their rituals or going on a short-term "expedition" in search of exotic artifacts, Malinowski actually lived with them.

He worked beside Trobrianders at everyday tasks: carving a canoe, grinding sea shells into elaborate ornaments, playing a game, welcoming the return of the fleet after a long sail around the island ring. Later scholars would label this method "participant observation," but it was Malinowski who laid out its basic logic, with a candid account of his own experiences in the field. It began with "hopelessness and despair," he said; you started out with a sense of confusion and disorientation, with the "imponderabilia of actual life" rushing in, exhaustingly, upon you. You might read a few novels to take your mind off your sense of inadequacy. You needed to gather the courage to start learning how to be a proper human being all over again, according to someone else's rules of good and bad behavior. To know *people*, much less *a people*, you had to "get out from under [your] mosquito net" and do your best to see the world as your hosts saw it. That, in turn, required really being there, for an extended period of time, learning from scratch how to act in ways that made sense inside the communities you were trying to understand.

As Mead waited in Honolulu for the ship to Samoa, she could not help but feel trapped in Malinowski's shadow. People could already sense that *Argonauts of the Western Pacific* was a milestone, a fundamental shift in how experts thought about the role of the anthropologist in the field. Malinowski was charting a new way of doing anthropology itself. Mead, too, wanted to know about people's lives: how they thought about childhood and aging, what it meant to be an adult, what they thought of as sexual pleasure, whom they loved, when they felt the sting of public humiliation or the gnawing sickness of private shame. But her own work plan had a twist. She aimed to do all this with the invisible mass of people whom anthropologists, including Malinowski, always seemed to miss—women and girls. She would have to take Malinowski's method, apply it to new questions, in a new setting, and hope that the results were something other than a jumble of village gossip.

IN HAWAII, MEAD PREPARED as best she could. She arranged for language lessons and made contacts with scholars at the Bernice P. Bishop Museum, the renowned repository of Polynesian culture and natural history. She had planned to do some collecting for the museum once she reached Samoa. In late August, she was at sea again, on board the steamship *Sonoma* on the middle leg of its passage to Sydney, Australia. She lay in bed with severe seasickness, sleeping up to sixteen hours a day and rarely venturing on deck except for meals. At last, on the final day of the month, the ship rounded a headland on Tutuila, the main island of American Samoa, and anchored off the crescent expanse of the village of Pago Pago.

Mead was immediately thrown into the chaos and excitement that accompanied the arrival of any passenger ship—now amplified by the welcome given to the destroyers and support craft of the U.S. fleet, which had arrived that day as part of a grand naval tour. Over the previous two decades, Pago Pago had become the navy's principal station in the South Pacific. It was the natural partner of Hawaii, more than two thousand nautical miles to the north. Both island chains had come into American possession at the turn of the century and had the feel of colonial acquisitions, drawing missionaries, merchants, and the military alike.

Admiral Robert Coontz, the fleet commander, was met from his flagship, USS *Seattle*, by Mauga, the Samoan governor of Tutuila, and other local dignitaries, all wearing elaborate headdresses and grass skirts, their bare torsos oiled to a fine glow. Sailors crowded the village common, or *malae*, to witness the formal presentation of gifts to the American guests: an assortment of coconuts, finely woven mats, strings of beads, and pieces of painted *tapa*, or bark cloth. The admiral expressed gratitude on behalf of himself and President Calvin Coolidge, while a group of young men and women prepared for the *siva*, or welcoming dance. Barefoot villagers crowded in closer, the men dressed in long *lava-lava* sarongs and the women in boxy dresses made from cheap imported cloth. Sailors pushed their way through to snap photographs. Black cotton umbrellas, the common Samoan shield against rain and sun, hovered like a cloud over the proceedings. When it was all over, some of the officers decamped to their cruiser, USS *Marblehead*, for dinner in the mess, while sailors, sprawled before a makeshift cinema screen on deck, were treated to Richard Dix and Frances Howard starring in *Too Many Kisses*.

Mead had brought along an evening dress in case such occasions presented themselves in the South Seas, and she joined in the festivities on board. That night she found herself enduring an impromptu lecture from a navy officer, her escort for the evening. "He told me what he thought about language, instincts, race, inheritance and a few allied subjects," she recalled, "and I discovered that the most boring thing in the world is to listen to someone talk to you about your specialty." She was eager to get moving, to begin discovering Samoa for herself, rather than to hear about it secondhand from a voluble seaman. Soon her letters to friends and family would arrive on newly printed letterhead that replaced the old version she had used in Bucks County. It now read, exotically, "Margaret Mead, Pago Pago, Tutuila, Samoa."

Mead was staying for the moment at Pago Pago's only hotel, along with a smattering of other *palagi*, or foreigners, and she used the time to acclimate to the local diet of sea urchin, wild pigeon, and the gluey taro root that formed the staple of Samoan cuisine. She was getting in the habit of describing everything she saw, writing it up in a series of "bulletins" for her friends and family back home: the strange mixture of Polynesian and American dress, the local government's belief that it was bringing civilization to this backward outpost, the power of a gift—*alofa*—to cement relationships, the smell of frangipani blossoms, the feel of a baby freshly rubbed down with coconut oil. When she first stepped down from the *Sonoma*, the crowd of Samoans had seemed a great undifferentiated mass, but within a few weeks she realized how absurd that impression had been. "Individuality is writ large on their faces," she said. She continued her language lessons by sitting cross-legged on the pebble floor of an open-sided Samoan house, holding her instructor's child in her lap while concocting labored sentences about cooking and manners.

From Pago Pago, Mead could take short journeys to inland villages—a formal trip known as a *malaga,* which was accompanied by speech making, ritual gift giving, and the ceremonial making of *'ava,* the Polynesian drink prepared from the roots of the kava shrub. In Vaitogi, a village across the island from Pago Pago, she was made a *taupou,* an honorary virgin, a position of esteem that she would carry with her in her other travels in Samoa. But none of that guaranteed the kind of access she would need to make her research a success.

Mead was already experiencing how hard it was to do fieldwork without really getting out from under the mosquito net, as Malinowski had phrased it. You had no way of knowing whether you were asking good questions or stupid ones. Informants tended to say what they thought you wanted to hear. "When a chief's son is tattooed they build a special house don't they?" she asked a man named Asuegi, one of the village chiefs in Pago Pago. "No. No special house," he replied.

Are you sure they *never* build a house?
Yes. Well, sometimes they build a small house of sticks and
    leaves. Yes.
Was that house *sa* [taboo]?
No, not *sa.*
Could you take food into it?
Oh, no. That's *sa.*
[Could you] smoke in there?
Oh, no. Very *sa.*
Would anybody go into the house who wished [to go in]?
Yes, anybody.
Anybody at all. Just anybody?
Yes, everybody could go in.
No one was forbidden to go in?
No.
Could the boy's sister go in?
Oh, no. That's taboo.

By mid-October, Mead had decided that the island of Tutuila had little more to offer. The only sizable villages were "over-run with missionaries, stores, and various intrusive influences," she wrote to Boas, and were much corrupted by the influence of the Americans. The governor's plan for increasing literacy involved printing up a collection of European fairy tales, as if Samoans had none of their own. The whole American administration seemed to think of local people as "a suggestible lot of children" and treated them accordingly. The *palagi* at the hotel spent their time complaining about how hard it was to get good help.

On November 9, Mead caught a steamer to a more remote set of islands about a hundred miles from Tutuila, the Manu'a group. From there she continued by canoe to Ta'u, a small island in the chain. She had barely begun her work with adolescents, which was supposed to be the focus of her study, and Ta'u seemed to have them in abundance. It was also sufficiently off the beaten path to have no worrisome missionaries. She took up residence with an American family on the island, the Holts, whose white clapboard house served as the local clinic. She had worried that this might not constitute real fieldwork. As she wrote to Boas, she was torn between the desire to live like a native and the need to have enough quiet time to write notes and reflect on her experiences, something that would have been difficult in an open-sided, communal Samoan house.

She might have been doing anthropology from the veranda—her room consisted of half of the Holts' back porch, screened off by a thin bamboo barrier—but she was never short of informants. Children and teenagers flocked to her for conversation and impromptu dance parties, arriving as early as five in the morning and staying until midnight. She hung a picture of Boas on her wall and decorated it with red hibiscus, taking it down occasionally to show the gaggle of children whenever they asked about the strange-looking man she seemed to revere. She soon took to signing her letters "Makelita," the pronunciation of her name in Samoan. "I find I am happiest here," she wrote in one of her bulletins, "when I am alone with the natives, either bathing or lying on the floor of a Samoan house watching the sea, or making long flowery speeches to some old chief."

Still, as the hot summer began—winter back in New York—she worried that time was slipping away. She had collected little of value, at least not enough to justify the National Research Council fellowship or the considerable money that Edward Mead had spent for the passage on the *Matsonia* and *Sonoma*. Her old life was intruding as well. Sapir continued to send tortured letters, by turns pleading and insulting, calling on her to give up the farcical trip and return to his side. She wanted to burn them but decided she couldn't do it, at least not yet. She wondered whether they were in fact documentary proof that she had made a terrible mistake—confirmation from a great scholar that traipsing off to the far side of the world had been a fool's errand all along.

At the same time, Sapir kept up his correspondence with Benedict, urging that they work together to force Mead to get professional help when she returned. Full institutionalization might even be required. "Truly, my dear Ruth, Margaret is not well, and the physical part of it is almost negligible in comparison with the psychic," he wrote. "Margaret's most insidious enemy is her zestfulness, her unflagging interest in things. . . . A girl as frail as Margaret has simply *no right* to accomplish what she does."

IN MID-DECEMBER, A DAY before her birthday, Mead wrote to Benedict as well, but the subject was not Sapir. She wanted to report on an inkling of an insight, the first time in months that she had a real sense of purpose. She began to suspect that there might be an actual big idea hidden somewhere among the palm trees.

Any student who paid attention in an introductory anthropology class, Mead said, knew that the main contrast between primitive and modern societies was the matter of formalism. Modern civilizations were fluid and adaptable, given to seeing the world in pragmatic ways based on factual evidence. Primitive peoples, however, believed in rules and rituals. Abiding by these formal dictates kept their world in balance. They gave society a clear set of procedures for summoning a rain god, calling forth a spirit to strike down an enemy, preventing marriages between the wrong individuals, and sanctioning the proper partners for princesses and priests. Polynesians were usually presented as the textbook case, with their taboos and intricate family trees of chiefs, "ritual virgins," upon whose chastity the community's well-being depended, and "talking chiefs," or public orators who spoke in place of the chief himself.

But Samoans didn't seem to behave this way at all, Mead reported. Her neighbors and acquaintances on Ta'u turned out to be rather ill-informed about the rules that were supposed to consume them. "The number of things that are optional and the ignorance of the general population of the things that aren't is amazing," Mead wrote to Benedict on December 15. "*Theoretically* the father's mother is supposed to name the first baby, but nine people out of ten will tell you anybody can name it anything." Rather than a deep concern with restrictions and ceremonies, the "general laissez-faire . . . attitude is too deeply engrossed in the culture." This attitude could not be easily attributed to the influence of the Americans or earlier missionaries; it wasn't, in other words, an instance of the cultural diffusion that Boas had identified in his own work and that Mead herself had written about in her dissertation. In their everyday lives, people seemed naturally to be making decisions in ways that were looser, more improvisational, than outsiders seemed to think.

Mead soon had a chance to see all this firsthand. The next month a hurricane swept over Ta'u and other islands. "All the houses in Vaitogi have been destroyed," wrote a close Samoan friend and honorary sister, Fa'amotu, from Tutuila, once the winds had died down. "Twenty-six houses have been damaged. . . . How about over there? Is everything okay or not?" Mead had hunkered with the Holt family in a concrete cistern, along with a roast chicken and a loaf of bread. When they emerged, most of the other houses on Ta'u had been leveled, even though the people were generally safe. Everyone now set about the task of cleaning up. Mead worried that this would ruin everything. It would be impossible to do ethnological work if there were no feasts or formalities to observe while people were busy rebuilding.

But she soon came to see things differently. An unexpected opportunity was unfolding right before her. What if the real way to understand people wasn't to gawk at their ceremonies or even to share in their most important work, as Malinowski had done, but to be beside them in their most unguarded moments—sweeping up debris, rebuilding a house, reweaving a damaged mat, comforting a wailing child? Even Mead's frailties had turned out to be providential. People somehow wanted to take care of her, especially when the wind and water rose or her old broken ankle gave her trouble. Vulnerable and dependent, she was something of a child herself. It was a condition that enabled a kind of intimacy that a fitter, more commanding figure might never have known. She called her accidental method the "ethnology of activity."

Mead rushed to get things down on paper. In the wake of the storm, she returned to the small group of children who had typically gathered on her veranda, mainly young girls, and began to ask them about their lives. She wrote out notecards on each of them: their views about growing up, how they related to boys, what they did when boys made rude gestures or rubbed up against them during impromptu dances. She took down life histories and began to fill up the fifty-cent reporter's notebooks she had brought from New York, sometimes using her own version of Samoan, sometimes recording the words of an impromptu interpreter. None of this was ethnology as she had learned to perform it. There was little talk of demons and taboos, fishing practices or basketry techniques. Instead, she was making inroads into a sovereign but previously hidden world: the inner lives of girls and women, with intimations of lust and love.

"Most wives are faithful to their husbands," she scribbled. "Very few husbands faithful to their wives. Masturbation universal among boys, from little ones to married men." Girls, too, knew many varieties of sexual pleasure, and oral sex was a well-known preliminary to intercourse. All the children she interviewed had seen intercourse and knew the basic mechanics. No particular taboo surrounded sex during menstruation, and the concept of female "frigidity," much discussed by psychologists in America, was unknown, as was male impotence (although old men were said to tire more easily than younger ones). Same-sex intimacy was present though not widely talked about, but it was possible for a boy to take on girl's tasks, like sewing or washing, without being shamed for it. The public deflowering of ritual virgins—an important practice in former times—had ceased, but if an unmarried daughter happened to get pregnant, the family would insist on a private marriage without any public celebration. Sexual freedom still had its limits.

The months sped by, with breathless letters to Benedict, occasional field reports to Boas, regular correspondence with Samoan friends on Tutuila, and periodic bulletins back to family whenever the mail boat managed to arrive. Mead worried that the time was rushing by too quickly to yield anything of value. There was so much she seemed to have left undone: the width of a grass basket, the name of this or that feast, how many fires were kindled at a death ceremony, the proper kinship term for your mother's brother. A bout of tonsillitis had lately kept her bedridden. She had let local friendships fall by the wayside. "I've never forgotten you," wrote Faapua'a, one of the girls living across the island. "I always remember you and how kind you have been to me. I'll always remember your love for me during all those many days when we were going around together. Don't you ever forget our great relationship." Mead wrote to Benedict that she would probably never become a really good fieldworker.

In May she left Ta'u by canoe, taken through the surf under a baking sun by a crew of nine Samoan men, chanting as they rowed. Back in Pago Pago, she caught a ship for the first leg of an around-the-world voyage. She had agreed to meet Cressman in France and to attend an anthropology conference with Benedict. But her head was still in Samoa. She doubted that her time in the field had been very productive, no matter how many headlines she inspired along the route to Europe—a lone female traveler returning from the remote South Seas. "Few lead more interesting lives than Dr. Margaret Mead, one of Uncle Sam's most brainy women, and a world authority on ethnology, who arrived here yesterday on the *Sonoma*," a local newspaper enthused when she arrived in Sydney. She soon boarded the steamship *Chitral* for the long journey west, via Ceylon and the Suez Canal.

Things would be complicated enough once she arrived in France, what with seeing both her husband and her lover after an extended absence from them both. But that wasn't the half of it. On board the *Chitral,* with long days on deck and evenings spent seasick or at boring dinners with tourists, she met someone else—a tall, rugged New Zealander with the odd name of Reo Fortune. She would have to figure out how to manage all this once she got to Marseilles.

Chapter Eight

COMING OF AGE

....

How is your trip?" wrote Fa'amotu to Mead that summer. "Have you recovered? Are you weak from travelling on the sea?" She had in fact spent much of the sail in a deep depression, seasick, with the neuritis reappearing in her arms. Her eyes were red with conjunctivitis, ringworm encircled her nose, and she felt generally "unequal to taking up all the threads of a complex existence again," as she wrote at the time. She fretted that her field notebooks, the treasure born of her months away, would be lost at sea. She worried that Edward Sapir had been right all along about her self-centeredness. Maybe she really was inherently defective when it came to settling down.

Reo Fortune—a kind of miracle when he appeared on deck, with his bubbling eagerness to talk poetry and radical politics—might easily have stood as witness for the prosecution. His first name, Maori for "the word," was a gift from his father, an Anglican missionary in New Zealand. His mind scurried in multiple directions at once, an energy that Mead found magnetic. If she had placed an ad for someone to accompany her on this next stage of her life—from vicar's wife to world explorer—Fortune would have fit the bill perfectly: fiery, prone to flights of fancy, pinging from one philosophical idea to the next, beautiful in a slouch hat, a William Blake in safari cottons. During the seven weeks it took to reach Europe, Mead fell in love, fighting it "with both hands," as she said, and sliding into the warmest sense of contentment she had felt in years.

Her arrival, however, turned out to be as nightmarish as she had feared. Cressman met the *Chitral* when it docked in the South of France but was left to cool his heels dockside while Mead said her goodbyes to Fortune. At lunch she confessed to her husband about her newfound love. The married couple nevertheless continued with their travels as they had planned, through Bordeaux to Paris, where Fortune reappeared, at the concierge desk of their hotel. Cressman met him in the lobby, calmly introduced himself, and told him discreetly that Mead was expecting him upstairs. Cressman soon decided to return to England, where he had spent the year on a fellowship, while Mead and Fortune continued to Poitiers. There they met up with Benedict, who had to be brought up to speed on the new entanglements. Mead continued to Florence and Siena and then Rome, where she once again saw Benedict, who now "melted," Mead recalled, into a jealous fury.

She assured Benedict that she still loved her, too, and that this was simply another test of her theory that it was possible to latch on to several people at once, with "demonstrative affection" flowing to each in different ways. Benedict's earlier eruption now burbled into acceptance. She was glad to see Mead happy at last, even if there would be no grand reunion with her in the way she might have hoped. At the end of the summer, they returned to the United States on the same ship, the matter of Mead's possible future with Fortune, for the time being, put off. "Tell me what to do!" Mead had screamed at Cressman before they parted. It was the only occasion he remembered seeing her cry.

When she got back to New York, she had plenty to occupy her time. A new job was waiting for her. Boas had recommended Mead to his old institution, the American Museum of Natural History, for a position as an assistant curator in charge of Africa, Malaysia, and the South Pacific. An academic lectureship seemed unlikely; there were no offers from any college or university, despite her completed doctorate and a better part of a year's fieldwork to her credit. A curator's smock would be a stopgap and would help move her research in new directions. "It appeals to me more than sticking at sex permanently," she told Benedict.

At the beginning of September 1926, she arrived at the museum's roseate facade on West 77th Street, much as Boas himself had done exactly thirty years earlier. Ascending past the public exhibition spaces to the fifth floor, she passed down a hallway lined with wood and plate-glass vitrines, the core of the anthropology collection. It was the longest continuous corridor in New York, an entire city block of baskets, ceremonial masks, beadwork, war clubs, textiles, ceramic figurines, and human and hominid bones—thighs and metatarsals, tibias and fibulas—all tucked away on movable trays.

At the west end of the corridor, she turned the corner and trudged up a steep cast-iron staircase, feeling the temperature rise as she moved into the stuffy attic. It was more of a double catwalk than a full floor. Two narrow passageways were flanked by a series of metal doors, a sort of elevated catacomb that served as the museum's bulk storage area. Pipes fed into small chambers flanking the catwalks. Each one was outfitted with heavy hardware that ensured the doors could be sealed tight from the outside. The system was designed to protect humans from the toxic gas that was regularly pumped into the rooms, a death sentence for the pests that would otherwise devour the precious artifacts.

Tucked beneath the riveted iron beams that supported the roof, the space looked more like a prison than a museum. But a few stairs higher, the museum's only female assistant curator finally opened the door to a small room with double-hung windows looking out over the red slate roof and up Columbus Avenue. Furnished with just a few metal cabinets, a bookcase, and an old rolltop desk that had been banished from one of the lower floors, it would suffice for the two or three years she planned to stay in the job. As it happened, she would end up working in the same cramped space for more than half a century—an aerie among gas chambers where she later said she felt secure and at home.

Mead had a full slate of curatorial duties: cataloging collections, writing leaflets, organizing public exhibitions. But that autumn she also began writing up the results of her time in Samoa. She had come to see her research as involving "a particular psychological problem," as she told a colleague, "that of the adolescent girl in an alien culture." The study would likely be of little interest to experts on Polynesia, since she had never intended to write the kind of detailed description of a specific culture or people that constituted an "ethnography," a term then coming into use for what earlier generations of anthropologists had typically called ethnology. A proper treatment of the culture of the Manu'a island chain would have to wait for another volume. This book, she said, was meant for theorists and psychologists. By December she declared that the manuscript was nearly complete. Its main aim would be to mix "propaganda for the ethnological method" with "human interest."

In early 1927, Mead presented her manuscript to Boas. Not long afterward he summoned her to a luncheon to discuss it. She was anxious about his reaction. Her work had, after all, turned away from analyzing cultural diffusion. Apart from collecting some physical artifacts for the Bishop Museum, she had spent rather little time doing the kind of descriptive ethnography Boas's students were doing elsewhere. And, of course, there would be no way to avoid talking to Papa Franz about sex, a subject that wound through her manuscript like a Polynesian tattoo.

As they sat down at the table, Boas, august and avuncular as always, cleared his throat. He had only one comment to make, he growled in his pebbly English. She had not adequately distinguished romance from physical passion, which he imagined would be corrected in a revised draft—but, that said, they could now proceed with the meal. Mead was both amused and mildly embarrassed to hear her gray-haired adviser talking candidly about sex. "THAT from Papa Franz!" she told a colleague afterward. She was also delighted when he agreed to write the book's foreword.

COMING OF AGE IN SAMOA appeared the next fall in the catalog of William Morrow, a new publisher who saw a grain of potential in the work. The title had been a compromise. Mead wanted something more academic, "The Adolescent Girl in Samoa," while Morrow preferred something catchier. The cover design was certainly aimed to attract. A topless girl and a young man, running hand in hand from the underbrush, were splashed against a tropical moon beneath arching palm trees. Samoan women didn't usually go about blouseless or in grass skirts, as Mead well knew, and surreptitious lovemaking was probably no more common in Samoa than it was in Barnard dormitories. But Morrow's aim had been to take advantage of the recent upsurge in interest in the Pacific while at the same time emphasizing sex, adolescence, and primeval freedom as core themes of the book.

In 1926 a silent film called *Moana* had played in cinemas around the country. It told the story of everyday life in Samoa (although in the British-held portion of the island chain rather than the American one), with scenes of hunting, fishing, fruit gathering, and flirtatious courtship. Its director, Robert J. Flaherty, had earlier pioneered the genre that would come to be called documentary, with a similar film set in the Arctic, *Nanook of the North*. The films purported to reveal real life in primitive societies but usually involved having locals stage ceremonies or don outmoded styles of dress. Flaherty's work offered adventure tourism at a distance, delivered with impeccable cinematic skill and, in both *Nanook* and *Moana*, glimpses of bare female breasts.

William Morrow aimed to ride the wave of public interest in getting to know savage societies from the inside. He also felt that coupling Mead's experiences in Samoa with a provocative take on the United States would be a major selling point. The suggested subtitle—"A Psychological Study of Primitive Youth for Western Civilization"—made the case explicitly, and he pressed Mead to add chapters pulling out the deeper meaning of her research for Americans. A press pamphlet for the book featured yet another topless woman, however.

Coming of Age in Samoa was meant to be about a specific society, the three villages on Ta'u that Mead had come to know well. But in the introduction, she set out her more general aim. Babies come into the world cultureless, she wrote. They know none of the rules of good behavior, what constitutes beauty or ugliness, how to be a proper person. Over the course of their lives, humans learn these things from the people around them. We call that process education, and in many societies we formalize it in a designated location, with rows of desks and dusty chalkboards.

But in reality, education takes place all the time, from the most intimate interactions with parents and caretakers to the rough-and-tumble of children at play. In their social lives, babies don't so much grow up as learn how to *be* grown up. The point of examining Samoa was to see the schemes that people halfway around the world, in a very different environment, climate, and culture, had devised for rendering children into adults.

Birthdays are not of much importance in Samoa, Mead continued, in part because there is no mystery attached to the process. Births are public, or at least not private, which would be impossible in an open-sided communal house. From their earliest moments, children must be taught a code of right behavior: to stay out of the sun, to avoid tangling the weavers' strands, to steer clear of the drying coconut, to shy away from the fire, to sit down when speaking to an older person, and to leave untouched a ritual *'ava* bowl. Older siblings, especially older sisters, have primary responsibility for rearing their younger charges. When girls are old enough to carry heavy loads and perform other physical labor for the family, they are relieved of the duties of babysitting—and with it, the frustrating interactions with the petty tyrants who might cry, pout, plead, or pee their way to acquiescence. If she can put off marriage for a while, the adolescent girl is suspended in a kind of ideal world, midway between the hard work of sibling childcare and the strict social role that comes with gaining a husband.

She also discovers a sense of her own social power. In contrast to some other Polynesian societies, Mead wrote, there are rather few ways that Samoan women are thought to be harmful. She will ruin the *'ava* if she is menstruating, of course, and she should refrain from touching fishing tackle or canoes, which she will likewise pollute. She should avoid places where chiefs are gathered. But the degree to which even these prohibitions were enforced seemed to differ from person to person. In fact, Mead found it rather difficult to assess whether Samoans considered there to be any innate gender differences at all when it came to ability and personal drive. "In those social spheres where women have been given an opportunity, they take their place with as much ability as men." You didn't have to *imagine* a world in which females might succeed in tasks typically assigned to males. You just had to spend some time in a Samoan village, where girls were accustomed to seeing their mothers and aunts take on public speaking roles and express their opinions in great assemblies.

As for sex, Samoan girls knew as much about it as their counterparts in New York, probably more. "Romantic love as it occurs in our civilisation, inextricably bound up with ideas of monogamy, exclusiveness, jealousy and undeviating fidelity does not occur in Samoa," Mead wrote plainly. Monogamy, where it did exist, was "brittle," especially for men. Dalliances did not necessarily threaten the institution of marriage, which was seen more as a matter of achieving a good match—in terms of wealth, social rank, and mutually reinforcing skills and talents—than as a guarded realm of exclusive sexuality. In great contrast to Americans, Mead wrote, Samoans were unfailingly candid about their actions but secretive about their emotions and motivations. American girls might say, "Yes, I love him but you'll never know how far it went." A Samoan girl might say, "Yes, of course I lived with him, but you'll never know whether I love him or hate him."

But what was coming of age actually like? Samoan children had intimate and early knowledge of those facets of life that were thought, in the West, to be part of the torturous process of getting through adolescence. They knew the many functions of the human body. Youngsters might scour the underbrush to try to catch secret lovers in the act. Masturbation was universal, and among boys it might even take place in groups. Same-sex encounters were casually accepted, although it was expected that one would grow out of them once marriage loomed on the horizon. None of these things was considered wrong. It was just that they were unseemly if practiced at an inappropriate time or indulged in too readily. In the end, adolescence was a period not of stress or crisis but rather of freedom and possibility. "To live as a girl with many lovers as long as possible and then to marry in one's own village, near one's own relatives and to have many children, these were uniform and satisfying ambitions."

Mead was careful to stress that not everyone experienced Samoan society in this way. There were girls who were troubled, whose reputations suffered, or who were regarded by their neighbors as bad seeds. But in terms of what she called "native theory"—the way local people made sense of their own society—the contrasts with the United States were manifest. Americans, she said, seemed to organize their intimate lives around an idealized sex experience. Sexual intercourse should be preceded by an elaborate courtship and driven by publicly expressed romantic love; it should take place solely between a postadolescent man and postadolescent woman who had gone through a formal, state-sanctioned ceremony called a wedding. Samoans saw things another way. Native theory on Ta'u had no such model at its core. As a result, everything else about human relationships was also organized differently. Age appropriateness, social rank, sexual skill, and physical pleasure were all concepts as much in use, and as widely celebrated in everyday conversations, as a chaste engagement and a dreamy honeymoon in America.

The chapter titled "Our Educational Problems in the Light of Samoan Contrasts" ballooned to the largest of all. In contrast to the United States, in Samoa it was hard to identify who precisely the adolescents were, Mead wrote. You certainly wouldn't know them by their rebellion, their angst, their peevishness, or their desire to break free of the suffocating strictures supposedly laid down by their parents. There was no youth culture and no widespread delinquency, at least not as a recognized phase of a person's second birth into adulthood. The reason, she concluded, was the road maps that Americans had devised for getting a child to full personhood. American adolescents experienced freedom as a rejection of the values, behaviors, beliefs, and habits held dear by their parents. Becoming an adult depended on struggling valiantly against the rules laid down by a puritanical, individualistic, prudish world. In a society that forced its young people to choose from among a number of exclusive pathways at once—to smoke or not, to marry or be a loose woman, to be a layabout or a company man—it was little wonder that social strain was the result. "The stress is in our civilisation," Mead wrote, "not in the physical changes through which our children pass."

The solution was not to make Americans into Samoans, of course, but rather to begin to see one's own logic and common sense as only a sampling of the many possible ways of shaping the social world, each with consequences that got played out in the lives of real people:

> Whether or not we envy other peoples one of their solutions, our attitude towards our own solutions must be greatly broadened and deepened by a consideration of the way in which other peoples have met the same problems. Realising that our own ways are not humanly inevitable nor God-ordained, but are the fruits of a long and turbulent history, we may well examine in turn all of our institutions, thrown into strong relief against the history of other civilisations, and weighing them in the balance, be not afraid to find them wanting.

Coming of Age in Samoa was full of bravado and overstatement, loose argument, and occasionally purple writing—very much like every other work of anthropology written at the time. Mead had few compunctions about drawing grand conclusions from a small sample set, fifty girls in three small villages on one island in the South Pacific. Samoans themselves were sometimes perplexed by her methods. "All these people from Fitiuta that you talked to, they are all fools," wrote a Ta'u chief. "This is why I'm telling you, if you want to write my statements for a newspaper or in your writings and publicize them to the whole world, and you send it to be read by these people of Fitiuta and the whole of Manu'a, then I will be very happy, especially if they read it." But the annals of anthropology were filled with male anthropologists doing exactly that: repeating what a male chief or shaman had told them about a folktale or relying on the ad hoc assistance of male fixers, much as Boas had done on the Northwest Coast.

Mead was trying something new. Samoa was a mirror that she aimed to hold up to her own society. Her basic point was not that she had found an outpost of free love where everything worked peaceably and well. She knew of Samoan cheating husbands, unhappy relationships, and island marriages that didn't last. Even people at the time knew that she hadn't set off in search of paradise. As a Philadelphia newspaper put it, Mead was "seeking to prove that the much reviled 'flapper' is not a modern phenomenon but has existed in all civilizations since the world began." Her basic claim was that her Samoan interlocutors did not conceive of adolescence in precisely the same way that Americans tended to see it: as a unique period of transition to adulthood that was necessarily anxiety-ridden. And when it came to understanding the lives, fears, passions, and worries of adolescent girls, Mead understood that the best way to proceed was actually to talk to them. The true experts on the crisis of adolescence were the girls who were said to be in the throes of it.

Her book came packaged with endorsements from leading scholars and public figures, from Clarence Darrow to Bronislaw Malinowski himself, who found it "an absolutely first-rate piece of descriptive anthropology." It quickly garnered reviews in major newspapers and magazines. The only sour notes tended to come from some of the men in the Boas circle. Alfred Kroeber managed a backhanded compliment. "While some people complain that you do not give enough data to allow them to check up, this leaves me cold," he wrote to Mead. "Somehow I have confidence that your diagnoses are right even when your facts are few or not printed in full." Sapir, still obsessing over his old flame, told Benedict that he found it all "disturbed and rather cheap," unworthy of the author, humiliating even. He stressed that he had borrowed the book and hadn't actually bought it.

Within a few months of publication, *Coming of Age in Samoa* sold more than three thousand copies—a stunner by academic standards—with promises of even stronger earnings into the future. Mead had little time to reflect on any of this when the book appeared on store shelves, however. She was far away from New York at the time, on leave from the American Museum of Natural History and back in the South Pacific on another fieldwork expedition. She had also started to inform colleagues that her title should now be given as "Miss" or "Dr." but no longer as "Mrs."

———

"PHILADELPHIA GIRL PLANS CANNIBAL SOJOURN," reported Mead's hometown newspaper just as *Coming of Age in Samoa* was arriving in bookstores. For some time, she had been plotting out a new expedition with Reo Fortune, with whom she had been in regular contact since they first met aboard the *Chitral*. Fortune had been working on postgraduate research at the University of New Zealand. His interests lay in Melanesia, especially the islands off the coast of New Guinea.

Melanesia was some three thousand miles away from Samoa. If they were to go there together, Mead had little chance of making a return visit to Tutuila or Ta'u, which she had hoped to do as a follow-up to her earlier research. But as she told Fortune at the time, "You know it's your career I'm thinking of first." The matter of Cressman had been resolved a few months before *Coming of Age in Samoa* was published. She had obtained a divorce decree in Mexico, a quick, inexpensive, and discreet way of dissolving a marriage that was accepted as legal in the state of New York.

A year younger than Mead, Reo Fortune had graduated from the university in Wellington. He had spent a year earning an anthropology diploma, a degree just short of a doctorate, from Cambridge University, where he had met Malinowski and studied with other leading researchers on Melanesia. One of his mentors, A. R. Radcliffe-Brown, was emerging as a major figure in what would eventually be called social anthropology—an attempt to understand the stable social habits around the world, from the uses of different kinship systems to the ways rituals reinforced collective values. While Boas and his students were more likely to use the term *culture* to describe their main interest, their British counterparts tended to think in terms of systems and functions. Some societies placed childrearing burdens on brothers-in-law rather than fathers. Others emphasized cross-cousin marriage: the practice of perpetuating particular clan relationships by ensuring unions between male and female offspring from different branches of one family tree. Some societies had religious systems that transported a gifted practitioner into another world to manipulate unseen forces, as in a shamanic trance. Others had practitioners who were expert in summoning otherworldly forces into the here and now, such as priests or sorcerers. All these systems yielded different but predictable social relationships, which researchers attempted to define and map. As anthropologists at Cambridge, Oxford, and the London School of Economics saw things, the web of possible social connections in any society was a direct product of the way that society wielded basic concepts such as family, power, and order.

In practice, however, British and American researchers worked on many of the same topics, with the same techniques, exchanging ideas across the Atlantic in a grand quest to define a discipline that was still only a few decades old as a recognizable science. Fortune was a neophyte in all this, with some field experience but no research degree. Still, he offered a kind of intellectual partnership that Mead had never before found in a man, someone who shared her enthusiasms but, given his Cambridge studies, added a different way of approaching complex social problems. Together they settled on a new field site in the Admiralty Islands, north of New Guinea. There Fortune could continue his work on Melanesian societies while Mead could study adolescents in a new cultural setting—an Antipodean-Yankee team that would put to use anthropological methods emanating from both the British and American scholarly worlds.

Mead was now set to strike out on the first expedition she had ever undertaken with someone else, arranging to meet up with Fortune in the South Seas. But she was leaving Benedict behind yet again. Their relationship, she wrote en route to the West Coast, would always be independent from any she might have with a man. Love affairs could trundle along on wholly separate sets of wheels. Benedict, however, was the centerpiece, a "beautiful walled palace," she said, "the ineradicable root, the one homosexual thirst there is no getting by." The next month, in October 1928, she and Fortune were reunited in a registry office in Auckland, New Zealand, where they became husband and wife. She cabled Benedict to tell her the news. To Mead it felt like a sudden calm after a leveling storm: the return to New York, the new job at the museum, the drawn-out collapse of her marriage to Cressman, and all the worries over the next steps in her career. On a moonlit night, six weeks after departing from New York, she and Fortune finally arrived in Pere, a large village on the island of Manus.

Pere was "a perfect little rustic Venice," she reported back to Benedict. The sea dwellers of Manus built houses on pilings in a calm lagoon, surrounded by mango swamps. The men wore their hair long, gathered in a topknot, while the women shaved their heads and adorned their necks and arms with the bones of dead relatives. Children spent their lives perched above the shallow sea, "independent little water rats" who learned to swim not long after birth and managed great distances even as toddlers. To get from one household to the next, you had to climb down from your own dwelling, risk plunging into the water from a rickety ladder, and launch out in a boat. There was no such thing as social life without this sense of peril. Mead knew this from firsthand experience. Her weak ankle, still causing trouble after the taxi accident years earlier, snapped again. She took a twelve-hour canoe ride to the regional capital of Lorengau, only to be told that a native bonesetter would do a better job than a trained physician. For weeks afterward, she hobbled about on shore on homemade crutches. She still had not learned to swim.

Mead and Fortune made a study of the local language and mapped out the various households in Pere, with their complex kinship networks. They worked independently on their own writing. Fortune polished some field research he had completed earlier on the island of Dobu to the south, while Mead gathered material for what she hoped would be a new study of the few dozen village children. She tried a new technique of distributing pencils and paper to the children, the first time many of them had ever seen such things, and asking them to draw whatever they wished. The drawings soon piled up, some thirty-five thousand of them, curling in the tropical heat and humidity.

Manus turned out to be even better suited to her interests than Samoa had been. But this had little to do with its remoteness. Rather, in watching a group of children intently—seeing them play and fight, jump confidently into the lagoon, and record the world as they saw it, in pictures and symbols of their own devising—Mead was honing in on a problem that had perplexed educators and social reformers for decades: which behavioral traits are we born with, and which ones are the product of the life circumstances in which we happen to end up?

THE PROBLEM OF THE innateness and heritability of mental properties was one of the fundamental problems occupying the social sciences for the entire time that Mead had been associated with the Boas circle. At Columbia she had written a master's thesis on whether intelligence tests might mistake cultural knowledge for brainpower. By studying a sample of Italian and American schoolchildren in Hammonton, New Jersey (the field site of her mother's never-finished dissertation), she found that intelligence scores seemed to mirror the test takers' facility in English. Knowing the rhyme scheme of a sonnet, say, or who Rubens was—the type of question not uncommon on intelligence tests of the era—had little to do with one's ability to solve a problem or reason clearly, she argued. Even completing word puzzles or problems in logical reasoning depended on having a clear understanding of what was being asked. Psychologists who thought they were modeling the universal human mind were actually doing a kind of anthropology—measuring a subject's facility with language and the special knowledge that fluency brings. They certainly weren't measuring a subject's mental acuity. With typical confidence, she wrote to the makers of the intelligence test that she used for her study—the Otis Group Intelligence Scale—trying to point out what seemed to her an obvious problem with the design. The maker wrote back to her, a mere master's student, with a brush-off that ended the correspondence.

Boas, too, had long been skeptical about grand claims that smartness followed one's lineage. One of the "fundamental aims of scientific anthropology," he wrote in a new book, *Anthropology and Modern Life*, published just as Mead and Fortune were setting off for Melanesia, was "to learn which traits of behavior, if any, are organically determined and are, therefore, the common property of mankind, and which are due to the culture in which we live." The "if any" was a crucial aside. As Boas knew, a large body of scientific opinion was pressing in precisely the opposite direction, toward confirming the theory that nearly *all* behavior, by individuals as well as by groups, was inheritable. Our predispositions to act—morally or with venality, after rational forethought or with instinctual emotion—were said to be lodged in the deepest recesses of the human organism. Our children come into the world already bearing the propensities that we, unwittingly, hand off to them.

In 1905 a British biologist named William Bateson had invented a new word—*genetics*—to refer to the way living beings pass on their deepest traits from parent to offspring. A few years later, other researchers coined the term *gene* to denote the quantum of information that flowed down family lines with predictable regularity. Whether your irises were blue or brown, whether an earlobe dangled or clung to the side of your head, whether you could curl your tongue—these variations seemed to follow the pattern of Mendelian inheritance, named for Gregor Johann Mendel, the nineteenth-century botanist who had first proposed it. There was little reason to doubt that other traits, from mental ability to leadership skills, flowed along the same pathways from parents to offspring.

No one had ever seen a gene, of course, but then again no one had seen an atom or a thing called gravity. Science proceeded by positing a theory that purported to account for observed reality and then sticking to the theory until some piece of evidence showed it to be false. To any person well versed in the latest scientific advances, it was clear that breeding was, to a very large degree, destiny. And if you needed a specific example, it lay in the story of a young woman named Emma Wolverton, better known to the American public as Deborah Kallikak.

Wolverton was a resident of the New Jersey Home for the Education and Care of Feebleminded Children. She had come to the school as an eight-year-old, in 1897, with beautiful, wide eyes and a pleasant disposition. But as she moved into adulthood, her capacities seemed to stall. She walked with a strange, jerking gait. She could play the cornet and hammer together furniture in the woodshop, but her ability to reason or perform complex tasks remained essentially that of a child.

She was, according to Henry H. Goddard, the school's director of research, a high-grade moron (a scientific label that he had invented). The more Goddard learned about her case, the more he suspected that the origins of her condition might be found inside her family tree. While reconstructing her lineage, Goddard discovered that Wolverton descended from a Revolutionary War officer who had fathered two distinct family lines: one from his legal spouse and another via an affair with a barmaid, a woman who was said to be mentally defective. Goddard then stumbled upon a remarkable fact. The soldier's legitimate descendants were upstanding members of a prominent New England family. The illegitimate ones were in general backward, poor, and delinquent—alcoholics, criminals, social pariahs, or just the pleasantly dim, like Emma Wolverton.

It was as close to a natural experiment as Goddard could imagine. He immediately realized that Wolverton and her antecedents were a test case for the origins of mental aptitude, structured like a medical trial. All the relevant parameters were held constant except for a "treatment," that is, the officer's illicit affair. He wrote up the story in *The Kallikak Family*, published in 1912. Goddard had received his doctorate from Boas's old institution, Clark University, and his book bore all the hallmarks of the scientific principles that G. Stanley Hall had tried to instill in his students: careful observation, experimental research design, close analysis of real data. The family name— Kallikak—was a pseudonym Goddard pulled together from the Greek roots for "good" and "bad," the normal seeds and the damaged ones, lying alongside each other in the descendants of one man. Had it not been for one wayward barmaid, the logic went, the state of New Jersey would have been saved the expense of incarcerating, monitoring, and housing scores of substandard human beings. The fate of Emma—or Deborah, as he called her in the book—had been sealed long before she was born. "Rather good-looking, bright in appearance, with many attractive ways, the teacher clings to the hope, indeed insists, that such a girl will come out all right," he wrote. "Our work with Deborah convinces us that such hopes are delusions."

An entire shelf of popular books had employed similar methods:

The Jukes (1877), about degenerate upstate New Yorkers; *The Tribe of Ishmael* (1888), on itinerant thieves in Appalachia; *The Nam Family* (1912), dealing with a clan of prostitutes and grifters. New terms— *dysgenics* or *cacogenics*, which meant what they suggested—had been coined to encompass the field, the obverse of studying good breeding, or eugenics. But *The Kallikak Family* was different. It told a compassionate and ultimately tragic story, with the fate of one young girl hanging in the balance. Its specific findings also fit neatly with recent scientific speculation about intelligence. A few years before Goddard began his work, the French psychologist Alfred Binet had pioneered a test that could produce an "intelligence quotient"—an IQ—as a measure of mental capacity. Goddard had now demonstrated how that stealthy number worked its dark logic down through the generations. Other researchers delved into the life histories of people classed as morons, idiots, and the insane, as well as the different policies that countries might pursue to educate them or isolate them from the general population. All used some version of Binet's intelligence test, much the way anthropometrists had adduced the cranial index to determine race. If a concept could be measured, it could also be observed, and if it could be observed, it must be a *thing*—handed down from person to person as predictably as the kink in a hair or the slope of a brow.

Goddard's work went into multiple printings and editions. It included photographs of Emma/Deborah, bright-eyed and happy, as well as of her extended family, all low foreheads and drooping jaws. (The images, it was later pointed out, had been touched up to make the family look especially brutish.) The book seemed to offer proof of what could be achieved when people like Emma/Deborah were dealt with in humane ways—corralling them in an institution, providing instruction in practical skills, and most important, preventing them from passing their cacogenic traits to new human beings.

Goddard's timing was impeccable. He was working at a time when policy making and population research were perhaps more closely linked than at any point in American history. In 1910 philanthropists at the Carnegie Institution of Washington established a special institute to push forward new research on populations, abilities, and breeding. Located in Cold Spring Harbor, New York, the institute set about collecting masses of data on how inheritance worked, from the banal traits of animals—the feather coloring of chickens, for example—to the ones that might be of particular interest to educators or criminologists, such as physical prowess and mental deficiency. The longer-term goal was to design public education programs for family improvement and racial advancement. Well funded and endowed with a bevy of hands-on researchers, the Eugenics Record Office, as it was known, used the latest statistical techniques to show that government-organized science could help reduce the reproduction of defectives, improve the biological stock of the most advanced races, and produce a healthier, more productive American society.

Nature, after all, did not lie. As Charles B. Davenport, a Harvard-trained zoologist and the office's director, wrote in one of its numerous reports, "Laws restricting marriage selection are designed, on the one hand, to protect the rights of the consort who would suffer through helplessness or ignorance and, on the other, to prevent the legal consummation of such matings as are calculated to produce physically and mentally handicapped children—those deprived of the 'right to be well-born.'" Entering the world full of potential and set on the path of normalcy, rather than shackled by the inadequacies of previous generations, Davenport believed, was in a way the ultimate human right. State legislatures agreed. In the first two decades of the century, a wave of forced sterilization laws, designed to prevent bad parents from producing another generation of bad children, swept the country: Indiana in 1907; California and Connecticut in 1909; Nevada, Iowa, New Jersey, and New York in 1911 and 1912; and Kansas, Michigan, North Dakota, and Oregon in 1913.

The ideas of Goddard and Davenport were widely shared by America's—and the world's—scientific and political elite. When the global community of eugenicists got together to share data and policy ideas, it was Boas's old employer, the American Museum of Natural History, that served as host. Two grand international congresses on the subject were held at the museum, with addresses by Alexander Graham Bell and invitations mailed out by the U.S. Department of

State. For the Second International Congress of Eugenics, in 1921, two of the museum's floors were refitted with new displays on the ill effects of racial interbreeding, the dire impact of race-alien immigration, the positive outcomes of mandatory sterilization, and amateur studies by teachers, pupils, and freelance researchers—a vast science fair dedicated to rooting out the causes of criminality, insanity, poverty, and national decline. A chart by the Eugenics Record Office clearly showed the twenty-six types of eugenic genius and the ten categories of "socially inadequate persons"—said to constitute about 10 percent of the population—ranging from the inebriate to the "cacaesthenic," that is, those with defective sense organs, such as the blind and deaf.

A year before Mead and Fortune set off for New Guinea, in 1927, the practical application of eugenics had its most important impact on American justice. In a precedent-setting case, *Buck v. Bell,* the U.S. Supreme Court upheld forced sterilization as a matter of constitutional law. It had been fully justifiable, the court ruled, for the Commonwealth of Virginia to sterilize Carrie Buck, a young, allegedly disabled woman in the state's care, in order to prevent the transmission of her mental shortcomings to future generations. "It is better for all the world, if instead of waiting to execute degenerate offspring for crime, or to let them starve for their imbecility, society can prevent those who are manifestly unfit from continuing their kind," wrote Justice Oliver Wendell Holmes Jr., in the majority opinion. "The principle that sustains compulsory vaccination is broad enough to cover cutting the Fallopian tubes. Three generations of imbeciles are enough."

As it turned out, Carrie Buck was probably not intellectually challenged or learning disabled, even by contemporary standards. She had become pregnant at the age of seventeen—the reason for Virginia's sterilization order in the first place—probably as a result of rape and family abuse, not the "sexual license" said to be habitual among the feebleminded. Still, the *Buck* ruling caused sterilization rates to soar from a few hundred in each state to thousands afterward. By the early 1930s, twenty-eight of the forty-eight U.S. states had laws authorizing "eugenic sterilization" of people deemed by authorities to be morons, idiots, imbeciles, or insane, in addition to castration or tubal ligation already practiced as punishment for certain classes of convicted criminals. By 1941 more than thirty-eight thousand such "asexualizations," in the legal language of the time, had taken place, nearly two-thirds of them involving women. By the 1960s, the figure had nearly doubled, with the practice continuing long afterward.

EUGENICISTS WERE IN NO sense on the scientific fringe. They were the establishment: well resourced, armed with a battery of statistics and test results, and with an outsize influence on law, education, and popular culture. The American Eugenics Society, founded in 1926, became one of the primary conduits for communicating the work of the Eugenics Record Office and other bodies to broader audiences. The society reached out to churches, women's clubs, schools, and state fairs with the message of clean living and cleaner breeding. Its "Fitter Families" contests assembled panels of historians, physicians, and dentists to evaluate mothers, fathers, and children for eugenic fitness. "While the stock judges are testing the Holsteins, Jerseys, and White-faces in the stock pavilion," declared one of the society's administrators, "we are testing the Joneses, Smiths, and the Johnsons."

Science and history seemed to arrive at the same conclusions. Just as racial theorists such as William Z. Ripley and Madison Grant were mining the historical record for civilizations that had collapsed in the face of unchecked alien immigration, eugenicists were revealing the inner flaws of body and mind that, if uncorrected, would spell doom for American society. The lessons they gleaned were so appealing not because they were reactionary—Grant, Goddard, and Davenport would all have been shocked by that label—but rather because they were deeply, committedly progressive. After all, their work offered both a diagnosis of and a course of treatment for most of the ills that reformers had identified. The American foundational stock of well-bred Anglo-Saxons was being corrupted by ill-planned reproduction and open borders. Family planning advocates, physicians, immigration opponents, and many others soon found that they had a common basket of concerns: to cleanse American society, to halt the decline of its master race, and to prevent "dysgenic breeding," as Margaret Sanger, founder of the American Birth Control League—later known as Planned Parenthood—put it. One of the most popular birth control devices of the era, a cervical cap developed by the British family planning advocate Marie Stopes, was marketed under the name Pro-Race—the idea being that, if people couldn't control their sexual urges, they could at least avoid misprocreation. Even in their most intimate moments, American couples were enacting their duty to build better versions of themselves.

A year after the *Buck* decision, Boas took aim at the frenetic American project to curtail the unfit. "Types" are no more than abstractions, Boas wrote in *Anthropology and Modern Life*, whether we mean races or any other social category, such as the eugenically sound or the deviant. The aim of social science, he argued, should not be to rummage around for humanity's atomic units, the unbreakable categories into which all human beings supposedly fall. Rather, we should try to hold two things in our heads at once: first, that all people are individuals, with their own talents and tribulations, and second, that we are social beings who cling desperately to the sense of reality in which we are reared. "We cannot treat the individual as an isolated unit," he wrote, characteristically mixing plain speech with his own more convoluted, academic style. "He must be studied in his social setting, and the question is relevant whether generalizations are possible by which a functional relation between generalized social data and the form and expression of individual life can be discovered; in other words, whether any generally valid laws exist that govern the life of society."

One of the goals of anthropology, from John Wesley Powell forward, had been to garner enough data to fashion general claims about the natural evolution of human societies as they crawled their way from savagery to civilization. Boas's career had been aimed at trying to bury this idea. But now, in the wake of the Kallikaks and

Buck v. Bell, it seemed to have more life in it than ever. The drive to uncover the universal laws that determined the shape of individual lives—such as the consequences of dysgenic breeding, as with Emma Wolverton or Carrie Buck—seemed to be the obsessive purpose of many biologists, social scientists, and public policy advocates. For this reason, Boas said, "almost every anthropological problem touches our most intimate life." When we think we are studying people out there, we are really making claims about people right *here*—about us and our neighbors, about our sense of the normal, the evident, and the standard.

"We classify the variety of forms according to our previous experiences," he wrote. Every society trains itself to see categories. Whom you love, whom you hate, the kind of person you'd be disgusted to see your daughter marry—none of these problems follow universal rules of attraction or repulsion. They are instead notions fired in the crucible of culture. The mobilization of sham science to justify bigotry might be said to be a deep characteristic of only one culture: that of the developed West. Northern Europeans and their diaspora, having conquered much of the world, predictably sought to remake it in their image. They filled it with imagined races and subtypes, imbeciles and geniuses, primitives and civilized men. They then declared their intellectual artifice to be deeply, provably natural, as unshakable as a god-made Valhalla.

It was here, Boas said, that there had to be a "parting of the ways of the biological eugenicist and the student of human society." It was easy to show that criminals sometimes clustered *in* families. But it was a great leap to claim that the essential traits of criminality or deviance were the products *of* families—much less that these traits were transmitted from parent to child, as Goddard had tried to show with the Kallikaks. After all, societies differed on the basic definition of what constituted criminal behavior. Criminologists, for example, tended to pay scant attention to rich criminals or well-placed miscreants: the tax cheat, the unscrupulous businessman, the corrupt politician. Their theories of innate criminality seemed to be based exclusively on the poor: the pickpocket, the public drunkard, the street prostitute. That fact was itself evidence of how culturally determined the definition of *crime* was in the first place.

The only thing the eugenicists had proven, Boas concluded, was "how easily the human mind is led to the belief in an absolute value of those ideas that are expressed in the surrounding culture." Had the British managed to capture George Washington, their modern-day eugenicists would likely have developed a theory of the inherited deficiencies that made him so criminally rebellious. There might well be general patterns to human development, but they certainly weren't the kind that could tell you which families were likely, for all time, to produce substandard human beings.

RESEARCHERS SUCH AS GODDARD and Davenport imagined themselves to be some combination of physician and psychologist, bridging the study of the human organism and of human society. They peered into family lineages as a way of understanding the workings of the human mind. Anthropology had flourished as a discipline by attempting to do something similar. When Boas joined Columbia, anthropologists and psychologists shared quarters in the same department. His students, including Sapir, Benedict, and Mead, typically took seminars with psychology professors in addition to their study of kinship systems or indigenous languages. In American universities, psychology as a scholarly field was older than anthropology, but both were concerned with uncovering the essential patterns of human development: for individuals in the case of the former, or for entire peoples in the latter.

Boas had worked alongside psychologists since his days at Clark University. President G. Stanley Hall had been a student of the Harvard philosopher William James, whose *Principles of Psychology* (1890) had laid the foundation for an experimental science that would seek to systematize the study of emotion, reason, and will. Hall himself had played a major role in bringing European psychoanalysts such as Sigmund Freud and Carl Jung to an American audience. At one of Hall's academic conferences, a group photograph showed a young Boas amid some of the era's foremost psychological researchers, a wry and self-satisfied smile on his face, as he stands in the same row as James, Freud, and Jung. But Boas tended to keep his distance from theorists whose work was unmoored from hard data. He carried on a robust correspondence with most of the prominent intellectuals of the day, but Freud and Jung were apparently not among them. Still, the upsurge in interest in psychoanalysis was impossible to escape. It was Freud himself who had laid out a clear statement for how he thought his field could contribute to the work that anthropologists were doing. In his *Totem and Taboo*, first translated into English in 1918, Freud proposed to interpret primitive societies through the lens of neuroses and obsessions. Primitives, he speculated, seemed to display some of the same behaviors as neurotics in modern societies. What was a taboo, after all, but a compulsive desire to avoid being soiled by an imaginary pollutant? Other psychologists, such as Jean Piaget in Switzerland and Lucien Lévy-Bruhl in France, took similar approaches. Anthropologists tried to understand bizarre people around the globe—distant villagers, with their thunder gods and loincloths—while psychologists tried to diagnose the deviants down the street. Yet the two projects, these thinkers proposed, might actually be versions of the same thing.

Freud was no experimentalist. He piled up hypotheses into pyramids without ever actually testing them, as Boas's student Alfred Kroeber put it in a review of *Totem and Taboo*. Mead, too, had been reading the book before she left with Fortune on their voyage to the South Seas. She found it intensely stimulating, but one aspect bothered her. Children, neurotics, and savages, Freud proposed, might be understood as variants of one type. They were all individuals who were either preadult or somehow retarded—literally, in the sense of being slowed down along some developmental pathway—by biology, history, or circumstance. Individuals and entire cultures could be stuck in the same way, as if waiting for a delayed train to sweep them on toward the next station. The difference was that children eventually grew up. Neurotics and savages needed other interventions, such as the analyst's couch and the ministrations of civilized educators, to make their way on down the line.

Mead had proposed to study this problem on Manus, which was how she had pitched her work to one of her funders, the Social Science Research Council in New York. Island villagers shared the landscape with wood sprites, demons, and the spirits of their ancestors. They were hovered over by embodiments of the jealous wishes of their neighbors, which might spoil the fishing or send a rogue wave crashing into the lagoon. The sea dwellers lived amid a host of social taboos, more even than in Samoa, especially regarding sex, marriage, and property. A cascading array of travails would befall anyone who broke the rules.

Many of these rules were associated with the quick transition from childhood to the age of marriage. That moment seemed to plunge young men into a state of worried despondency, with an extreme sense of shame and jealousy. "They are quarrelsome, uncooperative, aggressive, unable to organize any community undertaking, or to develop any sort of society with central authority," Mead wrote from the field in the spring of 1929. "Even the pigs live and die without bearing litters because no one is willing to raise a boar which will sire freely the pigs of their neighbors." The complex code of behavior among the adults of Pere was a kind of handbook for negotiating a world infused with unseen doom. But abiding by its dictates was precisely the thing that seemed to spur such inordinate unhappiness and unneighborliness.

Yet in her hours and hours of interaction with the children of Pere, looking at their drawings and talking with them as they tumbled over her lap, Mead found these younger villagers to be blissfully unaware of the complex rules and beliefs that seemed to animate their parents and older relatives. They were either wholly ignorant of, or just unconcerned with, the spirits that enveloped the adults. "For them the dark is less peopled than for their elders who know the names, the very face and stature of scores of the ghost population," Mead wrote. The children acted more like normal adults, while the adults acted rather more like children or neurotics, as Freud would have understood them. These primitives weren't like children, precisely because their *own* children weren't like primitives.

And if children didn't seem to go through a stage of magical thinking in the way they conceived of the world, it was hard to argue that an entire society went through such a stage either. Human minds had infinite potentialities, Mead realized. It took a society to sift through the possibilities and name some of them good and others bad. Children were simply versions of human beings who were as yet undisciplined by the categories, obsessions, and social rules into which they were born. On Manus, people who might be labeled insane in New York—people who were convinced, for example, that bad fishing was the result of a visitation by the ungrateful dead—could find a way of leading perfectly healthy lives on the pole stilt houses in the lagoon. There was also a deeper truth here, Mead discovered, something that she had observed in Samoa as well: even the adults seemed to talk about the rules of correct behavior more than they actually followed them. "One of the principal characteristics of the culture is an extreme flexibility in practice," she reported in early 1929.

Much of the anthropological literature had treated people in primitive societies as younger, more naïve versions of civilized ones. They were all children, of a sort, and their gods and demons were figments of a fantastic but simple mind that modern education would eventually sweep away, much as a school-age child might be weaned from believing in Santa Claus. Mead found little support for this approach. "I would suggest that the solution lies rather in the fact that every human culture is built up by a process of rather severe selection," she reported to the Social Science Research Council.

> Only by emphasizing certain aspects of the human endowment at the expense of others can a culture assume form and shape. . . . These neglected potentialities will show up most sharply in children who are as yet undisciplined by the culture, in those individuals who draw more upon their innate equipment than upon their culture, poets and artists and in those ungifted psychological non-conformists whom we call neurotics. . . . This potential-

ity of the human mind is dynamic in our society just as man's more affective and less disciplined thinking is dynamic in other societies; neither is childish in a developmental sense, rather both appear in childhood, imperfectly mature and soon to be shaped and distorted by the categories of any given culture.

The people of Manus had simply chosen to emphasize a specific mode of thought in defining adulthood—obsession with the dark imaginary—that Mead's own culture happened to associate with childhood. Their children had to be *taught* to behave this way, through an elaborate and often painful transition away from the carefree existence they enjoyed until the age of marriage.

"All social relations require short canoe journeys," Mead wrote in her field notes. Among the people of Manus, perched above the water in their houses on stilts, that was literally true. But there was no better metaphor to illustrate the general principle that was coming to inform Mead's work. Really understanding another place and its people required a leap out your own front door and some hard rowing before you got to someone else's hut. Anthropology was science, she believed, but it was also an act of translation. You had to use the imperfect language of your own society to try to make sense of another.

Like Boas in his work on sound-blindness decades earlier, Mead was discovering that we necessarily interpret foreign ways with the intellectual tools we have closest at hand: the mental boxes that are meaningful in our own time and place. All cultures are "experiments in what could be done with human nature," she later wrote. The way to understand these experiments was not to imagine yourself as a white-coated scientist, as Goddard had done with the Kallikaks. It was instead to launch your canoe into the world, throw yourself into an unfamiliar setting, and try to understand how local customs make sense to the people who engage in them—even those who might appear neurotic or dim, with dog's teeth for currency and the bones of their father hanging from their arm. If you were going to sterilize someone on the basis of your science, as had happened to poor Carrie Buck, you should want to get it dead right.

MEAD AND FORTUNE ARRIVED back in New York in September 1929 to the unexpected good news that she now had $5,000 sitting in her bank account. *Coming of Age in Samoa* was a best seller. William Morrow, her publisher, offered an advance of $500 for a follow-up book concerning her new adventures on Manus. It appeared the next year as *Growing Up in New Guinea*, with a dedication to Reo Fortune. The new book sealed her position as an outspoken, even scandalous public scientist, given her frank discussions of sex and her refusal to acknowledge the self-evident superiority of Western civilization. She had become, seemingly overnight, one of the country's foremost experts on the relevance of the most remote parts of the globe for understanding what was happening back home.

She wrote quickly and well—twenty-five hundred words a day, by her own account—and rushed off short essays to magazines with opinions on education, child rearing, adolescence, and other subjects. Letters poured in from supportive readers and exasperated ones alike. "Your book, next to the Bible, is the most interesting book that I have ever read," wrote one fan. "It is the only book costing more than a dollar that I have bought for a long time," wrote another. Authors of girls' adventure books hailed her as a model, a daring explorer traveling the world, the first "white woman" to set foot in the remotest regions—a wild exaggeration, of course, but one that Mead did little to discourage. She hired an agent to arrange speaking engagements where she could regale audiences with news from the far side of the globe. *The Saturday Evening Post,* however, rejected a barbed essay on the deficiencies of American education. The world around us, not the universe within, mapped the twisted pathways from childhood to adulthood, Mead had said. "We can't stomach such a sweeping blow at practically everything we stand for," the editor wrote back.

Cressman had remarried, taken off to Oregon, and started a new career as an archaeologist. Sapir had married a woman he met while Mead was in the South Seas and had become a father again, with a new chair waiting for him at Yale. Fortune was still working on his doctorate on another Melanesian people, the Dobu Islanders. But Mead was famous. Not yet thirty years old, she had already done more to introduce the reading public to the word *anthropology* than anything since Boas's efforts at the Chicago world's fair more than three decades earlier. Fortune would later complain that, harnessed to a genius, his ongoing study of Dobu would be "the last book I'll ever write alone." Mead recalled their household as "stable, though rather tempestuous." It would get worse.

Chapter Nine

MASSES AND MOUNTAINTOPS

....

By the time Mead and Fortune returned from Manus, virtually anyone teaching anthropology or running a natural history museum in
the United States could claim one of two intellectual fathers: Harvard's Frederic Ward Putnam or Columbia's Franz Boas. At Harvard,
Putnam had curated one of the country's great collections, the Peabody Museum of Archaeology and Ethnology. He had boosted the
study of Native American sites and trained new teams of researchers
in rigorous field methods and preservation, much as he had done with
Boas himself at the Chicago fair. But his death in 1915 signaled the end
of an entire generation, one that had included John Wesley Powell,
Otis Tufton Mason, and other scholars with whom Boas had tangled.

Harvard and Columbia continued to compete for graduate students and research funding, but in terms of sheer numbers, Boas was
winning out. He had been an energetic behind-the-scenes promoter,
helping his graduate assistants land jobs in key universities. By now
his former students—and students of students—populated anthropology departments, museums, and research institutes across the
country. They were beginning to shape an entire discipline according
to his vision, as physical anthropologists, ethnographers, linguists,
and archaeologists worked together on common problems.

Boas's program produced students who resembled their department chair in other ways, too: contrarian, opinionated, with a sense
of the urgent necessity of anthropology as a public science. Its practitioners saw themselves as destined to venture out of the laboratory or

exhibition hall and into the fray. In a time of restricted immigration, racial segregation, and the apparent triumph of eugenics, the stakes of being schooled in Columbia's new science of humanity seemed higher than just winning a research grant or securing an academic appointment. Every year Boas's students recruited budding anthropologists with a zeal approaching that of a nascent religion, much as Benedict had done for Mead.

Gladys Reichard had taken over some of the introductory classes at Barnard, where she lectured to classrooms of eager undergraduates. Melville Herskovits had moved from the Free School to run some of the courses in physical anthropology, engaging Barnard students to carry out measurements and collate data. Benedict continued to oversee their work as a junior professor and Boas's effective lieutenant. Once you had been introduced to Boas's core ideas, it was impossible not to feel the weight of it all: the world-upending insights, the sense of common cause, and—for plenty of young women in particular—a new way to confound society's notions of proper behavior. "I began to treasure up the words of Dr. Reichard, Dr. Benedict, and Dr. Boas, the King of Kings," recalled one undergraduate. "We all call him Papa, too."

This particular student was unusual because she was thirty-four years old, although she claimed to be about a decade younger. By her own admission, she had a voice too big for polite company, a tendency "to stand and give battle," and a roll and ramble to her step that she said came from having been taught to walk by a sow hog. Her Barnard class photograph had her near the center of the frame but half hidden by a tree branch, "a dark rock surged upon, overswept by a creamy sea," as she described herself—the college's only African American student. A recent migrant from Florida, she had bounced from one pursuit to another: as a dresser with a traveling Gilbert and Sullivan company, then a manicurist, then a night school attendee. The closest she had ever come to anthropology was a brief stint waiting tables at John Wesley Powell's old Cosmos Club in Washington, D.C., joining other black servants in an atmosphere of "paternalistic affection tempered by budgetary caution," as the club's official history put it.

In a room of people just back from some foreign expedition, the most arresting thing about her was the name one of her mother's friends had given her—Zora. No one knew where it came from, but there was suspicion that it had been swiped from a Turkish cigarette label.

ZORA NEALE HURSTON WAS born in Alabama, probably in January 1891—she was hazy about the details—but grew up in Eatonville, north of Orlando, Florida. The area around the town was pitted with sky-blue lakes, giving it the feel of a spider's web of dry land stretched over an inland sea. Spanish moss drooped from the trees. Ospreys and turkey vultures circled over the minor ripples in the landscape that passed for hills. It was a place where sinkholes could open up and swallow a cow or where an entire lake could simply disappear, sucked down a natural drainpipe formed in the porous limestone. The region's gritty, ash-gray topsoil, whipped up by a tropical storm or a passing buggy, dusted Sunday clothes and seeped through window frames, as if Floridians had established themselves on top of some older, burned-over civilization and were now paying the price.

Eatonville had the distinction of being the country's first incorporated African American city, "a pure Negro town," as Hurston called it. Maitland, its mainly white counterpart down the road, with fancier homes, was distant enough for propriety but not off limits. Hurston was one of Eatonville's well-born, if one could say that about a black woman in the era of Jim Crow. She was only two generations removed from chattel; all four of her grandparents had been enslaved in Georgia and Alabama. Her father, John Hurston, was a Baptist minister and town mayor who helped preside over Eatonville's unofficial city hall, the front porch of a store run by Joe Clarke, another local notable. On the creaky floorboards, neighbors would joke, lie, and carry on, women and men together, trading stories and one-upping one another with well-placed insults—specifying and signifying, as people called it.

Her mother, Lucy, balanced things out with a commitment to education, books, and ambition. Jumping at the sun, she told her eight children, will at least guarantee you get off the ground. But Lucy's death, which occurred when Hurston was barely a teenager, changed things. Her father quickly remarried, to a much younger woman, and Hurston was sent to school in Jacksonville in the coastal pinelands upstate. This break with a familiar world, and with her father, would stand as the defining shock of her early life.

Traveling geographically north in Florida meant going culturally south. It was in Jacksonville, she said, that she first realized she was "a little colored girl." Reality seemed designed to convince her of that fact. Official signage sorted people, Noah-like, into whites and blacks, just as you might mark off a cattle egret from a tawny-breasted grackle. You could see the quick reaction in a white person's face when your talk strayed toward the frontier of sass. Hurston was traded among various family members, now in Nashville, again in Jacksonville, then north to Baltimore, until she was old enough to step out on her own.

When her father died unexpectedly, his car crushed by a train in Memphis, she stayed away from the funeral and instead started planning her future. She became part of what would come to be called the Great Migration: the flow of African Americans from south to north, seeking jobs and an escape from the strictures of totalitarian local governments, ones that frequently halted northbound trains or jailed people simply for trying to move across state lines. She ended up in Washington, lured in part by the prospect of studying at the country's premier integrated institution, Howard University.

The distinctions between Jacksonville and Washington, however, were less stark than Hurston might have anticipated. President Wilson would soon proclaim freedom and self-determination to be bedrock principles of world affairs, but at home his administration was the first to insist on Jim Crow restrictions in the federal workforce. African Americans were dismissed from appointed posts or reassigned to separate Negro units. "Colored" toilets appeared in some federal buildings lining the National Mall. African Americans formed more than a quarter of Washington's population, and the U.S. Congress—which ruled the city through an appointed commission rather than an elected council or mayor—used its influence to ensure that racial segregation by law and custom remained in force in restaurants, hotels, cemeteries, and other public facilities. The only space where black and white Washingtonians regularly interacted was on the mixed streetcars, and it was clear who had the upper hand. In 1908 James Thomas "Cotton Tom" Heflin, an Alabama congressman, had shot a black man on a streetcar for using foul language. Never jailed, Heflin was still legislating on Capitol Hill when Hurston first arrived in the city. A few years later the committee organizing the dedication ceremony of the majestic Lincoln Memorial would require that African American attendees sit in a cordoned section far from the stage. Not long after that, the Ku Klux Klan moved its national headquarters to the city, now friendlier than ever to the organization's aims.

In the summer of 1919, just as Hurston was preparing to begin college, as many as two thousand armed whites, mainly uniformed soldiers and sailors, swept through black neighborhoods in search of two men who had allegedly tried to steal a white woman's umbrella. After three nights of violence, six people were dead, scores were injured, and hundreds—mainly black men—were confined to the city jail while federal troops patrolled the city streets. But as classes resumed that fall, Hurston discovered that Howard University was in many ways an oasis. In the redbrick buildings around a swath of lawn and willow oaks that students knew as the Yard, the classrooms brimmed with what W. E. B. Du Bois had called "the talented tenth"—the women and men who would demonstrate in their own lives the possibilities of black achievement. For the first time, Hurston felt she was at the center of something and not at life's dusty edge. She fell immediately into the circle of Howard's esteemed professors such as Lorenzo Dow Turner, head of the English department, and the philosopher Alain Locke, who had been the country's first African American Rhodes scholar. "I felt the ladder under my feet," she recalled.

It was at Howard that she began to write stories, essays, and poetry, first for a campus publication and later for *Opportunity*, one of the magazines that would soon help channel a new outpouring of black literary talent. She was rarely an outstanding student, however.

There were classes taken and missed. Progress toward her degree stalled, restarted, and then stalled again. Tuition bills piled up. She soon found herself broke. Hurston's literary work had already gained some notice, and with introductions to the right people, she reckoned that she might eventually make her way as a writer. Just as it had for Mead, New York seemed to beckon. "Zora's greatest ambition is to establish herself in Greenwich Village where she may write stories and poems and live an unrestrained Bohemian," read the caption in her Howard yearbook, for which she had chosen a saccharine but not inaccurate quotation as her motto: "I have a heart with room for every joy." In the first week of January 1925, she stuffed her belongings into a bag, along with $1.50 in cash, and set off north.

HURSTON SLIPPED EASILY INTO the galaxy of writers, publishers, and wealthy white philanthropists, many of them women, who formed the essential patronage network for New York's budding black artists—the "Negrotarians," as Hurston dubbed these supporters. That summer she managed to garner the second prize in a literary contest run by *Opportunity*. At the awards dinner, she met Annie Nathan Meyer, the founding benefactor of Barnard, who offered to arrange a place for her at the college during the next academic year, along with financial support. Hurston was also introduced to one of the first-place finishers, a man from the Midwest, ten years her junior but already acclaimed for his poetry. In Langston Hughes she found an immediate traveling companion within the world she had first encountered at Howard, a swirl of ideas and experiment, of words that poured out hot onto the page. It was all an unexpected windfall—the place at Barnard as well as the prospect of becoming a serious writer at the same time—especially given her middling grades and unfinished bachelor's degree from Howard. She decided to enroll that fall.

With the blessing of Meyer and of the college's dean, Virginia Gildersleeve—the same person who had offered Boas a refuge across Broadway after his outspoken opposition to the First World War—Hurston was almost immediately a person you needed to say you knew. Young women fell over one another to propose lunch. Hurston knew she was a whetstone for sharpening one's progressive sensibility, a role she would reprise virtually every time a white benefactor took an interest in her advancement. "I became Barnard's sacred black cow," she later wrote. She had already perfected her signature form: a retiring standout, an obsequious bullhorn, a loud, brash, and brilliant self-doubter—"cross eyed, and my feet aint mates," as she wrote to the poet Countee Cullen not long after arriving in Manhattan.

Her feet, more and more, were taking her in new directions, away from the quiet quads of Morningside Heights. By the end of 1925, her former professor Alain Locke had selected one of her stories, along with work by Hughes and other young writers, to appear in a volume he was editing titled *The New Negro*. The book would stand as a kind of signal fire for the Harlem Renaissance, a time of white patronage as well as overt exploitation, of artistic boldness and intense anxiety, a sweeping experiment in redefining blackness in a country that had been built on defining it for you.

Hurston threw herself into Harlem, not just the neighborhood but also the lifestyle. She lived mainly on 131st Street, although she moved frequently, and reveled in the circle of writers and artists clustered around the small journals and Saturday evening parties shaping the new cultural movement: Cullen and Hughes, her essential partner; the actor and singer Paul Robeson; the writers Arna Bontemps, Dorothy West, and Wallace Thurman; the heiress and impresario A'Lelia Walker; the white writer and photographer Carl Van Vechten, whose portraits became a kind of celluloid monument to a brief, burbling moment, a time when "the Negro" was more in vogue than at any previous point in American cultural history. Hughes remembered Hurston as "certainly the most amusing" of these contemporaries, "full of side splitting anecdotes, humorous tales, and tragic-comic stories . . . who had great scorn for all pretensions, academic or otherwise."

She seemed to know everyone. It was the kind of life that Mead and the Ash Can Cats could only have dreamed of for themselves a few years earlier. Hurston was a real writer, and she made sure people knew it. At a Barnard luncheon, she hosted her friend and sometime patron Fannie Hurst, a best-selling novelist—which at the time was roughly the equivalent of a college freshman casually walking into the dining hall with J. K. Rowling. "It made both faculty and students see me when I needed seeing," she told Hurst in a letter. Hurston's writing was already being published in the leading Negro periodicals, even if her term papers and exams suffered in the process. It seemed hard to find a major party north of Central Park where she wasn't present, smoking cords of Pall Malls, dressed in bright scarves, crackling beads, or anything else that would turn heads when she swept into a room.

Still, traveling the distance between a Barnard lecture hall and a Harlem rent party was like shedding a skin, or perhaps slipping into one. Both worlds had their own constraints. For older black intellectuals like Locke and Du Bois, the blossoming of African American literature was not simply a matter of art. It was the leading edge of what might become a broad reevaluation of black potential—proof positive that African Americans could produce great work that spoke not just to their own condition but to general problems of humanity. "I do not care a damn for any art that is not used for propaganda," Du Bois wrote in 1926. Art would be liberating not in the sense that black voices would at last be heard but rather that black writers would now be seen as intellectuals with common claim to universal themes. Race was a route into art, and art was an escape from a racial straitjacket. Elevation, advancement, refinement, polish—these were the keys to proving oneself before the white cultural establishment and staking out a version of blackness that was stylish, bold, urbane, and modern. All these qualities were what was meant to be new about the work showcased in Locke's *The New Negro*.

But Hurston was skeptical. She chafed at the idea that black experiences had to be pronounced worthy of being expressed in art rather than be depicted exactly as they were: in rounded vowels and her own booming voice, with cutups and jokes and ecstatic prayers and poor man's food, through grammars and vocabularies that contained their own brand of genius. Hughes and other younger writers shared some of her views, but they sometimes found her personal style grating, even offensive. She could take things too far, they thought. "To many of her white friends, no doubt, she was a perfect 'darkie,'" Hughes later said, "in the nice meaning they give to the term—that is a naïve, childlike, sweet, humorous, and highly colored Negro." Speaking *for* the people didn't mean you always had to speak *like* them.

Within only a few months after her arrival in New York, Hurston emerged as the Harlem Renaissance's greatest internal critic. She had grown up with supreme confidence in the Eatonville version of herself—a town where it was possible to be both black and in charge—and for all its pretensions to progress, Harlem wasn't quite that, she felt. A person new to the city could climb out of the subway at 135th Street and find a world where every job was held by a person of color, from the policeman to the butcher to the schoolteacher. But its artists seemed intent on trumpeting that fact as somehow unusual. "Negroes were supposed to write about the Race Problem. I was and am thoroughly sick of the subject," she later wrote. "My interest lies in what makes a man or a woman do such-and-so, regardless of his color. It seemed to me that the human beings I met reacted pretty much the same to the same stimuli. Different idioms, yes. . . . Inherent differences, no." It was a mental framework that she was gradually picking up at Barnard, a fancier way of saying what she had, from her earliest days, thought about herself: that she was born "a child that questions the gods of the pigeon-holes."

Hurston was majoring in English, but when a college adviser suggested that she broaden her coursework, she signed up for a class with Gladys Reichard. Hurston's story was that Reichard called one of her papers to Boas's attention. More likely, in the small circle of fieldworkers and lecturers surrounding Boas, Hurston couldn't resist being caught up in the enthusiastic wave. If she had arrived in New York as a would-be writer, after only a few months at Barnard she was coming to see herself as a social scientist, too, a budding Parsons or Benedict. She likely heard about another promising student who was off doing fieldwork in Samoa. Presiding over it all was Boas himself, the regal but warm father figure she had never quite had in Florida. "Of course, Zora is my daughter," Hurston recalled Boas saying at a department party, with probably a fair bit of her own embellishment. "Just one of my missteps, that's all."

Already by the spring of her first year at Barnard, Hurston felt like part of the club. She took to calling Boas "King" rather than "Papa Franz" in letters to friends and associates. "I am being trained for Anthropometry. . . . Boas is eager to have me start," she wrote to Mrs. Meyer. She had been entrusted to Melville Herskovits for the anthropometry course, which was still a required subject in the field. Before long, she was leaving her apartment in Harlem and standing on street corners, calipers in hand, inquiring whether passersby would mind having their measurements taken. Herskovits had even instructed her to assess gradations of skin tone by coding the lightness or darkness of the inner triceps, a question that predictably caused many subjects to turn and walk the other way. Still, there were few people who could "stop the average Harlemite on Lenox Avenue and measure his head with a strange-looking, anthropological device and not get bawled out for the attempt," recalled Hughes, "except Zora, who used to stop anyone whose head looked interesting, and measure it."

While Hurston was still completing the requirements for her degree, Boas arranged for her to take on a field expedition back to Florida. She was to work on assembling, systematically, the kinds of stories with which she had regaled friends in Harlem—folktales and jokes, verbal quips and half-true lies. It was a source of tremendous pride that she had been asked and that Boas arranged a fellowship to cover the costs. In February 1927, she set off for the South, this time as a bona fide apprentice anthropologist—"poking and prying with a purpose," as she would later describe it. It was the first time anyone had paid her to do something that came so naturally, to sweep up the stories that fell like wood shavings all over Joe Clarke's porch, and it was heady beyond belief. She was bound for a place that was both intimately familiar and newly, magically strange.

AT BARNARD AND IN Harlem, people knew of Eatonville from Hurston's tales and barbs, but plenty of people had already come across her section of Florida. Anyone who was paying attention had read the newspaper reports about a neighboring town, not quite twenty miles from her childhood home, called Ocoee.

On November 2, 1920, Election Day, a local man named Mose Norman had come to the polling place in Ocoee to cast his ballot in the presidential race. The contest offered a choice between two Ohioans—Senator Warren G. Harding and Governor James M. Cox—and it was the first presidential election in which women in every state had the right to vote. A massive voter registration drive aimed not only to bring women to the polls but also to increase participation by African Americans. In Florida a person like Norman was easily turned away. Across the state, white election officials conspired to challenge black voters' registration credentials, a common method of voter suppression. Norman protested but was chased off by a white crowd.

Word went out that Negroes were rioting. White reinforcements arrived from neighboring towns. Norman took refuge in a house owned by a man named July Perry, which was soon set upon by the growing mob. After shots were exchanged, white attackers worked their way street by street, ransacking houses and torching churches. Perry was dragged from a car and hanged from a telephone pole along the highway. Norman escaped, but other stragglers were pursued into the brambly woods and shot.

Every black family that had not been killed was beaten, burned out, or forced to leave. The death toll was uncertain, since there were few people around who cared about identifying bodies or ensuring proper burials, but the figure perhaps ran into the dozens. "White children stood around and jeered the Negroes who were leaving," wrote one eyewitness. "These children thought it a huge joke that some Negroes had been burned alive." The five hundred or so survivors could be seen trudging along the highways miles from town, like refugees from an undeclared war. The *New York Times* carried the news as a front-page story.

Ocoee would turn out to be one of the bloodiest and most unsparing antiblack pogroms in American history. It ushered in a new wave of massacres that the newspapers routinely mislabeled as "riots": murderous patrols by white citizens in nearby Orlando and Winter Garden; the storming of black neighborhoods in Tulsa, Oklahoma, in 1921; the racial cleansing of the town of Rosewood, Florida, in 1923; the destruction of black businesses in Little Rock, Arkansas, four years later. With the addition of further lynchings and innumerable one-off beatings and indignities, it was the largest upsurge in organized antiblack violence at any point since the end of slavery.

It would take Hurston a decade to write about Ocoee, in an unpublished essay unearthed only after her death. But she knew the world to which she was returning in 1927—alone and with only a vague plan for collecting ethnographic material, perhaps doing some writing in the morning and some anthropology in the afternoon, as she told Annie Nathan Meyer. As she made her way south, she kept correspondents abreast of her safety as well as her progress. Florida had not gotten any friendlier in her absence. She found poor whites to have "the harshest and most unlovely faces on earth," staring out with "aggressive intolerance," even though she reported no particular troubles along the way. "Flowers are gorgeous now, crackers not troubling me at all," she wrote to one correspondent, using the term in common use for Florida's rural white residents.

In the time she had been away, nearly half a million new inhabitants had come to the state. The Atlantic and Gulf coasts were booming with migrants from the North, mainly white, via a rail system that ran eastward from Chicago and southward from Boston, New York, and Philadelphia—the "Orange Blossom Special," as a popular fiddle tune was called at the time. Still, Jim Crow authoritarianism drew sharp lines between the public lives of blacks and whites. Not a single school was racially mixed before midcentury. A combination of the poll tax and the so-called white primary—in which political parties were treated as private clubs that could exclude African Americans and decide the election for southern Democrats well before polling day—kept blacks from exercising the right to vote. Even the state's beaches were strictly segregated.

By the 1920s in Florida, unlike in other southern states, blacks and whites were close to parity in their shares of the population. As a result, the white community tended to see its own position as somehow under threat, the politically and socially dominant now recasting themselves as victims. Violence was often the preferred way of rectifying the perceived imbalance. Between 1890 and 1930, Florida had, per capita, more public lynchings than any other state in the country, almost exclusively of African Americans—twice the number in Mississippi and Georgia, three times that in Alabama. Yet before the mid-1930s, not a single person in the state was convicted of lynching. Unpunished mob violence such as the Ocoee massacre seemed to embolden terrorist groups such as the Ku Klux Klan, which witnessed a new upsurge in recruits.

Outside the towns and resorts that were growing along the coasts, Florida was the heart of darkness: a landscape of dense timberland and open scrub prairie, sparsely populated, where white sheriffs and mayors ran their jurisdictions like petty fiefdoms. The region's major industries—cutting down virgin timber, boiling up turpentine from the endless pinewoods, pulling natural phosphate out of the ground for use in chemical processing and artificial fertilizers, and tending the burgeoning orange groves—demanded enormous amounts of human labor. Floridians had long understood that their jails and prisons were full of it.

Convicts had routinely been "leased" to local developers and industry leaders, in a form of labor bondage that amounted to a new kind of enslavement. Florida abolished convict leasing in 1923—one of the last states to do so—but the privatization of imprisonment in the service of big business continued. Chain gangs could be sent out to work on rural roads as a form of rehabilitation. Tenant farmers could be imprisoned for nonpayment of rent—a criminal offense under Florida law, not a civil one—and then forced into a private labor camp to work off the debt. Few of the state's major industries could have functioned without this cheap, guaranteed, and captive labor source, one that consisted overwhelmingly of African American men. "We used to own our slaves," said one farmer as late as 1960. "Now we just rent them."

Hurston knew of the brutal, mosquito-bitten reality of Florida's interior. It was in fact exactly where she was headed. Her aim was to do some systematic collecting of folktales, sayings, stories, and other ethnographic material among black communities in the state's northern and central counties. Her financing had come from a foundation devoted to Negro culture, but she was traveling on Boas's suggestion and under his aegis—which is why she decided to list him as a reference when she financed a used car for the journey. Boas was later surprised to be contacted, out of the blue, by a Jacksonville loan company. "You certainly ought to have written to me about this matter so that I may know why you want the money," he wrote to her, the first hint of the exasperation that would wind through their correspondence over the years. But it all became clear when she informed him that it would be impossible to get to the best field sites without an automobile.

By March 1927 she was tooling through the back roads, headed farther south into the wrinkled landscape, her Nash coupe—"Sassy Susie," as she had named it—kicking up a gray cloud behind her. She hit Palatka, on the muddy St. Johns River upstream from Jacksonville; Sanford, where many of the Ocoee refugees had fled; Mulberry, on the edge of the central lake district; Loughman, with its labor camp workers sweating in the dense underbrush; as well as Eatonville—John Hurston's daughter now back home and made good.

The landscape seemed designed, in one way or another, to sting, stick, bite, or scratch. Sunlight filtered through spiky palms. Great stands of cypress stood up on their octopus legs out of the swampy muck. Poinciana trees bloomed into burning bushes, while swarms of gnats and mosquitoes hung stationary in the breezeless air. Public bathrooms were restricted to whites, as were most motels and restaurants, which was why Hurston, like any African American traveler of the period, headed straight to the black side of town at the end of each day's travels, the only place likely to offer her a bed and a meal. Just in case things went wrong, she had a chrome-plated pistol at hand.

It took her a while to figure out how to be a working anthropologist. "Pardon me, but do you know any folk tales or songs?" she recalled asking in what she called her "carefully accented Barnardese."

Like Mead in Samoa, Hurston even brought along a handful of printed stationery—hers with the Barnard College seal—which she used as an incongruous vehicle for dispatching news from the field. She had grown up hearing stories at Joe Clarke's store, but that was in a community she knew, with family and friends. This was different. You couldn't just roll into town in a sputtering car, sidle up to a bunch of strangers, and ask them to tell you everything they knew on the spot. It took time to understand people, to demonstrate your good faith and get them to trust you.

She contemplated writing a novel about lynching, based on an interview with a victim who had miraculously survived and then crawled four miles to find a black family that would nurse him back to health. But she was coming to feel "lost to Bohemia forever," she wrote to Dorothy West. She had found her calling in fieldwork.

Soon she shipped back to Boas a typescript, the first draft of what she hoped would be a detailed study of the folk life of Florida. If she had the chance to do more collecting, she said, she might extend it to all the Gulf states. She had even more material in pencil and hoped to be able to type it up soon. She had been trained in anthropology as the art of salvage, and she now understood what that meant. The first thing people would often say to her was that they had forgotten all the "old stuff." With enough conversation and prompting, they might open up. But it was all disappearing fast. Their "negroness" was being "rubbed off by close contact with the white culture," she told Boas. To make sure she got it all down, she took notes in phonetic spelling, with *the* as *de* and *that* as *dat*, in a way that would have scandalized some of her old professors at Howard.

Hurston was gradually giving a scientific gloss to a gut feeling, something that had always bothered her about the way the older generation of black intellectuals regarded people like her. What if all the stories and the stomping, the porch banter and the ax-swinging work songs, were placed alongside Samoan tattooing or Kwakiutl wood carving as activities that constituted their own system of rules, rituals, and routines? A fully formed yet unappreciated recipe for living as a human being seemed to be lurking in the dense pinelands and lakeshores of northern and central Florida—something as yet uncataloged, as Boas or Benedict might have put it in their lectures. To Hurston, the ways of life that white people made into frolicking blackface, and that black "race leaders," as she called them, would rather not discuss, were coming to look more and more like the very thing she had heard Boas's other students talk about: a culture, with an aesthetic sensibility and moral order all its own.

Over the next few months, Hurston remained in Florida and then, in the summer, gradually made her way to New York, traveling for part of the journey in Sassy Susie with Langston Hughes, who had been making his first visit to the South. On her outbound trip, she had acquired a husband, Herbert Sheen, a University of Chicago medical student whom she had married hastily. But now he was noticeably absent. She told Hughes the next spring that she and Sheen were ready to call it quits, since "he tries to hold me back and be generally obstructive," although the divorce would not be registered until several years later.

She had rather little to show for her time away. She eventually wrote up a slave narrative that she supposedly collected in Mobile, Alabama, and published it in the *Journal of Negro History*. Much of her text, however, turned out to be plagiarized from an older published source, a fact that escaped academic reviewers at the time. She consulted Boas about what to do with the other materials she had amassed, but a meeting with him reduced her to tears. He had urged her to be more systematic, to pay particular attention to the transmission of proverbs, myths, and musical forms from European planters to African slaves, and she had failed to follow that advice. Her field notes and interview data, he told her, contained little that wasn't already known. The only way of rescuing the six months she had spent in the field was to go back and do more.

After a short period in New York, she headed south again. This time she traveled under the aegis of a patron, Charlotte Osgood Mason—or "Godmother," as she insisted on being called. Mason lived in a twelve-room Park Avenue apartment filled with antiques, bone china, and African art, the latest issues of Harlem Renaissance publications fanned conspicuously on the side tables. She and her late husband, a noted physician, had otherworldliness as their vocation. They cultivated salons where telepathy, hypnosis, spiritualism, and primitivism—the idea that the ills of modernity could be cured by a retreat into the premodern past—were explored.

Like several other white philanthropists of the era, Mason believed that black intellectuals had a special facility for tapping into humans' most ancient and authentic practices and beliefs. She was an early supporter of Alain Locke and, through him, became benefactor to a wide circle of Harlem writers and artists. In return, she demanded intense loyalty, even obedience. She agreed to take on Hurston as a formal employee, with a $200 monthly salary. It gave Hurston a financial stability she had never known but obligated her in new ways. She could continue her collecting while also pursuing some of the literary work that had languished while she was in the field. Any material Hurston collected, however, would belong to Mason.

Boas had been urging Hurston to write a real ethnography, but as weeks turned to months, her scientific work amounted to little more than piling up reams of notes, ideas for books, and even film reels, since Mason had furnished her with a camera to record folk life as she found it—something that neither Mead nor Benedict had managed in Samoa or the Southwest. When she was on the move, she worried that it would all be lost in a house fire or flood. In 1928 and 1929, she was back in Eatonville and Maitland, then in turpentine camps and lumberyards, later a swing through Alabama and an autumn and winter in New Orleans, then another cold season in Florida, later still an excursion to the Bahamas. Her work wasn't so much about capturing a dying culture as trying to understand the here-and-now of a ferocious, angular way of being. Don't tell Godmother, she wrote back to Hughes, but "Negro folk-lore is still in the making."

Not until the spring of 1930 was she again in the New York area for any length of time, promising Boas that she was working hard on at last producing something of value out of the fieldwork that had occupied her, off and on, for three years. Her luggage was stuffed full with notes and tales, stories and character sketches, from more than a hundred different people: phosphate miners, domestics, laborers, boys and girls, Bahamian plantation owners, shopkeepers, ex-slaves, sawmill hands, housewives, railroad workers, restaurant keepers, laundresses, preachers, bootleggers, along with a Tuskegee graduate, a "barber when free," and a "bum and roustabout," as Hurston noted. But her reports were usually disappointing. "At last I come up for air," she wrote to Boas that summer. "It's been very hard to get the material in any shape at all."

FOR ALL HIS PUBLIC attacks on racial scientists and eugenicists, even Boas tended to see faraway peoples as laboratories and nearby ones as pathologies. In 1906 he had assured his listeners at Atlanta University that Negroes were as fully capable as people who called themselves white; it was just that their innate talents had yet to be fully realized. After all, he said, Africans had smelted iron, cast intricate bronzeware, crafted complex judicial codes, and commanded conquering militaries long before the arrival of European colonizers. But Boas himself saw little value in what Africans had become once they were forcibly removed to the Americas. "There is nothing to prove that licentiousness, shiftless laziness, lack of initiative, are fundamental characteristics of the race," he wrote five years later, in *The Mind of Primitive Man*. "Everything points out that these qualities are the result of social conditions rather than of hereditary traits." It was indicative of Boas's own limitations, as well as the historical moment, that he never questioned whether these qualities in fact described African Americans.

Even if there was nothing essential or innate about black inferiority, Boas felt, when it came to the idea of black culture, it was hard to see anything except a degraded form of whiteness. Some of his older students took the argument further, coming close to repeating a version of Madison Grant's nose-on-your-face common sense about race and history. "It is of course not fair to argue from cultural accomplishment to racial faculty," Alfred Kroeber concluded in *Anthropology*, a popular textbook he published in 1923. ". . . But the consistent failure of the Negro race to accept the whole or even the main substance of the fairly near-by Mediterranean civilization, or to work out any notable sub-centers of cultural productivity, would appear to be one of the strongest of the arguments that can be advanced for an inferiority of cultural potentiality on their part." For the white Berkeley students who took Kroeber's courses, and the countless others who used his textbook in most other—almost exclusively white—American universities, a class in anthropology often ended up confirming the racial hierarchy that they took as obvious. Cultural inferiority now stood in for the biological inferiority preached by the generation of Madison Grant.

It was beyond irony, of course, that this view developed precisely at the time of the staggering achievements of the Harlem Renaissance. Yet even for black intellectuals, it was perfectly possible to believe in both the equality of races and the backwardness of black folkways. Booker T. Washington had famously encouraged young black men to focus on agriculture and craftwork, the primary subjects taught at his Tuskegee Institute, founded in 1881. Centuries of enslavement had produced human beings who would need to be remade from scratch, keeping to their place in America's racial strata until they had rendered themselves worthy of advancement—stepwise and someday. W. E. B. Du Bois, on the contrary, had urged that there was no need to wait. Black men and women were already showing themselves to be as creative, talented, and ambitious as any other segment of American society, even in a political and economic system designed to convince them of their natural weakness. Yet for both Washington and Du Bois, to be black was to be perfectible. By definition, then, black minds and bodies had to be set on a path away from an imperfect present. Old ways of being and doing would need to be cast aside, like the manacle and the whip. White Americans had a culture, most people seemed to believe, but black Americans had a condition.

When the lives of real black people found their way into white public consciousness, it was often through one of the cousins of anthropology, the field known as folklore. People who called themselves folklorists had been around since the 1840s, when the term was first coined by the English writer and antiquarian William Thoms, but their major tasks had been defined decades earlier. The label referred to the body of sayings, just-so stories, proverbs, and children's rhymes that any randomly selected person in a given society might be expected to know. These tales and fables were of interest because they were thought to form the spiritual and intellectual essence of a people. Anyone can tell a story, of course, but if lots of people seem to tell the same one over and over again, the plotline, characters, and core message might reveal something about the unique genius of their cultural group. If you paid attention, you might just glimpse the *Volk* as it wafted up from the speech acts of ordinary folk.

In the first half of the nineteenth century, the brothers Jacob and Wilhelm Grimm had pioneered the field in Germany. They traveled around the rural districts near their hometown, in the principality of Hesse, compiling and editing the stories they heard along the way. When they published their first collection, *Children's and Household Tales,* in 1812, they took a giant leap not only toward preserving an oral tradition but also toward defining what it meant to be authentically national. In the absence of a country called Germany—which wouldn't come into being for more than half a century—to be German meant in part to be the kind of person who knew one of the Grimm tales, from "Hansel and Gretel" to "Cinderella." And if you didn't already know one, the Grimms' book laid it out for you. They had created nothing less than a primer in the right way to be knowledgeably part of a collective *us*—the Germans.

The stories people told, folklorists believed, told the story of a people. Powell's Smithsonian researchers had compiled songs, legends, and rituals on the Great Plains. Boas and Parsons had done similar work in their field expeditions in the Pacific Northwest and the desert Southwest. In the mid-1920s, Benedict began a long stint as editor of the premier scholarly outlet for this research, the *Journal of American Folklore,* which had been around for nearly half a century. "The types and distribution of the whole body of folk-tales and myths must form the subject of our inquiry," Boas once wrote in the journal.

"The reconstruction of their history will furnish the material which may help us to uncover the psychological processes involved." Folklorists were particularly good at using the results of their work to deflate the self-conceptions of Europeans and Americans who thought of their own society's mores as deeply rational and enlightened. "More than any other body of material," Benedict wrote on the subject, folklore "makes vivid the recency and the precariousness of those rationalistic attitudes of the modern urban educated groups which are often identified with human nature." But when it came to African American collecting, folklore was always tinged with a gloss of the less-than—allegedly the work of a simple, childlike people whose wisdom, where it existed, lay in a facility for avoiding hard work, thumbing a nose at authority, and somehow coming out on top. From the late nineteenth century forward, generations of white children had been schooled in precisely these ideas through a collection of stories that became a kind of American answer to the Grimms' fairy tales. Anyone who knew of Cinderella probably also knew of the adventures of a sly, ambling, and deeply American hare and his comrades.

Brer Rabbit, Brer Fox, Brer B'ar, and their narrator, a kindly old man called Uncle Remus, were the product of Joel Chandler Harris, a white Georgian journalist. His collection of stories, *Uncle Remus: His Songs and Sayings,* was published in 1880. Harris had picked up the raw material for his stories from enslaved women and men on a Georgia plantation, where he worked as an apprentice printer. When he eventually moved to a reporter's desk at the *Atlanta Constitution,* he could look back on what he recalled as an Old South of harmonious relations between owners and owned. The person at the heart of *Uncle Remus* is not a black man or an animal but rather a young white boy, carefully illustrated in watercolor in the first published edition of the book, sitting regally before the bent-over Uncle Remus.

The stories were allegedly about African Americans, and some of Chandler's tales probably did have African roots. But their audience was literally there on the page: a white person gazing at an allegedly black world, uncomplicated, tricksterish, full of wily creativity. Each night at bedtime, millions of white schoolchildren heard their parents twist their mouths around Chandler's rendering of dialectal speech. "One day, whiles dey wuz all settin' an' squottin' 'roun', jowerin' an' confabbin'," one of the stories went, "Brer Rabbit, he up 'n' say, sezee, dat ol' Mammy-Bammy-Big-Money tol' his great gran'daddy dat dar wuz a mighty big an' fat gol' mine in deze parts, an' he say dat he wouldn't be 'tall 'stonished ef 'twant some'rs close ter Brer B'ar's house." What they received in the bargain was an easy-to-swallow lesson in the essential otherness of black people. It was as if "Hansel and Gretel" were required to be rendered with the *ja*'s and *und*'s of a Hollywood German.

In addition to the Uncle Remus tales, other collections of supposed black folklore appeared in the nineteenth century, most of them comic and nostalgic in equal measure, with homespun puns, exaggerations, and remembrances of a bygone South. By contrast, when scholars sought to understand black communities, they tended to turn to Africa. It was a way of connecting what was considered to be a substandard culture nearer to home with a richer, more authentic one farther away. Hurston's old professor at Howard, Lorenzo Dow Turner, was among the first to document the linguistic connections between West Africa and the creole-speaking Gullah communities along the Georgia and South Carolina coasts. The historian Carter G. Woodson, who oversaw the foundation that paid for Hurston's first collecting expedition, mapped the connections between songs and folk beliefs in the New World and older forms among sub-Saharan peoples. "The author considers the Negro as human," he had to state at the beginning of his heavily footnoted study of transoceanic history, *The African Background Outlined* (1936)—that is, as people with histories, triumphs, and influences as recognizable as those attributed to Europeans. Africans, too, it turned out, could be seen throughout history "advancing when free to go forward and lagging behind when hindered by obstacles not encountered by others."

In a pathbreaking article in 1930, Boas's student Melville Herskovits, who had sent Hurston on her first anthropometric outings in

Harlem, defined the essential research questions for this new area of study, which he called the problem of "the Negro in the New World." But his version of the field's major questions still amounted to a kind of forensic pathology. African cultures and histories were valuable to the degree that they offered hints as to why African Americans were so persistently problematic today. "Why did the Negro acquiesce in slavery itself as complacently as he seems to have done?" he wrote in the flagship *American Anthropologist.* "Was it something essential in his make-up, or was it because the only cultural fact that was familiar to him in the civilization of the Americas was that of slavery?"

What is the significance of the great family solidarity of the Negroes, something noted by all who have had contact with them? . . . Why in the United States is there such great objection among Negroes to allow their children to be cared for in institutions? Why is it that families, themselves almost on the poverty line, will take under their wing a homeless child rather than give him to strangers? What is the relation of the phenomena of religious hysteria so familiar to students of the Negro in the United States, Haiti, the Guianas and the West Indies to similar African phenomena? And to what extent is the folklore of the Western Negroes today . . . deflected by the culture of the whites? Until we know more of African folk-material we cannot adequately answer these questions.

It was his old research assistant "Zora Hurston," Herskovits suggested in a letter to a colleague, who had first prompted his thinking along these lines. Her speech patterns, her way of walking, and her style of singing were all brilliant examples of how a "typically Negro" woman could embody discrete behaviors that mirrored their transoceanic originals. By looking back to Africa, in other words, you could not only map the tenacity of things such as religion or music—how they resisted change even in the face of massive social and economic upheaval—but also tap the ur-source for the behaviors that made black Americans so odd or troubled right now.

Most progressive thinkers would have agreed. The "Negro problem" was a matter of culture, which could be changed, not of biology, which presumably couldn't. The more radical idea—that African Americans had devised for themselves coherent folk cultures that were worth studying on their own terms, not simply as an echo of a silenced past—was much harder to imagine. In the white-dominated human sciences, enlightened anthropologists commonly approached the behaviors and beliefs of Samoans and Admiralty Islanders as puzzles to be understood, not as social diseases that needed curing. Doing the same thing in the American South, or even north of Central Park, was close to unthinkable.

HURSTON CAME BACK TO New York with "my heart beneath my knees and my knees in some lonesome valley," as she recalled. She struggled to make sense of the material she had gathered and to transform it into something other than a random assortment of anecdotes. Collecting was essentially stenography, she felt. Anthropology had to be more.

She worried that she was a disappointment to Boas as well as to her benefactor. Boas had wanted her research to be systematized somehow, to reflect broader theorizing about how stories were transmitted from place to place or how folk symbols changed over time, from Africa to the Americas. Mason had wanted unadulterated, primitive art, which she had vaguely intended to use in some of her own work as a would-be folklorist.

Hurston continued to correspond with Boas, providing periodic updates on her note-taking and academic writing. Her relationship with Mason gradually soured. The stock market crash made Mason less generous with her patronage, which eventually dwindled to nothing. Hurston once more found herself looking for means of support: an application for a Guggenheim Fellowship (denied), a proposed chicken-based catering business for wealthy New Yorkers (never launched), a stint producing musical revues (barely covering her costs). Even her relationship with Langston Hughes, which might

Franz Boas aboard *Germania*, en route to Baffin Island, summer 1883. Boas had written in a schoolboy memoir that his life had been defined by the desire to make comparisons among things he observed in the natural world. In the Arctic, he aimed to do that with the people he was already calling "my Eskimos."

Boas with his wife, Marie Krackowizer, in the year of their marriage, 1887. "Mama Franz," as Boas's students would eventually know her, was part of the sizable community of German speakers in New York in the second half of the nineteenth century.

John Wesley Powell, director of the Bureau of American Ethnology at the Smithsonian Institution, ca. 1890. Powell's explorations of the American West and his energetic lobbying and scientific organizing helped define the way that museums, schools, and government agencies understood the frontier and its indigenous peoples.

The Anthropology Building at the Chicago World's Fair, 1893. The building temporarily housed the world's largest exhibition of ethnological artifacts, but the poor attendance disappointed Boas. He vowed "never again to play circus impresario."

Kwakiutl dancers (identified only as John Drabble, second from left, and Mrs. Drabble, third from left, the remainder unknown) at the Chicago World's Fair, 1893. They were asked to demonstrate tribal ceremonies next to the Leather and Shoe Trades building, seen in the background. "Stop it! Stop it! This is a Christian country!" exclaimed one tourist.

Boas demonstrates the Kwakiutl *hamatsa*, or "cannibal dance," to assist Smithsonian curators in constructing a diorama of the secret ritual, ca. 1895.

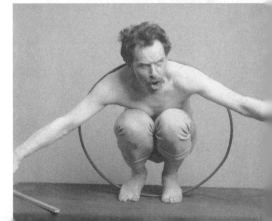

SMITHSONIAN INSTITUTION
United States National Museum

Tribe. *F. Boas.*   Sex.

Measurements.		OBSERVATIONS.	

No. _____ Age. *68*

Deformation of head _*+*_

BODY:

Stature _*167.4*_

Max. finger reach _—_ *(disab.)*

Height sitting _*88.3 — 5274*_

HEAD: *c. limb 79.1*

Length _*17.6*_   *@ 3. 77. 1~5*

Breadth _*15.2*_

Height _*10.6 — 3.1 = 12.6*_
    a. m. 15.8

FACE:

Length to nasion _*11.3*_

Length to crinion _(hair cut)_

Breadth, bizygom. _*13.4*_

Diam. front min. _*10.3*_

Diam. bigonial. _____

Nose:

Length to nasion _____

Breadth _____

Mouth:

Breadth _____

Left Ear:

Length _*7.6*_

Breadth _*4.2*_

MISCELLANEOUS.

Chest:

Breadth at nipple height _*30.2*_

Depth at nipple height _*23.3*_

Left Hand:

Length _*19.5*_

Breadth _*9.—*_

Left Foot:

Length _*26.4*_

Breadth _*9.8*_

Left Leg:

Girth, max. _____

Weight of Body: _*163*_
(With shoes, but without outer garments.)

Color of skin _*+*_

Color of eyes _*d. br.*_

Color of hair _*v. d. br. (aft ½ br.; aft 2/3 yr.*_

Nature of hair _*+*_

Moustache _—_

Beard _—_

Forehead _*+*_

Supraorb. ridges _subm_

Eye-slits _*+*_

Malars _subm._

Nasion depress. _*+*_

Nose _sl. conv._

Nasal septum _n. hor. (sl. 1. y.*_

Lips _*+*_

Alveol. progn. _sl. ab. med._

Chin _*+*_

Angle of l. jaw _*+*_

Body and limbs _*+*_

Toes _*+*_

Breasts _____

PHYSIOLOGICAL.

Pulse _____

Respiration _____

Temperature _____

Time of day _____

State of health _____

Strength:

Pressure { r. hand _*28.5 (rt. hand T)*_
          { l. hand _*21.5*_

TEETH

1st { upper { r. _____
            { l. _____
    { lower { r. _____
            { l. _____

2nd { upper { r. _____
            { l. _____
    { lower { r. _____
            { l. _____

A typical anthropometry inventory sheet, in this case Franz Boas's. His head and body measurements were taken down as part of a Smithsonian project to determine whether America's leading intellectuals were biologically superior to average Americans. (It turned out they weren't.)

(Below) Ruth Benedict in 1924, when she served as Boas's assistant in his lecture courses at Barnard College. "The discovery of anthropology—and Dr. Boas—proved to be her salvation," her sister would later recall. Although still married, Benedict lived a life largely separate from her husband's. Boas's classroom became a surrogate home. As she told a friend, "I don't have children, so I might as well have Hottentots."

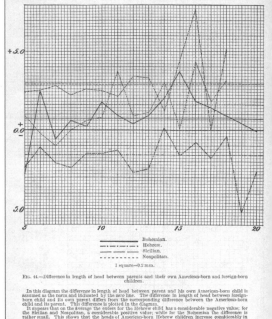

Bohemian.
Hebrew.
Sicilian.
Neapolitan.

1 square=0.2 mm.

FIG. 44.—Difference in length of head between parents and their own American-born and foreign-born children.

In this diagram the difference in length of head between parent and his own American-born child is assumed as the norm and indicated by the zero line. The difference in length of head between foreign-born child and its own parent differs from the corresponding difference between the American-born child and its parent. This difference is plotted in the diagram.
It appears that on the average the excess for the Hebrew child has a considerable negative value; for the Sicilian and Neapolitan, a considerable positive value, while for the Bohemian the difference is rather small. This shows that the heads of American-born Hebrew children increase considerably in length, while those of Sicilian and Neapolitan children decrease in length.

(Above) A page of data from Boas's report for the Dillingham Commission, 1911. "The adaptability of the immigrant seems to be very much greater than we had a right to suppose before our investigations were instituted," Boas concluded.

(Right) A tabletop display used by the American Eugenics Society, 1926, with flashing lights illustrating the financial and social costs of people "with bad heredity such as the insane, feeble-minded, criminals, and other defectives"

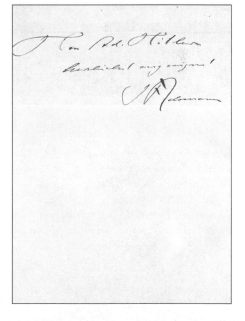

Madison Grant *(above)* and Adolf
Hitler's copy *(above right)* of Grant's
Passing of the Great Race (German
edition, 1925), with a dedication to
Hitler from the publisher *(below right)*.
Well into the 1930s, Nazi scholars
and policymakers were learning how
to construct a race-based state by
studying the American experience.

Margaret Mead as a girl in Pennsylvania, ca. 1912. According to family lore, she learned to pronounce the words "sociology" and "economics" before even knowing what they meant.

Margaret Mead as a student at Barnard College, Columbia's institution for female undergraduates, ca. 1923, sitting on a footbridge above Amsterdam Avenue. "For the first time, I felt that I had found something really better than myself, and was happy," she later remembered.

Edward Sapir, probably late 1920s, "the most satisfactory mind I ever met," as Mead would remember him. She and Sapir had begun a relationship shortly before she departed for Samoa. His heartbreak over the end of their relationship translated into lifelong disdain for her work.

The house of the Holt family, with whom Mead lived during her time in American Samoa. Her room—the veranda to the right—was largely destroyed by a hurricane in early 1926.

Margaret Mead with Fa'amotu, a Samoan friend and informant, American Samoa, ca. 1926, both in festive attire. Mead spent most days on the island of Ta'u surrounded by the teenage girls and children who formed the basis for her study of adolescence—*Coming of Age in Samoa*—which would soon be a sensation.

Reo Fortune with boys of Pere village, Manus, 1928. Fortune would complain that, now harnessed to Mead, a best-selling author, his own research would be "the last book I'll ever write alone."

Margaret Mead with children in the lagoon of Pere village, Manus, 1928. The book that resulted from her research, *Growing Up in New Guinea*, concluded that all cultures are "experiments in what could be done with human nature."

"Flowers are gorgeous now, crackers not troubling me at all," Zora Neale Hurston wrote during her first fieldwork expedition, in her native Florida. She carried a chrome-plated pistol for protection. "Pardon me, but do you know any folktales or songs?" she asked in what she called her "carefully accented Barnardese."

"It's Gregory Bateson of course," Mead wrote to Ruth Benedict at Christmas 1932. An anthropologist, Bateson had read *Growing Up in New Guinea,* and Mead fell for him almost immediately when they met in a remote village.

Ella Deloria, 1920s, while an instructor at the Haskell Institute in Lawrence, Kansas. Back at Columbia, where she served as Boas's research assistant and, later, coauthor, she was one of the few people who could claim to be both objective observer and object of study.

ANTHROPOLOGISTS FROM NEW GUINEA.

Bateson, Mead, and Fortune, captured by an Australian newspaper photographer on their way back from New Guinea, summer 1933. Their stormy love affair had exhausted them all. But some of the ideas that emerged there would later structure Mead's thinking about sexuality and gender.

From left: Mr. G. Bateson, Dr. Margaret Mead, and Dr. Reo Fortune, who arrived from New Guinea yesterday by the Macdhui.

Felicia Felix-Mentor, the woman photographed by Hurston in Haiti—the first recorded depiction of a zombie, as the *Life* magazine caption had it. In Haiti talk of zombies "seeps over the country like a ground current of cold air," Hurston recalled.

THIS IS THE ONLY ZOMBIE EVER PHOTOGRAPHED

Hurston, by the noted Harlem Renaissance photographer Carl Van Vechten, 1938. Research was a kind of "formalized curiosity," she later wrote. "Just squat down awhile," she said, "and after that things begin to happen."

The anthropologist observed: Bateson and Mead enjoying a meal inside their mosquito netting, while Iatmul villagers look on, New Guinea, 1938. "I feel like a frightful pig to have such a lovely life," Mead wrote to one of her friends.

The anthropologist observing: Hurston with musicians Rochelle French and Gabriel Brown, photographed by Alan Lomax, 1935. Dragging along a tape recorder, Hurston and Lomax netted stories, work songs, spirituals, and blues numbers for the Library of Congress.

FIFTEEN CENTS

May 11, 1936

TIME

The Weekly Newsmagazine

R. H. Hoffmann

ANTHROPOLOGIST FRANZ BOAS

He translated the world's gestures.

(See SCIENCE)

Volume XXVII

Number 19

Circulation Office, 350 East 22nd Street, Chicago.   (Reg. U. S. Pat. Off.)   Editorial and Advertising Offices, 135 East 42nd Street, New York.

Circulation this issue more than 600,000

By the 1930s, Boas was a widely known public intellectual whose views on current affairs were solicited around the world. His looks probably bolstered his image as a genius of the social sciences. As many as twenty-five hundred letters flew off his desk each year, passed back and forth between New York and wherever his students, colleagues, and field agents happened to be, along with acceptances and regrets to editors, journalists, civic leaders, and foreign dignitaries.

Benedict, ca. 1931. To Mead, she was a "beautiful walled palace . . .
the ineradicable root, the one homosexual thirst there is no getting
by." Benedict kept the Columbia department running as Boas's
effective lieutenant. Her own star would begin to shine with the
publication of *Patterns of Culture* in 1934.

Interned Japanese Americans at the racetrack in Santa Anita, California, June 1942. Their recitation of the Pledge of Allegiance was accompanied by the "Bellamy salute," a widely used gesture until its similarity to the Nazi salute became an embarrassment. Robert Hashima, a crucial informant to Benedict, began his journey into the U.S. concentration camp system here.

Mead once tried to make a map of all her relationships in the Boas circle, both personal and professional: narrow lines for minor influences, thick lines for major ones, double lines for lovers, and then Benedict, the twin sun at the center of her galaxy.

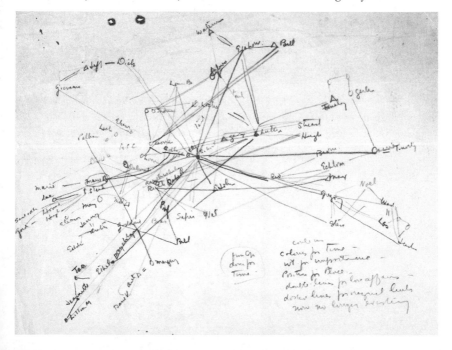

Mead in her office in the American Museum of Natural History. It was the one place where she claimed to feel secure and at home. Her workrooms were a nest of field notebooks and tagged artifacts, handwritten letters and typed mimeographs, lecture notes and photos, thousands upon thousands of pages and objects.

have yielded the most dynamic collaboration of the Harlem Renaissance, faded, the casualty of a failed effort to produce a play drawn from Florida folklore. But now shed of Mason, Hurston was free to pursue fiction even as she was chasing down ethnological facts. "I have kicked loose from the Park Avenue dragon and still I am alive!" she wrote to Benedict. "I have found my way again."

While living in Florida, she had sketched out a story line loosely based on her own experience as the daughter of a troubled southern preacher. She wrote and rewrote a text, then borrowed $1.83 in postage to send the typescript to a publisher, Bertram Lippincott of Philadelphia. Sometime later a telegram arrived announcing the novel's acceptance—on the very day, it turned out, that she received an eviction notice. Still, the news came like a sun shower on a muggy Gulf Coast day or, as Hurston later described it, as more thrilling than finding your first pubic hair. The novel, *Jonah's Gourd Vine,* appeared in 1934. It was hailed as a fine "Negro novel," with good reviews and praise for Hurston's emerging role in the company of Hughes, West, and other black writers.

Lippincott's advance against royalties was less than half of what another first-time author, Mead, had received six years earlier. It was hardly enough to pay rent, much less to found a career. Hurston would have to find a line of work to sustain her between book contracts and one-off writing projects. In January 1935 she enrolled as a doctoral student at Columbia. That path had previously been blocked by the overbearing Mason, who had insisted that an advanced degree would be a waste of time and energy. Boas signed on as her mentor. The Julius Rosenwald Fund, a philanthropic group that supported black artists and scholars, promised a fellowship to cover her studies on "the special cultural gifts of the Negroes." "I might want to teach some day and I want the discipline for thoroughness," she told Boas.

Later that year Hurston managed to wrench into some kind of order the sheaf of notes, transcripts, and stories she had hauled back and forth between New York, New Orleans, Eatonville, and points in between, her mind lurching from "corn pone and mustard greens" to "rubbing a paragraph with a soft cloth," as she said. "Thanks and thanks for fixing up the MS so well," she wrote to Benedict, who had offered comments and editorial suggestions. Lippincott published it in the autumn as *Mules and Men*. A friend of Hurston's, the Mexican painter Miguel Covarrubias, provided the illustrations, with silhouetted bodies wrapped together in a juke joint scrum or with hands raised in agonized worship. After some pleading by Hurston—"I am full of tremors" in even asking, she said—Boas agreed to write a foreword, just as he had done for Mead's *Coming of Age in Samoa*. He praised Hurston's book as the first attempt anyone had made to understand the "true inner life of the Negro."

Folklorists had previously thought they were getting at the hidden essence of a community, but what they often ended up with, Hurston believed, was offhand pleasantries and made-up tales. It was little more than lint-rolling passed off as science. *Mules and Men* was the first serious effort to send a reader deep inside southern black towns and work camps—not as an observer but as a kind of participant, as Hurston had been. Since 1927 she had spent more time on the Gulf Coast than Boas, Mead, and Benedict had ever spent in their own field sites. She wrote from the perspective of someone eager to hold up the entire tapestry of local culture, with its stories and dialects, its insults and wisecracks, as a work of communal genius that could be understood as well as appreciated.

She hadn't returned to her "native village," as she called it, in order to flaunt "a diploma and a Chevrolet." Rather, she wanted to comprehend a way of life that had been too close to her before she started off northward, a culture in which she had swum ever since she had "pitched headforemost into the world." Folklore was "the boiled-down juice of human living," she would later say, and on page after page, she joined in on the boiling-down. She abandoned grammatical detachment and used the first person to tell of meeting people, talking to them, even narrowly escaping a knife fight, the dust roiling behind her car as she sped out of town.

Mead had done a version of the same thing, although often in the second person—telling a reader what *you* see when *you* first come upon a Samoan village or a Manus stilt hut. For the same reason, Mead also wrote in what would come to be called the ethnographic present. Samoans and Admiralty Islanders were grammatically frozen at the moment she had observed them—*swims, eats, tells, knows*. They were relevant to Americans precisely because they could be imagined as unchanging yardsticks against which to measure one's own hidebound society.

But Hurston wrote about Eatonville and Loughman, with their loggers and turpentine boilers, bootleggers and juke crowds, in the past tense—*ran, hollered, fell, cut*. She was offering readers a creative, interpreted record of things she had witnessed and heard about, with her informants situated in time and space. She communicated her science exactly the way she had performed it: as a conversation in which she, the observing intelligence, was also part of the action. She was making data, not just gleaning it, and she wanted the reader to understand that fact. In doing so, she put on permanent display one of the deepest of Boasian messages: that all cultures change, even while anthropologists are busy trying to write up their field notes about them.

Mules and Men was a collection of sorts, organized into two sections, one on folktales and another on folk religion, or hoodoo. Her prose didn't just repeat other people's stories—about romantic courtships and the origins of race, about the hidden lives of animals or the interminable conflicts between Baptists and Methodists. It actually took you straight into a sweaty room, with flies buzzing and liquor being passed around the circle. It was a grand unspooling, the stories arranged not so much by chronology or theme as by their own poetic imagery. A single word from one story might suggest a new one on an entirely different theme, the way one storyteller would pick up where another had left off. "Ah know another man wid a daughter," someone would say, or "I know about a letter too," and you'd be away on another tale, one flowing into the next.

Folklore wasn't about exposing some hidden essence of a society, Hurston realized, but about the way real people interact with one another, over time, repeatedly, in a long arc of conversations, fights, and reconciliations. Stories get told by people, and those people are in places, together. "Many a man thinks he is making something when he's only changing things around," she wrote. The basic logic of legends, tales, and folkways was not to suspend them in time but rather to try to communicate to a reader an appreciation for storytelling as a communal act: the slippery logic, the quiet genius of taking a sliver of someone else's account of the world and conjuring it into your own, a jazz ethic before anyone thought to call it that.

"I think it is not saying too much to state that Miss Hurston probably has a more intimate knowledge of Negro folk life than anyone in this country," her old instructor Melville Herskovits wrote of her after the publication of *Mules and Men*. But Herskovits was reading Hurston through his own academic interests. The whole point of *Mules and Men*, as with her growing body of published fiction, was not to talk just about black people or to embalm Negro culture for future study in a classroom. Rather, she imagined it as a grand project to confirm the basic humanity of people who were thought to have lost it, either because of some innate inferiority or because of the cultural spoilage produced by generations of enslavement.

Hurston didn't claim to speak for all black people or to have captured some deep, essential blackness. But she knew that no one on Joe Clarke's porch thought of himself as speaking a bastardized version of English. None of those people imagined themselves to be in the dim twilight of African greatness. In *Mules and Men* she had tried to show, in plangent prose and revved-up storytelling, that there was a distinct *there* to be studied in the swampy southeastern landscape she knew from childhood—not a holdover from Africa, or a social blight to be eliminated, or a corrupted version of whiteness in need of correction, but something vibrantly, chaotically, brilliantly alive.

Chapter Ten

INDIAN COUNTRY

....

W hile Hurston was making her way along the Gulf of Mexico and Mead and Fortune were planning new projects beyond Manus, Boas was more or less stuck in New York. He was by now an eminence: one of the acknowledged greats in anthropology and a public authority on race, inheritance, culture, world affairs, and virtually any subject that a newspaperman, museum director, or average citizen might raise. The responsibilities that came with his status meant that he would never again do the kind of fieldwork he had managed as a younger, more obscure scientist.

As many as twenty-five hundred letters flew off his desk each year, page upon page passing back and forth between New York and wherever his students, colleagues, and field agents happened to be, along with acceptances and regrets to editors, journalists, civic leaders, and foreign dignitaries. A parade of secretaries, usually drawn from among his graduate students, was kept busy sorting, typing, mailing, and filing the correspondence. The public relations department of Proctor & Gamble asked whether Boas might undertake a comparative study of "the utilitarian and aesthetic differences among the hands of various peoples." A student at Brooklyn College wrote in to ask whether it was true, as his teacher had said, that "the Negro race was far inferior . . . to the White race . . . and that the brain size of the Negro is smaller than that of the normal White man." "What your instructor told you is all nonsense," Boas replied the next day. Did Negroes make better boxers because they matured faster than whites? inquired the sports editor of the *New York Sun*. There was no evidence for such a thing, Boas wrote back matter-of-factly, with perhaps an exasperated sigh.

Life at Columbia involved seminars and tutorials, conference planning and editorial meetings, administrative battles and interpersonal spats. The department was small compared with others, but that meant Boas spent a lot of time defending its existence. "There is something in administrative positions that contaminates even decent people," he once said. The double anxiety of insecure research funding and infighting among academic bureaucrats could give him nightmares. He told Mead about one: he was pounding nails into a wall for a new curtain rod only to find that what he was actually hanging up was a bag of wriggling mice, each one biting the back of another.

The pace of departmental business was all the more extraordinary given Boas's age and health. He was entering his seventies when Mead and Hurston published their first books. There were recurring stomach problems, heart ailments, and the fatigue of managing too many commitments. "He looks weak and bent still," Ruth Benedict wrote to a friend in the spring of 1932, "and probably if you saw him you'd still be shocked." During the time when Boas's students had launched some of their most important projects, his personal life had been laced with tragedy. His daughter Gertrude had died in 1924, a victim of polio. His son Heinrich was killed the next year, his car crushed by a locomotive. Since the death of baby Hedwig decades earlier in Chicago, Boas had now managed to outlive more than half his children.

Then there was Marie, or as his students knew her, "Mama Franz." She had been the consummate host at their parties in Grantwood, passing around plates of oatmeal cookies to poorly fed postgraduates. On a wet, foggy day in December 1929, just before Christmas, she had gone into Manhattan to do some shopping. As she was crossing a busy avenue on her way home, a car came right at her. It was impossible to move out of the way in time. Boas, who had been at academic meetings in Chicago, rushed back east, with Edward Sapir keeping him company on the journey. He arrived home to find Marie's coffin in their living room. For the entire night, he sat at the parlor piano and played Beethoven, just as he had done when their family was larger and more complete.

The department had recently moved to more spacious quarters, joining the other natural sciences on the fourth floor of Schermerhorn Hall. When students arrived for classes, they walked beneath an inspiring inscription from the Book of Job: SPEAK TO THE WORLD AND IT WILL TEACH THEE. That is what most of them had been doing. A class session might involve handling baskets, quivers, or human bones in the department's dedicated laboratory space, but the stuff of science was elsewhere. The real objects of study—the people of Zuñi, Samoa, New Guinea, the Gulf Coast—were separated from the seminar room by a train or steamship schedule.

A change had recently taken place along the department's hallway, however. The field was increasingly coming to the fieldworkers. Native informants were turning up in New York for a semester as visiting scholars, dropping in to provide language lessons or pore over an old vocabulary list or indigenous folktale. Not since the Chicago world's fair, when a Northwest Coast village had alighted on the shores of Lake Michigan, had anthropologists and their subjects been more closely intertwined. But Boas already had firsthand experience of the narrowing distance between homework and fieldwork. A memory had been ghosting him for many years, one that illustrated the terrifying costs of building a science of humankind. It was a moment of his life that he said hung around his heart like a stone.

IN FEBRUARY 1898, more than two decades before Mead or Hurston arrived in New York, a younger Franz Boas had gathered with a group of men in the courtyard of the American Museum of Natural History. One by one they picked up rocks and placed them solemnly on a cloth shroud. As the Ninth Avenue elevated train clattered along nearby, Boas spoke up to pay his respects to Qisuk, an Inuit man from Greenland, who had died of tuberculosis. Qisuk's seven-year-old son, Minik, stepped forward and made a mark in the dirt on the north side of the burial cairn, a final sign of farewell.

Qisuk and Minik were part of a group of six Greenlanders whom Boas had found living in the museum when he returned from one of his summer expeditions to British Columbia. They had been brought there by the renowned Arctic explorer Rear Admiral Robert Peary. Boas had earlier requested that Peary recruit an Inuit who might help catalog some of the items in the museum's expanding collections. Instead, Peary had returned with several. They joined a revolving cast of indigenous people who had been brought to the museum as expert informants. Some were already living there when Boas first joined the museum two years earlier. One later found employment in a Coney Island sideshow. Still others fell ill and, like Qisuk, died downtown at Bellevue Hospital while under the museum's care.

What everyone except young Minik knew, however, was that the entire ceremony was a fake. There was no body left to bury. Qisuk's remains had been dismembered by medical students at Bellevue. His brain had been removed, weighed, and preserved in formaldehyde, his body flayed, and his bones bleached in the sun by the museum's building superintendent. His reassembled skeleton—labeled "An Eskimo"—was placed in the anthropology collection. A detailed analysis of his brain was later published in the *American Anthropologist*, with the conclusion that "a further study of Eskimo brains" would be "very desirable."

A few years later, when the teenage Minik attempted to retrieve his father's body, a scandal erupted in the New York press. The story of the museum's grotesqueries and the plight of an orphaned child— by this stage, English-speaking and Christian—made sensational headlines. Boas was defensive about his own role. The ritual, he claimed, had simply been an attempt to comfort a boy distraught over the loss of his father. The outcry eventually faded when Minik himself died, a victim of the great influenza epidemic of 1918. The whole affair had little effect on anyone's career. The Inuit men had worked closely with Alfred Kroeber, then one of Boas's graduate students, but Kroeber felt little power to change their circumstances. The disposition of Qisuk's body and the study of his brain fell to Aleš Hrdlička, the Czech anthropometrist who would go on to become one of the dominant figures in American physical anthropology. The memory of the sham funeral and the fates of Qisuk and Minik remained with Boas for years, but public outrage was only a blip, not unlike the objections to his performing anthropometrical studies on Worcester schoolchildren years earlier. Not until 1993 were the bodies of four of the six Inuit who had arrived with Admiral Peary—Qisuk, Nuktaq, Atangana, and Aviaq—returned to Greenland for interment.

Boas's ideas were often ahead of his practice. Ethnology could be a kind of blood sport, the domain of young, adventure-seeking researchers, almost entirely men, whose primary orientation was the acquisition of what they called data. Individual informants were valuable mainly for what they had to say about their cultures and societies. They were the wellspring of evidence that could be worked through and classified by the inquiring mind of a well-trained scientist, almost always one of European descent. Boas's own work had depended on turning real people into exemplars of something beyond themselves: Signa and Betty on Baffin Island, George Hunt in the Pacific Northwest, and countless other men and women who gave up stories, told family lore, revealed sacred secrets, and served as brokers between their own social worlds and that of a nosy, overconfident foreigner.

The effects on these partners could be inconvenient or embarrassing, even dangerous. A year after he staged Qisuk's burial, Boas received a worried letter from Hunt, his Northwest Coast fixer, about another brewing scandal. A Kwakiutl chief, Hemasaka, had heard a rumor that Boas had misused the information he gathered on the important "cannibal dance," a ceremony of induction into one of the main Kwakiutl secret societies and the ritual that Boas himself had modeled, in his underwear, for a Smithsonian photographer.

> Someone told him a speech that you had made about that you have been all round the world, and seen everything changed for the best, except the Kwakiutl tribe, that they eat dead people, and I was called into a feast and after [Hemasaka] told this news, all the people told me that they don't want you or me to see dances

of any kind again. . . . Now you are the only one I have now. The only thing I am wishing for is my life to be spared.

Hunt derived much of his livelihood from gathering information and artifacts for museums and ethnologists. His standing in his home community depended on good relations with his neighbors, which now seemed imperiled. Boas quickly wrote back denying he had ever said anything about real cannibalism. Actually ingesting human flesh, if it ever happened, was a secret guarded by the Kwakiutl society. But he had revealed the dance to public audiences and scholarly readers, he said. He asked Hunt to set up a feast for all the chiefs, at Boas's expense, and to explain his high regard for the Kwakiutl. The feast went off as planned, and by April, Hunt wrote back to say that the show of goodwill had worked. The hurt feelings had been repaired. His only regret, Hunt reported, was that one of his small daughters had recently died, which put him behind in his work for the great scientist.

In one form or another, a long continuum of exploitation ran from Kwakiutl villages and other anthropological field sites to Coney Island and beyond. Certain categories of people could expect to be put on display: the obese or the interestingly disabled, the hirsute, the very tall or the very small, and individuals from societies that white Americans still regarded as leftovers from an earlier version of humanity. Museums and circuses alike had difficulty distinguishing between an artifact and a person. During the Chicago fair, Boas had relied on Hunt and others to staff the Kwakiutl houses with a small community of women and men who performed for the crowds. A few years later, in 1897, some twenty thousand people came to the Brooklyn docks to see the arrival of the *Hope*, Admiral Peary's sailing ship, with Qisuk, Minik, and the other Greenlanders on board. Not long after that, the American Museum of Natural History briefly played host to Ota Benga, a Congolese pygmy man who would later be placed on public view, alongside apes, at the Bronx Zoo.

None of this was unusual. "Have totally wild southern Yana at museum," Alfred Kroeber wired excitedly to Edward Sapir in the autumn of 1911. Kroeber, by then a professor at the University of California, was relaying news of an indigenous man, emaciated and nearly naked, who had appeared one day in an animal enclosure near a slaughterhouse. He was soon taken in by anthropologists at the university, who identified him as the last of his California tribal group, the Yahi. Kroeber gave him the Yahi name Ishi, meaning "man," and assumed responsibility for his well-being. Kroeber strictly controlled Ishi's comings and goings around the city and arranged for his long-term accommodation in the university's museum in San Francisco, inside a converted exhibition hall. When Ishi died in 1916, still a resident of the museum building, his brain was removed for further study, just as Qisuk's had been. It was eventually donated to the Smithsonian, where it remained for the better part of a century.

The Yahi were not in fact a lost tribe. Their reduced condition was the product of modern history, not a relic of some mist-shrouded past. Driven from their land first by Mexicans and then by white settlers, they were among the 120,000 California Indians deported, abducted, starved, or massacred over the middle decades of the nineteenth century. The survivors lived as vagrants, taking canned goods or other necessities from non-Indian households, or turning up, as Ishi had, for scraps of meat at an abattoir. They were not holdovers from prehistory but rather refugees from a brutal present. By the time he came into Kroeber's life, Ishi was speaking a native language infused with Spanish, one of the many discernible legacies of conquest, adaptation, and displacement that the Yahi had experienced over the past two centuries. The research on Native American linguistics and culture that Ishi enabled was critical to the making of Kroeber's career and, to a degree, that of Edward Sapir, who also worked closely with him on a grammar of Yana, the Yahi language. Sapir had also documented traditional crafts in photo shoots that were staged to seem as if Ishi had walked straight from the Stone Age onto the Embarcadero. "I killed him by letting Sapir ride him too hard," recalled another California anthropologist, Thomas Waterman, who considered Ishi his best friend.

Asking informants to engage in hard work for little or no compensation, or to enlist their relatives in the same unpaid project, was often anthropologists' standard way of operating. "Dear friend I hope you come down here in summer I will very glad to see again . . . I tell my mother in law to rember all the storys she know," wrote Ignacita Suina, one of Benedict's sources, from the Southwest. Back in Manhattan, Melville Herskovits casually spoke of the "coons" he was enlisting in his anthropometric studies, people whose bodily measurements enabled his rise as one of the fathers of African and African American studies. Mead also depended on intense relationships that quickly faded once she left South Seas. "But just one thing, where are you now?" wrote Fa'amotu, Mead's essential partner in her Samoan work, two years after Mead had gone away. "We haven't received a single letter from you. Why haven't you written to us? I wish you would write to us. We love you so much and we still remember you."

The fates of these people ranged from the merely tragic—debts unpaid, letters unanswered, assumed friendships left to decay once the anthropologist departed for home—to the grisly. By the time Mead joined the museum as a junior curator, she walked to work every day past an entire graveyard of human remains. Drawers and vitrines held the bones of real people who had ended up as museum artifacts only because their families and neighbors hadn't been powerful enough to stop it.

The American Museum of Natural History, like the Smithsonian in Washington, had maintained an energetic collecting program since its foundation: an organized plan of grave robbing and surreptitious cadaver flaying in the name of scientific progress. The assumptions of racial science drove the collecting efforts. The museum housed more than a thousand human skulls, including the heads of at least 350 Inuit, 250 Indians of the American Southwest, 600 indigenous Bolivians and Peruvians, and 350 Mexicans. The accent was always on the non-European and exotic, with human remains placed within neat racial categories, the better to demonstrate the supposed divisions of humankind. One report cataloged the crania of "2 Pygmies, 3 Australians, 2 Japanese, and 1 New Zealander" to be found in the collections—but no Anglo-Saxon or Teuton ones, apparently.

Indigenous people were not just the subject of anthropological research—they were the reason for its existence. From the moment anthropologists crossed grasslands and oceans to study them, a silent procession of the unnamed and unburied marched alongside: people whose words, belongings, and bodies were the evidence that shaped an entire science of humankind. This was, of course, the field's great failing—a fact that we can see now, with the power of hindsight, much as Boas and his students understood the idiocy of scientific racism in their own day. But at the time, it was a moral problem that bothered its practitioners only infrequently.

What concerned them was not so much the ethical problem of relying on local informants—how could you study Samoa without talking to Samoans?—as the conceptual problem of counting on them to tell the truth. "Many persons who practice [conjuring or hoodoo] will tell you at first that there is no such thing, and laugh at the ignorant who spend their money on 'root,'" Hurston reported to Boas from Florida. "They are terribly afraid of being thought ignorant and superstitious fools and of being laughed at by the more advanced Negroes, and so they dissemble."

The same worry had tugged at Boas on the Northwest Coast, then at Benedict among the pueblos, and then at Mead and Fortune in the Pacific. How did you know that the things people were telling you weren't just their opinions, fantasies, or, worse, outright lies? Could you really claim to know an entire culture if you had to depend on only a few individuals to explain it to you? In working through these problems, anthropologists owed an outsize debt to one group in particular: an indigenous community that, for the better part of a century, had been relegated to a federal reservation on the Missouri River— the Omaha.

LIKE MANY TRIBAL GROUPS on the northern prairie, the Omaha were relatively recent migrants to the region. At some point in the seventeenth century, they had gradually moved from the eastern woodlands and down the Ohio and Wabash rivers, perhaps because of conflicts with the Iroquois. Over time they split from and coalesced with other neighboring peoples, many of whom also spoke languages derived from the common Siouan family. By the early eighteenth century, French cartographers and fur trappers found them on the upper Missouri. They had developed the semi-nomadic horse culture that would come to define the lifestyle and economy of many Plains peoples.

Because of their geographic location—as one of the easternmost of the Plains tribes—the Omaha were often the first aboriginal people encountered by traders and explorers setting out for the American West. That also meant they were typically among the earliest Plains societies to see their tribal hunting grounds shrink. Every year their lands were crisscrossed by new sets of oxen tracks and wagon ruts. Despite a basketful of treaties with the U.S. government—in theory, a protection against exploitation and expropriation—the Omaha were removed to reservation lands as early as the 1850s. From that point on, white Americans were more likely to associate their name with the capital of Nebraska, the state into which most of their reservation fell after its admission to the union in 1867, than with the aboriginal society itself.

The reservation system attracted physicians, schoolteachers, missionaries, and later in the century, amateur researchers eager to contribute to the work of John Wesley Powell's Bureau of American Ethnology. One of them was James Owen Dorsey. An Episcopalian minister originally from Baltimore, Dorsey spent the early 1870s living and working among both the Omaha and the neighboring Ponca. He was particularly taken with the Omaha's complex kinship structure. Like many Native American societies, the Omaha were divided into two major lines of familial descent—or "moieties," as ethnologists called them. Social custom prohibited marriage inside the same moiety and prescribed the types of relationships that were possible within or across these lines. Like European royals' debating which pairings of cousins would be appropriate and which unthinkable, the Omaha had a spectacular ability to work out endlessly complex family connections, the permissible as well as the prohibited, based on this scheme.

Dorsey had begun as an unschooled enthusiast of native peoples, much as Lewis Henry Morgan had been earlier in the century. He thought Indians might be one of the lost tribes of Israel. They might even have retained elements of Hebrew in their native languages. Actually living with them, however, convinced him otherwise. Through the detailed collection of word lists, testimony about religious rituals, and oral histories of migration and warfare, he was able to assemble one of the most sensitive, detailed, and historically minded studies one could have imagined. He was pleased when Powell's bureau agreed to publish it. The work appeared in 1885 with the simple title *Omaha Sociology*.

In a discipline that was still in a state of becoming, Dorsey's research achieved the status of a classic. Any student of American anthropology was soon expected to have read it. In doing so, early generations of professional ethnologists ended up placing the Omaha among the small pantheon of peoples—Malinowski's Trobrianders would become another—routinely cited as evidence for some theoretical claim. Boas lectured on Omaha kinship relations. Benedict referenced them in her seminars. Even Mead and Fortune briefly tried their hand at Omaha research after returning from Manus, only to find the Nebraska reservation's dusty roads and grinding poverty deeply unappealing. "If this is field work in America, no wonder everybody thinks it's a penance instead of a privilege," Mead wrote to Benedict. "It's just nothing at all. A thing like this isn't a culture, hardly even the remains of one."

Edward Sapir also recalled poring over Dorsey's *Omaha Sociology* in his student days. It was like hitching an express train right outside the doors of the Columbia University library. Dancers pushed themselves to the limits of physical endurance. Great herds of buffalo ran at full tilt before a mounted lancer. Family trees intertwined in impossible braids and curlicues. Folktales twisted back on themselves, ending where they started or starting where you thought they had stopped.

You had magic at your fingertips, if you knew the right words or the correct sequence of rituals.

Sapir couldn't help but notice one annoying feature of Dorsey's style, though. Dorsey would report something about the Omaha with great confidence and authority—and then report exactly its opposite. For example, one of Dorsey's most important passages involved a long description of the buffalo dance among the Omaha and other Siouan-speaking peoples. The dance was a sacred rite performed by members of the Buffalo Society, who were thought to have supernatural ties to the bison. A session might be called to induce rainfall, especially when the tribe's cornfields seemed to be withering in a drought.

But then came Dorsey's qualification, often in parentheses: "(but Two Crows denies)." Two Crows, an Omaha chief and one of Dorsey's major informants, appeared throughout *Omaha Sociology* as a nagging naysayer, an ethnographical balloon deflator. As soon as you were sure you had a handle on whether to translate a name as "Dried Buffalo Skull" or "Dried Eagle Skin," or on whether the Thunder People were independent or an offshoot of the Lion clan, or on whether they were part of the same moiety, Two Crows would pop up at the end of a sentence and dismiss the claim.

Variants of the word *deny* appeared twenty times in Dorsey's study and *doubt* six, along with many other words or phrases in which Two Crows and other informants threw suspicion on the whole enterprise of trying to get things accurately squared away. Sapir recalled being taken aback when he read this. If you trawled through field reports and other classics of anthropological fieldwork, Sapir said, "embarrassing questions as to the factual nature of the evidence which led to anthropological generalizations" seemed to be "courteously withheld by a sort of gentlemen's agreement." But Dorsey was refreshingly different. He reported the facts as he had gathered them, complete with denials and contradictions. Even as a student, Sapir could see Dorsey's style for what it was: evidence of honest self-doubt by an observer who realized how hard it was to pin down anything at all about someone else's culture.

"We see now that Dorsey was ahead of his age," Sapir later

observed. Social science was not like physics or mathematics. No matter how vehemently a Two Crows might deny that eight and eight are sixteen, his denial would not change reality. But for just about anything you might wish to know about the *social* world, you were invariably prisoner to whatever Two Crows or people like him had to say. There was no figuring out this dance or that planting ritual, this hunting totem or that healing chant, except by actually talking to someone about it. And in doing so, you immediately opened yourself up to disagreement about the facts of the case. The social world was nothing, Sapir continued, apart from the "consensus of opinion" about it. And even then, you still had a problem. Even if you could get a majority of people to agree on when the buffalo dance occurred or which moiety subsumed which clans, a Two Crows might nevertheless come along and deny that such a thing was true.

Anthropology had imagined itself as a science, committed to getting things right. Merely taking a majority vote on truth and calling it a day wasn't good enough. That was why it was supremely important to think of people as people first, Sapir thought, not as mere data generators—a lesson he might have given to an earlier version of himself in his work with Ishi. If you focused enough on your informants, you might figure out what something like "Two Crows denies" really meant. Perhaps Two Crows had been present at a buffalo dance that took place during a rainstorm, which would have contradicted the idea that its function was necessarily to relieve drought. Or maybe he was in a long-term feud with another chief and had reason to paint his rival as inept and ill informed. Perhaps he simply misunderstood the question, or maybe you misunderstood his answer.

The more you really looked at things, the more you might see that Two Crows had "a special kind of rightness, which was partly factual, partly personal," Sapir wrote. The data you thought you were gathering would inevitably get changed once you started talking to people about what *they* thought the relevant facts were. What this meant in practice was something that Mead and Hurston were already discovering in the field, and that Sapir was able to give, as he often did, an elegant theoretical gloss.

Instead, therefore, of arguing from a supposed objectivity of culture to the problem of individual variation, we shall, for certain kinds of analysis, have to proceed in the opposite direction. We shall have to operate as though we knew nothing about culture but were interested in analyzing as well as we could what a given number of human beings accustomed to live with each other actually think and do in their day to day relationships.

Sapir was driving a new nail into an old coffin. Boas himself had argued along similar lines nearly a half-century earlier in his public spat with John Wesley Powell and Otis Tufton Mason. Cultures didn't live out there, floating above the heads of their practitioners. They weren't "superorganic," as Sapir remarked in another context. You should therefore give up the idea of ever arriving at a once-and-for-all definition of what this or that society is *really* like. What you should do instead is to come clean, to admit that the closest you, as a stranger, can ever come to an account of social reality is to report on what an expert—someone who *lives* that reality—happens to think it is. Culture, for Sapir, was mainly a theoretical abstraction that both insiders and outsiders—Two Crows as well as pith-helmeted anthropologists—claimed as an approximation of what some collectivity of people did, thought, said, and felt.

Any given number of human beings accustomed to living with one another, as Sapir put it, could constitute such a collectivity, regardless of whether they wore buckskins or ball gowns. A factory could be a culture. A middle-class street could be one. A Methodist church group and a wattle-and-daub village both had their rituals, obsessions, common understandings, and—crucially—their internal disagreements about what constituted right behavior. Understanding the social lives of any of these people wasn't about one grand theory or one summer's fieldwork. What you needed was repeated and respectful conversations with the real human beings whose worlds you were straining, as best you could, to comprehend.

SAPIR WAS WRITING FOR his fellow anthropologists. To most other people, it would have come as a surprise that there was any argument at all about what constituted Omaha culture. Most white Americans had never met *an* Indian, but they were pretty sure they knew *the* Indians: a single primitive type, divided into named tribes, with a more or less common mass of "legends" and "lore" said to be characteristic of once-upon-a-time communities from New England to the Pacific Ocean. To be American was, in part, to be convinced that you basically had Indians figured out.

From early in the republic, fraternal orders of merchants and civic leaders made use of tomahawks, headdresses, and aboriginal terminology in their secret ceremonies—*sachems* for lodge leaders, *wampum* for club dues—much as Morgan had done with his failed revival of the Iroquois Confederacy. The Indian Wars had produced on-the-spot reportage about the perils of stagecoach travel, the barbarisms of horse-mounted warriors, and the ruthlessness of hero-bandits, from Cochise of the Chiricahua Apache to Red Cloud of the Oglala Lakota.

But after the major armed conflicts wound down around 1890, American aborigines came to occupy a central place in the way white people imagined their own racial future. Just as Madison Grant and his colleagues were warning of the decline of the Anglo-Saxon race, Indians were increasingly held up as examples of the middle-class values that might rescue it: stoicism, hard work, and knowing one's purpose—bravery and adventure for boys, crafting and hearth-tending for girls. Rather than savages resisting the westward expansion of the United States, Indians were now portrayed as wise, noble stewards of nature, a kind of vanished civilization whose virtues, like those of ancient Greece, might offer lessons for the present. White Americans could imagine an extinct and foreign world as somehow deeply present and intimately theirs: on the Midway Plaisance at the Chicago world's fair, with its war dances and craft stalls; in museum exhibitions and Wild West traveling shows; and in the work of the photographer and amateur ethnologist Edward S. Curtis, whose arresting portraits filled the pages of his monumental *The North American Indian*, the first volume of which appeared in 1907.

One of the most prominent spokesmen for seeing Indians as useful models was Clark University's G. Stanley Hall, who believed they had a special role to play in helping white children navigate the rocky shoals of puberty. In his influential study *Adolescence* (1904), Hall reckoned that the aging process of an individual human recapitulates the progress of humankind from savagery to civilization. This was one of the established theories that Mead had attacked in her research in Samoa. But Hall's work had another component. Individual development, he believed, was deeply tied to the progress of races. From infancy to adulthood, humans themselves went through the same physiological phases that marked off darker-skinned, primitive peoples from the lighter, civilized ones. The tendency of children to pick at scabs, for example, was a throwback to the need for savage races to pick lice; likewise, while adults could stand up to a snarling animal, children would look for the nearest hiding place, just like their primitive ancestors. "Most savages in most respects are children, or, because of sexual maturity, more properly, adolescents of adult size," Hall wrote. "If unspoiled by contact with the advanced wave of civilization . . . they are most virtuous, simple, confiding, affectionate, and peaceful among themselves, curious, light-hearted, amazingly religious and healthful, with bodies in nearly every function superior to ours."

The natural impulses of each phase of development had to be allowed to run their full course. Our own primitives—that is, boys and girls—had to be given space to act like primitives; to do otherwise was to deter them from their natural course of development. Boys should be free to romp and holler in the woods. Girls should be encouraged to cultivate their inchoate mothering instincts. Both should be given opportunities to pursue these ends unhindered by the strictures of city life. "The power to throw with accuracy and speed was once pivotal for survival, and non-throwers were eliminated," Hall said. "This makes, for instance, baseball racially familiar, because it represents activities that were once and for a long time necessary for survival."

Hall believed that Morgan's old hierarchy of savages, barbarians, and civilized societies had things more or less right. The coda he offered was that Morgan's schema could be applied equally well to a person and to an entire people, especially white Americans. Since these children were likely the product of many different stocks—English, French, German, Dutch, and others—they risked falling victim to "an unsettled . . . body of national customs, traditions, and beliefs" in their progress from benightedness to enlightenment. Hitting a leather ball, building a wigwam, erecting a totem pole—all were essential elements not only of growing up well but also of furthering a vigorous, ambitious race at ease with its less refined origins.

Physical fitness and racial fitness, in other words, were simply versions of the same thing. Theorists like Hall thought American Indians provided a route toward achieving both. White Americans had no better way to manage their own hometown primitives—their children—than to educate them about the savage cultures that had once flourished right on their doorstep. An entire movement soon took this idea as its foundational precept. The Boy Scouts of America and the Camp Fire Girls, both established in 1910, adopted faux Indian rituals and wound them into their ceremonial orders. White children took up "Indian crafts"—beading, leatherworking, making dream catchers and God's eyes—at summer camps, which were given names that harked back to aboriginal communities: Camp Algonquin and Camp Tecumseh in New Hampshire, Camp Iroquois in Vermont, Camp Katahdin and Camp Wigwam in Maine, Camp Wampanoag in Massachusetts.

Science had clearly shown the advantages of Indian life for teens and preteens, camp enthusiasts declared. "Margaret Mead and a whole group of pupils of Franz Boas . . . have helped us to an understanding of the problems that face us in handling adolescents and in our changing moral standards," noted the preeminent parents' guide to summertime, Porter Sargent's *Handbook of Summer Camps*, in 1935. "Though [primitive peoples] know nothing of clothing, shelter or agriculture, they have most elaborate customs, traditions and rituals, and no lack of virtues." When former campers went to college and beyond, they took their imaginary Indians along as well. In the 1920s, more and more sports teams across the country, from segregated universities to whites-only professional clubs, began to call themselves Braves, Indians, Warriors, and Chiefs. Young white men were kitted out in buckskin and feathers to stoke their teams' warrior ethos. "Chief Illiniwek" first appeared at the University of Illinois in 1926. "Big Chief Bill Orange" ran onto the field for the first time at Syracuse in 1931. The Boston Braves first snapped a football in 1932, before moving five years later to become the Washington Redskins—the national capital gaining both a football team and a racialized totem. Only a few decades beyond the conquest of the West, white Americans now found it entirely normal to invest time and energy toward disguising themselves as the very people their forebears had worked hard to obliterate.

THERE WAS ONE PERSON in the Boas circle who found all this particularly troublesome, both for herself and for her budding profession.

To anyone who encountered her in Morningside Heights, she looked at once pensive and expectant, and not quite placeable, with a round face, long dark hair, and eyes that trailed downward. "I stand on middle ground," she once wrote, "and know both sides." On the Great Plains, where she was from, she was known by multiple names, including Anpétu Wašté Win, or Beautiful Day Woman. In Manhattan, she was called Ella Cara Deloria.

In a university department that was a revolving door for visitors, informants, and collectors, she was one of the few people who could claim to be both objective observer and object of study. Just as Hurston was working through what it meant to study a culture you had known from the cradle, Deloria was running at full tilt trying to save one that seemed dangerously close to disappearing entirely. More than anyone around her, she understood the difficulties of zeroing in on the truth about a specific society—especially one that seemed, each year, to be slipping further and further into history.

Deloria was born on January 31, 1889, the same year that Boas had begun setting up his anthropometry lab at Clark University. Had he known her then, or during his data collecting for the Chicago world's fair, he might have seen her as a stellar example of just how hard it was to pigeonhole indigenous people, either as specimens of a specific "American" racial type or as representatives of a single, timeless culture. Her birthplace was the Yankton Indian Reservation in southeastern South Dakota, but she grew up on Standing Rock, one of the largest tribal reservations in the United States and a homeland of the Hunkpapa Lakota, Sihasapa Lakota, and Yanktonai Dakota subgroups of the larger Sioux nation.

Her mother was of mainly European descent. Her father, Philip Deloria, was of predominantly Dakota heritage. He was a hereditary chief in the tribe's intricate hierarchy but spent his later life as a locally prominent Episcopal minister. "He knew the race, as a race, was doomed, insofar as they failed to adjust themselves to conditions brought on by European civilization," she recalled. He insisted that his daughter speak both English and Dakota, in all three of its dialects, even learning the church catechism in both languages.

The world, she thought, was large. "In some of the countries the people have very strange ways," she wrote in a schoolgirl essay, "and are very queer themselves." She dreamed of someday visiting Holland. Instead, her parents sent her to an Episcopal boarding school in Sioux Falls. She managed an A-plus in ancient history, a middling C in mathematics, but solid B's in English, Cicero, and "Life of Christ," the last probably something of a disappointment for a preacher's daughter.

After graduation, she began college at Oberlin, a rare but not unheard-of opportunity for an Indian from the Plains. A generation earlier an Omaha man, Francis La Flesche, had worked closely with members of the Bureau of American Ethnology, earned degrees from George Washington University, and published his own study of Omaha society in the tradition of James Owen Dorsey. Others had followed a similar path. Like La Flesche, the son of an Omaha chief, Deloria was safely ensconced inside the provincial elite, the daughter of a reservation notable and a baptized Christian. Opportunities tended to come her way. Like Mead—an ambitious Episcopalian squirming inside the social strictures of a midwestern college town—Deloria soon set her sights on New York.

Teachers College was Columbia's training institute for elementary and secondary school instructors. Its roots ran back to the 1880s, when the imperious Nicholas Murray Butler, later Boas's administrative nemesis, had been its first president. Its mission was to create a cadre of instructors for the children of the urban poor. Deloria enrolled in 1912 to finish the degree she had begun at Oberlin. She was one of a small army of women and men who were meant to realize the college's mission in remote postings: back on Indian reservations and in community schools that catered to indigenous populations. In its students, the college was shaping civilized aboriginals, as might have been said at the time, who would become credits to their race and help elevate their charges out of poverty and paganism.

In New York, Deloria was separated from the Great Plains by geography but not really by history. The end of the western frontier was still a recent memory. Her father had been among those who had tried to mediate between reservation authorities and Sitting Bull, the legendary Sioux chief who had prophesied the defeat of George Armstrong Custer at Little Bighorn. Just before her second birthday, agency police had killed Sitting Bull on the same reservation where she grew up. In the same month, December 1890, an attempt by U.S. cavalry to disarm Lakota Sioux at Wounded Knee Creek in South Dakota left more than two hundred men, women, and children dead—the century's last large massacre of Indian civilians by agents of the United States. Deloria was living at a time when American views of Indians were shaped not only by the recent experience of violent conquest but also by the refashioned memory of it: a world of dime novels, cigar-store statues, and Buffalo Bill's Wild West Show, which unrolled its arena-sized version of American history until 1913 when, during her junior year, it finally went bankrupt.

As she was completing her studies at Teachers College, Deloria received an unexpected summons. Professor Boas wished to see her. She soon made her way the short distance down Broadway to Columbia's main campus. Boas had heard that Teachers had enrolled a Sioux woman. He wondered whether she might be helpful in several ongoing projects. He quizzed her on Dakota grammar and, convinced that she did in fact know the language, hired her to help with a Dakota class three times a week, which she did for the remainder of her senior year. She would later remember the stipend Boas arranged for her as the first real paycheck she had ever received.

After graduation, Deloria left New York and returned to teach at her old school in Sioux Falls, just as a Teachers College alumna might be expected to do. She eventually moved on to a position at the Haskell Institute in Lawrence, Kansas. Haskell was part of the web of federally run boarding schools for tribal children, the leading edge of a national system that encouraged assimilation through the mandatory reeducation of boys and girls, often in harsh conditions. Uniformed and trained in military drill, they were regularly arrayed in ranks outside the stone facade of Hiawatha Hall, the institute's main building.

In time Deloria came to oversee physical education courses among the female pupils. The classes sometimes amounted to a perfect union of the imaginary Indians from American summer camps and the real people still living on the Kansas prairie. In one of them, the children were outfitted in appropriate Indian attire—buckskins courtesy of Lyon Curio Supply of Clinton, Nebraska—for a pageant showcasing "Indian Progress," the old, wandering life giving way to citizenship as settled, educated, Christian Americans. As Deloria's script went:

> *Dear comrades, who with us have traced the road*
> *O'er which our race has journeyed through the years:*
> *Have seen how gifts of Church and School and State*
> *All helped usher in our newer day.*

It was perhaps an underuse of her Columbia degree, but the connection with Haskell turned out to be fortuitous. In the spring of 1927, almost by chance, Boas came across her in Lawrence during one of his trips to the West Coast. He remembered her assistance from more than a decade earlier and was eager to hire her again, if she had time to spare. "She always appealed to me as unusually intelligent," Boas told Elsie Clews Parsons, "but I lost sight of her completely." At the end of the year, she decided to resign her teaching position and pick up where she had left off back in New York. She arrived in February 1928, just as Mead was finishing *Coming of Age in Samoa* and Hurston was on her first collecting expedition in the South.

Boas had plenty for Deloria to do. He set her to work checking the research of nineteenth-century linguists and travelers on the Plains. The annual reports of the Bureau of American Ethnology and the many publications of the American Museum of Natural History were brimming with details of vocabulary, ritual, and belief systems. But little of it had ever been corroborated by an Indian, with any discrepancies properly cleared up in a new scientific publication. Boas soon realized the remarkable opportunity that Deloria provided. He directed her to tackle the earlier findings of James R. Walker, a reservation physician and one of the last great amateur collectors in the tradition of men like Dorsey.

Walker had served in the Union army during the Civil War and later earned a medical degree from Northwestern University. In 1896 he took up a position as agency physician at Pine Ridge in the South Dakota grasslands, the second-largest reservation in the country. For the next eighteen years, Walker treated tuberculosis cases, worked to improve sanitation, and learned to cooperate with local healers in the treatment of disease among the agency's more than seven thousand residents, mainly Oglala Lakota. In 1902 a chance encounter with Clark Wissler, an associate of Boas's at the American Museum of Natural History, then visiting Pine Ridge, turned Walker into an amateur anthropologist. Like Dorsey among the Omaha, he was drafted into service as an informant on Oglala language and religion and a part-time measurer of Sioux men, women, and children for the museum's collections of anthropometric data. In 1917 the museum published Walker's *The Sun Dance and Other Ceremonies of the Oglala Division of the Teton Dakota,* an exhaustive study of one of the principal ceremonies among several Plains tribes. Walker was careful to credit a range of local informants—Little-wound, American-horse, Bad-wound,

Short-bull, No-flesh, Ringing-shield, Tyon, and Sword—who had participated in the rites they described. But all this needed checking, rechecking, and updating by someone who knew the local scene well. With money from Boas, Deloria set out for Indian country. While Hurston was scouring the Gulf Coast for folktales, Deloria spent the summer back on the Plains, talking, writing, and compiling. During the academic year, she was again in New York, trying to organize, cross-reference, and confirm. By 1929 she had wrangled her notes into a scholarly manuscript, which she submitted to the *Journal of American Folklore,* where Ruth Benedict was then serving as editor. The article appeared that fall. It immediately cast doubt on much of what Walker had claimed.

At the very least, Deloria said, it was difficult to nail down one unambiguous form for Sioux ceremonies, especially the Oglala Lakota version of the sun dance. Among several tribal groups, young men sought sacred visions by enduring painful trials, such as suspension from lodgepoles by rawhide ropes threaded through the skin of their chests and backs. But making once-and-for-all conclusions about how the ritual was performed, when, and by whom—as Walker had seemed to do—was nearly impossible. She suspected that Walker, like most outsiders, had a difficult time confirming things that people told him. He was at the mercy of only a few informants who, even if they were chiefs or other notables inside a community, might nevertheless have narrow or biased viewpoints.

Again and again, at Boas's request, Deloria returned to the Walker material. Each time she did, the more doubt she seemed to cast on work that had lain at the foundation of white Americans' understanding of the Sioux. Walker seemed to have made things up, as best she could determine, or at least reported things as fact that no one she encountered had ever heard of. Some of his stories seemed to be glosses on biblical themes and therefore clearly influenced by Christian missionaries. Other elements were things that might have been believed or practiced in the old days, when Walker was collecting, but had no traces now. Even if some of Walker's accounts might have been true at the time he recorded them, Deloria said, Sioux society seemed to have moved on. The Sioux were a living people, she stressed, not some disembodied culture preserved in amber.

Boas was exasperated. Walker could not have simply invented things, he insisted in letters to her. There must have been something behind his ideas. Traces of the details he cataloged must still exist somewhere on one of the Sioux reservations, if only Deloria would work a little harder to try to find them. Everything had to be approached carefully, she responded; you couldn't just turn up unannounced and demand that people tell you whatever stories they knew, as Walker had apparently done. What you were likely to get was equally unrepresentative and ephemeral. The world was full of people like Two Crows of the Omaha, denying this and claiming that. It took time and local knowledge to figure out what a great many people in a community actually believed or thought, and what, on the other hand, someone claiming to speak on the community's behalf made up whole cloth.

"I cannot tell you how essential it is for me to take beef or some other food each time I go to an informant," Deloria wrote to Boas one summer. "The moment I don't, I take myself right out of the Dakota side and class myself with outsiders." You had to know precisely how to make a gift, how to make the right kind, how to eat properly with people, how to call them by the correct kinship terms—uncles, brothers, sisters, aunts, cousins, and the many variants of each that existed in Sioux languages. Only then could you go back, another time, and hope to get stories or information about a long-ago ceremony. But "to go at it like a white man, for me, an Indian, is to throw up an immediate barrier between myself and my people." As if to prove her point, she shipped back a parcel of muskrat tails, considered to be the source of some of the best sinews for adorning a garment with fine porcupine quills. To extract the sinew, she instructed Benedict in a cover letter, all you needed to do was pop the tip of the tail between your teeth and pull.

———

DELORIA WAS WELL KNOWN in the department, even if she was now more frequently in the West than in Manhattan. She relied on Boas for guidance in her fieldwork, and she turned frequently to Benedict, effectively his aide-de-camp, for editorial cues and advice. She became acquainted with Mead at some point in the winter of 1930–31, once Mead and Fortune returned from their work among the Omaha. She and Hurston worked on common projects sponsored by other Columbia faculty, although they probably never met in person.

Since Deloria was not enrolled in the graduate program, her training was limited to what she managed to pick up in quick lessons with Boas or Benedict in their offices or along the departmental hallway. However, given Boas's teaching style, that instruction was probably not much less than his regular students typically received. She might sit in on a lecture when she happened to be in New York or jot down Boasian reminders about how best to organize her work. "Get nowhere unless prejudices first forgotten," she noted at one point. "Cultures are many; man is one. Boas."

When she wasn't back on Standing Rock, she blew through a succession of addresses: small apartments in Manhattan and New Jersey, a short-term rental in Iowa, a friend's house somewhere in South Dakota, and from time to time her car. On one occasion, she reported that she could count only six items as her real property, none of which was a typewriter, a critical piece of equipment for a collector of words. Like many other women connected to the Columbia department, Deloria was in essence an itinerant social scientist, with no academic position and nothing by way of research support except for the piecework assigned to her by Boas or Benedict. But bills had to be paid. To eke out an income, she wrote and directed grand pageants of indigenous music and dance that were staged across the country, much as she had done at Haskell. Some were for paying tourists, while others were for white children at summer camps—pretend Indians being coached by the genuine article. In time, however, a new project came along that promised to provide more stability than ever before.

For more than two decades, Boas had been working on a comprehensive treatment of Native American languages. It had begun when he first approached the Bureau of American Ethnology about sponsoring a series of handbooks on indigenous speech. The first one had appeared in 1911, the year that marked the real flowering of his thought and his emergence as a public scientist. The second came out in 1922. It featured Edward Sapir on the Takelma language of southwestern Oregon, along with scholars tackling the languages of the Coos of the Pacific Northwest and the Chukchi of Siberia, among others. It demonstrated the linguistic connections between the aboriginal peoples of North America and those of Eurasia, bolstering the theory of an early peopling of the Americas by migrants from beyond the Bering Strait. By the time the third volume was ready, in 1933, the bureau's interest in the handbooks—a publication series that promised to be interminable—had withered. Boas turned instead to a small New York publisher to print what remained of his team's work, including Gladys Reichard on the Coeur d'Alene of Idaho and Ruth Bunzel on Zuñi, the community that had been so central to the Boas circle's findings earlier in the century.

Much of the funding for Boas's ambitious project came from the Committee on Research in Native American Languages, supported by a grant from the Carnegie Corporation of New York. From its establishment in 1927, the committee had been working on a shoestring budget, about $80,000 total, disbursed a few thousand dollars at a time to cover train fares, lodging, and stipends for native collectors. The list of grantees read like a shadow history of the entire profession, peopled by part-time assistants, field agents, amateur linguists, and committed aficionados who never gained a professorial title or other university appointment. Deloria was among them. Boas promised to channel some of the funds toward her field research and living expenses while she worked on Sioux materials. The money that eventually came her way—paid out in dribs and drabs, often delayed, with checks sent to the wrong address—was sometimes the difference between a rented apartment and a night in her car.

The entire project was bewilderingly complex. Boas was managing field researchers and academic specialists from across the United

States and around the world, all of them rushing to track down native speakers, compile vocabulary lists, and work out complex grammatical structures before the last fragments of a language crumbled to dust. In many cases, the anthropologists were a collective Brothers Grimm, archiving stories and ways of speaking so that they would no longer depend on the transmission from parent to child, the traditional way languages survived. In many cases, they were creating, from scratch, a standard form for languages that had no written version or were spoken in an enormous array of dialects. Opening one of the volumes of the *Handbook of American Indian Languages* could be a magical encounter: coming across a speech form you had never heard of, with its own logic, rules, and beauty, its own perfectly formed way of seeing the world—a route into the coded secrets of people who had previously been regarded as exotic natives or, worse, frontier savages.

Among this far-flung team, Deloria was different. "In all his work with American Indians," Benedict later wrote, "Professor Boas never found another woman of her caliber." She was a native speaker of Dakota and its dialects, with little education as a linguist apart from the informal sessions that Boas or Benedict might provide. But her instincts and on-the-spot grasp of field methods, Benedict said, probably amounted to more expertise than many doctoral students had at their disposal. "Her knowledge of the subject is unique," Boas wrote plainly in a recommendation letter, one of many he would write over the years.

Margaret Mead had found her own stint in a Native American community, the Omaha, to be mainly an exercise in what she called "too-late ethnology." Anything of interest seemed to her long dead, killed off by poverty and white invasion. But Deloria knew this couldn't be the case. After all, what would that make her, except a ghost with a cardboard suitcase? Even an experienced fieldworker like Mead could be guilty of what Deloria called "armchair anthropology." A better method was to give up trying to identify the dying embers of an older civilization and instead get to know the living, right-now culture of the people you were actually surrounded by—women and men who weren't stuck in history but, like Deloria herself, were feeling their way through it. There was no need for nostalgia about the past if you could uncover the kaleidoscopic richness of the present. It was just that the present might take forms that you found surprising or frustrating, even disappointing.

That was why understanding a language was so crucial, Deloria believed. Speech, too, was constantly changing. Like tree rings or an archaeological dig in the middle of a city, it was most important not as a record of a single bygone moment but rather as an archive of change, an endlessly creative confluence of past worlds with the present one. Native American languages prized wit, puns, juxtapositions, intentional mistakes, wordplay, and jokes well told—the same things that any other language might allow. The trick was to begin to *hear* it all, to regard the living languages that still dotted the Plains not as a dreadful remnant but as a thing existing in the real, quickened now. To write properly about Indians, you had to stop using the past tense.

In field trip after field trip, on Standing Rock and elsewhere, Deloria worked to write it all down. Her aim was to pull together, out of the mass of notes and interviews, something that would describe the way her Dakota family and neighbors actually spoke, without at the same time rendering it inert, as Walker and other reservation agents had seemed to do years earlier. As Boas and Deloria traded letters and manuscript pages, their conversations about Dakota speech were often highly technical. How could you best explain the language's wealth of demonstratives—the many forms of *this, that, those*? What about Dakota's astonishing ability to express time, place, and the speaker's point of view using only one word? How could you render the possessives that distinguished parts of the body that we easily control—such as the eyes or the foot, but also, as the Dakotas believed, the spirit—from those that were thought to be tougher to rein in, such as the thumb or the jaw? Sentence by sentence, phoneme by phoneme, they were working to map an entire cosmos of meaning. They wrote treatments of the speech forms of men and the different ones applicable to women, a general feature of Siouan languages; the panoply of ways to indicate approval, disapproval, or indifference; the deep significance encased inside a complicated structure—the ability, for example, to say succinctly something like "My sister gave me a stone instead of bread" while also saying "It was a very bad thing that she did so, and now our relations are ruined." Complex social connections could be collapsed into a single grammatical form.

To describe a language was to peer into a community's unique ways of corralling experience, of parsing it into understandable, communicable units. Throughout all this, Deloria was inhabiting two realms at once. "Her childhood among [the Dakotas], her privileged position in the tribe, and her command of the language made possible an intimate and otherwise impossible account of this important group," wrote Benedict in a research report. But Deloria could also feel the disadvantages of this way of making a living. "I am very sad today because all the things I had planned have fallen thru so far and I am without work," she wrote to Boas toward the end of 1938, using old hotel stationery. It was now a decade since she had begun assisting Papa Franz. Her labors on the language project had dragged on for years. "I can't get any federal work, because I have the reputation of being so educated!"

The next summer Boas had news that he thought might perk her up. "You will be glad to know that [our work] will be published by the National Academy of Sciences," he told her. The country's premier institution in the natural sciences would soon send along the page proofs, he said, which he would need her to help check for accuracy. The end result, called simply *Dakota Grammar*, at last arrived from the printer in 1941. Like other excursions in technical linguistics, it was a formidable piece of scholarship and not a book for the fainthearted. But much in the way mathematicians might describe a complex equation as being elegant or ingenious, a descriptive grammar could be a work of communal art. It was a route into a civilization that had once stretched across the entire northern Plains, one that was still refashioning itself, as Deloria knew, on the reservations and beyond. Deloria's perfect command of the language, Boas said in the book's preface, her strong sense of nuance and minute differences of expression, her extensive vocabulary, and most important, her gift for the language's "emotional tone" were vital to the research.

More than Minik, searching for the bones of his disappeared father, or Ishi, who died as a literal museum piece, or even Two Crows, preserved for posterity inside parentheses, Deloria's achievement was at last to verify Boas's foundational theory: that the people whose remains had been put on display, whose cultures were made over as pop primitivism, were fully human after all. All this also provided a glimpse of a deeper America, one obscured by its obsessions with racial fitness and linear cultural evolution. If you wanted to know what Sioux chiefs had said after the Battle of Little Bighorn or to understand the anguished wail of mothers when their sons' bodies were brought home from Wounded Knee—if you wanted to discover, in other words, the inverse of American history as it was normally taught in schoolrooms and summer camps—Boas and Deloria were showing the way.

The trailhead was right there on the title page. Boas had written forewords for some of his students' first major books, notably Mead's *Coming of Age in Samoa* and Hurston's *Mules and Men*. But with Deloria he did something much rarer. "So many people are asking about our grammar," she wrote to him the year after publication. "I feel very proud to be your co-author." For the first time with any of them—in fact, for one of the very few times in his career—he shared a byline.

Chapter Eleven

LIVING THEORY

....

Over the course of the 1930s, amid the demands of writing, advising, editing, and fund-raising, Boas decided to make a change in how he taught. The occasional gatherings of graduate assistants and visiting scholars that he had hosted when Marie was alive would now become regular seminars. On Tuesday evenings throughout much of the decade, he presided over sessions where students and colleagues were invited to discuss their latest discoveries. The old forest in which the Boases had built their gabled house was morphing into a suburb, connected to Manhattan by the newly opened George Washington Bridge. Each week Benedict would fold herself into a car along with a couple of doctoral students and head over to New Jersey.

They had plenty to report. Between department meetings and dissertation advising, Benedict had been reworking her earlier field research in Zuñi and editing articles for the *Journal of American Folklore*. Most of a recent issue had been taken up with a hundred-page study by Hurston on folk religion in New Orleans and the Gulf Coast. Mead and Fortune were writing up their work among the Omaha. Alfred Kroeber visited during a sabbatical from Berkeley, where he had become the country's leading authority on Californian tribal peoples.

The venerable Bronislaw Malinowski would occasionally make an appearance on a visit from London, perhaps angling for a job were Boas ever to vacate his professorship. "He is vain as a peacock and as cheap as a saloon story," Benedict gossiped to Mead. He could plow through department parties with single-minded determination, "a belligerent romanticist," as Sapir once called him. On one occasion he allegedly slipped money into Hurston's stocking as an apparent invitation to an affair. For her part, Mead could feel an undercurrent of disregard whenever Malinowski entered the room. He had praised her Samoan work in letters to her, but she was convinced that Sapir had turned the great Pacific scholar against her.

Sapir knew how to worry an old wound. "She is . . . a loathsome bitch flattened out to a malodorous allegory," he wrote to Benedict after reading *Coming of Age in Samoa,* "a symbol of nearly everything that I detest most in contemporary American culture." He soon published a thinly veiled attack on "free women" who failed to understand that jealousy was a universal human emotion. "Love having been squeezed out of sex, it revenges itself by assuming unnatural forms," he wrote in the *American Journal of Psychiatry.* "The cult of the 'naturalness' of homosexuality fools no one but those who need a rationalization of their own problems."

Mead responded in kind. Jealousy, she said in her own article on the subject, was in her experience frequently found among old men with small endowments.

The slights and betrayals, the underground flings and seething animosities, the granite friendships as well as roiling rivalries, were as much a part of the seminar evenings in Grantwood as Dakota verbs and New Guinean masks. But whether they were discussing sex, success, or any other aspect of social life, Boas had taught his students to resist making grand schemas or big conclusions. He had long been clear on what he saw as "the most difficult problem of anthropology," as he called it: were there universal laws to human cultures, and if so, how might one go about discovering them? Reo Fortune's former professor, A. R. Radcliffe-Brown, once pressed Boas to derive at least one generalization from his decades of expeditions, collecting, and publishing. The only thing Boas would hazard was a single sentence: "People don't use anything they haven't got."

It was a simple but profound summation of his thought. Importing ideas, concepts, frameworks, and mental categories from your society into a very different one might tell you something important, of course. Birth rates and death rates on Ta'u, how the soft palate lowers to form a Dakota nasal consonant, the moments when an Eatonville story veered from the factual into the fantastic—these were all things that an outsider could count or identify. But you shouldn't mistake your own gaze for unproblematic truth. The place to start your analysis was with the intellectual tools that made sense to those who actually used them. If you came upon a society where people didn't seem to recognize a thing you called a "first cousin," an "illicit romance," or a "migraine," there was no good insisting that they nevertheless had them.

Anthropology should be a conversational science, Boas felt. It ought to be a dialogue between one's own way of seeing things and someone else's. Where it led was toward specific histories and unique experiences, toward a particular community—this one *here*—and its most precious ways of understanding its place in the world. To be an anthropologist was to be committed to the critical refinement of your own experience. That was the whole point of purposefully throwing yourself into the most foreign and remote of places. You had to gather things up before you refined them down. Anthropologists should be innately skeptical about jumping too quickly from their own culture-bound schemas to pontificating about the Nature of Man. Boas had seen the awfulness that could result when racial theorists and eugenicists confidently pronounced that they had all of humanity figured out.

Some of Boas's older students chafed at their mentor's reluctance to play the generalization game, however. Lowie, Kroeber, and Sapir, in different ways, wanted theory to drive science, or at least to stand as an ultimate goal. "It is clear that Dr. Boas' unconscious long ago decreed that scientific cathedrals are only for the future, . . . that only cornerstones, unfinished walls, or even an occasional isolated portal are strictly in the service of the Lord," Sapir wrote in a testy review of Boas's *Anthropology and Modern Life*. That was a pity, Sapir thought. Stacking up stories, legends, kinship charts, and native vocabularies had little use if they weren't placed in service of an overarching conclusion. Since anthropology had become a popular science, he said, it was now in danger of being made "cheap and dull, like Margaret Mead's *Coming of Age in Samoa.*"

The quest for general laws had animated Lewis Henry Morgan and John Wesley Powell. They had championed the idea of a common pathway along which all cultures were treading. It was a central assumption of psychologists like G. Stanley Hall, who aimed to plumb the deepest recesses of the human mind. By the time Boas began his Tuesday seminars, it was also central to sociology, the discipline that was developing as a kind of sibling to anthropology: the former seeking to understand the allegedly more complex societies of the developed West, the latter focusing on the supposedly simpler ones everywhere else.

In the United States, sociological research had recently been galvanized by *Middletown* (1929), a study of life in an unnamed, and supposedly typical, American town (in reality Muncie, Indiana). "To many of us who might be quite willing to discuss dispassionately the quaintly patterned ways of behaving that make up the customs of uncivilized peoples, it is distinctly distasteful to turn with equal candor to the life of which we are a local ornament," wrote its authors, Robert and Helen Lynd. "Yet nothing can be more enlightening than to gain precisely that degree of objectivity and perspective with which we view 'savage' peoples."

Using statistical tables and well-spun stories, the Lynds examined the nature of work, home life, education, religion, and leisure among the town's inhabitants. They offered not just an ethnography of small-town life but also a general theory about it. Cultural habits, they wrote, seemed to lag behind shifts in material conditions. Middletowners found it easier to accommodate indoor bathrooms, for example, than women working outside the home. The Lynds ignored many important facts about their field site. Despite the presence of plenty of black citizens in Middletown, the word *Negroes* appeared on only three pages of their book. But they had shown that statistics, careful interviews, and historical research could add up to the very sort of innovative general theories that Sapir and others desired for anthropology.

Even Mead was feeling the tug toward a more ambitious, all-encompassing science. She could claim no theoretical advance as her own, no broad finding that people would recognize as a signature contribution. "I find I am growing more and more cynical all the time about good work winning through," she complained to Benedict in early December 1932. She had been reading Dostoyevsky and feeling very low about her own career. Her salary as an assistant curator was a little under $2,400. Benedict at least had an academic job; she had been elevated to an assistant professorship at Columbia the previous year, earning about $3,600—although this was still far less than the salary of a male visiting scholar. (She also wasn't allowed to use the Columbia faculty dining room, which was reserved for male professors.) Mead worried that she herself was fated to be little more than a popularizer or, as she had once complained, "that awful animal a 'lady scientist.'" "I don't think having the worst paid job in the Museum, and never having been offered another job, and having been panned or damned with faint praise in all the journals of my own science, is wonderful recognition," she wrote. You needed academic prestige to make your ideas stick, and so far that was very much lacking.

At worst, she might be spending her life learning how to do little more than throw convention up in the air. Anthropology could be thrilling but also exceptionally dangerous and very possibly not even worth the price. One had only to look at the recent example of Henrietta Schmerler, one of Boas's newer students. Schmerler had taken off for Arizona in the summer of 1931, with dreams of becoming the Mead of the Apache, embarking on detailed studies of puberty rituals in the American Southwest. "The country here is simply beautiful," she wrote to Boas in July, "and even though at times I've been frightfully discouraged which, I suppose [one] must expect on one's first field trip, I'm enjoying my work tremendously." Later that same month, she was found dead, murdered by a young Apache man on the way to a dance. It was hard to walk into someone else's backyard and demand that they give up their secrets. It was even harder to do so while letting your own guard down. Fieldwork required people to twist themselves into being intrepid and vulnerable in equal measure.

That Christmas found Mead wrestling with her ambition in one of the remotest places in the world. She was back in New Guinea with Reo Fortune, this time in a soggy river port on the mainland. She would soon be in the throes of what she believed would mark her greatest achievement as a thinker and writer, a genuine theoretical breakthrough on par with the most profound insights in the social sciences. It would also usher her toward the brink of madness.

MEAD AND FORTUNE HAD been eager to get back to the field. Fortune had eventually transferred to Columbia for his graduate studies and submitted a dissertation on the social organization of Dobu. Mead had written two popular books and other serious ethnographies, none of them, she believed, tackling a mainstream problem in anthropological theory. In the spring of 1931, they set off on a return expedition to Melanesia, one they envisioned as a long-term research project among the peoples living along the Sepik River.

The longest river on the island of New Guinea, the muddy Sepik snakes its way from the central highlands eastward to the Bismarck Sea. The German name was a holdover from the European explorers who, in the 1880s, had first mapped the Sepik's lower reaches. After the First World War, the eastern half of the island passed to Australian control, while the west remained under its colonial overlords, the Dutch. Because of this imperial heritage, New Guineans played an oversize role in anthropological research, especially among British, Australian, and New Zealand writers. As with Native American tribal groups in the United States, countries tended to build their theories of human nature on the alleged savages closest to hand.

Mead and Fortune were in search of a place as remote as possible, without the corrupting influences of missionaries and merchants. They were soon "as placid as kittens," Mead reported. They settled in the uplands north of the river, among a group of people they called the Arapesh, who had experienced rather little contact with outsiders. (Their name, in fact, was Mead's invention based on the local term for "human beings.") She would wake into a cool dawn, lying in bed long enough to hear the plaintive bird calls outside the mosquito netting. Breakfast was a cup of tea, and then the workday began: hours of conversation, language lessons, typing up notes, running about to see a ceremony or check on a newborn baby, until the anthropologists closed up shop at sundown. They would have kept going into the night, she wrote to Benedict, but for the fact that they had brought along no lanterns.

Fortune might go away with some of the men on a hunting expedition, while Mead would remain behind with the women and babies, tending the yam gardens. "I'm more than ever convinced that the only logical place for the anthropologist is in the field—most of the time—for the first ten years, or even fifteen years of his anthropological life," Mead wrote. "Aside from adding to the sum of knowledge and catching it in time, it's the most perfect way of building up judgment and laying a solid basis for theory." She missed Benedict dreadfully and had hung a photograph of her in their hut. The local children thought Benedict must be a very important person to have such a large picture on the wall.

The more she got to know the Arapesh, the more Mead was convinced that they had "solved the sex problem." As far as she could tell, there wasn't much in the way of a concept of adultery. People seemed puzzled when she asked about sex outside marriage. They couldn't quite fathom what she was talking about or why she might be interested in such a subject. She talked with just about everyone in the local community and knew of many cases in which wives had left husbands or a man had tried to start a relationship with a married woman. But the attitude of the Arapesh about these issues seemed wholly pragmatic. "Yes, the woman's husband whom she had deserted for her brother, was angry because he had paid that brother lots of rings and pigs for her," she told Benedict, "the brother was obligated to protect his rights and in the old days he might have fought with him." But there was no invoking of religion, deep morality, or some theory of natural rights to explain or condemn the transgression.

Mead and Fortune spent eight months in the highlands before deciding to try out a different field site along the lower Sepik River.

They moved from the land of the Arapesh into the domain of a low-land group they knew as the Mundugumor. It was a place and a people Mead loathed, as she later recalled. Even sex seemed always to be accompanied by biting and scratching. People would copulate violently in one another's yam plots just to spoil the vegetables. The Mundugumor were known to engage in cannibalism and typically preyed on swamp dwellers living in a neighboring region. "Yes, I have eaten human flesh," a child told her, "just a very little of the Kalengama people. It was so small that I could not really taste it."

Where the Arapesh had seemed bathed in ideas of freedom and openness, the Mundugumor lived life in the imperative, hemmed in by an elaborate system of prohibitions. The first thing a child learned was the local equivalent of *Don't!* Even among cannibals, life could be a bore. Mead saw little ritual, art, or myth to interest an anthropologist. And then there were the mosquitoes, hordes of them, descending like vampires on any piece of exposed flesh. Mead walked around with a broom in her hand in a vain effort to fight them off. After three months in these conditions, with meals of corn fritters and crocodile eggs, Mead and Fortune decided they had seen enough and made plans to head up the Sepik.

They had a lifeline of sorts. Gregory Bateson, an old acquaintance of Fortune's, knew the region well. A fellow anthropologist, a sometime lecturer at the University of Sydney, and a Cambridge don, Bateson was then conducting his own studies along the river, and he offered to help them scout a locale for their new research. They had all agreed to spend that Christmas together in Ambunti, a port town deep inland, where the Sepik makes one of its many switchback turns. Mead and Fortune boarded the government pinnace, a small steamer that delivered mail and supplies, and set off with luggage and field notes in tow.

On the way to Ambunti, they stopped to pick up Bateson at his field camp. "You're tired," he said when he first saw Mead, offering her a chair. Mead would remember that moment as the first inkling of attraction. During the year she and Fortune had been away, they had gone through their ups and downs, but things were now going reasonably well between them. This new feeling seemed to come like a bolt from the blue.

Just after Christmas, Mead sat down to bring Benedict up to speed. "I've got a lot to tell you," she wrote. "It's Gregory Bateson of course."

BENEDICT KNEW BATESON BY reputation, as did Mead. No anthropologist of his generation could claim a more illustrious scientific lineage. His father, William Bateson, was the Cambridge University biologist who had first coined the term *genetics*. His mother, Beatrice, was part of a family line of noted intellectuals that included her sister Edith Durham—Aunt Dick to the family—the formidable adventurer and Balkan travel writer. Gregory carried his pedigree even in his name. He had been christened for Gregor Mendel, the Austrian monk who pioneered the study of inherited characteristics; the elder Bateson had helped to introduce Mendel's pathbreaking work to the wider scientific world. As a schoolboy at Charterhouse, a training ground for Britain's elite, Bateson had demonstrated a passion for botany and insect collecting. During school holidays he and his father would traipse across the French Alps, with knapsacks and butterfly nets, in search of new specimens. When his two older brothers died tragically—one as a soldier in the First World War, the other in a dramatic suicide in Piccadilly Circus—he became the sole bearer of his family's considerable legacy.

Slightly younger than Mead and Fortune, Bateson was studiously unkempt, with mussed hair and worn clothes, a style he maintained even when not in the field. He was also enormous, lumbering but not ungainly. He talked a mile a minute at their first meeting. Shortly after Mead and Fortune arrived at his field site, he pulled out a copy of her *Growing Up in New Guinea* and challenged her on a specific point about menstruation. She was smitten.

Bateson had a compelling air of "vulnerable beauty," Mead told Benedict, which was all the more touching for his size. At some six feet five inches tall, he had to stoop to engage in conversation and seemed to wrap himself around Mead in the process. Fortune felt in no way threatened, Mead reported, and she hoped everything would work out fine, without "any gunpowder in the situation." Everyone was an adult, after all, and if she and Fortune needed an example of how all this could be worked out in a straightforward, rational way, they had only to look downriver at the Arapesh. She and Fortune had just spent months living among people who seemed to have built an entire society out of not getting too worked up over the intricacies of love. "I do think I've learned once [and] for all that sex need not be permitted to spoil things," Mead wrote.

The holiday season found the three anthropologists in a swirl of expatriate parties in Ambunti—crowds of remote-post foreigners, by turns giddy and combative, fueled by gin and whiskey, the verbal barbs flying, then fists, then apologies all around and some quiet. The night after Christmas, Fortune got roaringly drunk. In all their years of marriage, Mead had never seen him in that state. She, too, downed four cocktails and then fell into bed to sleep it off. Fortune kept at it the next day, with more drink and a steady-state slur. Mead and Bateson decided that a trip upriver might do everyone some good.

They all loaded into a pinnace and chugged upstream to a village that they had wanted to scout as a field site. It took six hours to get there. The heat was nearly unbearable, lessened only by the small breeze kicked up by the slow-moving boat. Fortune slept off the booze while a portable record player he had brought along competed with the rattle of the engine. Whenever Fortune woke up and saw Mead and Bateson talking or sharing a cigarette, he flew into a rage.

No sooner had they arrived than news came that a neighboring community was set to attack the village. They spent the night in constant worry. A loaded Webley revolver was their only line of defense but also, Mead and Bateson feared, an unsettling temptation to an addled Fortune. No attack ever materialized, however, and the trio soon set off on the ride downriver. Mead and Bateson would later mark the journey back to Ambunti as the moment it all started: the unraveling of her marriage to Fortune and the first moments of a new relationship with Bateson.

"I love you terribly," one of them said on a veranda when they returned. "I know," said the other.

These developments had complicated things, of course. But one couldn't know what the future might hold, and until it arrived, there was work to be done. By early January, Fortune and Bateson had patched things up well enough that Bateson could conduct them to their next field site. It was among people they called the Tchambuli, who lived around a lake that linked up with the Sepik River during flood season. The Tchambuli inhabited low-lying fenland, among floating islands of peat and tall grass that could drift around the lake and alter its contours from one day to the next. The peaty water shone like polished enamel, inlaid with bright water lilies, an occasional blue heron sunk knee-deep in the murk.

The Tchambuli, no more than five hundred people in all, tended their taro gardens and fished the lake from dugout canoes. They built large ceremonial houses with crescent-shaped rooflines, where they held elaborate rituals in carved masks and headdresses made from cassowary feathers and shells. They seemed to live in a world of ease and plenty, one that Mead saw as a relief after months among the Mundugumor. "I've climbed mountains and gone about in the sun and I feel pleased with the country at last," she told Benedict shortly after arriving. "It's come to have a character of its own and I've got my feet down in the soil as I've not had them for a dozen years." There was now yet another language to learn, another kinship system to chart, handfuls of lotus seeds providing a quick snack along the way.

Once Bateson departed back to his camp, Mead kept up a regular correspondence with him, their notes written on typing paper cut into rectangular strips and rowed upriver by messengers. In Mead's eyes, Bateson had emerged as a kind of fantasy protector, a spirit guide. He had brought her to a place where she could be happier as an anthropologist than she had ever been. Now, if only they could solve the personal problems that had started back in Ambunti. "The truth of the matter is we had learned how to do field work without enjoying it," Mead wrote to Bateson from Tchambuli, "a bad lesson you have helped us to unlearn." As they made the rounds from house to house to acquaint themselves with the Tchambuli, Fortune would ink family genealogies on his forearm so that he would not mistake important kin relations and create a minor scandal. The language was no less complex, with a surfeit of grammatical genders—"lots of them," Mead reported to Bateson. More and more, Mead was coming to see the lakeshore as a place where she could tackle something big and wonderful: clawing culture away from nature, as she put it. She was starting to see human beings with a clarity she had never imagined.

Things with Fortune went from bad to worse, however. Living inside a small house with a single mosquito net, they had no place to escape. There was no bathroom door to lock until a fight had subsided. Bateson would occasionally visit from his own field site, which stretched the quarters even further—and underscored to Fortune that his relationship with Mead was now unquestionably changing.

Mead soon contracted malaria, with fever and stomach pains. Her mental haze was broken only when Fortune, in another drunken stupor, shouted at a child or picked a fight with a local man. "And Reo and I go to bed to argue, wake in the night to argue, get up in the morning to argue," she wrote to Benedict. This was not only the end of her marriage, she felt, but also the start of a new way of thinking about herself. The last year in the field had more or less forced her into an exclusive romantic relationship for the first time in her adult life, and she was coming around to the view that she had no talent for it. Part of her soul was going numb in the process. She was best suited to open love, she decided, with different kinds of people in different ways. Fortune would have to adapt himself to it if he wanted to remain with her, much as she had insisted with Cressman years earlier.

"So I do feel that I've given monogamy, in an absolute sense, a pretty fair trial and found it wanting," she told Benedict, "and now it's fair for him to try 'my culture' for a change, if he can do so without violence to his own temperament."

MEAD AND BATESON WERE both straining to understand what was happening between them. How did you make sense of feeling terrible, they wondered, when it was hard to find anyone in particular to blame? Individuals were born with innate dispositions of personality that got socially expressed in particular ways, Mead reckoned. They consisted of traits such as boldness or laxity, assertiveness or passivity, boastfulness or modesty. In any given society, conceptions of gender tended to standardize some subset of these temperaments, to cluster them just so, and to imbue them with a sense of propriety and naturalness. Yet in all societies that Mead, Fortune, and Bateson had studied, there were people whose temperaments seemed to run against these standards.

As they talked, late at night under kerosene lanterns, Mead and Bateson came to realize that they were the deviants in their own cultures—a woman, yet assertive and adventurous; a man, yet somewhat retiring and unprepossessing, despite his commanding stature. Fortune, by contrast, was masculinity in a bottle: tough, harsh, vindictive, believing himself to be reasonable but given to anger and petulance when things failed to go his way. In his culture, he was the right kind of man. Here on the Sepik, he was literally the odd man out.

Toward the end of March, Mead wrote to Benedict to inform her that she was now overcome with excitement, more positive about life than she had been in many months. The reason was a breakthrough that she regarded as her greatest contribution yet, a "discovery of great magnitude," she said. In a gin-fueled, malarial fog, Mead and Bateson had scribbled out a schema that they believed would explain how individuals relate to the culture into which they were born. It was a framework for making sense of themselves—and, they thought, the world—that would at last bring some clarity to the swirl of emotion, hurt feelings, sex, and passionate conversation they had experienced along the lakeshore. They called it the "squares."

People naturally came in four basic types, or "temperaments," they reasoned. "Northerners" tended to be rule-oriented and in control of their emotions. "Southerners" were passionate and experimental. "Turks" were mysterious and contemplative. "Feys" were expansive and creative. Surveying their own lives and the personalities of their friends and family, they found that everything seemed to fall into place. Everyone they knew could be placed neatly into one of these boxes: Fortune, a clear Northerner, with his hardness and will to dominate; Boas and Benedict, probably Northerners, too, with their boldness and calculating sensibilities; Sapir, a Turk, always seeking the key to the universe; the Ash Can Cats and Leonardo da Vinci, Feys the lot of them. Friends, intimates, old flames, teachers, parents, the famous and obscure, they were all now revealed in their truest essence, rooted and understandable.

"We moved back and forth between analyzing ourselves and each other, as individuals, and the cultures that we knew and were studying," Mead later recalled. Fortune and Mead had not been able to make a go of it in their marriage because they were constitutionally unsuited, as she had been with Cressman. She and Bateson, by contrast, fit together like hand and glove, their innate temperaments complementing each other rather than being in inherent conflict. As for Mead's enduring love for Benedict, her inability to settle down to one kind of relationship, whether with one person or with one gender, these now seemed less like problems inside herself than a simple mismatch between her own temperament and the society into which she had been born.

They had only to step outside the mosquito net to see it all in action. Mead and Fortune, and now Bateson, had spent months living among people who did things differently. The Arapesh had many gender categories in their language, not just masculine and feminine; they saw no sharp divisions between what Western societies saw as normal and deviant sexual behavior. The Mundugumor showed what a society could become when it gave itself over to suspicion and jealousy. The women of Tchambuli tended the crops while the men made art. Like the morning sun rising over an ebony lake, the world seemed to stretch before Mead and Bateson in a new, clarifying light. They had arrived at a theory of themselves and the societies in which they now resided that upturned old ways of thinking while offering a fresh, liberating explanation for their own predicament. "This is the climax of the work I've done this last year," Mead wrote to Benedict, "a combination of anthropology and reviewed biography."

The language of the squares now looped through the notes Mead and Bateson sent to each other when they were apart. Fortune, too, initially signed onto the project. He drafted a letter to Luther Cressman telling him how clear everything had become, now that he and Mead had worked out precisely why they had been destined to fall in love on her journey from Samoa. Even Fortune and Bateson might be in love, they all speculated, the two men's mutual affection refracted through their joint obsession with Mead.

But Fortune soon developed doubts. Mead and Bateson had shared their deepest secrets in front of him. They spent long hours quibbling over their new theory while he was left to get on with the practical fieldwork. After his initial excitement about the squares, he came to feel more alienated than ever. It was the worst kind of betrayal, he said to Mead, in friendship or in marriage, to share a partner's intimacies with someone else. She had even told Bateson where Fortune kept his revolver, which Bateson then took away from him; he worried again that Fortune might turn to it in a fit of drunkenness. The squares, Fortune decided, were lust masquerading as science—a crude, ridiculous exercise in label making with no real aim other than to get rid of him, an unstable triad painfully resolving itself to a harmony of two.

By the spring of 1933, the situation in the tiny household had gone from tense to unbearable. The squares had become a private cult, with Mead inventing entire art forms, rituals, even cuisines that she thought characterized the various temperaments. When Mead was away visiting a Tchambuli household, Fortune and Bateson passed the time playing chess, the shapes on the board a stark reminder of the mental world Mead and Bateson had been designing for themselves. At some point, in the middle of yet another fight, Fortune knocked Mead to the ground. It turned out that she was pregnant at the time. A doctor had earlier told her it would be nearly impossible for her to conceive a child, and she would later say that the incident caused a miscarriage. Fortune's response, she recalled, was to blame Bateson. "Gregory ate our baby," he said dementedly.

Malarial hallucinations, biting mosquitos, the click-click of a typewriter, the lazy spin of a wind-up record player, the dark forest and the black lake, the dank tribal lodges with their terrifying carved masks, the ecstasy of discovery, and always the remoteness, upriver from nowhere, a deep sense of being profoundly alone—the three anthropologists had descended into a mad spiral of shouts and absences, then reunions and a chilling peace, all of it adding up to an invented vision quest that they believed represented a new kind of science. "There was a large amount of religion in all our hearts," Mead wrote to Benedict, "and everything seemed clear."

IT COULD NOT CONTINUE.

Fortune was suffering from a fever. Mead was recovering from a scorpion sting and was generally incapacitated. Even for Bateson, work was impossible. Later that summer they decided it was time to move out of the field and try to sort through things—the squares, Mead and Fortune's marriage, Bateson's possible future with Mead— in a more sedate and familiar setting.

Boarding a schooner for the trip downriver, they traveled slowly under the power of sail. From the coast they caught a steamer to Australia. The voyage was "ghastly," Mead later reported. Fortune met an old girlfriend on board and resolved to stay with her when they reached port. Mead hoped this new interest would open up space for her to be alone with Bateson. A news photographer captured their arrival in Sydney, all of them smiling slightly, Mead sandwiched between the two men in her life, everyone having traded tropical cottons for tweeds, slipping back into their old skins. But just then one of Bateson's former girlfriends walked up along the quay and took him by the arm, leaving Mead to watch uncomfortably as both he and Fortune walked away from the docks with other women.

They were all soon reunited, however. They took apartments in the same building: Mead and Fortune on one floor, Fortune's quondam girlfriend next door, Bateson a floor below. Mead saw Bateson mainly at restaurants, in groups of friends. The bickering and arguing with Fortune continued. At one point, in the middle of another fight, Mead started screaming at him in Samoan. He hit her hard, probably across the face. She had "forced [his] hand," Fortune later told her, but he was sorry for doing it. Sometime later, at the end of August, she made a festive lunch for him at their apartment. He put on a new suit and bought flowers, sherry, and cheese. For that hour or so, things seemed back to normal. But after they ate, Mead simply walked out—straight to the docks, up the gangplank of a steamer bound for Hawaii, and then toward home.

"Oh, Ruth, it's so wonderful, it's so wonderful to be coming back to you," she wrote to Benedict from somewhere in the Pacific. "It's so wonderful to love anyone so surely." Back in Sydney, Bateson and Fortune played more chess, coolly trying to make the best of the horror they had all produced, until they too moved on, both eventually finding their way to Britain. "They say there are devils in New Guinea," Bateson would later explain to a friend. "If so they may have helped create the crazy atmosphere."

On board her ship, Mead walked the decks alone, talking to no one, except for dull conversations at mealtimes. She took in a movie now and then but mainly spent her time turning over everything in her head: Fortune and Bateson, her future career, the doomed marriage and the burgeoning affair that she was keeping secret from nearly everyone. When she finally arrived back in New York, she tried to explain things to the one person she knew would understand—Benedict—but the only language Mead could conjure to describe it all was the squares: the impossibility of "diagonal marriage" between Northerners and Southerners; the natural happiness of "endogamy" inside one's own square group; the perversity of continuing with a match that seemed to run fundamentally counter to her own temperament. Benedict was baffled by what any of this was supposed to mean. She was concerned about Mead's health and about her academic reputation if she ever dared put any of it in print. "I find that I am worried only at the point where I dread your being reviled professionally for your succession of husbands," Benedict said.

Mead had earlier described the year after her return from Samoa as her "one from Hell." Her marriage with Cressman had melted, and she had writhed with desire for Fortune. But now she was in the very same place again, with Fortune casting himself in the role of jilted partner. Every few days Mead or Fortune would rush off an impassioned note to the other about the tumultuous time on the Sepik. Weeks would go by before the letter arrived, and then weeks more before a zinging reply. Sometimes the letters came in great batches, written at different times and in different moods, delivered by the postal service in a single tranche and read by the recipient in a binge of anguish and pique.

They relived the pain, exhilaration, and betrayal, going over it all with the obsessive forensics common to disintegrating marriages. She tried calm persuasion and firmness. He would stab the page with the nib of his fountain pen, rutting the paper with rage and then settling back into a stream-of-consciousness account of his own emotions. He could hurl barbed arrows with the accuracy of a New Guinean warrior, sometimes fletched with social theory or the latest findings in psychology.

> Don't make up any more constructions of temperament to draw circles about your preferences—keep your preferences clear as preferences to fuck whom you will at the moment— don't make up sagas or heroics about it, don't damn X's character merely because you want to fuck Y. If you can't get Y without that, do without him. I don't particularly want to be fucking you at the moment—you need a rest for your mind, and you keep it too near your devices for loving.

Her theories, Fortune spat at her from across the world, were no more than rationalizations for her own bad behavior. He in turn made a bonfire of his field notes, one of several he would light in fits of anger or indifference over the course of his career.

Walking the streets of Manhattan, Mead felt a catch in her heart whenever she saw a tall man in the crowd. She wondered for an instant whether it might be Bateson, descending like a hero from a Zuñi folktale to save her. He told her they would look back on all this and see it as their own personal *ecdysis*, a word he knew from childhood outings with his father: the process by which a snake sheds its old skin for something new.

EVER SINCE MEAD JOINED Fortune in their first expedition to Melanesia, she and Benedict had been joined in a bargain about their own relationship. They professed eternal love for each other, something no marriage or shipboard romance could ever shake. Physical intimacy might happen between them—maybe—but that would be left to circumstance. Benedict's own marriage to Stanley had by now effectively ended. They had long been living independently, with their own encounters, and had separated formally by 1930.

For the entirety of Mead's time in New Guinea, Benedict had been her polestar—the person with whom she shared insights and triumphs, news from the field, confusions about her future with Fortune, and the maddening, wondrous appearance, out of the blue, of Bateson. Benedict in turn kept up a steady stream of letters and packages, with gossip from the department, newspaper stories, some volumes of Virginia Woolf, some Dostoyevsky. She also sent along portions of a manuscript she had been working on, which she hoped Mead, Fortune, and Bateson would read.

While the trio on the Sepik were puzzling through the squares, Benedict had been working out her own contribution to grand theory. Much as Mead and Bateson had been trying to organize the intimate data of their own passions and discontents, Benedict hoped to make sense of the mounds of ethnographic detail that her friends and colleagues had collected over the years. She was not for drawing up boxes or putting people in newly invented categories, as Mead and Bateson were insisting. The more modest term she used was *patterns*.

Benedict had not been in the field since the late 1920s, but she had long been a friend, confidant, and perpetual agony aunt to people who had, many of them trying to talk over one another at the Tuesday seminars at Boas's home: Fortune's adventures among the sorcerers of Dobu, Ruth Bunzel's work among the pueblos, Mead's travels among the Samoans and the stilt-dwelling people of Pere, even Boas's own long-ago note taking on the muddy coast roads of the Pacific Northwest. "Anthropology is the study of human beings as creatures of society," Benedict stated flatly at the beginning of her manuscript. Over the next few hundred pages, she laid out exactly why that insight mattered.

There can be no real analysis of human societies without the prior assumption that one's own way of seeing the world isn't universal, Benedict said. Every society, including our own, suffers from the tyranny of the capital letter: we tend to equate our own behavior with a thing we label Behavior and the ways that seem natural to us with a thing we call Human Nature. But all societies are in fact just snippets of a "great arc" of possible ways of behaving. Which particular snippets a society develops depends on a whole host of accidental factors, from "hints" provided by geography, environment, or basic human needs to more or less random borrowings from neighboring societies. These choices might be reasonably durable, which allows anthropologists to study them in context—to write down, in a given society, how babies are born, how boys are ushered into adulthood, or how girls are married off well and expeditiously. But they are never glued in place. All societies change.

At the same time, Benedict continued, cultures are not random assortments of traits—"a mechanical Frankenstein's monster with a right eye from Fiji, a left from Europe, one leg from Tierra del Fuego, and one from Tahiti." They make sense to themselves; they have coherence, a sense of integration, that allows for individuals inside that society to find their way from childhood to adulthood. Being a well-adjusted member of a society means understanding its essential patterns of life—its basic "cultural configurations," or *Gestalt*, Benedict called it, borrowing a German term from psychology: the wholeness of a thing, the sum of qualities that make it uniquely itself. She borrowed two further terms from another German source, the philosopher Friedrich Nietzsche, who in turn had taken them from Greek mythology. "Apollonian" societies were those whose cultural configurations stressed order, rules, community, control, and boundaries.

"Dionysian" societies were those that stressed disruption, freedom, individualism, expression, and limitlessness.

It would be absurd to cut any complex human society down to "the Procrustean bed of some catchword characterization," she warned. But paying attention to broad patterns enabled one to grasp what made a society both different from all others and intrinsically meaningful to itself—its way of seeing social life, custom, and ritual, of defining the goals and pathways of life itself. Benedict then illustrated how all this worked in chapters on the people of the pueblos, of Dobu, and of the Northwest Coast—the first one Apollonian, the other two Dionysian.

By the end of her manuscript, Benedict had come around to her real insight. Her work wasn't really about Zuñi or the Kwakiutl at all. It was a grand illustration of what an anthropological outlook on life might entail. Social scientists had tended to treat the analysis of culture as taking place inside a geographical box. You could examine this culture *here* or that culture *there*. These units typically got labeled as tribes, peoples, villages, or ethnic groups. Anthropologists had sometimes referred to these things as "culture areas"—a piece of real estate covered by a single broad culture—and museums might arrange their collections accordingly: a room for the Pacific peoples, for example, or a vitrine showing tribesmen of the Great Plains dragging a travois, just as Boas had urged long ago in his dispute with the Smithsonian.

But this was not the only way of seeing things, Benedict said. Some cultural patterns might well be marked off by geography. An isolated village in a remote forest, with little outside contact, might represent its own culture area. But as Edward Sapir had suggested, a Ford factory or Greenwich Village might have its own well-integrated ways of behaving, a sense of moral order, agreement on right and wrong ways of dressing and speaking, a complex set of commonly understood procedures and rules. For an outside observer, the key was to make oneself what Benedict called "culture-conscious": fully aware of the ways in which one's own gut-level response to difference—a catch in the throat, exasperation at some other society's stupidity, even visceral disgust—was in fact a clash between two worlds, each with its own unique patterns. No institution, no habit, no way of acting that any given society saw as basic, obvious, and normal was ever inevitable. They were all—even Rotary Club luncheons and High Table dinners—selections from "the great arc of potential human purposes and motivations."

None of this should throw anyone into despair, Benedict concluded. Rather, it offered a deep sense of hope about humanity and our ability to comprehend ourselves. She had been working up to her final paragraph for the entire manuscript and, in a way, for her entire life. "The recognition of cultural relativity," she wrote, clearly naming the Boas circle's central idea for the first time in a book-length manuscript, "carries with it its own values, which need not be those of the absolutist philosophies.

> It challenges customary opinions and causes those who have been bred to them acute discomfort. It rouses pessimism because it throws old formulas into confusion, not because it contains anything intrinsically difficult. As soon as the new opinion is embraced as customary belief, it will be another trusted bulwark of the good life. We shall arrive then at a more realistic social faith, accepting as grounds of hope and as new bases for tolerance the coexisting and equally valid patterns of life which mankind has created for itself from the raw materials of existence.

In a few sentences she managed not only to land on a concise statement of cultural relativity but also to provide a clearer definition than anyone before her of how social science could be its own design for living. Her travels in the Southwest, her reading of the fieldwork of other anthropologists, the long cloying letters from Mead, Fortune, Sapir, and other friends, her own sense of being ill at ease nearly everywhere she went—she had finally distilled it all into a code that was at once analytically sharp and deeply moral.

"Ruth's book is finished and isn't very good," Mead wrote to Bateson after seeing a draft. Mead wanted more ambition, more theory, more sweep, the things that the male colleagues in the circle had long been calling for and that she herself had been trying to achieve with the squares. In fact, Benedict's *Patterns of Culture*, published by Houghton Mifflin in 1934, would have a more enduring impact than anything any of them would write. It would become arguably the most cited and most taught work of anthropological grand theory ever, as well as "propaganda for the anthropological attitude," as Alfred Kroeber put it at the time. Through her book, Benedict introduced "the doctrine of cultural relativity" to the reading public, said a reviewer in the *New York Times*, using the term for the very first time in a national newspaper. At its core, Benedict believed, was a foundational ethic that applied as much to individuals as to entire societies. It was the thing she had been fighting to say, in one way or another, from childhood, through the screams of her distraught mother, her second-class status as a lady professor, and her unnamable love for Mead: there is no such thing as a defective human being.

"IT'S FUNNY, YOU KNOW I am perfectly willing to admit the extraordinarily abnormal state in which I did that Sepik thinking and the number of false analogies and impossible constructs which I built up," Mead wrote to Bateson just as Benedict was preparing *Patterns of Culture* for the publisher. The whole thing had been a kind of mock religion, she felt, and she was still trying to make sense of what had happened. "It was of course a form of madness, a rate of thinking and feeling that one couldn't keep up for more than a week or so without snapping into something too remote to matter; but I think it was the kind of madness out of which, if one doesn't snap altogether and has some brains and some intellectual background, one can bring new ideas." It helped that they had all been in love with one another, she said, a weird triangle of obsession, physical passion, and intellectual giddiness, with everyone struggling to fit it into some kind of sensible frame.

Fieldwork was the destroyer of worlds. Marriages failed. Old relationships faded. Youthful ambitions came to look quaint. To do anthropology well, you had to alienate yourself from everything familiar. You had to throw away what passed for your own version of common sense as you strained to take on the local knowledge of another place. Anthropology could produce its own intellectual vertigo. The payoff was a liberating and original way of seeing your own society, denuded of its specialness, as just one of a number of ways of structuring the social world. And if you had always felt somehow out of kilter in your own culture—an "abnormal" or a "deviant," a sexual "invert" or a "mixed type," as Benedict put it in her own work—you might acquire a new set of tools for figuring out why your own life had been such a struggle.

For Mead and Benedict, these insights helped make sense of the relationship they had maintained for more than a decade: at times physical, at times not, but always the two of them tied together, bound and eternal. "The kind of feeling you have classified as 'homosexual' and 'heterosexual' is really 'sex adapted to like or understood temperaments' versus 'sex adapted to a relationship of strangeness and distance,'" Mead had written to Benedict from the Sepik. "I believe every person of ordinary sex endowment has a capacity for diffuse 'homosexual' sex expression, and specific climax—according to the temperamental situation. To call men who prefer the different expression 'feminine' or women who feel only the specific 'masculine,' or both 'mixed types' is a lot of obfuscation." Everything was to some degree potentiality, until it got channeled in a specific direction by circumstance and the rule-scape into which one was born. Mead could see that in herself, in her own yearnings and desires, and she witnessed it in others whenever she went into the field.

The price of this method, though, was a kind of intentional madness. If your sense of reality was shaped by a particular time and place, the only way to free yourself was to go out of your mind: to step outside the mental frameworks that you knew to be real, true, and obvious. "We were well away on a voyage of discovery without cultural landmarks to guide us," Bateson told Fortune, reflecting on the Sepik. "There is a heavy price attached to all expeditions of that sort and we all more or less went through hell." But it was the kind of insanity that, with just enough control, could produce new ideas, even new people—ones schooled in the art of embracing a foreign way of being. "Before I was nothing, a child," Bateson said, "now I am more or less grown up and an anthropologist. . . . Whether the price was worth paying I don't know—new knowledge can probably only be got by departure from culture (old knowledge) and many do that without gaining any of it."

And what about the squares? Mead and Bateson had kept up their intense correspondence since she left Sydney, using the same slips of paper they had exchanged for months in New Guinea. They typed up general descriptions of the squares theory and drew complicated diagrams showing each of the four principal types. But it was no good. The theory was unmoored from observable data, Benedict felt. Fortune insisted the whole thing was an embarrassment, amateur science at best, fantasy at worst. "You got so excited by its usefulness to your purpose that you thought it true," he wrote Mead. "I hope to goodness you've not told Boas anything of it." She hadn't.

But just a few months after returning from New Guinea, Mead was writing to Bateson about a new line of thought that had descended out of the mess on the Sepik. What if the key issue wasn't which box individuals fit into but rather the ways different societies standardized specific temperaments in individuals? It was the mirror image of the problem that Benedict had been getting at in *Patterns of Culture*. Benedict wanted to know about the dominant forms that a society might be said to take. Mead wanted to know how those forms structured the lives of individuals—which, at its core, was precisely what the wild theorizing about the squares had been about.

All this was easiest to see, Mead said, when it came to women and men. In New Guinea they had recorded men who dressed as women, women who took on the social role of men, and everything in between. But describing things that way felt like a conceptual straitjacket. Mead was trying to explain an entirely different social world relying only on the binary categories of male and female that she knew from her own society. Her society—"our own modern cultures," as she put it—had selected a thing it called sex to be the container in which an individual's core temperament resided. Biological men and women were said to have essential qualities that everyone in the culture could describe fluently. Boldness, aggressiveness, and dominance got cataloged as male; gentleness, motherliness, and creativity got cataloged as female. But no one in her society tended to associate being big-eared or green-eyed with inherent traits of character; claiming that people with protruding ears were naturally weak-willed, for example, would seem plain silly. Her culture, she said, had evolved in such a way that being male or female was a basic, binary, and deeply meaningful way of classifying reality. Having prominent ears or green eyes wasn't.

But you could imagine a very different way of setting up a society. The squares had been one attempt at doing so, made up whole cloth in a malarial funk. The Arapesh, the Mundugumor, and the Tchambuli were others. Now Mead had found a way of tying all of these examples together in one sweeping insight.

Her new book, which she called *Sex and Temperament*, was published a year after Benedict's *Patterns of Culture*, in 1935. It was dedicated to Boas and contained a generous acknowledgment of Fortune—to whom Mead was still married and, at least to everyone but her closest friends, seemed to be married happily. William Morrow again packaged the book for a wide audience. She sent a copy of the book to Fortune. He wrote back to say he thought it was "brilliant."

Sex and Temperament represented Mead's most serious attempt to bring fieldwork together with grand social theory. It was also an effort to link up the ways Boas had taught his students to think about race with her own thinking about sex and gender. Our society makes a heavy investment in sex differences, she wrote. It expects men and women to behave very differently, from birth forward, simply on the basis of their biology. It "plays out the whole drama of courtship, marriage, and parenthood in terms of types of behavior believed to be innate and therefore appropriate for one sex or for the other." We build our slang, our jokes, our poetry, our obscenity, even our medicine around the belief that sex and social behavior go together. People who don't fit their designated type—people who get called effete men, say, or manly women—seem at odds with the natural order of things.

Western societies thought of differences between men and women as being natural, God-given, and obvious. All societies assigned specific social roles to biological men and women. But it was not a universal feature of human cultures that these social roles must be strictly tied to biology itself, she observed. Even if you could demonstrate that, on average, biological men were disposed to behave one way and biological women to behave another, you were still left with the twin problems that Boas had long ago identified about race. First, the degree of difference within each category was likely to be greater than between the categories. No great gulf of behavior separated all men from all women. Second, there was no easy way of distinguishing the behaviors that were a product of social factors from those that were supposedly innate. The only thing that was universal, Mead said, was the independent existence of sexual roles and of differences in personality, or what she called temperament. Where societies differed was in how they drew lines connecting these two things—in other words, what specific temperaments a society *assigned* to maleness and femaleness. You couldn't begin to talk about deep differences between the sexes until you also understood the alleged qualities a society attributed to each sex. Indeed, you'd also want to know whether a society bothered much with assigning unique qualities to the sexes at all. She had at her fingertips three very different societies that, on her account, just didn't.

Consider the Arapesh and Mundugumor, she continued. Both communities assigned different roles to men and women. The Mundugumor thought fishing was an occupation appropriate mainly to women, while the Arapesh considered painting in color to be the exclusive purview of men. But neither society seemed to believe that these roles had anything to do with differences of natural temperament between the sexes. Women were better at carrying heavy loads, the Arapesh would say. But that was only because they thought women's heads were harder and stronger, not because they believed women were inherently suited to servile tasks. Child rearing was a job in which men and women cooperated, but not because both sexes were believed to be naturally "maternal"—on the contrary, the Arapesh also practiced infanticide. Rather, in the local understanding of things, procreation was the result of multiple sex acts between a man and a woman. Children were shaped and "fed" by the couple, via sexual intercourse, over the period of gestation. It was only natural, then, that the parents would continue to work together on raising the child after birth.

Had the Arapesh been pressed to explain their conception of an ideal person, it would be someone who was, using a Western vocabulary, gentle, nurturing, and oriented toward the good of the community. The Mundugumor, by contrast, seemed to have taken things in precisely the opposite direction: they regarded aggression, acquisitiveness, and suspicion as ideal qualities. It was a society of rivalry and distrust, Mead reported, divided into long, complex lineage groups that held property in common and defended it against an array of assumed aggressors. The only thing that seemed to unite the community was a headhunting raid against neighbors. But all the societies' preferred traits were thought to be dispersed equally among women and men.

And then there were the Tchambuli. They tended to put men in the role of artists who spent their days making elaborate paintings, carving wooden masks, and dancing—a *sing-sing*, as they called it—while the women went about the tasks of fishing and food preparation. Yet again the Tchambuli made no distinction between men and women as to the inherent distribution of their potentialities. In fact, they would regularly stage festive events that overturned sexual identities, grand masked balls where men dressed as women and women pantomimed intercourse.

Where did all these social roles come from? Mead asked at the end of her study. Western societies had learned over time to associate specific temperaments with the social roles into which they placed the biological sexes. Since women were by and large given the role of nurturing mother, it was convenient to believe that women were by nature careful, attentive, and focused on the well-being of children.

Since men were given the roles of politician and war-maker, it was equally convenient to believe that biological men possessed discernment and bravery. But to see this alignment of sex and temperament as the only possible way of organizing society was to mistake effect for cause. Sex roles, Mead argued, came first, the product of a long and complex process of cultural borrowing, compromise, change, and chance. Only later came the "standardization of sex-temperament," as Mead put it, to fit these preexisting roles.

The real question to ask of her own society, she concluded, was how far people might be willing to open themselves to the idea that human potential did not come prepackaged with one's sex organs. Following the social science usage of the time, Mead never employed the term *gender* in anything other than a linguistic sense. All the languages that she had studied in New Guinea had multiple genders— not just nouns classed as masculine, feminine, and neuter, but also more than a dozen other grammatical categories into which a plant, a bird, or a crocodile egg might be placed. But in *Sex and Temperament*, she sought to draw a bright distinction between sex-as-biology—this brand of genitalia or that array of secondary sexual characteristics, say—and sex-as-social-category. The first could be thought of as a class of biological facts, at least for all but a small portion of human beings. The second, which would now be called simply gender, was the product of a specific time and place—the discrete social positions that a given society assigned to men and women, or alternatively the menu of roles, behaviors, attractions, and potentialities that it made available to people, with little reference to biological sex at all.

It was a version of the argument Boas had made years earlier about the difference between observable physical differences and the social category of race. Mead's conclusions were the result of what she had called, in correspondence with Benedict, her practice of "reviewed biography," that is, using social science theories as tools of critical self-analysis. It produced the maniacal theorizing on the Sepik and then, back in New York, the academic writing that would become *Sex and Temperament*. At last she had a way of understanding her own mixed-up, misfit fate. It also gave her a way of talking about the tragedies and passions of many of the women and men she had known in her life, from Barnard forward, of Benedict and Fortune, and now of her newest, most liberating love, Bateson.

Cultures are cunning tailors. They cut garments from convenience and then work hard to reshape individuals to fit them. Benedict had concerned herself with the cultural patterns of a given society. Mead was interested in how societies restrict and channel individual temperaments. Real liberation wasn't necessarily about making women more manly or allowing men to be effeminate. It was about unleashing human beings' potential from the roles that society had fashioned, seeing each person as a parcel of possibilities that might get expressed in many creative ways. Cultural change came about when enough people began to see that the old clothes simply didn't fit.

Western society was obsessed with seeing people as "types" of some deeper, innate reality. Gender was no more than another version of race or head shape—one more way of reducing individual ability by corralling it. "A civilization might take its cues not from such categories as sex, race or hereditary position in a family line," Mead concluded in *Sex and Temperament*, "but instead of specializing personality along such simple lines recognize, train, and make a place for many and divergent temperamental endowments." To do otherwise wasn't at base a matter of injustice or oppression (as it would later be labeled), although it produced plenty of both. It was just a terrible waste, a vast squandering of talent, energy, and aptitude, all bottled up inside people who were forced to live their lives as tragically less-than.

Chapter Twelve

SPIRIT REALMS

....

Mead's *Sex and Temperament* appeared in the same year as Hurston's *Mules and Men*. Mead's book was marketed as a bold statement about sex and ability. Hurston's was treated as a black writer's account of black culture, or as a reviewer for *The New Republic* put it, about "the life of the unsophisticated Negro in the small towns and backwoods of Florida." Volumes on Samoans or New Guineans were hailed as commentaries on the universal features of human society. One about African Americans was a quaint bit of storytelling.

Still, Hurston was at the height of her power as a writer and intellectual. She had published two books that were reviewed in the major newspapers. She was working toward a doctorate. Fannie Hurst, the best-selling author and Hurston's old friend, asked her for an autographed photo when *Mules and Men* came out. She had done more collecting back in the South, this time with a young college student named Alan Lomax. Dragging along a tape recorder, Hurston and Lomax netted stories, work songs, spirituals, and blues numbers for the Library of Congress, a kind of sonic accompaniment to Hurston's own research. The year after *Mules and Men* was published, in 1936, she was finally awarded a Guggenheim Fellowship, a prize that had eluded Margaret Mead in the previous cycle. On the application, Hurston had declared her field to be "literary science." It was a good title for what she most wanted to do: to write creatively and to use folklore as a tool for understanding how people crafted meaningful lives inside their predicaments.

While Mead, Fortune, and Bateson were still sorting out the next phase of their careers, Hurston set off with $2,000 in Guggenheim funds—more money than she had possessed at any point in her life—for another fieldwork site. She planned to undertake what the Guggenheim trustees described in their announcement as "a study of magic practices among Negroes of the West Indies." Research was no more than a kind of "formalized curiosity," she later wrote. Your prejudices would melt if you just allowed yourself to access the trove of secrets inside any human community. "Just squat down awhile," she said, "and after that things begin to happen." That spring she stepped off a ship and onto the docks of Kingston, Jamaica.

KINGSTON WAS THE FIRST stop in what Hurston saw as a yearlong process of self-education. The Columbia department seemed be built for people like Sapir, Benedict, and Deloria, with their focus on Native American cultures. It was harder going for those with other interests. "Papa Franz knows the Indian, etc. but there was nothing to help me in my study of the Negro," she complained to Melville Herskovits, by then a professor at Northwestern University.

Like Boas and Mead in their early expeditions, Hurston quickly made local headlines as a foreign researcher arriving to receive instruction from the natives. She cut a dashing image by tooling around Kingston in jodhpurs and riding boots. Even for someone practiced in the art of self-reinvention, Jamaica seemed to Hurston a place where people could be nearly anything they wished—"a land where the rooster lays an egg," as she put it.

"Everywhere else a person is white or black by birth," she claimed, "but it is so arranged in Jamaica that a person may be black by birth but white by proclamation." With enough visible pink or red in your skin tone, you could change your circumstances by sheer willpower. Any Jamaican in that category seemed to be able to take on the airs of the English, from received pronunciation to tea at four. In her own country, Hurston was intimately aware of the phenomenon of passing—the ability of people to inhabit two racial categories at once: a private one known only to themselves and their family, and a different, public one with which they moved through society. Passing, she realized, almost always took place in one direction: toward social power. Jamaica seemed to be reproducing the racial hierarchy inherited from white colonizers, purposefully obscuring black lineages beneath a veil of perceived whiteness. People could convince themselves of the most remarkable things if the society in which they happened to live made it hard for them to do otherwise. She hadn't expected to learn much new about race, a subject that she had tried to avoid in her own writing. But being in Jamaica put it all in starker relief. Culture wasn't just a set of rules or rituals, she realized. It could also be a set of chains that individuals dragged around with them after the prison wardens more or less fled the scene.

Before long, Hurston got out of Kingston, driving with friends over the Blue Mountains to the north shore of the island and the parish of Saint Mary, looking for something interesting. The sea was a celestial blue. The rocks and grasses on the shoreline were lifted straight from the world as it might have been at creation. In one village, a country wedding was in full swing. Hurston was soon in the middle of things, amid the music and the dancing, the unveiling of the bride, and plates of cake and curry goat bobbing from hand to hand.

Farther west, in Saint Elizabeth parish, she spent time among the Maroons, descendants of escaped slaves who had mixed with indigenous islanders. She joined a boar hunt that stretched over several days, traipsing up and down the mountain slopes, slogging along in her riding boots, the hunters' dogs yelping when they got too close to the boar's razor-sharp tusks. Then she was back on the other end of the island, in Saint Thomas parish, where she attended a nine-night ritual, a kind of wake meant to appease the spirit of the deceased. On this occasion, the corpse was nailed tight to the interior of the coffin to prevent its coming back to life and visiting mischief on the people of the village. Death, for the Jamaicans Hurston was surrounded by, wasn't so much an end as a change of condition. The trick was to make sure that the dark matter inside any person—the *duppy*—didn't take flight in the process. Nine-night was all about keeping a cadaver in the grave or, failing that, finding a way to satisfy the malevolent urges of the *duppy* once it was abroad in the community.

It didn't take effort to see the shreds of Africa in all these beliefs and practices. Hurston was well versed in the work of the many people who had done so: Elsie Clews Parsons, who had published research on Caribbean religion a decade earlier; Carter G. Woodson and James Weldon Johnson, whose research, because of the racial segregation in American academia, had appeared mainly in so-called Negro journals or with Negro book publishers; and, of course, Herskovits, who had been hard at work on his own studies of the religious, linguistic, and folkloric bonds between West African societies and the New World. His classes at Northwestern were already gelling into what would become the first program in African studies at a historically white college or university.

From her time in New Orleans, Hurston had seen for herself some of the African roots of black cultures in the Americas. But in Jamaica it was impossible to escape the British overlay, even in the countryside. From ideas of race to everyday manners, the island could seem like a made-over England. She soon realized that it would be hard to cut beneath the veneer of empire. If you really wanted to see what had been lost and gained as people were trafficked out of Dahomey or the Gold Coast and set down half a world away to hack down forests and raise up sugarcane, there was one place you had to go. In late September, Hurston packed her bags and caught a ship to Port-au-Prince.

FREDERICK DOUGLASS, WHO SERVED as the U.S. minister and consul-general in Haiti, once said that tracing the country's history was like following a wounded man through a crowd: you just needed to follow the blood. In 1791 enslaved people in the French colony of Saint-Domingue, on the western half of the island of Hispaniola, began an armed revolution against slave owners and colonial authorities. The uprising led to independence, as the Haitian republic, in 1804; but the price of victory was national indebtedness and isolation. European powers forced the new government to compensate France for the cost of its freed slaves. Periods of relative stability and reform alternated with coups, assassinations, a peasant revolt, brutal suppression, and finally, in 1915, a military occupation by the United States, which had intervened to support American investors then in control of Haiti's national bank. By the time Hurston arrived, in the autumn of 1936, U.S. troops had been gone for only two years, having handed power to a newly elected president.

"Funeral met funeral at the door," Hurston later wrote about Haiti's recent history. But the past was already giving way to what local elites were calling its second independence. The country's three million inhabitants were reasserting their power. Americans who had held posts in government, the military, the police, and educational institutions were replaced by Haitians. Each evening, along the streets and avenues of Port-au-Prince, Haiti's high society passed in review before porticoed buildings, the cathedral with its twin bell towers, the Place de l'indépendance, and the beaux arts Palais National, its white concrete facade set off against a backdrop of green hills.

Hurston set up shop on the outskirts of the capital. She worked to master the Creole language and made plans for further visits inland. The country was really two places, she said: the one of the Champ de Mars, the fashionable center of Port-au-Prince, with its French architecture and light-skinned clientele, and the one of the Bolosse, the poorer district near the municipal cemetery, with its shanties for the darker-toned. To know the place, you had to step out from the porticoes. By December, Hurston was on La Gonâve, the dry, sparsely populated island lying inside Haiti's pincer-shaped western coast. From the sea, the island's landscape resembled a reclining woman. The quiet village life, the calm water, and the simple meals of stewed goat made Hurston feel, in spite of the undeterrable mosquitoes, "a peace I have never known anywhere else on earth."

In early January she moved back to the main island, to Arcahaie, which she would make into one of her bases for the rest of her time in Haiti. Her host, a man named Dieu Donnez St. Léger, lived in a compound that encompassed several buildings and a large house. He governed entire plantations and reaped the rewards, which were on display in his elaborate surroundings: an entrance archway painted with bright stripes of green, white, blue, and orange, with green and red walls all around the compound, and a whole clan of workmen, underlings, and children running back and forth in the dust. The thing that gave Dieu Donnez such power was not the wealth from his farms but something that Hurston felt wound through Haitian society like a secret electrical grid. It was Haiti's indigenous source of energy and the aspect of local culture that outsiders seemed to understand least: the practices and convictions that Haitians called *vodou*.

NOT LONG AFTER HURSTON left the United States for the Caribbean, Melville Herskovits published his own study of rural Haiti, which he titled *Life in a Haitian Valley* (1937). Co-researched by Herskovits's wife Frances, the book dealt in detail with the religious life of Haitian villagers. "'Voodoo,' or *vodun*," he wrote, using yet another spelling of the term, ". . . is a complex of African belief and ritual governing in large measure the religious life of the Haitian peasantry."

God was the ruler of the universe, but the world was also inhabited by saints or spirits, *loa*, who could assume control of the bodies of the faithful. They might mount a human as someone would climb onto a horse. Priests, called *houngans* or *mambos*, had unique access to *loa* and understood their ways, and this knowledge could enable healing, prophecy, and other extraordinary feats. Temples, or *houn-forts*, were spaces where ceremonies were performed that connected the visible world to the unseen one through offerings, sacrifices, and the playing of sacred drums.

Different villages or districts had different practices, Herskovits pointed out, and as soon as you thought you had nailed down a belief or ritual, you would find a Haitian—a kind of Creole Two Crows—who insisted that no right-thinking person could possibly believe such nonsense. But there was nothing special in this fact, Herskovits realized. Ask a practicing Christian or Jew, Muslim or Buddhist about their faith, and you would get an enormous range of opinion on correct belief, good ceremony, proper ethics, the right way to live, efficacious prayer, even the number of gods. Catholics *said* they believed in only one, for example, but to any anthropologist, Catholics *practiced* a religion that seemed to have several. The Trinity, the Virgin Mary, and all the saints looked an awful lot like a grand polytheistic bazaar, each deity bearing a specific celestial rank along with unique magical powers.

Things sometimes attributed to *vodou* practitioners—such as snake worship or even cannibalism—were entirely the product of outsiders' imaginations, Herskovits wrote. Most Americans seemed to think that Haitians went about their daily tasks "in a universe of psychological terror." He was eager to correct this view. What he produced was perhaps the most sophisticated and sensitive portrait of Haitian village life published up to that time, an account infused with humanity and reasonableness—the best thing yet written on the country, as Ruth Benedict described it.

A deeper aim of *Life in a Haitian Valley* was to catalog what Herskovits called the "uncontaminated Africanisms" in language, magic, and social organization. He was, in a way, channeling Boas. Societies have histories, and those histories account for the practices and habits that one sees today. In Haiti's case, that history ran back through the era of independence, past centuries of enslavement, to ways of life that, an ocean away in sub-Saharan Africa, were still alive and well. Herskovits would later rank Haiti as second only to the Guianas, along the northeastern coast of South America, as a venue for studying the African origins of the cultures of "New World Negroes."

The fact that Herskovits could identify a word, a phrase, a deity, or a drum technique as Dahomeyan or Senegalese, Nigerian or Angolan—not just as a timeless primitivism—was a point he felt needed special emphasis. It ran against the grain of what most of his white readers would have thought about a black society. "If the life of the Haitian Negro peasant today presents aspects of harshness or instability," he wrote, "it would seem proper to ask how much of this might be ascribed to the examples which these Negroes were set by their masters, rather than unequivocally to assume inherent racial tendencies to account for them, as is so often done." A few years later he would make the case more forcefully in *The Myth of the Negro Past* (1941). The book's title contained an implied double negative. He wasn't attacking the myth that Negroes *had* a past but rather the opposite: the idea—affirmed by both slaveholders and white historians—that they didn't. The claim that black people were part of a long cultural lineage, one that could be reconstructed even across the canyon created by enslavement, was not particularly original. Herskovits owed much to thinkers such as Du Bois and Woodson, who had made similar points much earlier, although often for black readerships via segregated journals and publishing houses. Still, he pushed the argument further than nearly any white author at the time. Black people had a history worth remembering, he insisted, and its legacies could be mapped in the present. Even white southerners, Herskovits pointed out, recalled Africa in the way they sang, cooked, talked, and worshipped. After all, what was a white Protestant camp meeting, with its pounding piano music and emotional adherents walking a sawdust trail down to the altar, but a form of spirit possession with partially African roots?

Yet like many white researchers of the time, Herskovits was looking not so much at Haiti as through it. It was difficult to see Haitians as people if your science told you to see them mainly as embodiments of tenacious traditions—no matter how progressive that idea might be as compared with its racist alternatives. *Life in a Haitian Valley* tracked what Herskovits called the "amalgam" of Haitian culture, the suffusing of African roots with French borrowings. However, it was nearly silent on the great change that had defined the lives of the people Herskovits encountered day after day in his fieldwork: the occupation by the United States military. "As concerns the inner life of the people of this valley," Herskovits wrote, referring to his field site of Mirebalais, not far from Hurston's coastal Arcahaie, the occupation "seems to have passed without any discernible effect."

Yet the visible signs were all around him. He even reported on one himself. In the town square in Mirebalais, a lone old palm tree stood as a symbol of Haitian independence and a rallying point where townspeople gathered for public events. A U.S. marine had left behind a message carved into the soft trunk:

L. MARLOW

AUG. 13, 1920

U.S.M.C.

DRUNK AS HELL

All across the country, the American presence had cut deeply into Haitian society. The occupation forces had been obsessed with talk of false religion and its barbarisms. Marines bound for Haiti were given shipboard lessons on purported Haitian traditions, including casting spells and poisoning enemies. Local rituals that had been practiced for generations came under scrutiny as routes toward radicalization. Young Haitian men were thought to be particularly susceptible to the lure of underground priests. The American authorities officially banned *vodou* ceremonies and raided *hounforts*. Drums were seized and destroyed. *Houngans* were arrested or driven into hiding.

The marines who formed the bulk of the troop presence were both administering a country and fighting a local insurgency: the so-called *cacos*, or rural fighters from the interior uplands. "Probably all the caco chiefs are Vaudoux priests," wrote an American visitor, "and thus hold together bands which, freed from religious scruples, would abandon their purpose of brigandry." Junior officers and enlisted men charged with rooting out the guerrillas were given positions of immense power in the local administration. Their overweening authority, combined with racial prejudice, produced grotesque acts of violence, especially in remote postings. Forced labor, rape, and murders of civilians were widely reported. The common explanation was that these actions were required against a benighted and cruel people in the thrall of a hysterical religion. What could one do in a society riven with sorcery and dark magic, where naïve peasants were easily manipulated by high priests in league with *cacos* and unscrupulous politicians?

The U.S. invasion was the first episode in the twentieth century when a foreign occupier saw its chief enemy as an otherworldly one: a set of religious ideas, rooted in a specific culture, which in turn justified the violence used to eradicate them. Once the marines and the journalists who covered them returned home, their tales of island life convinced the broader American public of the exoticism of Haiti as well as its natural savagery. Soldiers' memoirs such as *The White King of La Gonave* (1931) and *Black Bagdad* (1933) charted the American effort to bring civilization southward. *The Magic Island* (1929), a bestselling travel book by the journalist William Seabrook, became one of the most influential depictions of "voodoo" enchantment. Ecstatic rites in Haiti were a throwback to an earlier time, a leftover from a primitive stage in religious customs when emotions were raw and the gods closer to hand. "Voodoo in Haiti is a profound and vitally alive religion," he wrote, "alive as Christianity was . . . when miracles and mystical illuminations were common everyday occurrences . . . despite up-cropping naïvetés, savageries, grotesqueries, superstitious mumbo-jumbo, and at times deliberate witch-doctor charlatan trickeries."

Hurston had read *The Magic Island* in preparation for her journey, but she was already well acquainted with "hoodoo" or "voodoo," as she called it in her own writings, the popular religion of certain black communities in the South. During her time in New Orleans, she had been initiated into secret rites by several expert practitioners. She had spent days lying naked in the summer heat, with candles burning at her head and toes. She had published the results of her research in Benedict's *Journal of American Folklore*.

Now in Haiti, Hurston fell in easily with priests whom she met casually through local friends and colleagues. In Arcahaie, her connection with Dieu Donnez provided a ready passage into this veiled society. She met some of the country's foremost *houngans* and *mambos* and watched as late-night ceremonies summoned an entire pantheon of gods—a holy conclave of Jesus and the saints, standing alongside unfamiliar deities such as Damballah Ouedo and Erzulie Freida. She saw people writhe and cry as they were mounted by a *loa*. She felt the urgency of grasping at another plane of reality—seeing wickedness and purity, the most venal things and the most exalted, all braided together, all making sense, no more bizarre or unreal, or less ecstatic, than a Baptist prayer meeting in Eatonville. As a lapsed Christian and minister's daughter, she knew something about the power of accessing other worlds.

Religion depended on categories, Hurston was coming to realize: the sacred and the profane, the ethereal and the earth-bound, the miraculous and the commonplace. In Manhattan, there were only two boxes, the living and the dead. But Haitians had added a third, a way of being neither one nor the other, or perhaps both at the same time. Seabrook's *The Magic Island* had already introduced Americans to the idea. It was the first book to standardize the English spelling of a condition that Haitians knew as *ʒonbi*, or as Seabrook had it, zombie.

A special type of creature haunted the Haitian landscape, Seabrook wrote, "a soulless human corpse, still dead, but taken from the grave and endowed by sorcery with a mechanical semblance of life." On their patrols, the American occupation forces had heard talk of zombies. An army of the walking dead seemed to inhabit Haiti's denuded hillsides and remote villages. They were perhaps responsible in some way for the *caco* insurgency. Maybe it was they, villagers suggested, who had carried out the unexpected nighttime raids that terrorized marine platoons.

A few years later, in 1932, audiences back in the United States could go to a local cinema and see zombies on the screen. *White Zombie* starred Bela Lugosi as a manipulative voodoo master who visits his evil powers on a vacationing American fiancée. Haiti's evils could infect anyone—even a white woman, hence the film's title—and the antidote was there on the screen. Lugosi's voodoo spell is lifted only when his character dies, plummeting from a cliff along with his black minions. Inspired by Seabrook's travel writing, *White Zombie* was both a horror film and a kind of ethnography at a distance. It was a

work of pure fiction that seemed to do for Haiti, in more sensation-
alized form, what *Nanook of the North* and *Moana* had done for the
Arctic and Samoa: rendering it understandable by suspending it in the
realm of the exotic.

In Haiti, talk of zombies "seeps over the country like a ground
current of cold air," Hurston recalled. She encountered zombie legends nearly everywhere she went, from Port-au-Prince to Arcahaie
and beyond. People would talk of zombies the way one might men-
tion the weather or an upcoming wedding, if perhaps in a quieter tone.
Everyone Hurston knew had met one, or knew someone who had met
one. But all that was talk. Nothing could quite prepare her for coming
face-to-face with such a creature herself.

AT ONE POINT DURING her stay, Hurston visited a Haitian hospital. In the yard near the fence, she found a woman who had just
been served dinner. Huddled in a defensive position, the woman had
barely touched her food. When she saw Hurston approach, she pulled
a branch from a nearby shrub and began to sweep the ground. She
kept her head covered with a cloth, wary and fearful, as if expecting to
be hit. A doctor pulled the cloth from her face, but she flung her arms
up, bending them around her head like a turtle retreating into its shell.

Her name, Hurston learned, was Felicia Felix-Mentor. She had
grown up in Ennery, a village on the road between Gonaïves and
Cap-Haïtien, where she and her husband had managed a small gro-
cery store. The stunning thing about this woman was that medical
records showed that she had died in 1907. Hurston snapped several
photographs of Felix-Mentor, at least one of which was later published. It remains the first known depiction of a person whom her Haitian neighbors knew as a zombie.

What had happened to Felix-Mentor? Twenty-nine years earlier,
her funeral had taken place. She had been mourned, but her family quickly moved on with life. Her husband took a new wife. Her
son grew into a man. But then, the autumn before Hurston visited,
gendarmes had encountered a woman walking naked along a coun-

try road. She had turned up at a local farm and pointed it out as a property that had once been hers, an inheritance from her father. The farmhands tried to shoo her away, but the owner soon arrived and, flabbergasted, declared that this was in fact his sister. Her former husband was sent for, and he also confirmed that it was indeed his dead wife, Felicia. There was no going back to the way things were before, however. In her absence, everyone, including Felix-Mentor herself, had become someone else. The brother was a prosperous farmer, with control over the old family property that might otherwise have been shared with her. The husband was a minor official in the postoccupation government, with a new family of his own. There was little to be done except to seal her up again, this time behind the walls of the hospital where Hurston found her.

Doctors told Hurston that Felix-Mentor was likely the victim of poisoning. A practitioner of dark magic, a *bocor,* might have given her a drug that simulated death, concocted from a secret formula passed down from priest to priest. The *bocor* could then summon her back to life, brain-damaged and only a shell of the person she had been before, with only "a mechanical semblance of life," as Seabrook would have put it. She might have wandered the countryside for years, or even lived in plain sight in a community that had more or less forgotten about her. Hurston was familiar with the condition, in a way, which is perhaps why she described her encounter with Felix-Mentor in detail. She had spent her childhood not quite believing in her own mother's death. Her father, by contrast, had known how to draw the lines between worlds in ink. He had been an expert in trading his old family for a new one.

Hurston toyed with the idea of tracking down the formula for the poison and uncovering the secret of the zombie phenomenon. Maybe she could even dig more deeply into Felix-Mentor's past and reconstruct those lost twenty-nine years, or recount in detail how she ended up among the living dead. But when Hurston suddenly came down with stomach problems that summer, she backed off. Perhaps she was getting too close to some secret knowledge. Could she herself have fallen victim to the poison vial of a *bocor* worried that she was edging up on a hidden truth? She decided she had learned enough. "What is the whole truth and nothing else but the truth about Zombies?" she would later write. "I do not know, but I know that I saw the relic, or refuse of Felicia Felix-Mentor in a hospital ward."

The key to understanding zombies, Hurston concluded, lay not in finding a secret potion or in debunking another people's mythology. It was actually believing in them. Felix-Mentor wasn't a person who was *said to be* a zombie. She wasn't a make-believe one, like her fictional counterpart in a Hollywood film. She really *was* one. If you could twist your brain into seeing that fact, then you had taken a giant step toward seeing Haiti—and most important, its spirituality—from the inside. At base, zombies were an object lesson in native categories. They were a way of dividing up reality that spoke volumes about how people in the Haitian countryside inhabited their world. In New York, people thought about death as a finality, the end of everything; reality came in two flavors, now and nothingness. Haitians, however, lived in a society that had opened up a condition not quite here but not quite on the other side of death either, a middle ground between being alive and not.

You could search for the deep origins of this way of seeing things in West Africa, as Herskovits had done. But to see it as the dimly remembered customs of people torn away from their cultures and forcibly resettled in the New World was to mistake history for the present. That insight was the simple equivalent of finding, for example, that Christianity had its roots in Palestine. To really see a religion, you needed to have your eyes not on the heretofore or the hereafter but on the here and now. *Vodou*, like all forms of faith, was about the present moment, about how one understands social power and makes sense of *this* world, the out-of-kilter one. Governments rose and fell. Powerful countries invaded and then left. Violence descended out of the hills or came stealing into a village under darkness, dressed like a *caco* or a U.S. marine. A woman disappeared—conveniently, for her brother and her husband—and then reappeared and started causing trouble until she was put away in a mental institution, cowering, distraught, wordless, no longer herself, alive yet dead. Religions survive not because people love the faith of their fathers but because they help us navigate the world as we find it.

Magic, Hurston had learned from Ruth Benedict in her seminars, is essentially the practice of setting a pattern for a desired event. If you want your son to grow up strong, you give him a name that signals strength. If you want to kill an enemy, you stuff a piece of his clothing down a dead snake's throat. Magical thinking was as close to a human universal as you could imagine, and it existed in modern societies, too. Gambling, the stock market, even the concept of private property—the belief that I can expand my sense of self to include an inanimate object, the loss of which would induce deep displeasure and anxiety—all depend to a degree on magical belief systems. They are ways of summoning the unlikely and the invisible in order to control the tangible world. They differ only in how we join the natural plane to the supernatural one, which in turn depends on history and local conditions.

Hurston could see in Haiti exactly what her professors had been getting at. It didn't take instruction in the dark arts to grasp any of this, although Hurston had already had plenty, both in New Orleans and now in Arcahaie. All you needed to do was open your eyes to a world of unmoored forces, sudden miracles, and windblown tragedies. People who "play the zig-zag lightning of power over the world, with the grumbling thunder in your wake," Hurston later wrote, never had to think about such things. But people who walked in the dust did. If your society commanded the oceans and could make people bow down before you, it is likely that your gods could, too. If you were beholden to the whims of fate, torn from one place and plopped down, dazed, into another, tossed this way and that for reasons that seemed incomprehensible, then your gods behaved in the same way—capriciously, with their darker and lighter personas struggling for dominance and, from time to time, requiring feeding and appeasement.

"Gods always behave like the people who make them," Hurston wrote in her notes from Haiti. A boisterous spirit could say the thing a peasant couldn't. A person mounted by a *loa* could curse a field boss or a pith-helmeted American. Possession by unseen forces, escaping into a kind of death, could be a way of being truly, deeply alive, especially in places where it was hard to speak the truth in any other way. That was the real story of Felicia Felix-Mentor. Put away, disregarded, institutionalized, forgotten, willed by others to be effectively dead—her condition was very much like that of many people Hurston knew, the black women and men she had met from Florida labor camps to whites-only universities. It was just that Haitians had invented a word for it.

But if Hurston needed to feel the powerful sense of magic at work, she didn't have to turn to zombies. It had come at her already in her first weeks in Haiti. A thing had been "dammed up" in her, she said, and now came rushing out in one great spirit-fueled wave. It was a novel into which she had deposited a preserved passion—the remnant of a past love now kept in a suspended state, between reality and memory, her own private experiment in living in between.

Not long after meeting Felix-Mentor, she wrote to the Guggenheim Foundation that she would soon be coming back from the Caribbean with two books in tow, "one for anthro. and one for the way *I* want to write it." It was the second one that would end up giving her something close to immortality.

HURSTON HAD BEEN IN Haiti nearly four times as long as Herskovits. Her visit had been interrupted by a short return trip to New York, but with the help of a second Guggenheim Fellowship, she had been able to return to complete her research. She now had almost a full year of Caribbean fieldwork to her credit. In the late summer of 1937, her publisher, Bertram Lippincott, wanted her back in New York. After staying long enough to attend one more *vodou* ceremony, she reluctantly agreed to sail north.

When she arrived in Manhattan, she was swept into a swirl of literary gatherings, congratulatory notes, newspaper reviews, and an entry in *Who's Who in America*. Years earlier Margaret Mead had once furtively joined other Barnard girls in leaving flowers at the doorstep of one of their idols, Edna St. Vincent Millay. Now it was Millay who sent a gushing telegram to Hurston. The reason was the publication that September of the novel that had poured out of her in Haiti. She titled it *Their Eyes Were Watching God.*

Hurston's journey to the Caribbean had been a self-imposed exile. Some months earlier she had fallen in love with a handsome Columbia graduate student, Percival McGuire Punter, whom she had first met while still married to Herbert Sheen. Punter was twenty-one years her junior, a fact she probably hid from him as artfully as she hid her age from most people. The spark was intense. They talked art, music, theater, and literature. He intrigued and challenged her. She sputtered and sizzled with him, rolling from besotted to enraged as soon as she caught his eyes following a woman on Seventh Avenue. "I did not just fall in love," she recalled. "I made a parachute jump."

Their relationship was carried on at a distance, but then she would return to New York and fall back into his arms. The two of them would settle into a turbulent bliss, with dishes flying and an occasional slap in the face—her slap, his face—then passionate forgiveness. He asked her to marry him, but she felt it wasn't possible. The age difference, her commitment to her own work, and his desire for a particular kind of wife, one she knew she could never quite be, all stood in the way. The Guggenheim came at exactly the right time, and she had set off for the Caribbean leaving Punter well behind.

When she arrived in Port-au-Prince, the words came tumbling out onto the page. The result was a fictionalized memoir not only of her love for Punter but of many other things besides—all of it "embalmed," as she said, in the story of a woman, her search for self-knowledge, and the difficulty of finding real companionship. "Ships at a distance have every man's wish on board," she wrote in the first sentence, an aphorism that would become one of the most famous first lines in American literature. And the oldest human longing, Hurston said of her main character, Janie Crawford, is self-revelation. Janie comes upon her identity gradually, much as Hurston had done when she first traveled outside Eatonville. Married off by her grandmother to a wealthy landowner, she bristles at the demands of farm work and house tending, her insides churning for something more.

She soon takes off with Joe Starks, a man who knows how to treat her right, to Eatonville. There she can listen to the stories on the storefront porch and, as the wife of a local notable, glory in the notoriety. But Joe can be a petty tyrant, with his keep-quiet mentality and public humiliations aimed squarely at Janie. When he dies, Janie is left a wealthy widow, now older and worldlier than she had been before. She soon becomes the object of the affections of Tea Cake, a younger, open-road gambler—a romantic version of Punter, perhaps—with whom she has some version of the companionship that has always eluded her. It doesn't last. A rabid dog bites Tea Cake; he flies into a manic rage, threatening her life; she shoots him dead to save herself and, acquitted of any crime, looks back over her life with a kind of satisfaction—innocence becoming experience.

The novel was a summation of the work Hurston had done in the South, fused with the understanding of place that she was gaining in Port-au-Prince and Kingston. As in some of her earlier work, the dialogue was rendered in dialect. She put the essential method of an anthropologist into the mouth of Janie Crawford. "It's uh known fact," Janie says, "you got tuh *go* there tuh *know* there." Hurston had done it herself from the moment she left for the South in Sassy Susie, loaded up with the vocabulary of science. She had sharpened her talents in ceremony after ceremony with a string of respected *houngans*. No other member of the Boas circle could claim to have gone as deeply into the lived experience of the people she was trying to understand.

Their Eyes Were Watching God was many things at once: a coming-of-age story, a meditation on the inner lives of women and the men they loved, a literary ethnography of the Gulf Coast. It was also a reimagining of geography. Hurston's South is really a north, an extension of the Caribbean, where racial prejudice and everyday apartheid look more like the leftovers of colonialism than the innovations of Jim Crow. Myth and religion are as powerful in her depiction of southern life as a *vodou* drum circle in Haiti. The fine gradations of racial belonging are as obsessed over as skin tone in Jamaica. After a devastating hurricane from which Janie and Tea Cake manage to escape, the victims are buried in separate graves; the white overseers insist that black workmen identify the right and wrong kind of dead people by the color and texture of their hair. It is hard to know where to start explaining, much less uprooting, such a system, Hurston suggests—a reality in which even corpses have a race. If you could believe in a thing like that, zombies were downright banal.

"NOVELISTS KNOW MORE ABOUT people than most scientists," Mead had confided in a letter to Bateson a few years before *Their Eyes Were Watching God* appeared. Writers had the freedom to mold language to their own purposes, and they couldn't hide behind professional jargon. They opened themselves to the possibilities of expression and, in doing so, had special access to the words, thoughts, and experiences of others.

There is no evidence that Mead read any of Hurston's fiction at the time it was published, however. The chasm of race separated Hurston from the other members of the Boas circle, even at a time when Boas's students were assiduously denying that race was a fundamental division in human societies. One of the most embarrassing moments of Mead's life came in the summer of 1935, when she lectured at an interracial conference in Pennsylvania. In describing her work in New Guinea, she referred to local infants as "pickaninnies," using what she claimed was the accepted pidgin English term. She immediately felt the African Americans in the audience bristle. Nearly in tears at her thoughtless gaffe, she quickly apologized and moved on with her talk. But the lesson she took away was not about her own insensitivity or casual prejudice—the fact that one needed a special word to distinguish black babies from white babies was the very definition of racism, after all. It was rather the ability of speakers to win over their audiences if they express remorse.

Hurston had little contact with Mead in the 1930s, a result of their long periods of fieldwork on opposite sides of the planet. On those occasions when Hurston was back in New York, she was more likely to be visiting publishers and old patrons than wandering around the anthropology department. In fact, she had given up on the doctorate almost as quickly as she had begun it. The financing turned out to be less generous than she had imagined, and in any case she was coming to feel that her deepest commitment was to art over science—or rather to art as a way of expressing the scientific collecting she had been doing for years. After her return from Haiti, she made further expeditions back to the American South to gather folklore and take notes on charismatic worship among Pentecostals. She remained an ethnographer in practice, even though she had no desire to move toward an academic career. The proceeds from writing helped finance her unrewarded science.

There had been a time when Mead imagined her life evolving in the same way. A younger version of herself had been convinced that poetry, not social science, would be her calling. Now, after her return from the Sepik, she was at something of a loss. She had her curator's job at the museum, but she seemed to be in a kind of limbo. Her relationship with Benedict was warm and friendly, but in the time Mead had spent abroad, Benedict had moved on to other passions, other relationships. Mead's marriage to Fortune was moving toward its conclusion. In the summer of 1935, she delivered the divorce papers to the Mexican consulate in New York, the second time she had used this route to end a marriage. She kept up her correspondence with Bateson; they would later remark on the special moment, in April 1935, when they switched from writing on slips of cut paper, as they had done in New Guinea, to using more conventional stationery. But managing this new relationship required tact and planning. They met surreptitiously and only when an encounter could be explained by another commitment: an unexpected reunion during a vacation in Ireland, say, or a conversation during a visiting lecture by Bateson at Columbia.

Especially given the public notice she was receiving for *Sex and Temperament*, Mead was careful to avoid any hint of scandal. Most people assumed that she and Fortune were doing fine, even though the two had not been living together since her return from the field. In any case, she needed good sales. The royalties would help to pay the legal fees for the divorce. She had not spoken to Papa Franz about any of this, of course. Only later that year did she finally get around to doing so—telling him that Fortune had rejected her, when the truth was closer to the opposite.

For months, she and Bateson had been working out, letter by letter, a scheme for meeting at a new field site and marrying as inconspicuously as possible once her divorce from Fortune was finalized that fall. They planned an expedition together, this time to Bali, where they would begin a project on mental illness and local religion, in addition to doing some broader work on culture and temperament. They devised an elaborate ruse to convince family, friends, and colleagues that they had met again by chance and fallen madly in love. The insanity of the Sepik would remain safely hidden from everyone except Benedict. "In any case I think [it] a very good thing to amuse the world for a month or two with the idea that we are working together and mutually jealous and disapprove of each other's methods and what not ad lib, to get them used to the idea of impending marriage before it happens," Bateson wrote to Mead just before Christmas 1935, as if scripting a screwball comedy. "Then the marriage itself is an acquisition of respectability, and not just a bombshell. Let them think us a little Bohemian for a month and then recover their respect for us when we get married."

By now she was no longer Margaret in his letters but rather "my grub." The next spring, when they both arrived on the island of Bali, she was already being referred to as "Mrs. Gregory Bateson." They had been married in Singapore, and Bateson soon wrote to inform his mother that she now had a daughter-in-law: an American, a gracious hostess, an anthropologist, an atheist by inheritance, and an Anglican by choice. In looks, Bateson reported, she even had an "almost female-Darwin face," a comparison that he must have reckoned his mother—if not Mead—would see as a signature compliment.

Mead and Bateson worked well together. They were tackling a new set of problems at the intersection of psychology and anthropology, mainly in the area of the cultural determinants of mental health, a theme that had intrigued both of them for some time. They were also interested in religious belief and practice, especially the phenomenon of trances in Bali, and they planned to record everything they could find. They had taken along masses of equipment—a dicta-phone, typewriters, cameras—and had planned to document their work from beginning to end, using film in much the way Hurston had been doing in the American South. In the months that followed, they would snap some twenty-five thousand photographs. Mead would remember it as "the perfect intellectual and emotional working partnership"—physically comfortable and in harness with a person she both respected and loved.

It was the longest she had ever spent in the field: two years in Bali and then, by 1938, another six months back on the Sepik, where she and Bateson could work on another New Guinea people, the Iatmul, free of the horrible love triangle that had cut short the earlier expedition among the Tchambuli. It was hard to concentrate, though. Radio reports spoke of war clouds in Europe. Austria had been joined to the Third Reich. That September a Chinese boat chugged upriver and delivered the news that the European powers had brokered an agreement allowing Nazi Germany to annex a portion of Czechoslovakia. "The crises are always past before we hear of them," Mead wrote, "and leave us hoping again that if they can stave war off long enough, something may happen, like a few well chosen deaths in high places."

Even in paradise, the outside world had a habit of intruding. She and Bateson burrowed into their fieldwork. They constructed a writing hut inside mosquito netting where they could type up their notes at a small double desk. Iatmul villagers would sometimes gather outside, looking in on them the way visitors to a zoo might examine the hyenas. "I feel like a frightful pig to have such a lovely life," Mead wrote back to one of her friends. "We are really so contented that we spend at least an hour a day just purring." The only drawback was that Mead had decided she was ready to try for a baby, something that had been denied to her and Fortune. The timing was distinctly inconvenient. "There is no doubt about it," she said, "the tropics is a poor place to breed in."

IN THE FALL OF 1938, just as Mead and Bateson were deep in their Iatmul research, Hurston published her fieldwork from Jamaica and Haiti. She called the new book *Tell My Horse*, a phrase used in *vodou* settings when an individual is possessed by a *loa*. It was not much of a success, despite the fact that it contained the picture of Felicia Felix-Mentor, the world's first photographed zombie. Hurston made sure to identify her by name and without putting her condition in scare quotes. The book was more ramshackle than Hurston's earlier work on the South, a mixture of memoir and ethnographic description. Reviews were mixed though not unkind. A British edition, retitled *Voodoo Gods* in hopes of moving copies, sold through its five-hundred-dollar advance in the first week and provided Hurston with a small income stream.

Over the next several years, she moved from one place to another, reappearing unannounced from time to time, apologizing to friends for being so long out of touch. There was a return to New York, another journey south, more collecting, a brief stint teaching college, a head-scratching marriage that lasted six weeks. The money from her two Guggenheims long since spent, she signed on for the Federal Writers' Project, a Depression-era program to assist out-of-work journalists and novelists. Like most federal programs of that era, the writers' project was separated into the regular staff—all white—and special "Negro units." Hers was charged with working on a guidebook to Florida as well as a companion volume titled *The Florida Negro*. With a team of folklorists and a large audio recording device, she returned to the phosphate mines and turpentine camps she had known years earlier, getting down blues songs, work tunes, and jokes, much as she had done with Alan Lomax before her trip to the Caribbean.

Like Mead and Benedict, Hurston was also acquiring a kind of antifollowing. A small group of critics, exclusively men, could be relied on to write a lukewarm or negative review just about every time she published a book. Richard Wright and Ralph Ellison, now succeeding Langston Hughes as younger writers taking on the problem of race in American society, both saw Hurston's portrayals of southern folkways as quaint at best, perhaps even embarrassing. Her old mentor Alain Locke joined the chorus of dismissers. *Their Eyes Were Watching God*, he complained in the pages of *Opportunity*, was no more than "folkloric fiction," too bled through with local color to be either a convincing portrayal of the main characters or a reliable account of race relations.

Locke's review cut especially deep for Hurston. It was his mentorship that had helped launch her from Washington to New York more than a decade earlier. "I get tired of the envious picking on me," she told James Weldon Johnson, echoing similar complaints by Mead and Benedict. All of them had published books and been reviewed—more than favorably—in the nation's major journals and newspapers. Yet most of the men in their lives still found them unclubbable. Giving as good as she got, Hurston fumed and spat in letters to friends. When she had a chance to review work by Wright and others, she returned volley for volley. She soon made what amounted to a formal break with Locke, much as she had done with Hughes.

She was in no sense isolated, however. Royalty checks came regularly throughout the 1930s: payments for her earlier novels, *Jonah's Gourd Vine* and *Their Eyes Were Watching God;* proceeds from the two ethnographies, *Mules and Men* and *Tell My Horse;* and in 1939 an advance for another novel, *Moses, Man of the Mountain*, a retelling of the biblical Moses story as if he were a creature of Eatonville. When this last book was published, Ralph Ellison insisted that it did nothing to move "Negro fiction" forward. That was the standard to which Hurston was usually held, at least among her fellow novelists: what had she managed to do for Negro fiction, as a Negro writer? In anthropology she found a professional community that, more often than not, saw her mainly as a fieldworker and a colleague, not merely as a representative of her race.

In the spring of 1940, she signed on with Mead and Jane Belo, an anthropologist whom Mead had come to know in Bali, to conduct research on trance behavior in southern churches. She was soon on her way to the low country of coastal South Carolina and Georgia. With Belo she recorded songs and filmed the worship services of so-called Sanctified churches, where cymbals crashed and tambourines jangled in ecstatic praise. Some of the film footage captured her in the shot: playing a conga drum wedged between her legs, shuffling along with maracas, praising God among the saints, an ex-believer among the converted.

Her field notes, which she typed up and sent to Mead, were modeled on the kind of work she had been doing in the Caribbean—getting into a community, really participating, straining to see it all from the inside. She and Belo had settled into Beaufort, South Carolina, where the palmetto trees screeched with cicadas and the sounds of a small "holiness" church wafted through the thick air. The worship was transporting, with impromptu prophecies and people speaking in tongues, the language of the angels gifted for a moment to human beings, the better to glorify God. Everyone prayed at once, lifting individual voices in a great cacophonous chorus, broken only by chanting or an exclamation of praise. "The form of prayer is like the limbs of a tree," she wrote, "glimpsed now and then through the smothered leaves."

Mead was unimpressed. She urged Hurston to be more systematic in her collecting, not just to describe the scenes as she saw them. What were the characteristics of the people who seemed to be in a trance? Did their behavior correlate with times of financial hardship or a love affair gone wrong? "I am sure it is going to be fascinating stuff," she said dryly. It wasn't clear to Mead at the time, but Hurston was in fact repeating, in her own poetic way, exactly the thing she had learned from Papa Franz many years ago. You might think you had captured the essence of religion, the trunk of a culture disappearing into a hidden root system. You might believe it could be characterized exactly, its essence defined, its core values dissected. But you could only ever do this imperfectly, Hurston insisted, half-blindly, with the leaves getting in the way. In fact, maybe the leaves were the things you should be paying attention to in the first place: the secret rituals, the insane asylum housing a zombie, the stomped-out rhythms of godly praise and inexpressible joy, an infilling of spirit flooding the humid night. In her own language, Hurston was reiterating Boas's code for how to be ambitious as a scientist and modest as a human being: jettison the search for universal laws and open your eyes to the people standing, singing, and chanting right before you.

While she was in South Carolina, in 1940, a kind of official history of the Harlem Renaissance was already on its way to the publisher—Langston Hughes's memoir, *The Big Sea*. In his telling, Hurston was a bit player, a difficult, colorful, brassy partier, not a thinker or ethnographic collector, certainly not a scientist. "Girls are funny creatures!" he concluded dismissively about his past disputes with her. That same spring Richard Wright's *Native Son* would open an entirely new episode in American literature. It eclipsed the work of older intellectuals and placed the predicament of black men—their social limits and their crushing frustrations, the world-heavy consequences of a system of reality crafted by white men—at the forefront of black art and social commentary. The Harlem Renaissance and its women were already fading into history.

Lippincott suggested that Hurston try writing her autobiography, perhaps as a response to Hughes, with her own take on her childhood, on Boas and his influential circle, on the faded glory of Harlem. It would be a chance for Hurston to look back over both her art and her science. Could you ever really know what it meant to be a person of faith if you had never felt the tug for yourself? Could you make sense of a community's mental universe if you didn't take seriously, at least for a moment, their perception of the worlds beyond? Hurston, with her unfinished doctorate, had abandoned the idea of making a career of these questions. But more than Mead, Benedict, or even Boas himself, she had glimpsed what it might mean to make them into a life. It was something that Mead had tried, briefly, on the Sepik: to let down your guard, to give yourself over fully to something, to suspend your commitment to lab-coat science long enough to allow your brain to slip entirely into another style of thinking. To really see people, unvarnished and stripped of your own prejudices, you needed to "love unselfishly," as Hurston wrote in the manuscript she was working on, and to "[fondle] hatred with the red-hot tongs of Hell."

She titled her memoir *Dust Tracks on a Road*. By 1942, however, when it finally appeared, her editor had chopped up the original text beyond recognition. Her deep criticisms of European colonialism were deemed too controversial. Her habit of pointing out the contradiction between Americans' support for national liberation abroad and government-supported racism at home was felt to be ill timed.

The United States was now at war, and Hurston found that it was harder than ever for people to live in the way that seemed most natural to her. She had named one of the excised chapters "Seeing the World As It Is."

Chapter Thirteen

WAR AND NONSENSE

....

When Boas retired from formal teaching in 1936, Benedict was ready to assume his role. No one was better prepared to lead the country's most highly regarded department of anthropology, with its alumni seeding most other major universities. She had spent her entire career under Boas's tutelage, first as a teaching assistant, then as a junior professor. "I am to be acting head of the department next year," Benedict wrote excitedly to Reo Fortune, who had been bouncing from appointment to appointment, finally landing a professorship in Guangzhou, China.

But there was one obstacle in the way, she said. "Being a woman is a big liability when it comes to getting official status at Columbia." When the university authorities finally decided on a new chair, the job went to a scholar from outside the department named Ralph Linton. He was the same Linton who, close to twenty years earlier, had withdrawn from Columbia's doctoral program and moved to Harvard. There could be no clearer sign that changes were in store.

Linton was certainly qualified for this new position. In his most recent academic job, at the University of Wisconsin, he had risen quickly through the professorial ranks. He was a recognized authority on indigenous societies from Madagascar to the Marquesas. At Wisconsin he had created a model for what good anthropology instruction should be: a way of weaning students from the certainty that their own cultural obsessions are universal. His introductory textbook, *The*

Study of Man (1936), would soon be sold in great stacks from campus bookstores.

But Linton had always been wary of the Boas circle. He felt that Boas's students—the women in particular—were mainly popularizers, shepherded by an antiquarian story collector rather than a real scientist. That opinion may have been precisely the thing that recommended Linton to Nicholas Murray Butler, then still Columbia's president. Butler had long seen the anthropology faculty as a haven for misfits and dissenters, the inconstantly patriotic, perhaps even the occasional Bolshevik. It was time for renewal. The university would at last be able to loosen Boas's cultish hold on the department.

After Linton's arrival, graduate students divided into "his" and "hers," some siding with Linton, others with Benedict. Boas was allowed to retain an office—a borrowed one—but was required to submit detailed memos justifying any secretarial expenses. Funds for his research had to be raised mainly from private donations that Benedict managed to pull together. "I'll have to get accustomed to the idea that the days of my usefulness are over," he told his old benefactor Elsie Clews Parsons.

In fact, he was about to embark on the greatest battle of his career. Every sham idea he had spent decades pulling apart in his adopted home was now congealing into state-sanctioned dogma in his old homeland. Although his immediate family was either safely in the United States or, like his parents Meier and Sophie, long deceased, Boas would soon face a shocking realization. German and Jewish, a disfigured immigrant surrounded by Negroes, primitives, women who loved other women, and still more Jews, he and those closest to him, had they been in Germany, would have been prime candidates for imprisonment or death.

Yet as Boas knew, there was an equally frightening fact about the country that had given him so much since his first visit in 1884. The ideology that would have sealed his own fate as a Jew, an immigrant, and a dissident intellectual—Nazism—rested on a set of pseudoscientific foundations that had a decidedly American stamp.

FOR YEARS BOAS HAD made almost annual summer visits to Europe, and he watched events on the continent with growing sadness. In Germany, Nazi thugs had wended their way into the institutions of the state, street brawlers and faux intellectuals becoming, seemingly overnight, a new political elite. In the spring of 1933, Boas wrote an open letter to President Paul von Hindenburg, begging him to prevent Adolf Hitler from creating a one-party dictatorship. He dashed off an essay on "Aryans and Non-Aryans" that picked apart Nazi fanaticism and bad science; translated into German, it was circulated widely in the anti-Nazi underground. He used every newspaper interview and conference speech to denounce Hitler and his policies. Once the Nazis were fully in power, there were immediate repercussions. The university authorities in Kiel rescinded Boas's doctorate. His books were pulled from German libraries, tossed on top of volumes by Marx, Freud, and other Jewish thinkers, and burned.

Soon letters began pouring into the anthropology department from German colleagues seeking a visiting professorship or any other route of escape. Boas would occasionally turn up unannounced at Mead's office at the museum, hoping that she or other colleagues might have a lead on how to help "his dispossessed Jews," as Mead called them. Along with Benedict and other university faculty across the country, Boas soon established the Committee for Democracy and Intellectual Freedom. Its aim was to combat racism, defend freedom of expression, and help find homes for the displaced academics whose institutions had been swamped by Nazism and its imitators in Italy and other countries.

In a series of national broadcasts on WNYC radio, Boas warned that the language of science was double-edged. It could be used to foster a sense of common humanity or to buttress dangerous doctrines of essential difference. "Intellectual freedom in many European countries has been destroyed by intolerance and political oppression," he said over the microphone, with his throaty German r's and muddled diction. But it had to be defended at home as well through what he called a campaign "to make our schools fortresses for democracy." His name soon appeared on the letterheads of special interest organizations, democracy promotion groups, and refugee assistance committees. He mobilized networks of friends and colleagues to do something, anything, to help people fleeing persecution abroad—as well as to stand up for liberal values at home. Manifestos against lynching, against the government's hounding of professors for alleged sedition, and against the removal of "immoral" literature from schools arrived in mailboxes across the country with his personal cover letter asking colleagues to sign and pass on to other friends.

As Boas saw it, the rising tide of intolerance wasn't in any sense unique to Hitler's Germany. At the time, any right-thinking American took many of the basic ideas the Nazis espoused as natural and well proven, even if they weren't accompanied by a swastika. The Germans had spent the 1930s not so much inventing a race-obsessed state as catching up with one. Most of the United States, not just the old Confederate South, had some form of mandatory segregation by race in schools, public offices, theaters, swimming pools, cemeteries, and public transportation. Most had prohibitions on marriage between racial categories or treated mixed-race couples as having committed a crime. Most used forced sterilization as a tool of eugenic betterment or a form of punishment for the incarcerated. In every jurisdiction, male homosexual behavior was against the law.

Paramilitary groups such as the Ku Klux Klan, often the de facto partners of local governments from Anaheim, California, to Dayton, Ohio, used public marches, arson, and murder to intimidate minority communities. America's domestic surveillance agency, the FBI, kept detailed records on academics, artists, writers, and journalists perceived as potentially disloyal, especially if they also happened to be black or Jewish. The country's immigration laws had been explicitly designed to increase the percentage of the population accounted for by people the Nazis called Aryans. On several occasions over the course of the 1930s, anyone walking past Madison Square Garden in New York would have bumped into a crowd of thousands of brownshirts filing into the arena and chanting slogans in support of "one hundred percent Americanism," once beneath a three-story portrait of George Washington. Some Americans had taken to using shorthand acronyms—such as MIAFA, for "My interests are for America"—to signal their support for the values advanced by the Klan and other self-defined patriotic organizations. And until the early 1940s, it was even common for American schoolchildren to begin their day the same way Germans did: with a mandatory stiff-armed salute pointed toward their flag. (The "Bellamy salute," as it was known, was the version recommended by the author of the Pledge of Allegiance, Francis J. Bellamy.)

Nazi jurists and policy makers examined in detail what they understood as America's nationwide race-ocracy, at the time the most far-reaching system of racial awareness and disenfranchisement practiced by any major power. Adolf Hitler himself had praised the American system in *Mein Kampf*. The country's commitment to racial betterment, its extermination policy against the primitive Indians, its attention to blocking race-alien immigrants from despoiling the nation, and its restrictions on mixed-race marriages, Hitler suggested, had all ensured that the Aryan settler would become master of North America: "He will remain the master as long as he does not fall a victim to the defilement of the blood." Hitler even kept a translation of Grant's *Passing of the Great Race*, bound in screaming yellow buckram, in his personal library. (It survived the war and is now housed in the rare books collection of the Library of Congress.)

For years German specialists had studied the theories of Grant and his successors, pored over the reports of the Eugenics Record Office, and attended the eugenics congresses hosted by the American Museum of Natural History. Heinrich Krieger, one of the major legal theorists whose writings shaped Nazi policy, had gained expertise in American race law as an exchange student at the University of Arkansas. In turn, German universities awarded honorary degrees to some of America's foremost eugenicists, including Henry Fairfield Osborn, president of the natural history museum and one of Boas's old detractors. In their journals and newspapers, Nazis cataloged the many ways that the United States used property requirements, poll taxes, literacy tests, election-day violence, and gerrymandered districts to shape national political institutions. "In most of the Southern states of the Union white children and colored children are sent to different schools following statutory regulations. Most Americans further demand that race be given in birth certificates, marriage licenses, and death certificates," reported a German scholar in the *National Socialist Handbook for Law and Legislation*, published in 1934. "Many American states even go so far as to require by statute segregated facilities for coloreds and whites in waiting rooms, train cars, sleeping cars, buses, steamboats, and even in prisons and jails." As these observers saw things, all Americans were born in a race, registered their children in a race, and died in a race—all meticulously superintended by federal, state, and local institutions from the Census Bureau to the neighborhood school. Long before American universities created "area studies" programs to help students develop expertise on foreign nations, the Germans were working diligently to understand how the United States had gotten racism so right.

In 1935, when the Nazi government passed its own race legislation, the so-called Nuremberg Laws, the new statutes rested on years of careful study of the "U.S. model," as Nazi officials called it. The difference, of course, was that Jews replaced African Americans as the object of fear. The Jewish race was defined as the product of a biological, inherited essence passed down from parent to child: pure Jews with three or four Jewish grandparents; *Mischlinge*, or mixed persons, with one or two; pure Aryans with none. (Nazi theorists had worried that the American version of race identification—the "one-drop rule," where any amount of traceable African ancestry was enough to categorize a person as Negro—would be unworkably radical if applied to Jews.) Marriages and sexual relationships across these lines were declared illegal. Citizenship was recast as the privilege of the *Deutschblütiger*, or people of "German blood," and their Nordic cousins. Repeat criminals, the mentally ill, the disabled, and homosexuals were the subjects of further laws that mandated imprisonment or sterilization for the unfit, or as German medical researchers called them, *Lebensunwertes Leben*—the lives unworthy of life. After all, as Rudolf

Hess, the Nazi Party's deputy leader, reportedly claimed, "National Socialism is nothing but applied biology." A new German translation of Henry H. Goddard's 1912 study, *The Kallikak Family*, which had helped launch the American eugenics movement, was praised in Nazi publications as pioneering research that justified Germany's new law on the eradication of feeblemindedness.

A German anthropologist had recently published work alleging that Jews had a definite and repulsive body odor, Mead wrote to Bateson the summer before the Nuremberg Laws came into force. "This is one of the bulwarks of race prejudice in this country," she said, referring to similar claims that white Americans made about Negroes. The logic that tied some alleged difference to a sense of repulsion seemed to work "so automatically once race prejudice gets started." In the United States, the Census Bureau had long deployed English equivalents of the German *Mischlinge:* the terms *mulatto* and *quadroon*, labels for people declared one-half or one-quarter black. These terms had appeared off and on in U.S. censuses but were finally dropped only in the 1930 count, when white government officials reshuffled African Americans into a single category for anyone possessing what was routinely called "Negro blood."

A few years later, at a conference in Paris, Boas saw firsthand what these ideas looked like in both their American and their German versions. In 1937, he watched as a representative of the American Eugenics Society told the assembled scientists and public policy experts of the advances being made back home. "It will be a fortunate nation which first discovers and makes effective those social conditions favorable to a high proportion of births among its ablest citizens," said Frederick Osborn, one of the society's founders. Osborn was followed by a string of Germans who argued along similar lines, their prepared papers addressing topics ranging from the detection of inherent defects in embryos to the susceptibility of particular races to psychosis.

When it came time for Boas to deliver his own paper, he concluded with a simple denunciation of most of what he had heard. "Our consideration of both the anatomical form and the functions of the body, including mental and social activities," he said, "[does] not give any support to the view that the habits of life and cultural activities are to any considerable extent determined by racial descent." The idea that anything at all, positive or negative, was inherent in a specific " 'race' "—he had started to put even the word itself in scare quotes—"is at best a poetic and dangerous fiction." If your basic definition of the nation-state was a place of, by, and for only one kind of community, you had already taken a step in the wrong direction. Once you latched on to the idea that your group or your way of life was bound to a piece of real estate by history and national destiny, no supply of free elections could change the outcome. The result was a world in which every society reduced itself to one people, one country, even one leader—each expressing its particular national will, wall-bound and suspicious.

It was one of the last major scientific congresses Boas would be able to attend. By the time war broke out in September 1939, he was already three years into his official retirement. He had grown thin and hollow-cheeked, with wisps of hair sticking up at all angles. For more than a year, he told Benedict, he had felt impossibly weak, with a racing heartbeat and shortness of breath. But in his writing and public lectures, he was still fiery and truculent. If American leaders easily recognized Germany's racism for the abhorrent ideology it was, he felt, that was in large part because the people being excluded, expelled, or imprisoned looked a great deal like them. In those moments, it was especially important to see yourself as part of the problem. You needed to understand the ways your own behavior mirrored the awfulness you saw in others. If you looked at American school curricula and geography textbooks, he told the *Baltimore Sun*, you would find a version of race theory akin to the very thing that the Nazis were teaching German schoolchildren. Both systems buttressed their prejudices with bad science. It was just that the local version assigned African Americans to the role that Nazis reserved for Jews.

The only unassailable moral positions, Boas believed, were those grounded in data. In the two decades since the First World War, German researchers had won more Nobel Prizes than those of any other nation. Now the country's scientists, like many of their American counterparts, put theory before observation. There was no evidence to support the claim that some groups of people were naturally inferior—less intelligent, less beautiful, less capable of world-altering achievements. But if your alleged science told you there were, what was left to keep you from segregating, oppressing, or even destroying them?

The discovery that human communities make mental boxes—dead people, living people, and zombies, as Hurston put it—is an important insight, Boas acknowledged. But the fact that we engage in this behavior in so many different ways means that we shouldn't take any society's categories, not even our own, as the only serviceable ones. The carving off of human beings into discrete classes is the product of our own imagining, not something derived from the laws of nature. And that division is dangerous. The belief in natural hierarchies implies a belief in dominance, whether it took the form of the "pitying smile" Boas had talked about in *The Mind of Primitive Man* or of the overbearing, cleansing state then rising in Germany. The strongest moral schemas rest on the proven truth that humanity is one undivided whole.

Boas found it perfectly compatible to believe both in cultural relativism and in democracy and representative government. Science pointed toward the progressive widening of the circle of people to whom we owed moral behavior, however we defined it, and liberal democracy was the best way of assuring that the circle would at least expand as far as your own country's frontiers. The next step was to figure out how to extend it to the entire planet. The United States held no particular expertise in these matters, Boas believed. He had seen how quickly America's open doors could close, especially in a time of war or fear, as had happened during the First World War and with the anti-immigration policies that followed. When your government placed a premium on loyalty and stoked the belief that your own society was providential and pure, it was all the more important to proclaim your allegiance to a set of principles, not to a flag or an anthem.

The first of the Nuremberg Laws, after all, declared the swastika to be the symbol of Germanness itself—the sacred emblem of an ethnic *Volk*—not just of the German state. The Kwakiutl and Samoans had their totems, too, but neither one had yet tied them to the institutions of a state, cloaked them in science, and imprisoned or killed those who dared offend them. It took one of the modern world's greatest civilizations to manage that.

As the conflict in Europe deepened—the autumn invasion of Poland, a long spring of hoping for peace, then the lightning attack on France and the Low Countries—neither Boas nor anyone else could have predicted the horrors that would eventually flow from Germany's nationalist passions. If the future was hard to see, though, it was because so much of it had already arrived. The mania for racial separateness, the treatment of immigrants as undesirable and potentially criminal, the drive to eliminate the unhygienic and inferior, the application of rickety science to the improvement of society—the Nazi version of these ideas was an extension of beliefs and practices already well established in the United States and other advanced countries. German refugees had a word for the preoccupation with communal purity and the state-sanctioned separation of peoples: *Rassenwahn*—"race madness." It was a word that Boas felt applied equally well on both sides of the Atlantic. "I will try to clean up some of the nonsense that is being spread about race these days," he said in his farewell address at Columbia. "Here also people are going crazy."

WHILE BOAS WAS PLAYING host to itinerant scientists and refugee academics, the lives of Mead and Benedict were changing in profound ways. Stanley, still legally Benedict's husband although the two had been separated for the better part of a decade, died of a heart attack in late 1936. Sapir died less than three years later, in early 1939, also felled by a long-standing heart ailment. Benedict wrote the official obituary for the *American Anthropologist*. She described him as both "brilliant" and "challenging," in a kind of private code that spoke volumes about a history that only she, Mead, and Sapir really knew. The true cause of his death, Mead later speculated, was "corroding resentment."

Mead's relationship with Sapir had unraveled in part over the issues of family and career. She was never going to become the kind of wife and mother that he demanded. Not long after she returned from Samoa, a physician had told her that she would never bear children. Now it was hard to ignore the eerie timing of departures and arrivals. In their final months in Bali, she and Bateson had been trying for a baby. Miscarriages received a matter-of-fact mark on the calendar. "I shall work very moderately at home and mainly be constructively lazy and eat Vitamin E," she told her mother-in-law after suffering yet another one. Once back in New York and ensconced in her attic office, she learned that she was pregnant again. "England declares war," she noted in her datebook on September 2, 1939, and then four days later: "*Saw* baby move for first time." That December, attended by a young pediatrician named Benjamin Spock, she carried to term. The new parents called their daughter Mary Catherine—an imperious, jolly, testy child, as Mead described her, and "not overfond of being held."

Family and the advent of war made fieldwork on the old model impossible. But as the months passed, Mead, Bateson, and Benedict all began to imagine a way of continuing their work without traipsing back to remote and dangerous postings. Benedict had been thinking more and more about her own society and its deficits, especially its embrace of racism. "The slogan of 'science' will sell most things today," she lamented in a succinct, accessible book, *Race: Science and Politics*, which appeared in 1940, "and it sells persecution as easily as it sells rouge." But what about other modern societies? Might an anthropologist be able to reveal their codes at a distance—to "crack" a culture, as Bateson put it—by observing some of the taken-for-granted ideas contained in its art, newspapers, films, and novels?

Just before the war, Bateson had tried out something along those lines, although in a premodern setting. In *Naven* (1936) he had built up an account of a people's self-understanding—in this case that of the Iatmul of New Guinea—by analyzing one of its central rituals (which gave the book its title). He saw the entire complexity of middle Sepik society laid out in a popular carnival that upended established roles of rank and gender through costume and dance. What a society made and did, if viewed anthropologically, might be a key to figuring out how individuals in that society thought. At the time, many other anthropologists, sociologists, and psychologists were already at work on what was coming to be called the "culture and personality" approach in the social sciences. Psychoanalysis, long-term fieldwork, experimental psychology, and standardized testing, it was thought, might together help map out how a specific society and its inhabitants understood reality. One might read up from individual behavior to arrive at conclusions about the dominant traits of a society as a whole, or down from society to the habits and proclivities of individuals.

As the war intensified, the need to understand both the battlefield and the home front gave culture cracking new urgency. Boas had always insisted that good scholarship should reach beyond the ivory tower, while avoiding being slavishly tied to the interests of government. Now for Boas's intellectual children and grandchildren, the stakes were high: the enemy was a set of powers—Germany, Japan, and their allies—that believed themselves to be naturally fitter and better than the nations that surrounded them. If you could uncover how average German citizens really thought and behaved—quite apart from the racist and nationalist myths that their leaders were foisting on them—you might be able to shape propaganda and military strategy so that they aimed at the right targets. The same approach might work at home as well. What were the main social divisions or sources of discontent? Were people likely to be supportive of a costly entanglement overseas? Would democracy and truth remain compatible with security in a time of global disorder?

Bateson and Mead soon went into action. They joined an advisory group to President Franklin D. Roosevelt, the Committee for National Morale, a cohort of leading researchers that included pollster George Gallup and psychologist Erich Fromm, all committed to using social science to combat Nazi misinformation. Mead's office at the museum became the new headquarters of the Council (later Institute) on Intercultural Relations, a body she established to administer research grants, organize her burgeoning pile of papers and field notes, corral her research assistants, and give Bateson—still with no permanent academic job—a business card. Through connections of Benedict's, she managed to secure a paid position with the Committee on Food Habits, a unit of the National Research Council tasked with studying food availability and distribution in the United States. What was more closely tied to a society's sense of itself than what it consumed? She would have to take yet another leave of absence from the museum and move to Washington, at least part-time, but it would be a chance to put into practice many of the ideas she had been working through for years—something she was already calling "applied anthropology." She learned of her formal appointment on December 7, 1941.

Mead arrived in Washington to find it crawling with social scientists. Perhaps half of all people who claimed the label of anthropologist—many of them schooled by Sapir, Lowie, Kroeber, and, of course, Boas—were employed in full-time government work. Their cultural knowledge and linguistic skills proved useful in nearly every executive branch agency. Their familiarity with foreign terrain fed the machinery of cartographers and descriptive geographers busy producing maps and manuals on every theater of war. The next summer Mead produced another book, *And Keep Your Powder Dry*, a breezy attempt to "crack" her own society. American life, she concluded, stressed success and movement, a quickness to violence, a particular obsession with virtue and sin, the urgency of the present over the past, and a real ambivalence about the value of other cultures. The book sold briskly, and Mead was featured in a new wave of magazine articles and on lists of outstanding women of our time.

For Mead, the routine of life now involved committee meetings, office visits, reports on Americans' nutritional habits, and regular trips between New York and Washington. Her two homes—a Greenwich Village town house where Bateson looked after Mary Catherine with the help of a nanny and family friends, and a residence near Washington's Dupont Circle—became grand experiments in communal liv ing and culture cracking. Famous social scientists might drop in for a visit. Bateson's two teenage goddaughters were sent over from Britain to escape the war. Mead made plans for a documentary on the concept of childhood trust, taking notes as Mary Catherine launched herself down hills in Central Park. It was perhaps as close as she had come since Samoa to realizing her ideal of a natural family arrangement: many-sided, geographically fluid, and at times chaotic, with children running through the house and threatening to upend a table of ethnographic photographs or index cards. She called it a "joint household organized for wartime."

BY THE TIME THE United States entered the Second World War, Boas was in his mid-eighties and in failing health. Invitations to serve on boards or to chair worthy causes had to be rejected. Letters on every subject continued to pour in, and he did his best to answer them. "I have just learned that according to the Bible Adam was the first man," wrote Leon J. Fish, seven and a half years old, of Cincinnati, Ohio. "If he was white I cannot imagine how there are colored people, and yellow, and brown people to-day." "My dear Leon," Boas wrote back with a hint of exhaustion. "We do not think that the Bible story must be taken to be real history."

He had lived long enough, by the first months of 1942, to see scientific racism fully triumph in his country of birth. Fascist governments of one form or another controlled most of Europe. Nazi killing squads had shot hundreds of thousands of Jews over ravines in the occupied Soviet Union. Many more would be gassed at new, purpose-built death facilities—places such as Belzec, Treblinka, and Auschwitz-Birkenau—which had been set up in subjugated Poland. That December the Allied powers finally issued a joint statement acknowledging that the Germans were "now carrying into effect Hitler's oft-repeated intention to exterminate the Jews of Europe."

A few days later, on December 21, a Monday, Boas gathered with a dozen or so colleagues at the Columbia Faculty Club. The occasion was a luncheon in honor of Paul Rivet, the distinguished founder of the Musée de l'homme, France's premier ethnographic museum. Ousted from his post by the German occupation of Paris, Rivet was one of the displaced academics Boas had been trying to help.

Boas was eager to catch up. He had recently read that German scientists were admitting how hard it was to find real data to support their theories of absolute physical differences among racial types. That was good news. "We should never stop repeating the idea that racism is a monstrous error and an impudent lie," he said to Rivet.

Just then Boas rose slightly and fell back in his chair, silent but for a low gurgling noise.

Attendees upset plates and glasses to rush to his side. One young French visitor, Claude Lévi-Strauss, would later claim to have been near at hand as Boas's breath became shallower and shallower—a mystical passing of the torch to the person who would later become one of France's foremost anthropologists and public intellectuals. But Lévi-Strauss did not know Boas well, and in any case the scene was probably chaotic, with people loosening Boas's tie, shouting in French and English, or running to call an ambulance. Within minutes, his heart had stopped.

News of Boas's death whirred around the world by telephone and telegraph. Newspapers carried prominent obituaries, many reflecting on the fact that Boas had gone away just when the planet was most in need of him. "He believed the world must be made safe for differences," Benedict wrote in *The Nation*. Letters of condolence flooded into the anthropology department, most addressed to Benedict, in the role of his professional next of kin. Other correspondence piled up unanswered—about unfinished manuscripts, research projects in train, homages and memorials being planned by groups around the globe. A Baltimore shipyard wrote in with the news that it had decided to christen one of a new class of cargo vessels being built for the war effort, a Liberty ship, the *Franz Boas*. "It would have pleased him," Benedict replied.

At Columbia, Boas's passing was keenly felt. Whatever protection his presence might have afforded Benedict and her graduate students was now gone. She was an associate professor, promoted to that rank in

1937, but still earned less than any other tenured faculty member. The department was effectively Linton's as chair. He loathed Benedict, and she returned the sentiment. Every rivalry in the profession seemed to play out along the hallway: Harvard versus Columbia; the men who held the professorial chairs versus the women who were given the research assistantships (or nothing at all); the anthropologist as confident gourmand, lapping up cultures and spitting out grand theories, versus the careful assembler of data from the field. Linton's supporters remembered him as, at the very least, "touchy." Benedict found him "a swine." She was probably a communist, Linton suggested, and misused research funds to assist her own doctoral students.

Among the wider public, Benedict was becoming something of a lightning rod, especially when it came to matters of race. Along with a younger lecturer in the department, Gene Weltfish, she had condensed some of her earlier writing on the subject into a short tract, *The Races of Mankind*, published in 1943. The pocket-size publication was a full-on attack on common misconceptions. "Some people have shouted that if we got into our veins the blood of someone with a different head shape, eye color, hair texture, or skin color, we should get some of that person's physical and mental characteristics," she and Weltfish wrote. "Modern science has revealed this to be pure superstition."

The response was massive and unexpected. Hate mail oozed into her departmental postbox. "The negro may be the equal of the Jews but not the whites," said one reader from Palm Beach. "They have always been slaves from the time of the Romans. I am sure the Jews there in New York paid you to put out this foolish report because they want social equality." The U.S. Army abandoned a plan to use it as an anti-Nazi morale booster. The USO ruled it subversive and incendiary. The pamphlet's message was well and good when it came to Jews, a Kentucky congressman insisted, but the idea that black and white Americans showed no race-specific intellectual differences was "Communistic propaganda." The FBI dispatched interviewers to check up on the Columbia department.

The public controversy spurred sales. Churches and civic groups would eventually place orders for as many as three-quarters of a million copies of *The Races of Mankind*, which became one of the most widely distributed texts on the subject of its time. Still, the poison-pen letters continued. "You are no better than the blackest one we have down here and I suspect stink a lot worse," wrote "a citizen of Mississippi." "The idea of getting up such a mess in these critical times. You should have been putting all your time to the war effort instead."

Benedict agreed with the recommendation, if not the reason for it. In the fall of 1943, she took the train south to join Mead in Washington.

IN THE BUZZING CAPITAL city, it was not hard to find something to do. Benedict quickly signed on with a government outfit called the Office of War Information, or OWI, established a little over a year earlier. Inside the country, its mission was to provide a clearinghouse for truthful information on the progress of the war. It liaised with journalists but also produced its own film, radio, and print campaigns on everything from life in enemy nations to morale on the home front. Its overseas branch focused on countering German, Italian, and Japanese misinformation and shifting public opinion abroad in favor of the Allies. Many of the classic black-and-white newsreels of the era, both those that evoked the chaos of battle and ones that offered warm reminders of the America that soldiers were meant to be fighting for, were produced by the writers, broadcasters, directors, and social scientists on the OWI's payroll.

Analysts in another bureau had taken on a label that might have applied just as well to Benedict's colleagues in the OWI: the "Chairborne Division." Journalists worked alongside tenured professors and advertising executives. Multilingual clerks rushed off translations. Radio technicians monitored overseas broadcasts. Reams of reports, transcripts, and recommendations for action rolled out toward strategists, diplomats, and frontline commanders. As the OWI's director, the Yale psychology professor Leonard W. Doob, remembered, when it came to analysis, "the swift and the glib" tended to win out. Benedict's role was to assemble studies of foreign societies, using some of the sensibilities she had developed as an anthropologist to characterize places she had never visited and whose languages she didn't know— the ultimate version of culture cracking at a distance, as Bateson and Mead had earlier imagined it. As soon as an OWI officer was given a new assignment, a team of assistants fanned out to grab whatever scraps of information they could find: interviewing foreign nationals of a particular country, talking to people who had recently been there, reading works of literature in translation, picking through whatever artifacts might be found in the Smithsonian. Lives depended on how well people understood the places they were being asked to bomb, liberate, and patrol.

In June 1944 Benedict's bosses shifted her work toward a detailed analysis of Japan. The war was entering a decisive new phase. The Allies were pointing their full force toward Germany, attacking from the west in Operation Overlord and from the east in the Soviet Union's Operation Bagration. In the Pacific, U.S. long-range bombers targeted the Japanese mainland for the first time in two years. Allied carrier groups were making inroads from New Guinea to Guam. Places that Benedict knew mainly from Mead's fieldwork letters were now battlefields or forward operating bases across the South Pacific.

She stacked up whatever information she could gather. Other colleagues drafted memos on Japanese history. John Embree, a Chicago-trained anthropologist and OWI analyst, had written an important book on Japanese village life, *Suye Mura,* published just as the war began. Geoffrey Gorer, a worldly, magnetic British anthropologist and close friend of Mead's, contributed psychoanalytic readings of Japanese culture, some of them too wildly speculative for Benedict's tastes. Then there were films, novels, plays, transcripts of radio broadcasts, travel guides, history books, recollections of missionaries, memoirs, stacks of haiku and riddles, accounts of Zen Buddhism—anything that might shed light on Japanese society.

The assignment was more complicated than anything Benedict had tried before, but that was in large part because of the iron wall of assumptions that encircled her own country's understanding of Japan and the Japanese. The standard view in the U.S. government, from the Department of War to the OWI itself, was that the conflict in the Pacific was essentially different from the one in the European theater. Germany was a normal, civilized society that had been overtaken by a devilish ideology and a barbaric dictator. Average Germans were, in their way, victims, good people who had either been duped or subjugated by a political elite bent on expansion and conquest. The war against the Japanese, by contrast, was nothing less than a struggle for racial dominance. "In Europe we felt that our enemies, horrible and deadly as they were, were still people," reported the celebrated journalist Ernie Pyle after his transfer to the Pacific. "But out here I soon gathered that the Japanese were [seen by American soldiers] as something subhuman and repulsive; the way some people feel about cockroaches or mice." If the war in Europe was about soil, the one in the Pacific was about blood.

American films, posters, novels, and newspapers routinely portrayed the Japanese as sneaky, treacherous Asians, untrustworthy in their essence and given to a militant, fanatical allegiance to kith and kin. Shortly after Pearl Harbor, *Life* magazine published a guide with the headline HOW TO TELL JAPS FROM THE CHINESE. Marked-up photographs detailed the physical clues you could use to distinguish a Tokyo saboteur from a Peking businessman: height, nose shape, eye contour, skin tone. Admiral William Halsey Jr., one of the major fleet commanders in the Pacific, regularly referred to the enemy in public statements as "monkeymen" and "yellow bastards." "The Japanese were a product of mating between female apes and the worst Chinese criminals who had been banished from China," he once explained at a news conference—rather complicating the how-to guide provided by *Life*.

For Benedict and other social scientists in the OWI, those views were not only blatantly wrongheaded but also counterproductive. Any racist statement by an American official was publicized in Japanese media as a way of inciting fear and bolstering the other side's commitment to victory. Japanese fighting morale could be as changeable as that of any other belligerent power, OWI analysts believed; there was no reason to think that the Japanese would fight to the end, or that average citizens were blinkered by an undying loyalty to the government in power. OWI analysts began to look ahead, toward an eventual end to the war and what might be done in the event of a massive Allied landing in Japan or a long-term occupation of the islands. Whatever traits Washington might have attributed to the Japanese emperor—in American eyes, a symbol of uncompromising war aims and culturally ingrained militarism—he was not viewed the same way by the Japanese themselves. Ending the war well depended on educating American policy makers and the public at large about a people they profoundly misunderstood.

Anthropology required many of the skills of military command: impeccable organization, a sense of intrepidness, the ability to intuit more than was visible with the naked eye. You had to be able to look out on the dip and draw of a battlefield—a regimental pennant here, a line of caps bobbing there on the far side of an embankment, calm and chaos—and then imagine all of it on a flat plane. Three dimensions deflated to two, symbols standing in for proper nouns. Messy reality solidified into neat abstraction, ordering itself into an intelligible description of a time, place, and situation, using terms and shorthand that could travel easily across the globe. A complex kinship system could be represented by a flowchart: triangles for men, circles for women, equal signs for reproducing pairs. A whole culture, in theory, could be mapped out as a set of core propensities, obsessions, and dispositions. It was all a way of trying to say in brief what made people's behavior here different from their behavior over there—not scary, benighted, or illogical, just different.

Benedict had done all this before—that technique had produced some of her key insights in *Patterns of Culture*. But among the gray desks and steel filing cabinets of the OWI, she was out of her depth. She was surrounded by old Japan hands who knew the language and, in some cases, had published important work on the country before the war. Still, as she worked her way through piles of reports and primary documents, she had at her disposal a secret weapon: someone who would become her essential partner in figuring out the enemy. He was, at least according to the U.S. government, an enemy himself.

———

TWO YEARS EARLIER, in 1942, hundreds of families had rolled off crowded buses at a stop northeast of Los Angeles. They pulled down bundles of clothes, cooking utensils, and carefully tended envelopes containing mortgage papers and bank statements. The San Gabriel Mountains rose, hazy and snowcapped, in the distance. On the valley floor nearby, art deco grandstands, painted in Persian green and yellow chiffon, led down to a circular racetrack. Peeking out from the top of the bleachers were the barrels of two machine guns.

Many of the passengers would easily have recognized where they were, even without noticing the sign for Santa Anita. Photographs of the place had been in all the newspapers. Not long before, a gangly, injured racehorse named Seabiscuit had craned toward the finish line on the same track, winning a gigantic purse and confirming Americans' belief in the underdog. Now thousands of Japanese American families were ushered past a barbed-wire barrier, through cordons of armed soldiers peering down from watchtowers, and toward the horse barn, which had been outfitted with cots.

On February 19, President Roosevelt had issued Executive Order 9066, which empowered the U.S. military to designate zones of the country from which anyone could be removed for reasons of national security. The next month military commanders along the West Coast ordered the "mandatory evacuation," in the language of the time, of Japanese citizens and people of Japanese ancestry. Their destination was a network of purpose-built camps located farther to the east, with places like Santa Anita serving as assembly points along the way.

"In the war in which we are now engaged racial affinities are not severed by migration," reported Lieutenant General John L. Dewitt, in charge of the removals, to Secretary of War Henry L. Stimson. "The Japanese race is an enemy race and while many second and third generation Japanese born on United States soil, possessed of United States citizenship, have become 'Americanized,' the racial strains are undiluted." Some of the country's most prominent figures agreed. "I think it's probable that, if Seattle ever does get bombed, you will be able to look up and see some University of Washington sweaters on the boys doing the bombing!" the journalist Edward R. Murrow told an audience. "I believe that we are being lulled into a false sense of security," agreed Earl Warren, attorney general of California, later governor, and later still U.S. Supreme Court chief justice, in testimony before Congress. "Our day of reckoning is bound to come."

A new government body, the War Relocation Authority, was organized to oversee a network of incarceration facilities for the displaced families. The Census Bureau provided the WRA with block-by-block addresses of people who had declared themselves to be Japanese on the country's race-oriented census forms. By the end of October, official figures counted 117,116 people who had been moved into temporary assembly centers or one of ten permanent camps carved out of fields and scrubland in Arizona, Colorado, Wyoming, Idaho, Utah, Arkansas, and other parts of California. The WRA, with its all-white leadership, was clear on how the system should be described. "The work areas . . . should be referred to as 'relocation centers' or 'relocation projects,' not as 'internment centers' or 'concentration camps,'" said one confidential directive. "Even the use of the word 'camp' should be avoided since it carries some implication of internment and close military surveillance." The population at Santa Anita quickly swelled to nearly nineteen thousand people before falling off as families were transported to the longer-term facilities. From the spring to the fall of 1942, 194 children were born in Seabiscuit's old stable block and in newer tarpaper barracks.

Robert Seido Hashima was in his early twenties when he arrived at Santa Anita. He had been born in Hawthorne, southwest of Los Angeles, but in 1932 his parents moved with him back to their ancestral village in southern Japan's Hiroshima Prefecture. Hashima graduated from a Japanese high school and began working at a teacher-training academy. In early 1940 he returned to California to enroll in junior college, working part-time as a field hand and hotel clerk to cover his expenses.

President Roosevelt's executive order made him subject to mandatory evacuation. He was given a number, 23146, examined by a medical officer, relieved of any straight razors or other contraband, and assigned to a bed. Since the outcome of the war was unknowable, there was no long-term plan other than to keep people like him imprisoned indefinitely. At the end of May 1942, he was transferred out of Santa Anita to Poston, a permanent camp in western Arizona. Poston was situated on a sprawling acreage in the middle of the Arizona desert. It was encircled by a barbed-wire fence, but the prospects of escape were so slim that the usual watchtowers were never constructed. Adobe buildings stood in for the wood and tarpaper barracks found in other camps. Irrigated fields provided supplements to the canned rations. That November a strike over inhumane treatment brought camp life to a standstill, with internees refusing to work and gathering in crowds before the camp's jail. Local newspapers reported that a "Jap riot" had engulfed the facility. During another strike the next month at Manzanar, a camp in central California, soldiers fired into the crowd, killing two people.

The situation at Poston was resolved peacefully, but the upsurge in tension convinced officials of how little they knew about the people they were meant to superintend. By the end of the year, each of the ten facilities had a permanent "community analyst" on staff to help devise strategies to prevent rioting and to ensure the smooth operation of factories, schools, and recreation centers. Public relations materials and government reports featured photographs of watermelon-eating contests, dungaree-clad teenagers, camp orchestras, and orderly transports by bus and train. "Great care was exercised for the comfort of the evacuees traveling from Assembly Centers to War Relocation Centers," as one summary stated. "Each train carried a Caucasian physician and two nurses." But the reports of social scientists on the ground were chronicles of shock, disbelief, and sadness. "A mass evacuation of people on the basis of Japanese ancestry . . . has created in many evacuees a sense of disillusionment or even bitterness in regard to American democracy," wrote one social scientist. "Armed guards, barbed wire fences, search-lights, visits of government agents, all engender the feeling of being in a concentration camp."

Poston soon became the centerpiece of the WRA's applied social science program. A psychiatrist and Naval Reserve officer, Alexander Leighton, gathered a battery of young non-Japanese anthropologists and sociologists, some with no more than a master's degree. Their task was to offer advice on the proper governance of a sprawling facility, none of whose inhabitants had any desire to be there. Leighton recruited inmates to administer surveys, write up field notes, and provide expert advice on everything from cultural norms to canteen food.

In the racial hierarchy of the camp system, *issei* were at the bottom: first-generation immigrants and therefore, given the 1924 race-restrictive immigration act, ineligible for citizenship. *Nisei* were U.S. citizens of Japanese ancestry, whose children were in turn *sansei*, or third-generation Japanese Americans. Those categories could determine access to better housing and medical care, and even to better day-to-day behavior from a military policeman or camp commandant. Hashima, however, was *kibei*, a natural-born American who had been educated in Japan, the very highest rank. In the chaos of 1942, with people piling bundles of belongings onto train cars, closing down their businesses, and desperately trying to find a white neighbor willing to look after a house or apartment, that label could make all the difference.

Through John Embree, one of the social scientists employed at Poston, Leighton made the acquaintance of Hashima and quickly realized the young man's potential importance beyond the fence. Hashima knew Japan and the United States from the inside and was uniquely suited to becoming a cultural interpreter. Not long afterward the camp authorities notified him that he was to be released on special assignment. He was soon on his way to Washington and a job on the staff of the OWI. That is where he got to know "a lady, who was slender and had beautiful silver hair," as he later recalled.

The two first met when Benedict appeared at his desk and asked him to translate a haiku. Over the next several months, Hashima became Benedict's sounding board. She had relied on the work of Embree and other experts and had consumed memos written by colleagues in the OWI. Hashima, though, was different. In conversations and written correspondence, "Bob," as she came to call him,

served as a private tutor on everything from the Japanese tea ceremony to the captured diaries of Japanese soldiers, from hazing rituals
in schools to popular movies. When her reports required a Japanese
term or phrase, handwritten in *kanji* characters, it was Hashima who
supplied them.

Throughout the spring and early summer of 1945, Benedict produced short research notes and memos, which she gathered into a
sixty-page classified summary on "Japanese behavior patterns," the
title echoing the book she had produced just over a decade earlier.
Then came news of the twin bombings of Hiroshima and Nagasaki.
Benedict began thinking about how to make some of her findings reach
beyond the halls of government. More than ever, the United States
needed an interpretive guidebook to the country it was preparing to
occupy. There were better and worse ways of being a victor power,
she felt, and American administrators—and average citizens—would
need to understand something about the advantages of restraint. One
society could never hope to remake another from the ground up, even
after military defeat.

On August 15, 1945, the day the Japanese emperor announced the
decision to end the war, Benedict was back on her family farm in Nor-
wich, New York. She wrote immediately to Hashima. She had cried
when she heard that the emperor was going to deliver the news over
the radio. "I wish I knew how to say to Japan that no Western nation
has ever shown such dignity and virtue in defeat and that history will
honor her for the way she ended the war." When she got back from
her summer holiday, she wrote, "You'll have to help me say it."

In the following months, she worked with her old publisher to
think through the different titles that a book-length study might take.
She already had the material, culled from her OWI report. She now
needed a way of packaging it. Titles such as *We and the Japanese* and
Japanese Character all fell to an editor's pencil, as did *The Enameled
Rod*. They finally settled on something that was both poetic and sug-
gestive, *The Chrysanthemum and the Sword*. "It embarrasses me,"
Benedict confided to Mead, but she was consoled by the fact that a
more sober subtitle, "Patterns of Japanese Culture," would be used in

all the marketing. When the book was published in the fall of 1946, Benedict sent a copy to Hashima. He opened the cover to find that he was the first person thanked in the acknowledgments. By then, he had left Washington and moved to Tokyo. But he was present, in one way or another, on nearly every page.

"THE JAPANESE WERE THE most alien enemy the United States had ever fought in an all-out struggle," Benedict began. The war in the Pacific had been not just about supply lines and beachheads but also about the perceived distance between Americans and their adversary. Every interaction across societies is an act of translation, of taking foreign concepts and forcing yourself to see them as ordinary. "The anthropologist has good proof in his experience that even bizarre behavior does not prevent one's understanding it," she wrote. "More than any other social scientist he has professionally used difference as an asset rather than a liability." The place to start was by embracing your sense of being "baffled," a word that Benedict would use repeatedly in the text. Disorientation was the essential bridge between your own feeling for the commonplace and someone else's.

There was no single key to understanding everything about Japan, Benedict felt. Like all societies, Japan's was contradictory and complex, with values and behaviors that appeared alongside one another, even when they seemed deeply incompatible. That was the point of the chrysanthemum and the sword in her title: a society that had delicate, refined ideas of beauty and creative expression could also value militarism, honor, and subservience. But contradictions aside, a "human society must make for itself some design for living," she said. Culture is no more than the repeated ways we interpret our behavior and that of our extended families, our long-term neighbors, and the people we consider to be like us. It is the way otherwise random beliefs, practices, rituals, assumptions, and ways of speaking get "geared into one another."

Benedict set her aim as surveying "the habits that are expected and taken for granted in Japan." The most important of these was what the war had actually been about. Japanese political and military leaders saw the world as suffering from a deep anarchy, stoked by Europeans and North Americans. What was required was the restoration of order, a new international hierarchy, with Japan playing the dominant role among Asian states. Americans should find such an idea rather familiar. It was no more than a translated version of the racial dominance that had animated American foreign policy from Theodore Roosevelt forward, the fitter, whiter races imposing their will on the lesser and darker. But in Japan, this sense of hierarchy was also repeated at home. Each individual had a clear, ranked place within a community or household. Succeeding in life meant being acutely aware of your place in a grander scheme, sticking to it, and doing it well. "Taking one's proper station" was the essence of relationships between people, between people and the state, and between the Japanese state and foreign countries.

Hierarchical relationships also entailed a complex system of duty and obligation, a sense of indebtedness expressed in the Japanese concept of *on*. For Benedict, *on* was a kind of burden that one bore in virtually any social interaction. It was contained in the responsibility one owed to a social superior, such as a financial creditor. It was the mutual devotion that spouses owed to each other. But *on* was always laced with a reciprocal sense of shame, Benedict said. It was the debt that could never be fully repaid, which in turn kept everyone in a state of mutual anxiety at the inadequacy of their responses. Hierarchy, honor, shame, the burden of indebtedness—for Benedict, these were not so much the secrets to "cracking" Japanese society as they were ideas that made one fluent in being Japanese—that is, in being the kind of person who could make one's way comfortably in Japanese society.

Societies that privilege the idea of guilt typically speak in terms of absolute moralities. They see an ethical life as one in which an individual struggles between the poles of good and evil. They have concepts such as transgression, unlawfulness, sin, and confession. Their rituals strive for expiation—the desire to expunge an act that has contravened an explicit code of conduct. Societies that privilege shame, on the other hand, see things differently. Bad actions are not those that step over an explicit line but rather those that are inappropriate, unseemly, or out of keeping with a given circumstance. Unlike guilt, shame is hard to relieve. No confession can mitigate it, no atonement can lessen it. A sense of shame is always the product of how others see your actions, which means that you are always on guard: it is impossible to be sure *exactly* which behaviors will be shameful and which ones not. All you have are the vague clues of suitability and fittingness, as well as, in the Japanese case, the concept of *on*, the obligations you owe to an overlapping circle of people. But since your obligations may well be in conflict—Do you stay late at the office or visit your ailing mother?—virtuous behavior is always a "dilemma," as Benedict put it. Being the person you are meant to be is an eternal quest to balance deep commitments, each forever at war with the others.

For Benedict, these ideas lay at the core of the most important Japanese political institution: the emperor himself. Emperor Hirohito's personal announcement of the war's end on August 15, a little over two weeks before the signing of the unconditional surrender on board USS *Missouri,* was unparalleled and historic. It was a critical moment, but not because the emperor was a living symbol of Japanese identity. Nor did the average Japanese citizen consider him to be a god, an idea that Benedict said was a product of Western ideas of divinity more than of Japanese spirituality. Rather, it was because the emperor stood at the top of a society-wide and utterly real hierarchy. He represented the essence of balance and virtue extending all the way from family relations inside a household to the way Japanese citizens explained their national traditions to themselves.

On this point Benedict was not breaking new ground. All the Japan hands at the OWI knew the reverence in which the emperor was held. She had made the same argument years earlier in some of her research memos, including one specifically on the place of the emperor in Japanese society. The U.S. occupation forces, headed by Gen. Douglas MacArthur, had already taken the monumental step of allowing the emperor to remain in place rather than forcing his abdication. That decision probably flowed from MacArthur's own proclivities, especially his view that the emperor was of no particular importance in a society that would, in any case, soon be transformed by the example of American democracy. But what Benedict offered was an argument for why all this made sense—that is, why the United States, a country that had been brutally attacked by a foreign power, should then respond in victory with a policy that was restrained, mindful of local custom, and limited in its ambitions. *The Chrysanthemum and the Sword* was, in this way, less a manual on Japan than a primer for a specifically American audience. It was a kind of antivenom: a way of counteracting the notion—inculcated in American culture since long before Pearl Harbor, then reinforced by the war and the U.S. government's internment of people because of their supposed "race," as Boas would have written the word—that the Japanese were by nature somewhere between inscrutable and awful.

Benedict acknowledged on the first page the book's debt to America's betrayal of its Japanese citizens. "Japanese men and women who had been born or educated in Japan and who were living in the United States during the war years were placed in a most difficult position," she wrote understatedly. "They were distrusted by many Americans." It gave her special pleasure, she said, to write a book that depended on taking seriously what they had to say about themselves.

In around three hundred pages, she had demonstrated the Boasian technique of turning otherness into difference—an idea that, only a year after the war, was its own kind of revelation. "Any reader of this book will have a new attitude toward Japan," wrote the Book of the Month Club to its members. For some readers, those who had lost a part of their lives behind barbed wire, the book was also a tiny bit of justice. "It's like a fog clearing," one Japanese American woman wrote to Benedict.

In the years that followed, *The Chrysanthemum and the Sword* had a good claim to being the most widely read piece of anthropology ever written. Within five years, it went through eight editions. A Japanese translation appeared in 1948. It sold in the millions. Japanese scholars disagreed with portions of Benedict's argument. She could be loose with her descriptions and generalizations, they pointed out. Her assessment of Japanese culture could sometimes look like an idealized portrait of the Japanese middle class or of its military elite, precisely the people whom Hashima and other informants knew best. But at a time when Japanese society was going through a deep reassessment of its own history and values, the book was a redemptive gift: an account by a far-off American struggling to learn something true about an old adversary.

Benedict's work was a grand monument to the promise and limitations of two societies looking squarely at each other, through a glass, darkly. Hiding there in its acknowledgments was a core irony. America's most influential book urging better treatment of an enemy country owed a great deal to people whom Americans themselves had locked up as an enemy race. Of course, it would have been even better had Benedict visited Japan and checked her findings on the ground. But she had in fact tried. Right after the war, she hoped to join General MacArthur's occupation forces, working alongside locals and foreigners in the transformation of Japanese government and society. Higher-ups denied her request. The reason was straightforward: her American bosses would not approve the transfer of a woman over the age of forty-five.

"Why didn't I transvestite when I was young?" she asked Mead.

Chapter Fourteen

HOME

....

I read with interest your publication that upset the brass-hats so, and smiled," Hurston wrote to Benedict in the summer of 1945, referring to her controversial book, *The Races of Mankind*. "Facts go down mighty hard with some folks." The Second World War was a global contest among nations, economies, and political systems, but the uncomfortable truth was that it was also a fight among intellectual siblings. As Boas had taught his students, the worldviews represented by Japanese nationalism, Nazi race-madness, and American eugenics sprang from the same source. They were all products of an intensely modern fiction: that the highway of human social development led straight to us. None of America's enemies saw themselves as opponents of American values. Not even Adolf Hitler claimed to be against freedom, justice, or prosperity. Rather, they saw themselves as better, more advanced versions of what they believed Americans had been trying to achieve. Real freedom would mean the subjugation of the racially inferior. Real justice would mean allowing the fittest individuals and countries to take their rightful place on the world stage. Real progress would mean cleansing and separating, pushing forward the able and advanced while sweeping away the primitive and retrograde.

Vanquishing an enemy wasn't the same thing as defeating a body of ideas that your own society had helped to author. For that reason, it wasn't always easy to be optimistic about the future. "The world smells like an abattoir," Hurston said gloomily. President Roosevelt had defined the United States as an "arsenal of democracy," but maybe he meant "Ass-and-All of Democracy," she wrote in the *Negro Digest*, a black version of the largely white *Reader's Digest.* "I am crazy about the idea of this Democracy," but "the only thing that keeps me from pitching headlong into the thing is the presence of the numerous Jim Crow laws on the statute books of the nation." Had the war really been about defeating one kind of tyranny in order to preserve another, from the Deep South to British-controlled India? "I will fight for my country," she declared in a passage edited out of her autobiography, "but I will not lie for her."

Hurston had jumped from houseboat to houseboat in Daytona Beach, Florida, occasionally giving lectures to black GIs on recreation leave, part of a program overseen by the wife of the governor. From that vantage point—talking to segregated soldiers in a state that had only recently begun to convict white defendants in lynching cases—the war looked very different from the one that had engaged Mead and Benedict. For Hurston, the signature home front event was the Detroit massacre of 1943, the murder of more than thirty civilians, most of them black, by police and federal troops. The killings seemed to have passed largely unnoticed by the other members of the Boas circle, except as a nuisance and an opportunity. "Disturbing as our 'ethnic minorities' are to our body politic," Robert Lowie told the American Anthropological Association the next year, "they offer rewarding and as yet inadequately utilized fields for research."

For Mead, the winding down of the war effort was a chance to return permanently to New York and get on with the business of science. She soon settled into the kind of unshakable relationship with Benedict that she had always promised they would forge. Bateson had been away for long stretches of the war, deployed to Ceylon and Burma for the Office of Strategic Services, the government bureau that would soon be transformed into the Central Intelligence Agency. The burden of distance, and Bateson's own romantic wanderings, took their toll on the marriage. The year after the war ended, he moved out of the family home; by 1950 they were divorced. "Marriage is like the New York subways," Mead later quipped. "You have to get on a train to find out if you're on the wrong train."

Mead went over the history of her relationship with Bateson with ethnographic care. She made field notes about remembered conversations, trying to figure out why the intoxicating thrill of those days on the Sepik had faded away. Benedict was again in the role of confidant and listener. Yet for the first time, largely because of the success of *The Chrysanthemum and the Sword*, Benedict's fame probably outshone that of any other member of the Boas circle. Ralph Linton, the department chair, had moved on from Columbia, taking up a professorship at Yale in 1946. After his departure, Benedict was at last promoted to the rank of full professor—the first woman to hold the title in any of the university's social science departments. The American Anthropological Association elected her its president. Research grants flowed in to support the type of work she had outlined in her study of Japan. Invitations came for conferences and lectures, including a demanding trip that took her through France, Holland, Belgium, and Czechoslovakia, a country that had not yet fully disappeared behind the Iron Curtain. She saw up close a very different social system in the midst of becoming, one that claimed to be about liberation and equality but that was quickly descending into its own brand of authoritarianism.

Benedict was at the height of her renown: a widely read author, a sought-after speaker, a leader among her scholarly peers, and one of the most publicly recognizable social scientists in the entire country. *Patterns of Culture* and *The Chrysanthemum and the Sword* were required reading among college students, diplomats, and the civically aware. Her hair had brightened to white. Her eyes were still mysterious and captivating, as they had been to Mead a quarter-century earlier.

But when Benedict returned to the United States from her European tour, in the summer of 1948, she looked pale and exhausted. A few days later, she suffered a heart attack and was rushed to the hospital. Mead spent days and nights by her side. Her hospital bed was ringed with old friends, who talked with her quietly about work and future arrangements. She died on September 17. It was the birthday of her father, the man whose own early death, she once said, had determined the entire course of her life. She had been doing anthropology nearly to the end. When friends went through the contents of her purse, they found the normal bits and pieces of everyday life—bank receipts, scrap paper—as well as a notebook with scribbled thoughts on how Austrians might differ from Norwegians.

Condolences were sent to Mead as if she were the next of kin. In most ways that mattered, she was. "The discovery of anthropology—and Dr. Boas—proved to be her salvation. That is where you came into the picture, Margaret," wrote Benedict's younger sister, Margery Freeman. "One of the deepest satisfactions of her life has been the privilege of stirring up your intellect, and then watching you carry the torch into fields where she could never go." Whatever intense private grief Mead must have experienced she spun into the matter-of-fact business of getting on with things. She steeled herself for the organizational and emotional tasks at hand, comforting family, commiserating with friends, and notifying as many people as she could—telegrams to those she could locate, longer letters to those harder to find, nothing to old colleagues whose whereabouts were impossible to trace.

Mead telegraphed Deloria about an upcoming memorial service. There was no way for her to afford the trip from South Dakota, however. Deloria said she felt an obligation to stay put and continue what she had been doing since publishing her Dakota grammar: helping to keep afloat the school her father once ran on the Standing Rock reservation. When Mead eventually sat down to work on her own form of public mourning—a hodgepodge of Benedict's academic writing, memoirs, and poetry, which Mead titled *An Anthropologist at Work*—she made sure Deloria got a copy. "And thank you also for calling me an Anthropologist," Deloria wrote in a return letter. Merely knowing that Mead thought of her that way, as someone who would want to read the gleanings of Benedict's scholarly and literary life, perked her up. It was among the last surviving correspondence between the two of them. Deloria continued with her own studies and writing, but most of it was still unpublished at the time of her death in 1971. Her last mailing address was a motel.

If Mead tried to reach Hurston to let her know of Benedict's funeral, no record of it remains. By the late 1940s, Hurston had lost touch with many of the people from her past, whether at Columbia or in Harlem. Over the years, she had occasionally hatched plans for a return to fieldwork. "Together we can do something that will make Dr. Margaret Meade's [*sic*] 'SAMOA' look like the report of the W.C.T.U."—the Woman's Christian Temperance Union—she told her old research partner, Jane Belo, in 1944. But life could feel like a Florida loblolly, sinking, sinking, with her toes never quite hitting solid ground. The year Benedict died she was arrested on false charges of molesting three neighbor boys. She was eventually cleared, but it was hard to find her way back. She fell into another depression and made plans for suicide.

It would be decades before a clue about Hurston's virtual disappearance happened to come across Mead's desk, via a surprising source: an article in *Ms.* magazine. In 1975 the young poet and novelist Alice Walker recorded her own efforts to follow Hurston's long trail away from fame. The piece surveyed Hurston's early work and reminded readers of the long-ago world of Harlem rent parties and Negro vogue. It placed Hurston squarely alongside the men, such as Ralph Ellison and James Baldwin, who had succeeded her as voices of the black experience. She was, as Walker put it, "one of the most significant unread authors in America."

From Walker's article, Mead learned that Hurston had continued to write short stories and newspaper columns, small essays, and plenty of queries to publishers about planned, but never completed, projects. Her novels and folklore volumes were long out of print. She had worked at odd jobs to tide herself over between small advances from editors. She had shelved books in a library, minded unruly students as a homeroom teacher, cleaned other people's houses, been evicted from her own, and then, after suffering a stroke, moved into a cinderblock rambler surrounded by a lawn of crackly swamp grass. It was a county-run home for indigents on the landward side of a small Florida coastal town—segregated by race, of course. By the time Mead read the magazine piece about her, Hurston had been dead for fifteen years. Her death certificate misspelled her name.

Mead slipped the article into her files, a kind of artifact from the old seminar room, dug up after all these years. Conversations among colleagues followed, a flurry of letters, remembrances of a name that had been all but forgotten, then efforts to locate Hurston's field-work notes and films, some of them socked away in file cabinets and museum collections across the country. Most of her manuscripts and personal papers had been lost over the years. A zealous janitor burned some of what remained after her death, until a passing sheriff's deputy grabbed a garden hose and doused what could be saved. "Ain't it a shame, how interesting people get after they're dead," said Alan Lomax, the country's preeminent collector of recorded folklife and Hurston's former fieldwork partner. "Poor Zora."

No one could have foreseen the renown that would eventually envelop her. Walker's essay reintroduced Hurston to a wider reading public. It was the beginning of a revival that would elevate her into the pantheon of great American writers, with an almost cultlike following. Walker had managed to track down the graveyard where she was buried, an out-of-the-way cemetery in Fort Pierce, Florida, but the actual gravesite was lost to time and bad record-keeping. She nevertheless paid for a headstone, its location approximate and fixed by Walker's own fiat. Today a visitor might find it scattered with old flowers, a liquor bottle, or a personal note to a writer whose reputation has exceeded that of Langston Hughes, Alain Locke, and other contemporaries in the Harlem Renaissance. Walker also arranged a very particular honor. Of all the central members of the Boas circle, Hurston's is the only grave marker that includes the word *anthropologist*.

MEAD HAD ONCE TRIED to make a map of all her relationships, both personal and professional, as if charting the kinship networks of a New Guinea village. There were narrow lines for minor influences, thick lines for major ones, double lines for lovers: to Luther, to Edward, to Reo and Gregory, both double-lined to each other. Pencil marks led to Boas, then to the Ash Can Cats, to other members of the Columbia department, then to circles and triangles, an ethnographer's symbols for unnamed women and men. Apart from them all stood Ruth—her own separate node, needing no lines at all—like a twin sun sharing space at the center of a galaxy.

Mead outlived most of them. Her rooms in the rafters of the American Museum of Natural History were a nest of field notebooks and tagged artifacts, handwritten letters and typed mimeographs, lecture notes and photos, thousands upon thousands of pages and objects—even Reo Fortune's old Webley revolver, which she and Bateson had hidden away long ago, during those insane months on the Sepik River. On weekdays she could be seen purposefully striding the hallways in her distinctive felt cape, an affectation of middle age. She had taken to using a tall, notched walking stick, the better to support the perpetually weak ankle that had dogged her since she first limped ashore in Pago Pago.

Her formal teaching was mainly as an adjunct or visiting professor, never as a tenured member of her old department. Yet it was through Mead that Boas's core ideas lived on and spread to a broader audience than Papa Franz could ever have dreamed. Her early books on Samoa and New Guinea each went through as many as seventeen editions and twenty foreign translations. Her typical year's output might include a scholarly book, articles in learned journals, essays in edited collections, encyclopedia entries, a bevy of reviews, and short pieces in *Camp Fire Girl*, *Good Housekeeping*, and *Redbook* that spun anthropological findings into practical, how-to advice. Newspapers and conference organizers solicited her views on childcare, sexuality, marriage, race, the Cold War, and virtually any other subject of popular concern. In turn her FBI file, one of many kept on public intellectuals during the era of J. Edgar Hoover, ballooned to nearly a thousand pages of tedious reports on her movements and friendships. As with Boas, people she had never met sent letters seeking her advice or expert opinion. "Dear Dr. Mead," went one from the Bronx in 1958:

> Your renowned authority on Anthropology has made me feel free to consult you.
>
> My problem is a "craving" to write a book because of factual material. However, the lack of talent prevents it.
>
> Is this normal behavior or a frustration deeply rooted in [my] African, American Indian, and Anglo-Saxon heritage?

Mead's response, a week later, was social science in action:

> I think you will find that it is very normal for people in every
> part of the world to have a feeling that they have a great deal of
> factual material they would like to put in a book, but lack a par-
> ticular talent for writing. I don't think you should feel this has
> any relationship to your very interesting ethnic heritage.

She became the face of her discipline, the epitome of an engaged
scholar, even if other prominent academics continued to treat her, as
they had done for decades, as somehow outside the mainstream. "The
whole world is my field," she said in a long profile in *The New Yorker*.
The article took as its title her phrase for teaching people to know
themselves: "It's All Anthropology."

The era was awash in new social science that upended old ways of
thinking. The methods and sensibilities that grew out of Boas's worldview were branching into nearly every domain. Just after the Second
World War, the Carnegie Corporation of New York commissioned
the Swedish economist Gunnar Myrdal to undertake a comprehensive
study of the race problem in the United States. With anthropological
incisiveness, Myrdal marshaled both stories and statistics to show the
practical effects, on real people, of American institutions that had been
designed to perpetuate racial difference and inequality. Myrdal's findings, jammed into his monumental *An American Dilemma*, would go
on to influence the Supreme Court's *Brown v. Board* decision ending
segregation. Alfred Kinsey cataloged the enormous variety of sexual
practices unspooling inside suburban bedrooms. William H. Masters
and Virginia E. Johnson conducted laboratory studies of human erotic
response that characterized same-sex attraction not as an abnormality
but as a form of sexuality to be understood. Their work would inform
the eventual striking, by the late 1980s, of homosexuality from psychologists' lists of diagnosable illnesses.

Just as Boas had corresponded with nearly every contemporary
specialist in the human sciences and beyond, Mead was at the center
of her own network of idea shapers. A typed list of her major corre-

spondents ran to more than a hundred pages. Her address book was a who's who of the era's greatest sociologists, philosophers, political scientists, psychologists, and political leaders. She could turn out a jottable quote, which made her a fixture on college campuses and television talk shows. She was a born evangelist, commenting incessantly on the civil rights movement, the sexual revolution, and the many definitions of mental illness, and a seemingly tireless booster urging a reckoning with her own society's cultural blinders.

In a time of rapid change, however, even she could appear conservative, her Episcopalian rectitude and Bucks County progressivism increasingly out of step with the views of more radical reformers. In 1963 Betty Friedan titled a chapter of *The Feminine Mystique* after her. She blamed Mead for her old-fashioned ideas of womanhood and for allegedly making too much of the biological differences between women and men. According to Friedan, Mead had "cut down her own vision of women by glorifying the mysterious miracle of femininity, which a woman realizes simply by being female, letting the breasts grow and the menstrual blood flow and the baby suck from the swollen breast." It was a caricature of Mead's work, but Mead declined to defend herself in any detail. She feared that a younger generation of feminists had lost sight of what was truly revolutionary about her earlier research. What she had been fighting for was women's full recognition as human beings, with the power to choose whatever social roles they wanted—mothers and caretakers as well as anthropologists and poets.

Her platform was global, with return visits to Samoa and Manus, sold-out lectures, appearances on lists of most-accomplished women, and controversies that she stoked with a well-honed appreciation for the outrageous. As time went on, Mead could find the limelight overpowering. Boas had taught her to resist saying too much until you have your facts straight, but she could be willfully ignorant, even cranky and exasperating, in her public appearances. She had an air of assumed authority, as *The New Yorker* put it, "that comes from many years of telling students, anthropologists, and other people things for their own good." With her regular engagements to speak about the great problems of the age, people knew of her even when they couldn't quite remember why. It was difficult, Mary Catherine Bateson once complained, to have "a mother who is 'half-famous' . . . because when I assume that people know who you are, so often they don't."

For her seventy-fifth birthday in December 1976, the *New York Times* featured a full-page announcement in her honor. Less than two years later, in the spring of 1978, Mead found out that she had pancreatic cancer. She died that November. In the decades that followed, there would be a U.S. postage stamp with her portrait and a Presidential Medal of Freedom, awarded posthumously for her struggle to show, as the White House citation read, "that varying cultural patterns express an underlying human unity." Her cape and stick were eventually placed on permanent display near the American Museum of Natural History's exhibit on the cultures of the Pacific. When visitors go there today, they enter under a sign welcoming them to Margaret Mead Hall.

IN 1987 THE PHILOSOPHER Allan Bloom published his treatise on the parlous state of American society and the country's misguided universities. *The Closing of the American Mind* became an instant best seller and a classic among conservative critics of American cultural life. It soon took its place as standard reading in an international movement—from the United States to Britain and beyond—aimed at pulling Western virtues from the jaws of what would come to be called multiculturalism and identity politics. The concept of cultural relativism was in the bull's-eye of Bloom's attack. "Almost every student entering the university believes, or says he believes, that truth is relative," Bloom wrote in the book's first sentence. He went on to name the people who had led young people into this amoral thicket:

> Sexual adventurers like Margaret Mead and others who found America too narrow told us that not only must we know other cultures and learn to respect them, but we could also profit from them. We could follow their lead and loosen up, liberating our-

selves from the opinion that our taboos are anything other than social constraints. We could go to the bazaar of cultures and find reinforcement for inclinations that are repressed by puritanical guilt feelings. All such teachers of openness had either no interest in or were actively hostile to the Declaration of Independence and the Constitution.

His book purported to survey the entirety of Western thought, yet Bloom could think of very few women worth mentioning. Margaret Mead and Ruth Benedict were among those he did, as were Jane Austen, Hannah Arendt, Yoko Ono, Erica Jong, and Marlene Dietrich— all of them part of the problem, as Bloom saw it. There had been a fundamental transformation in the intellectual outlook of the West, he believed. It involved turning away from tradition and embracing the wrongheaded idea that there was nothing special about the American experiment in democracy. Modern education, Bloom argued, had as its dark goal "to establish a world community and train its member— the person devoid of prejudice." The relativity of morality, history, and social reality had become the new orthodoxy, scotching the ability of young people to search independently for what constituted a good, authentic, meaningful life.

Had they been around, Mead, Benedict, and Boas would have been surprised by the news that they had triumphed. They had lived their lives as struggles. They got used to repeating the same philosophical points again and again. Every year seemed to produce another front in the battle against the purveyors of old certainties, a new frontier on which to try out the idea that difference was nothing to be afraid of. In their lifetimes they were confronted with things we now recognize to be great moral evils: scientific racism, the subjugation of women, genocidal fascism, the treatment of gay people as willfully deranged. Boas knew well that people who trumpeted European civilization and the superiority of "the West" had also designed Jim Crow, sterilized Carrie Buck, and sent trainloads of Jews to the camps. Bloom's manifesto would have left him unmoved.

"We have been the first to insist on a number of things," wrote the respected theorist and fieldworker Clifford Geertz, part of the generation of anthropologists who came along after Boas and Benedict and helped cement cultural relativism as the discipline's foundational philosophy. "That the world does not divide into the pious and the superstitious; that there are sculptures in jungles and paintings in deserts; . . . that the norms of reason were not fixed in Greece, the evolution of morality not consummated in England. Most important, we were the first to insist that we see the lives of others through lenses of our own grinding and that they look back on ours through ones of their own."

It should not be surprising that these ideas made many people feel—in fact, still make them feel—that the sky is falling. Virtually every member of the Boas circle was routinely denounced as naïve, uncivilized, unpatriotic, or immoral. Boas was a crank who denied American greatness. Mead was a trollop who insisted that sex wasn't necessarily private, perplexing, and vaguely wrong. Benedict was a harridan. Deloria and Hurston were, say no more, an Indian and a Negro. But their whole point was to be upsetting. Getting over yourself was bound to be hard. The payoff was to get smarter—about the world, about humanity, about the many possible ways of living a meaningful, flourishing life.

Some of Boas's specific findings have fallen to better research and better data. No one now does anthropology exactly the way Mead or Benedict did. Scholars today are skeptical about some of the generalizations that the Boasians allowed themselves. Fieldworkers would eventually come to question the entire concept of "culture" as a distinct *thing* that could be easily described and analyzed, as if fixing a moth wing to a microscope slide. (Two Crows denies it.) But from the 1880s to the 1940s, these thinkers helped herd human knowledge in a very particular direction: toward giving up the belief that all history leads inexorably to us.

The work on human communities goes on. Genetics is demonstrating what can and can't be said about human populations. Epigenetics is showing the multigenerational, gene-level impact of environmental conditions. We are all products of a particular ancestry, but these ancestries do not come shrink-wrapped into things called races or ethnicities, at least not as we have long understood them. Why we readily refer to our ancestors with labels such as Scots, Italians, or Koreans—but not as, say, Babylonians, Scythians, or Axumites—is an outgrowth of our history, not of our genetic code. How we define intelligence is the result of a social process, not a biological one. What we mean by things like appropriate gender roles, proper sexual behavior, or an abnormal mind is a creation of human beings in repeated interactions with one another—that is, of a society—not of our innards. The fact that we are still tempted by the desire to root our society-bound prejudices in something allegedly deeper than our own collective imagination is the best evidence of how relevant the Boas circle's ideas remain.

Distinguishing right from wrong is a matter of philosophy, yet it rests on a matter of fact: our prior conception of what is obvious or given, versus what is ludicrous or absurd. The expansion of our sense of morality depends on first enlarging the realm of the thinkable. And that in turn often requires, as it did for Boas and his students, to go bravely, awkwardly to places where we are sure to meet someone essentially unlike us—a frozen island, a rain forest encampment, or across town. Cultural relativism was a theory of human society, but it was also a user's manual for life. It was meant to enliven our moral sensibility, not extinguish it. All places of which we have knowledge have people you can kill and those you can't; people who are owed honesty and those to whom you must lie; people with whom sex is forbidden and those with whom it is encouraged. There might well be such a thing as a universal moral code, Boas taught, but no society—not even our own—has a lock on what it might contain. A given culture typically preens itself into believing that its foodways, family structure, religion, aesthetics, and political system are the truly logical ones. If there is any moral progress at all, it lies in our ability to break that habit: to develop an ever more capacious view of humanity itself—a widening web of beings who deserve our ethical conduct, whatever we deem ethical conduct to be.

"There is no evolution of moral ideas," Boas wrote succinctly in

1928. The only thing that changes are the people we believe should be treated as full, purposive, and dignified human beings. This is the scientific finding and ethical disposition that Boas and his students wanted to share with the world. Focus less on the rules of correct behavior—eat this, don't touch that, marry him, don't speak to her—and more on the circle of humanity to which you believe the rules apply. Work hard at distancing yourself from ideas that feed your own sense of specialness. Figure out what your own society thinks of as its best behavior, then extend that to the most unlikely recipient of your goodwill—someone who might be living around the world or just down the street. Do this no matter how distasteful their beliefs and practices might be to you.

With the benefit of hindsight, it is easy to see racial science, eugenics, colonialism, and the excesses of nationalism for the misguided things they were—and, in their modern guises, still are. The more difficult thing, even for committed cosmopolitans, is to recognize in oneself the errors that Boas and his students were trying to correct. "I have seen and heard," Hurston wrote in a passage deleted from her autobiography. "I have sat in judgment upon the ways of others, and in the voiceless quiet of the night I have also called myself to judgment." The most enduring prejudices are the comfortable ones, those hidden up close; seeing the world as it is requires some distance, a view from the upper air. Realizing the limitations of your own culture, even if it claims to be cultureless and global; feeling the power of prayer if you reject someone else's god; understanding the inner logic of bewildering political preferences; sensing the worry and depression, the disquiet and rage, caused in other people by the very outlooks on reality that seem wholly natural to you—these are skills built up over a lifetime. Their promise is that, with enough effort, we might come to know humanity in all its complexity, in fits and starts, with dim glimpses of a different world appearing through the mist of custom, changing us, unseating us, in a way destroying us—the baffling, terrifying liberation of home truths falling away.

ACKNOWLEDGMENTS

This book came out of conversations with my wife, Margaret Paxson, the anthropologist in our house. Every day with her is a wonder, and she led me through what turned out to be a kind of private seminar in social theory, fieldwork methods, and much else besides. I would never have thought of writing this book—nor could I have actually written it—without her. I now have some sense of how big ideas can flower out of the closest relationships, as they did for Boas and his circle. Thank you, my darling.

For the past five years, I have also had another Margaret in my life. We know a great deal about the Boas circle because Margaret Mead was its chief packrat. Her archive, housed in the Library of Congress, contains half a million items of every shape and description: an excused-absence note, a corset consultant's recommendation, an ex-husband's insurance policy, field notebooks and reports, and letters to, from, and among friends, lovers, and colleagues. My deep thanks go to Mead's assistants and her family, especially Mary Catherine Bateson, and now the specialists in the library's Manuscripts Division, who have preserved this marvel.

The other collections I consulted for this project are also rich in their own ways, and I am grateful to archivists and librarians in the following institutions: the American Indian Studies Research Institute, Indiana University; the American Museum of Natural History, especially Kristen Mable, Rebecca Morgan, Gregory Raml, and Diana Rosenthal, who gave me an enthusiastic tour of Mead's old offices and the labyrinthine attic; the American Philosophical Society, especially the keeper of the

Boas papers, Bayard Miller; the Columbia University Rare Book and Manuscript Library; the Keep in Brighton, Sussex; at Harvard University, the Peabody Museum, the Francis A. Countway Library of Medicine, the Houghton Library, and the Tozzer Library; the library and archives of Haskell Indian Nations University, especially Dacotah R. Hasvold; at Vassar College, the Archives and Special Collections division of the Thompson Memorial Library, especially Dean M. Rogers; the Lauinger Library of Georgetown University, especially the Booth Family Center for Special Collections and the interlibrary loan service; the Smithsonian Institution's National Anthropological Archives, especially Caitlin Haynes and Katherine Crowe; and the Rare Books and Special Collections Reading Room and Main Reading Room of the Library of Congress.

Collective biographies would not exist without biographies, and I am grateful for the detective work and interpretations offered by many authors before me. Although my own emphases and conclusions may differ from theirs, I could not have completed this project without their research. They include Lois Banner, Valerie Boyd, Margaret Caffrey, Douglas Cole, María Eugenia Cotera, Regna Darnell, Robert Hemenway, Jane Howard, Carla Kaplan, Hilary Lapsley, Herbert S. Lewis, David Lipset, Ludger Müller-Wille, Virginia Heyer Young, Rosemary Lévy Zumwalt, and the pioneering historians of anthropology as a science and a vocation, George W. Stocking Jr., Lee D. Baker, and David H. Price. Professor Zumwalt took time away from her own biography of Boas to read my entire typescript and, in the process, guide me around many crevasses.

Andrew Bickford and Marjorie Mandelstam Balzer, anthropologist colleagues at Georgetown, helped sharpen my ideas and my prose. Other people offered leads, insights, and helpful advice and were often exceedingly generous with their time. They include Kristy Andersen, Raymond Arsenault, Tom Banchoff, Katherine Benton-Cohen, Warren Cohen, Darcy Courteau, Desley Deacon, Philip J. Deloria, Lois Gaston, John Leavitt, Gary Mormino, Terry Pinkard, Charles Weiss, and Sufian Zhemukhov. Krisztina Samu of East-West Concepts handled the translations from Samoan. Special thanks also go to "our little group," as Boas would have called it—my research assistants over the years—who unearthed archival documents, compiled bibliographies, and otherwise moved the project forward: Abraham Fraifeld, Rachel Greene, Erum Haider, Rabea Kirmani, Andrew Schneider, and Andrew Szarejko.

I am very thankful for the support of my home institution, Georgetown University, especially its Edmund A. Walsh School of Foreign Service and Georgetown College, and deans Joel Hellman, Chester Gillis, and Christopher Celenza. Portions of this project were also funded by a National Endowment for the Humanities Public Scholar Award (grant number FZ-250287-16). Any views, findings, conclusions, or recommendations expressed here do not necessarily reflect those of the NEH.

My agent at the time this book was contracted, Will Lippincott, didn't run away when I told him I wanted to write a book about anthropological theory. He has been both cheerleader and counselor in this project's evolution from inkling to argument. Thanks also to Rob McQuilkin and Maria Massie of Massie & McQuilkin for handling the many aspects of the journey from idea to bookshelf. Rob was the first reader of the complete manuscript, and I can't quite imagine how any book would get produced without such a creative and sympathetic editorial eye. I feel unspeakably lucky to work with Kris Puopolo, magician and prose whisperer, at Doubleday, whose nudges have made the book far better than it might have been, and with Bill Thomas, who steered this book toward its audience. Janet Biehl, Maria Carella, Rose Courteau, Marina Drukman, Kathleen Fridella, Michael Goldsmith, Lorraine Hyland, Lisa Kleinholz, Diane McKiernan, Daniel Meyer, John Pitts, Carolyn Williams, and Michael J. Windsor were kind, prodding, and professional in exactly the right measures. Will Hammond at Bodley Head was a booster of the first order when presented with the proposal in London.

Honest writing means trying to use words the way they were used when they were originally spoken or written down, even if those meanings might be obsolete or wrongheaded now. In this book, I sometimes use the word *primitive* to describe what we would today call traditional or premodern societies, since that was the term normally used by Boas and his contemporaries. They, in turn, meant it somewhat differently from what their predecessors meant by it. Other words and phrases—*native*, *Negro*, *Indian*, and *feebleminded*, for example—appear in their own appropriate contexts. I have also adopted the collective names for indigenous peoples that the main characters in this book used when speaking of them or when I am ventriloquizing their ideas. In some instances, these names are not the ones now used by members of these communities, such as the Biwat (Mundugumor) and Chambri (Tchambuli) of Papua New Guinea, and the Kwakwaka'wakw (Kwakiutl) of British Columbia. The distance between this word and that one, between now and then, is history.

NOTES

Epigraphs: ZNH, *Dust Tracks*, 264 (from the deleted chapter "Seeing the World As It Is," included in this edition); Max Planck, *Scientific Autobiography and Other Papers* (London: Williams and Norgate, 1950), 33–34.

Chapter One: Away

1   In her steamer trunk: MM, "News Bulletin IX," Dec. 11, 1925, MM Papers, Box N1, Folder 5.

2   "the first serious attempt": FB to MM, Nov. 7, 1925, MM Papers, Box N1, Folder 1.

2   "The band of some ship": MM, "News Bulletin IV," Aug. 31, 1925, MM Papers, Box N1, Folder 5.

3   "And oh how sick": MM to RB, Mar. 29, 1926, MM Papers, Box S3, Folder 3.

3   "I've got lots": MM to RB, Mar. 29, 1926, ibid.

3   "I'm feeling perfectly": MM to RB, Dec. 15, 1925, MM Papers, Box S3, Folder 2.

7   "our little group": FB to MM, Jan. 25, 1926, MM Papers, Box N1, Folder 1.

10   "the work of enlightenment": "Student of Man," *New York Times*, Dec. 23, 1942.

11   "illumination that comes": RB, "Younger Generation."

12   "Courtesy, modesty": FB, "Foreword," in MM, *Coming of Age in Samoa.*

Chapter Two: Baffin Island

14   The thing that always: FB interview notes, RB Papers, Folder 115.2.

14   His favorite book: FB, "Curriculum Vitae," FB Prof. Papers, Box 13, File "Boas—Curriculum Vitae #2."

14   When a schoolmate drowned: Hedwig Boas Lehmann, memoir, FB Prof. Papers, Box 20, File "Lehmann, Hedwig Boas—Reminiscences of Franz Boas."

15   "the greatest man": Quoted in Wulf, *Invention of Nature*, 333.

15   "kingdom of shreds": Quoted in Clark, *Iron Kingdom*, 429.

16   exchanged gifts at Christmas: Hedwig Lehmann, memoir, BRC, Box 1, File "Boas—Biographical—Reminiscences of relatives"; Helene Yampolsky, memoir, FB Prof. Papers, Box 3, File "Boas—Boas Family Life"; Cole, *Franz Boas*, 13.

16   He shifted his career: Cole, *Franz Boas*, 16.

16   He could be depressive: Lehmann memoir, BRC.

16   He managed good marks: FB to parents, Feb. 20, 1869, FB Prof. Papers, Box 3, File "Boas—Corresp.—Early 1869."

16   If he had one overarching: FB, "Curriculum Vitae," FB Prof. Papers, Box 13, File "Boas—Curriculum Vitae #2."

16   When the family returned: Lehmann memoir, FB Prof. Papers.

16   He saved the carcasses: FB, "Curriculum Vitae"; Lehmann memoir, BRC.

17   "unknown and unregarded": Quoted in Cole, *Franz Boas*, 28.

17   He celebrated: Ibid., 37.

17   As a boy: Lehmann memoir, BRC.

17   But it was somehow: Cole, *Franz Boas*, 41.

17   In later life: Ibid., 61.

18   One of his sisters: Cole and Müller-Wille, "Franz Boas' Expedition," 39–40.

19   Boas read Kant: Clyde Kluckhohn and Olaf Prufer, "Influences During the Formative Years," in Goldschmidt, *Anthropology of Boas*, 8.

20   From a hired boat: Cole, *Franz Boas*, 52.

20   earning a degree: Ludger Müller-Wille, "Introduction: Germans and Inuit on Baffin Island in the 1880s," in *FBAI*, 6.

21   Not long after defending: See the document in FB Prof. Papers, Box 2, File "Boas—Arctic Expedition—Outline of proposed trip, 1883."

21   Boas spent months: Müller-Wille, "Introduction," in *FBAI*, 9.

22   "with the color": FB to parents, Jan. 23, 1883, in *FBAI*, 36.

22   Boas had done much: FB to Abraham Jacobi, Nov. 26, 1882, in *FBAI*, 33.

22   He trained to confront danger: FB diary entry, June 9, 1883, in *FBAI*, 42.

22   "Farewell, my dear homeland!": FB diary entry, June 20, 1883, in *FBAI*, 45.

22   Crowds cheered: Ibid.

23   Meier watched: Cole, *Franz Boas*, 71.

23   "*my* Eskimos": FB to sisters, May 14, 1882, in *FBAI*, 33.

23   "I shall also engage": FB, untitled synopsis plan for Baffin Island expedition, FB Prof. Papers, Box 2, File "Boas—Arctic Expedition—Outline of proposed trip, 1883."

23   "They eate their meate": Settle, *Laste Voyage*, n.p.

23   "Two women": Ibid.

23   They were the first North American: Vaughan, *Transatlantic Encounters*, 1–10.

24   "I would immediately": FB to Abraham Jacobi, Nov. 26, 1882, in *FBAI*, 35.

24   Barely two days: FB diary entry, June 22, 1883, in *FBAI*, 46.

24   "but he has a frightfully": FB to Marie Krackowizer, June 25, 1883, in *FBAI*, 48.

24   Weeks passed: FB to Marie Krackowizer, Aug. 17, 1883, in *FBAI*, 65.

24   Mirages loomed: FB, memoir written for his children, BRC, Box 1, File "Boas—Arctic Expedition—Reminiscence written for his children, n.d., #1." Written later in the style of an adventure story, Boas included details drawn from his letters and notebooks written at the time.

25   Inuit women, dressed in sealskin: FB, memoir written for his children, BRC.

25   "They are not as dirty": FB diary entry, Aug. 28, 1883, in *FBAI*, 72–73.

25   He plucked wild grasses: At least one of these specimens has survived, brittle but still green, among Boas's papers. See FB Prof. Papers, Box 2, Files "Boas—Arctic Expedition—Plants, c. 1883."

25   "After a few days": FB, "Year Among Eskimo."

26   He spent long winter nights: Cole, *Franz Boas*, 72.

26   His wife, whom the whalers knew: FB, memoir written for his children, BRC.

26   He used musical notation: Boas later published the songs in FB, "Poetry and Music," and other articles.

26   Then he wrote out entire stories: See the field notebooks in FB Prof. Papers, Box 22.

27   He made a rough census: Cole and Müller-Wille, "Franz Boas' Expedition," 52.

27   From his supplies: Cole, *Franz Boas*, 75; FB diary entry, Oct. 23, 1883, in *FBAI*, 126.

27   It was diphtheria: Cole, *Franz Boas*, 75.

28   "I keep telling myself": FB to Marie Krackowizer, Nov. 18, 1883, in *FBAI*, 140.

28   Children were now sick: FB to parents and sisters, Oct. 31, 1883, in *FBAI*, 130.

28   Napekin relented: Cole, *Franz Boas*, 76; FB diary entry, Jan. 17–20, 1884, in *FBAI*, 168–69.

28   "Do you know": FB to Marie Krackowizer, Dec. 13, 1883, in *FBAI*, 151.

28   "I often ask myself": FB to Marie Krackowizer, Dec. 23, 1883, in *FBAI*, 159.

29   The only way you could: FB, memoir written for his children, BRC.

29   "I believe that in every person": FB to Marie Krackowizer, Dec. 23, 1883, in *FBAI*, 159.

29   "my notion of": Ibid.

30   That winter in Anarnitung: FB to Marie Krackowizer, Dec. 21, 1883, in *FBAI*, 157.

30   Most nights found him: Cole and Müller-Wille, "Franz Boas' Expedition," 54.

30   chicken scratches: Douglas Cole, " 'The Value of a Person Lies in His *Herzensbildung*,' " in Stocking, *Observers Observed*, 16.

30   Even today, the blood: FB diary entry, Dec. 23, 1883, in *FBAI*, 159.

30   He and Weike had only: Cole, *Franz Boas*, 77.

31   He soon received: Ibid., 78.

31   Meier had given: Cole and Müller-Wille, "Franz Boas' Expedition," 42.

31   He might lead off: Kroeber et al., *Franz Boas*, 7; Ernst Boas, memoir, FB Prof. Papers, Box 17, File "Boas, Ernst—Reminiscences of his father."

32   Inside, the collections included: Hinsley, *Smithsonian and American Indian*, 65–66.

34   Between battles, he collected: Davis, *Biographical Memoir*, 14.

34   "The good people of Green River City": Powell, *Exploration of Colorado River*, 1.

35   By the mid-1880s: Davis, *Biographical Memoir*, 56.

36   Plans for further exploration: Cole, *Franz Boas*, 83–86.

36   Even as he spoke, the bureau's researchers: See *Fifth Annual Report of the Bureau of Ethnology, 1883–84* (Washington, D.C.: U.S. Government Printing Office, 1887).

36   This was at least something to show: Cole, *Franz Boas*, 83.

36   Two lectures that he was invited: Ibid., 86.

36   No museums or universities: Ibid., 85.

37   In March 1885 he set off: Ibid., 86.

37   It was a state of mind: Ibid., 88.

Chapter Three: "All Is Individuality"

38   "When he arrived here": Sophie Boas to Abraham Jacobi, Apr. 20, 1885, FB Papers (microfilm), Reel 1.

38   "the African negro": Tylor, *Anthropology*, 2.

39   Such a "science of Culture": Tylor, *Primitive Culture*, 1:12.

39   "Indeed, the primitive Aryan": Frazer, *Golden Bough*, 1:viii.

40   "religion of the woodman": Ibid., 1:ix.

41 Rituals were devised: Deloria, *Playing Indian*, 77.

42 The new confederacy's membership: Ibid., 79.

42 "To encourage a kinder feeling": Morgan, *League of Ho-de'-no-sau-nee*, 1:ix.

43 When he began to imagine: Darnell, *Along Came Boas*, 89.

43 "The course of human events": Quotations from Powell's speech are from Powell, "From Barbarism to Civilization." Although delivered in the spring of 1886, the text was not published until two years later.

47 Boas was one of nearly 1.8 million: Nadel, *Little Germany*, 19, 21.

47 Had the residents: Ibid., 1.

47 Rising in life meant rising: Cole, *Franz Boas*, 99.

48 His English was still so shaky: Ibid., 99.

48 "I see such a wide": FB to parents, Aug. 24, 1886, quoted ibid., 99.

49 "Vancouver makes": FB, "Letter Diary to Parents (1886)," entry for Dec. 16, in *EFB*, 76.

49 "The stranger coming": FB, "Boas' Introduction," in *EFB*, 5.

49 He estimated that the total: Ibid.

49 "their highly developed": Ibid., 7.

49 "I go about visiting": FB, "Letter Diary to Parents (1886)," entry for Oct. 23, in *EFB*, 45.

50 Over the next few months: Cole, *Franz Boas*, 102; and FB, "Letter Diary to Parents (1886)," in *EFB*, various entries.

50 George Hunt, a half-Tlingit: On the essential role of Hunt, see Isaiah Lorado Wilder, "Friends in This World: The Relationship of George Hunt and Franz Boas," in Darnell et al., *Boas as Public Intellectual*, 163–89.

50 She had thought: FB, "Letter Diary to Parents (1886)," entry for Nov. 18, in *EFB*, 61.

50 "He said a man had lain dead": Ibid., entry for Nov. 8, in *EFB*, 55.

51 Even then, the myths: Ibid., entry for Nov. 20, in *EFB*, 63.

51 "They always try": Ibid., entry for Nov. 6, in *EFB*, 53.

51 It was all that remained: Ibid., entry for Nov. 15, in *EFB*, 60.

51 He departed a minor celebrity: Ibid., entry for Dec. 16, in *EFB*, 77.

52 He told Marie: Cole, *Franz Boas*, 104–5.

52 "the life of man as far as": Boas, "Study of Geography," 137.

54 "How far does an influence": FB to J. W. Powell, June 12, 1887, in Stocking, *Shaping of American Anthropology*, 60.

54 "The longer I studied": Ibid.

54 "historical facts are of greater influence": Ibid.

54 "We cannot agree": FB, "Occurrence of Similar Inventions," 485.

55 "By regarding a single implement": Ibid.

55 "I think it is a growing conviction": Mason, "Occurrence of Similar Inventions," 534.

55 "The explorer who goes": Ibid., 534.

56 "All that stuff": FB, "Letter Diary to Parents (1886)," entry for Oct. 31, in *EFB*, 50.

56 "In ethnology all is individuality": FB, "Museums of Ethnology" (first 1887 article), 589.

57   "human activities which characterize": Powell, "Museums of Ethnology," 613.
57   Boas could do little: FB, "Museums of Ethnology," 614.
57   The entire affair: Cole, *Franz Boas*, 129.
57   He had been elected: Ibid., 115.

Chapter Four: Science and Circuses
59   He would be the first: Ross, *G. Stanley Hall*, 196.
59   In the fall of 1889: Cole, *Franz Boas*, 121, 138.
60   Its endowment: Ibid., 137; Hall, *Life and Confessions*, 291.
60   At his first lecture: Cole, *Franz Boas*, 138.
60   one tragedy after another: Hall, *Life and Confessions*, 293.
61   Every year administrators: Ibid., 296.
61   "I only wish": Quoted in Cole, *Franz Boas*, 140.
61   His first doctoral student: Kroeber et al., *Franz Boas*, 12.
61   At the end of that academic year: Cole, *Franz Boas*, 145; Hall, *Life and Confessions*, 296.
61   In November he packed up: Cole, *Franz Boas*, 154.
62   Boas had recently become: Worcester Superior Court, Worcester, Mass., Feb. 23, 1892, naturalization papers available at www.ancestry.com.
62   "a collection of the habitations": *Chicago Tribune*, May 31, 1890, quoted in Freed, *Anthropology Unmasked*, 1:121.
62   offered a generous budget: Ibid., 1:122.
66   "his scalp scarred": *Worcester Daily Telegraph*, Mar. 5, 1891, quoted in Cole, *Franz Boas*, 142–43.
67   He coordinated: Ibid., 154.
67   The monstrous Manufacturing and Liberal Arts: *Plan and Classification: Department M* (Chicago: World's Columbian Exposition, 1892), leaflet in PM, Frederic Ward Putnam Papers, Box 4, Folder 43.
68   Two full-scale longhouses: Cole, *Franz Boas*, 155.
68   The building's two floors: See Putnam Director Records, Box 9.
69   Patrons could see: FB, "Report on the Section of Physical Anthropology," Putnam Director Records, Box 8, Folder 8.
69   "the Vertical Head-Spanner": Ibid.
69   The head shapes of Tyroleans: Ibid.
70   Already in 1889: FB, "On Alternating Sounds," 47–53.
70   "It is found that the vocabularies": Ibid., 51.
71   "liable to be overlooked": *World's Columbian Exposition Illustrated* (1893), quoted in Curtis M. Hinsley, "Anthropology as Education and Entertainment: Frederic Ward Putnam at the World's Fair," in Hinsley and Wilcox, *Coming of Age in Chicago*, 26.
71   Despite the sizable: Handwritten note on fair expenditures based on auditors' report, Aug. 7, 1893, PM, Frederic Ward Putnam Papers, Box 4, Folder 39.
71   People seemed more drawn: Hinsley, "Anthropology as Education and Entertainment," 27.
71   Even a hastily arranged: Holmes, "World's Fair Congress of Anthropology."
72   The fair's director: Cole, *Franz Boas*, 156.

72 "Stop it! Stop it!": Photograph caption of Kwakiutl performers, PM, World Columbia Exposition Photograph Collection, Box 1.

72 "Scientifically, the summer has been": Quoted in Cole, *Franz Boas*, 156.

72 She died not long: Ibid., 158–59.

72 "an unsurpassed insult": FB to William J. McGee, Feb. 17, 1894, NAA, Bureau of American Ethnology Records, Box 264, Folder "Boas 1889."

73 To assist the Smithsonian: Hinsley and Holm, "Cannibal in National Museum," 306.

73 "What good is the consciousness": Quoted in Cole, *Franz Boas*, 172.

74 Leaving Chicago, the Boas family: Ibid., 185.

74 Established in 1869, the American Museum: Freed, *Anthropology Unmasked*, 1:31.

74 On June 20, 1874: Ibid., 1:41.

74 But even at the time: Ibid., 1:43.

75 Uncle Jacobi had secretly: Cole, *Franz Boas*, 213.

76 "These facts are very strong": FB, "Some Recent Criticisms of Physical Anthropology," 105.

77 "will not become fruitful": FB, "Limitations of Comparative Method," 908.

77 "answer two questions in regard": Ibid., 902.

Chapter Five: Headhunters

81 "The intellectual man": Nott and Gliddon, *Types of Mankind*, 50.

81 Beauty "predominates": Aleš Hrdlička, "Beauty Among the American Indians," in *Boas Anniversary Volume*, 38.

82 "the black, the brown and the red": Quoted in Harris, *Rise of Anthropological Theory*, 256.

82 "It is not against experience": Jefferson, *Notes on State of Virginia*, 155.

83 "In seeing their black faces": Quoted in Gould, *Mismeasure of Man*, 77. On Agassiz and his relationship to other contemporary thinkers, see Menand, *Metaphysical Club*, esp. chaps. 5–6; and Painter, *History of White People*, 190–200.

83 "Man has been studied": Darwin, *Descent of Man*, 190.

84 "Those naturalists . . . who admit": Ibid., 192.

84 Pardons of former Confederate: Anderson, *White Rage*, 17.

84 In 1878 a precedent-setting opinion: See López, *White by Law*.

86 "There are reasons why Ethnology": Nott and Gliddon, *Types of Mankind*, xxxii–iii.

87 In fact, had it not been: Spiro, *Defending Master Race*, 61–67. I am indebted to Spiro's exhaustive study for my understanding of the impact of Grant on American visions of race.

88 "walk down Fifth Avenue": Quoted ibid., 97.

88 A bibliography compiled: See Ripley, *Selected Bibliography*.

88 The statistician Frederick L. Hoffman: Stocking, *Race, Culture, and Evolution*, 52–53.

88 The German sociologist: Ibid., 60.

88 "Dolichocephalic Nordics": Quoted ibid., 61.

88 whom Grant probably heard: Spiro, *Defending Master Race*, 93.

89   "Beyond the Pyrenees": Ripley, *Races of Europe*, 273.

90   Bookstores shelved it: Spiro, *Defending Master Race*, 143–45.

90   "In America we have nearly": Grant, *Passing of Great Race*, 6.

90   "an unending wail": Ibid., 8.

90   "mankind emerged from savagery": Ibid., 6.

90   Science had long discarded: Ibid., 11.

90   The human nose: Ibid., 27.

90   "Thick, protruding, everted lips": Ibid., 27.

91   "it has taken us fifty years": Ibid., 14.

91   "an intricate mass": Ibid., 31.

91   "One of the greatest difficulties": Ibid., 19.

91   "The cross between": Ibid., 18.

91   "As soon as the true bearing": Ibid., 227–28.

92   Three-quarters of American universities: Spiro, *Defending Master Race*, 168.

92   By 1910 the foreign-born: Statistics from Singer, "Contemporary Immigrant Gateways."

92   At the time Donald J. Trump: Gustavo López and Jynnah Radford, "Statistical Portrait of the Foreign-born Population in the United States," Pew Research Center, May 3, 2017, www.pewhispanic.org/2017/05/03/facts-on-u-s-immigrants-current-data/.

93   Indeed, by the turn of the century: Singer, "Contemporary Immigrant Gateways."

93   "Recent attempts have been made": Grant, *Passing of Great Race*, 14–15.

94   "Neither Berlin with its five": FB to Zelia Nuttall, May 16, 1901, FB Papers (microfilm), Reel 4.

94   "With archaeology represented": FB to Nicholas Murray Butler, Nov. 15, 1902, ibid.

94   It soon became an informal: Helen Boas Yampolsky, memoir, FB Prof. Papers, Box 3, File "Boas—Boas Family Life"; Ernst Boas, memoir, FB Prof. Papers, Box 17, File "Boas, Ernst—Notes on a conversation with Franz Boas, 1940 or 1941."

95   "It is gratifying to note": FB to Nicholas Murray Butler, Nov. 13, 1908, FB Papers (microfilm), Reel 9.

95   He informed Boas: FB to Felix Adler, Jan. 6, 1908, ibid.

95   Things were in "a pitiable condition": FB to A. L. Kroeber, Jan. 6, 1908, ibid.

95   He contacted his old colleagues: FB to W. J. McGee, Apr. 20, 1901, FB Papers (microfilm), Reel 4.

95   In the 1907–1908 academic year: Untitled report on teaching in the Department of Anthropology, n.d. [ca. 1908], FB Papers (microfilm), Reel 9.

96   "I am endeavoring": FB to Booker T. Washington, Nov. 8, 1908, ibid.

96   Still, when they returned: On the Dillingham Commission, see Zeidel, *Immigrants, Progressives*; Benton-Cohen, *Inventing Immigration Problem*.

96   "the immigration of different races": Jeremiah W. Jenks to FB, Mar. 11, 1908, FB Papers (microfilm), Reel 9.

97   "The importance of this question": FB to Jenks, Mar. 23, 1908, ibid.

97   That fall the government: Jenks to FB, Nov. 20, 1908, ibid.

97   They lugged along: FB to E. B. Meyrowitz, May 25, 1908, FB Papers (microfilm), Reel 12.

97   At reform schools: *Reports of Immigration Commission: Changes in Bodily Form*, 81–84.

98   "entirely unexpected results": FB to F. W. Hodge, Mar. 14, 1910, NAA, Bureau of American Ethnology Records, Box 138, Folder "Blumenthal, Walter Hart-Boas, Franz."

98   "The adaptability of the immigrant": *Reports of Immigration Commission: Changes in Bodily Form*, 2.

99   "These results are so definite": Ibid., 5. Beginning in 1912 and continuing through the 1920s and 1930s, scholars reran Boas's data or added their own observations to it. Some confirmed his findings about cranial differences between parents and offspring, which they attributed mainly to environmental factors. Others found discrepancies in the measurements or in Boas's statistical analysis. Further studies were conducted as recently as 2002 and 2003. Two sets of scholars, working independently, came to different conclusions about the magnitude of the variability, but both confirmed the basic fact of cranial plasticity. As one research team pointed out, the revelation of any variance at all essentially falsified the central claim of scientific racists: "At the time Boas conceived the study, the prevailing view among physical anthropologists was that humankind consisted of a few, unchanging races or types. . . . Boas's immigrant study is significant because it treated this assumption as an empirical matter. The most important result was that the cephalic index . . . was sensitive to the environment. Given the prevailing faith in the absolute permanence of cranial form, Boas's demonstration of change—any change—in the cephalic index within a single generation was nothing short of revolutionary." Gravlee, Bernard, and Leonard, "Boas' *Changes in Bodily Form*," 331. No serious scientist would now accept the pre-Boasian view of race as a stable, inheritable, and anatomically measurable classification for individual human beings. For further discussion, see also Allen, "Franz Boas' Physical Anthropology"; Gravlee, Bernard, and Leonard, "Heredity, Environment, and Cranial Form"; Sparks and Jantz, "Changing Times, Changing Faces"; Sparks and Jantz, "Reassessment"; and Teslow, *Constructing Race*.

99   "a pitying smile": FB, *Mind of Primitive Man*, 4.

100   "In short," he concluded: Ibid., 17.

100   The most truly apelike: Ibid., 22.

100   "the indefiniteness of distinctions": Ibid., 33.

101   "When . . . we compare": Ibid.

101   "man cannot be assumed": Ibid., 44.

101   "The differences between": Ibid., 94.

101   "activities of the human mind": Ibid., 98.

101   "It is a common observation": Ibid., 226.

103   "The proper way to compare": Ibid., 107.

103   "It is somewhat difficult": Ibid., 208–9.

Chapter Six: American Empire

105 "We recognize thus": FB, *Handbook of American Indian Languages*, 1:14.

105 Now he and Du Bois: Weatherly, "First Universal Races Congress," 318.

105 "The assumption of an absolute": FB, "Instability of Human Types," in Spiller, *Papers on Inter-Racial Problems*, 99.

106 "deemed it reasonable to follow": *Reports of Immigration Commission: Dictionary of Races or Peoples*, 5:3.

106 "as a class far less intelligent": Ibid., 1:13.

107 Despite the upsurge: Jens Manuel Krogstad and Michael Keegan, "From Germany to Mexico: How America's Source of Immigrants Has Changed over a Century," Pew Research Center, October 7, 2015, http://www.pewresearch .org/fact-tank/2015/10/07/a-shift-from-germany-to-mexico-for-americas -immigrants/.

108 "born under other flags": Quoted in Luebke, *Bonds of Loyalty*, 146.

108 Some six hundred thousand German: Ibid., 255–56.

108 Louisiana, Kentucky: Ibid., 252.

108 Nearly half of all states: The Supreme Court case was *Meyer v. Nebraska* (1923), in which the court ruled that a 1919 Nebraska law prohibiting teaching in languages other than English violated the due process clause of the Fourteenth Amendment.

109 Soon the *New York Herald:* Adam Hochschild, "When Dissent Became Treason," *New York Review of Books*, Sept. 28, 2017, 82.

109 "No matter what the letter": FB, "Warns of German Wrath," *New York Times*, Dec. 11, 1915.

109 In fact, the United States had done so: FB, "Nationalism in Europe," 13–14.

110 "I have always been": FB, "Why German-Americans Blame America," *New York Times*, Jan. 8, 1916.

110 In early 1917, Boas denounced: "Professor Boas Dissents," *New York Times*, Feb. 9, 1917.

110 "What had been tolerated": Quoted in McCaughey, *Stand, Columbia*, 248.

110 "un-American": "Professor Boas' Views," *New York Times*, Feb. 13, 1917.

110 "anthropology, as construed": Quoted in McCaughey, *Stand, Columbia*, 253.

110 As bills piled up: FB to Pliny Goddard, July 15, 1915, Elsie Clews Parsons Papers, Series I, Folder 1.

111 "a Cassandric prophecy": Quotations that follow are from FB, "Inventing."

112 "impugn[ing] the veracity": W. H. Holmes et al. to J. Walter Fewkes, Dec. 24, 1919, NAA, Bureau of American Ethnology Records, Box 267, Folder "Boas, Franz—1919–1920."

112 Boas "now occupies a comparatively obscure": Quoted in Spiro, *Defending Master Race*, 318.

112 He had even written: Freed, *Anthropology Unmasked*, 1:431.

113 His oldest sister: FB to Elsie Clews Parsons, Nov. 26, 1925, Elsie Clews Parsons Papers, Series I, Folder 3.

114 The same year the Supreme Court: For an overview of anti-immigration legislation in this period, see Daniels, *Guarding Golden Door*, 49–58.

114 "We have closed the doors": Quoted in Spiro, *Defending Master Race*, 233.

114 Scribner's issued two more: Ibid., 166.

114 Application forms now required: McCaughey, *Stand, Columbia*, 269.

114 "of either the Anglo-Saxon": Ibid., 270.

114 "pronounce every name": Ibid., 267.

114 "my Bible": Spiro, *Defending Master Race*, 357; Kühl, *Nazi Connection*, 85; Ryback, *Hitler's Private Library*, 109–10. The authenticity of this quotation has been contested, since Grant's family destroyed his papers after his death, but Kühl located a reliable source: the unpublished memoir of Leon Whitney, an American eugenicist who recalled seeing the actual letter on Grant's desk. Grant was published in Germany by J. F. Lehmanns Verlag, which became the single most important book publisher on Nazi race theory and a major supplier of volumes to Hitler's personal library.

114 "in which at least the weak": Hitler, *Mein Kampf*, 439.

115 "A state which in this age": Ibid., 688.

115 His son Ernst had volunteered: FB to Ernst Boas, July 24, 1917, BRC, Box 3, File labeled "Box 79."

115 the worry would prove: Helen Boas Yampolsky, memoir, FB Prof. Papers, Box 3, File "Boas—Boas Family Life."

115 He saw it as a kind: FB to ECP, June 25, 1925, Elsie Clews Parsons Papers, Series I, Folder 3.

115 "like a board": FB to Ernst Boas, June 14, 1915, BRC, Box 3, File labeled "Box 79."

115 He neglected his teeth: Yampolsky memoir, FB Prof. Papers.

115 "face crippled": FB anthropometry chart, NAA, Aleš Hrdlička Papers, Box 127, File "Anthropometry Data Sheets on Members of the NAS."

115 "The disappointment of my life": FB to Ernst Boas, Nov. 15, 1917, BRC, Box 3, File labeled "Box 79."

115 "Whether that be family": FB to Ernst Boas, July 29, 1917, ibid.

115 "Must one always kick": FB to Ernst Boas, Nov. 15, 1917, ibid.

115 His department, downsized: Goldfrank, *Notes on Undirected Life*, 4; *AAW*, 344.

116 "It is very painful": FB to Ernst Boas, July 21, 1917, BRC, Box 3, File labeled "Box 79."

116 "I do not command": FB to Ernst Boas, July 29, 1917, ibid.

116 The undergraduate program in anthropology: Caffrey, *Ruth Benedict*, 100; Kroeber et al., *Franz Boas*, 15–16.

116 "vaudeville courses": Yampolsky memoir, FB Prof. Papers.

117 When he refused to pray: Meyer, *It's Been Fun*, 9.

117 "I had a shrewd theory": Ibid., 5. On the broader history of Barnard's establishment and women at Columbia, see Rosenberg, *Changing the Subject*.

118 Boas's teaching style: Darnell, *Along Came Boas*, 294; Kroeber et al., *Franz Boas*, 14–15.

118 He never used textbooks: Darnell, *Along Came Boas*, 295.

118 If someone needed instruction: LC, *Golden Journey*, 105–6.

118 They would learn: Kroeber et al., *Franz Boas*, 14.

118 When Ralph Linton: Kluckhohn, *Ralph Linton*, 238; Banner, *Intertwined Lives*, 379.

118   "Jewish Ring": Young, *Ruth Benedict*, 42.
118   For more than a decade: FB to Nicholas Murray Butler, Nov. 13, 1908, FB Papers (microfilm), Reel 9.
119   "I don't have children": Quoted in Goldfrank, *Notes on Undirected Life*, 36.
119   "I have had a curious experience": Quoted in Deacon, *Elsie Clews Parsons*, 255.
119   Ruth Fulton, as she was: RB, diary entry for Mar. 7, 1923, in *AAW*, 98.
119   "a cult of grief": Ibid.
119   From childhood forward: Ibid., 99.
119   She imagined that there might: Caffrey, *Ruth Benedict*, 94.
119   The home became the focus: Ibid., 81.
120   "All he asks": RB, diary entry for Oct. [n.d.] 1920, in *AAW*, 143.
120   "to keep suicide from becoming": Quoted in Caffrey, *Ruth Benedict*, 81.
120   When Stanley sought: Banner, *Intertwined Lives*, 138.
120   "Fear of change is a part": Parsons, *Fear and Conventionality*, xv.
120   "a perfectly fearless love": Ibid., 216.
121   "predisposition to classify": Parsons, *Social Freedom*, 8.
121   After a string of books: Caffrey, *Ruth Benedict*, 96.
121   A society that advocated: Banner, *Intertwined Lives*, 148.
121   "bewilderment of soul": RB, diary entry for Jan. [n.d.] 1917, in *AAW*, 140.
122   "All known classifications": Benedict, "Vision in Plains Culture," 21.
122   "psychological attitudes of the utmost": Ibid.
123   It took her only three: Caffrey, *Ruth Benedict*, 102–3.
123   "is not very promising material": Frank R. Lillie to Elsie Clews Parsons, May 23, 1924, RB Papers, Folder 1.1.
123   "Down behind the hill": Cushing, *My Adventures in Zuñi*, 14–15.
124   "a spiked fence": Quoted in Caffrey, *Ruth Benedict*, 110.
124   "a deaf": Quoted ibid., 109.
125   "One of the most striking facts": RB, "Anthropology and Abnormal," in *AAW*, 263.
125   "Normality, in short": Ibid., 276.
126   "the psychic dilemmas": Ibid., 275.

Chapter Seven: "A Girl as Frail as Margaret"

127   She could marshal: MM, memory book, 1914, MM Papers, Box A12, Folder 7.
127   She recorded the mental development: MM diary, 1911–1914, MM Papers, Box Q7, Folder 5.
127   She made lists: Ibid.
127   She was born: Howard, *Margaret Mead*, 23.
127   Afterward she asked Margaret: Geoffrey Gorer, "Margaret Mead," typescript (1949), GG Papers, SxMs52/2/3/10/5.
127   Edward, a professor: LC, interview by Jane Howard, Nov. 3, 1979, JH Papers, Box 38.
127   According to family lore: Howard, *Margaret Mead*, 22n.
128   At age eleven: Banner, *Intertwined Lives*, 75. The young Mead described the event, in late December 1912, as "one of the happiest days of my life." MM diary, 1911–1914, MM Papers, Box Q7, Folder 5.

128 She decorated her dorm room: Mead misremembered the revolutionary's name as "Catherine Bushovka." MM, *Blackberry Winter*, 87.

128 The Kappa Kappa Gammas: Howard, *Margaret Mead*, 37.

128 It was not a devastating rejection: MM, *Blackberry Winter*, 100.

128 The things in which: Ibid., 98.

128 "fraternity life, . . . football games": Ibid., 90.

129 "For the first time": MM, "Life History," 1935, MM Papers, Box S9, Folder 7.

129 Each year they would adopt: MM, *Blackberry Winter*, 103.

129 The one that really stuck: MM, "Life History," 1935, MM Papers, Box S9, Folder 7.

129 By the summer of 1921: John S. Wurtz to MM, May 14, 1921, and John S. Wurtz to MM, June 14, 1921, MM Papers, Box R9, Folder 8.

129 "various little lesbian friends": MM, "Life History," 1935, MM Papers, Box S9, Folder 7.

129 just "reddish": Melville Herskovits to MM, June 9, 1923, MM Papers, Box C1, Folder 8.

129 New York was energy: MM to Emily Fogg Mead, Nov. 19, 1922, MM Papers, Box Q2, Folder 7; dance card for "Class of 1923" dance, Feb. 4, 1921, MM Papers, Q7, Folder 3.

129 It all made up for the fact: MM, draft manuscript of *Blackberry Winter*, MM Papers, Box I204, Folder 4.

130 She drew detailed pictures: MM class notes, MM Papers, Box A15, Folder 2.

130 made the honor roll: MM Barnard transcript, MM Papers, Box Q14, Folder 8.

130 "in the least a 'grind' ": MM to Edward Mead, Feb. 6, 1923, MM Papers, Box Q1, Folder 17.

130 She had done well enough: MM to Emily Fogg Mead, Jan. 31, 1923, MM Papers, Box Q2, Folder 8; MM to Edward Mead, Feb. 6, 1923, MM Papers, Box Q1, Folder 17.

130 In early February 1923: Banner, *Intertwined Lives*, 177.

130 "It appeared that she had become": "Two College Girls Suicides Same Day," *New York Times*, Feb. 8, 1923.

130 Marie had been recovering: MM, "Life History," 1935, MM Papers, Box S9, Folder 7. See also MM, *Blackberry Winter*, 114–15.

130 "I was the best friend": MM to Emily Fogg Mead, Feb. 11, 1923, MM Papers, Box Q2, Folder 8.

131 "My dear Margaret": RB to MM, Feb. 8 [1923], MM Papers, Box B1, Folder 5.

131 "She rests me": RB, diary entry for Mar. 7, 1923, in *AAW*, 67.

131 A month later, in March: Banner, *Intertwined Lives*, 182.

131 "Professor Boas and I": MM, *Blackberry Winter*, 114.

131 "No-Red-Tape Fellowship": RB to MM, n.d. [1923], MM Papers, Box T4, Folder "Benedict, Ruth. Miscellany, 1923, Undated."

131 "fairy godmother": MM to RB, n.d. [Mar. 1923], MM Papers, S3, Folder 1.

132 They had a short honeymoon: LC, *Golden Journey*, 91–92.

132 "Naively we say": "Anthropometry" notes, 1924, MM Papers, Box A15, Folder 4.

134 "all special cultural forms": FB, "Evolution or Diffusion?," 340.

134 "We know of cases": Ibid., 341.

135 He seemed to take a special interest: Banner, *Intertwined Lives*, 226–27.

136 "a huge country parish": MM, "Life History," 1935, MM Papers, Box S9, Folder 7.

136 There she would have the advantage: MM, "Apprenticeship Under Boas," in Goldschmidt, *Anthropology of Boas*, 42.

136 The broken ankle that resulted: MM, draft manuscript of *Blackberry Winter*, MM Papers, Box I204, Folder 4.

136 When Mead met Sapir in Toronto: Banner, *Intertwined Lives*, 227.

136 "a brilliant mind": ES to RB, Sept. 1, 1925, MM Papers, Box S15, Folder 2.

136 completing each other's sentences: Banner, *Intertwined Lives*, 227.

137 In the spring of 1925: Ibid.; LC, interview by Jane Howard, Sept. 25 (no year), JH Papers, Box 38.

137 "the most satisfactory mind": MM, interview by Jean Houston, 1975, transcript, MM Papers, Box Q18, Folder 4, f. 426.

138 For all these reasons, language: See Sapir, *Language*, chap. 1.

139 "any socially inherited element": Sapir, "Culture, Genuine and Spurious," 402.

139 A culture might be thought of: Ibid.

139 "The genuine culture is not": Ibid., 410.

140 "A reading of the facts": Ibid., 413.

141 Later that summer Sapir sent: ES to RB, Aug. 8, 1925, MM Papers, Box S15, Folder 2.

141 a term she had picked up: ES to RB, Aug. 11, 1925, ibid.

141 "student marriage": Mead, *Blackberry Winter*, 116; LC, *Golden Journey*, 127.

141 People came and went: Howard, *Margaret Mead*, 63.

141 He went to his bishop: LC, interview by Jane Howard, n.d., JH Papers, Box 38; LC, *Golden Journey*, 82, 88–91.

141 He soon entered: LC, *Golden Journey*, 117–18.

142 "I am worried about her": ES to RB, July 17, 1925, MM Papers, Box T4, Folder "Benedict, Ruth. Correspondence. Sapir, Edward, 1922–1925."

142 "What's all this nonsense": ES to RB, Aug. 11, 1925, MM Papers, Box S15, Folder 2. Boas, for his part, was a consistent supporter of Mead's desire to go to Samoa. Sapir, he felt, had read "too many books on psychiatry." FB to RB, RB Papers, Folder 114.1.

142 Sapir and Benedict had corresponded: On Sapir's ambivalent relationship with Benedict, see Darnell, *Edward Sapir*, 172–83.

142 "Now the theory of polygamy": ES to RB, Sept. 1, 1925, MM Papers, Box S15, Folder 2.

142 She would later tell Mead: MM, interview by Jean Houston, 1975, transcript, MM Papers, Box Q18, Folder 4, f. 427.

143 Once she got abroad: Code sheets, MM Papers, Box N4, Folder 4.

143 Mead wept: Banner, *Intertwined Lives*, 233.

143 Benedict remembered kissing: RB to MM, Aug. 24, 1925, MM Papers, Box R7, Folder 13. The question of exactly when, and to what extent, Mead and Benedict became physically intimate has been the subject of considerable speculation. The most recent investigation, by Lois W. Banner, suggests that the two "had become lovers" by "the end of 1924." Banner, *Intertwined Lives*,

225. However, Banner does not give clear evidence of this timeline. Based on their correspondence, the summer of 1925 is more likely. The two clearly moved to a new phase in their relationship during the train journey west. Their contact up to that point, Mead wrote, had involved only "fantastic daydreams . . . hidden . . . so carefully even from myself at times." Yet by early August she finally felt that Benedict "care[d]" and that she could "feel it now, always." Benedict mentioned holding Mead in her arms during the train journey. See MM to RB, Aug. 6, 1925, MM Papers, Box S3, Folder 1; and RB to MM, Aug. 19, 1925, MM Papers, Box R7, Folder 13.

143 "Against that background": MM to RB, n.d. [early Aug. 1925], MM Papers, Box S3, Folder 1.

143 Benedict would later lie awake: RB to MM, Aug. 25, 1925, MM Papers, Box R7, Folder 13.

144 "You are taking notes": MM to RB, Aug. 6, 1925, MM Papers, Box S3, Folder 1.

144 "And always I love you": Ibid.

144 Mead had given herself: MM to RB, Aug. 6, 1925, MM Papers, Box S3, Folder 1.

144 She took the time alone: MM to RB, Aug. 1925 [no day, "4th day at sea"], MM Papers, Box S3, Folder 1; LC, Golden Journey, 131–32.

144 She devised a plan: RB to MM, Aug. 4, 1925, MM Papers, Box S4, Folder 6; MM to RB, Aug. 15, 1925, MM Papers, Box S3, Folder 1.

144 J in her secret telegraph code: Code sheets, MM Papers, Box N4, Folder 4.

144 "For the first time": MM to RB, Aug. 15, 1925, MM Papers, Box S3, Folder 1.

146 He worried that he might: Young, Malinowski, 292–93.

147 From Dumont d'Urville forward: See Douglas, Science, Voyages; Tcherkézoff, "Long and Unfortunate Voyage."

147 These "Oceanic Negroes": Chris Ballard, " 'Oceanic Negroes': British Anthropology of Papuans, 1820–1869," in Douglas and Ballard, Foreign Bodies, 157–204.

148 It began with "hopelessness and despair": Malinowski, Argonauts of Western Pacific, 18.

148 "get out from under [your] mosquito net": Ibid., 6.

149 She lay in bed: MM to RB, n.d. ("August 1925") [Aug. 30, 1925], MM Papers, Box S3, Folder 1; MM, "News Bulletin IV," n.d. ("5th day at sea") [Aug. 1925], MM Papers, Box N1, Folder 5.

150 When it was all over: MM, "News Bulletin V," Sept. 2, 1925, MM Papers, Box N1, Folder 5.

150 "He told me what he thought": Ibid.

150 Mead was staying: MM, "News Bulletin V," Sept. 14, 1925, ibid.

150 "Individuality is writ large": MM, "News Bulletin VI," Sept. 27, 1925, ibid.

150 She continued her language lessons: MM, "News Bulletin V," Sept. 14, 1925, ibid.

151 In Vaitogi, a village across the island: MM, "News Bulletin VII," Oct. 31, 1925, ibid.

151 "When a chief's son": MM, "News Bulletin VI," Sept. 27, 1925, entry for Oct. 3, ibid. Mead was inconsistent with her timekeeping and sometimes

named a news bulletin for one date but included entries from later dates in the same communication.

152 "over-run with missionaries": MM to FB, Oct. 11, 1925, MM Papers, Box N1, Folder 1.

152 The governor's plan: MM, "News Bulletin V," Sept. 2, 1925, MM Papers, Box N1, Folder 5.

152 "a suggestible lot of children": MM, "News Bulletin VI," Sept. 27, 1925, entry for Oct. 3, ibid.

152 The *palagi* at the hotel: MM, "News Bulletin V," n.d. ("Labor Day"), ibid.

152 On November 9, Mead caught: MM to FB, Nov. 3, 1925, MM Papers, Box N1, Folder 1.

152 It was also sufficiently: MM, "News Bulletin VI," Sept. 27, 1925, entry for Oct. 13, and "News Bulletin VIII," Nov. 14, 1925, both in MM Papers, Box N1, Folder 5.

152 As she wrote to Boas: MM to FB, Oct. 11, 1925, MM Papers, Box N1, Folder 1.

152 She might have been doing: MM, "News Bulletin VIII," Nov. 14, 1925, MM Papers, Box N1, Folder 5.

152 Children and teenagers flocked: MM, "News Bulletin IX," Dec. 11, 1925, ibid.

152 She hung a picture of Boas: MM, "News Bulletin XII," Feb. 9, 1926, ibid.

152 She soon took to signing: MM, "News Bulletin VIII," Nov. 14, 1925, ibid.

152 "I find I am happiest": MM, "News Bulletin XI," Jan. 16, 1926, ibid.

153 She wondered whether they were: MM to RB, Apr. 3, 1926, Box S3, Folder 3. Mead would later say that she built a large bonfire and burned all of Sapir's letters on the beach before she departed Samoa. MM, interview by Jean Houston, 1975, transcript, Box Q18, Folder 4, f. 429.

153 "Truly, my dear Ruth": ES to RB, Sept. 1, 1925, MM Papers, Box S15, Folder 2.

154 "The number of things": MM to RB, Dec. 15, 1925, MM Papers, Box S3, Folder 2.

154 "All the houses in Vaitogi": Fa'amotu to MM, Jan. 5, 1926, MM Papers, Box N1, Folder 4.

154 Mead had hunkered: MM, "News Bulletin X," Jan. 10, 1926, entry for Jan. 12, MM Papers, Box N1, Folder 5.

155 It would be impossible: MM to FB, Jan. 5, 1926, MM Papers, Box N1, Folder 1.

155 "ethnology of activity": MM, "News Bulletin XI," Jan. 16, 1926, MM Papers, Box N1, Folder 5.

155 "Most wives are faithful": See field notebooks in MM Papers, Box N2, Folders 1–2.

156 A bout of tonsillitis: MM, "News Bulletin XIV," Mar. 24, 1926, MM Papers, Box N1, Folder 5.

156 "I've never forgotten you": Faapua'a to MM, Apr. 17, 1926, MM Papers, Box N1, Folder 4.

156 Mead wrote to Benedict that she would probably: MM to RB, Mar. 28, 1926, MM Papers, Box S3, Folder 3.

156 In May she left Ta'u: MM, "News Bulletin XIV," Mar. 24, 1926, MM Papers, Box N1, Folder 5.

156 "Few lead more interesting lives": Undated newspaper clipping, MM Papers, Box Q2, Folder 8.

Chapter Eight: Coming of Age

158 "How is your trip?": Fa'amotu to MM, July 4, 1926, MM Papers, Box N1, Folder 4.

158 ringworm: MM to Sallie Jones, Dec. 21, 1926, MM Papers, Box I4, Folder 16.

158 "unequal to taking up": MM to RB, May 27, 1926, MM Papers, Box S3, Folder 4.

158 She fretted that her field notebooks: MM to RB, July 13, 1926, MM Papers, Box N1, Folder 1.

158 She worried that Edward Sapir: MM to RB, July 15, 1926, MM Papers, Box S3, Folder 4.

158 Reo Fortune—a kind of miracle: MM to RB, May 27, 1926, ibid.

158 If she had placed an ad: The Blake comparison is owed to Gregory Bateson, who would become Mead's third husband. GB to "E. J.," Feb. 27, 1936, MM Papers, Box S1, Folder 8.

158 During the seven weeks it took: MM, interview by Jean Houston, 1975, transcript, MM Papers, Box Q18, Folder 4, f. 438.

158 "with both hands": MM to RB, July 15, 1926, MM Papers, Box S3, Folder 4.

158 Her arrival, however, turned out to be as nightmarish: My account of the tangled circumstances of Mead's arrival is based on "Note by MM on What Really Happened," July 9, 1957, MM Papers, Box S11, Folder 1; LC, interviews by Jane Howard, Nov. 3, 1979, and Sept. 25 [no year], JH Papers, Box 38; Banner, *Intertwined Lives*, 245–47; and LC, *Golden Journey*, 175–81.

159 "demonstrative affection": MM to RB, July 15, 1926, MM Papers, Box S3, Folder 4.

159 She was glad to see Mead happy: RB to MM, Aug. 2, 1926, MM Papers, Box S5, Folder 1.

159 At the end of the summer: Banner, *Intertwined Lives*, 247.

159 "Tell me what to do!": LC, interview by Jane Howard, Sept. 25 [no year], JH Papers, Box 38.

159 "It appeals to me more": MM to RB, July 17, 1925, MM Papers, Box S3, Folder 1.

160 As it happened, she would end up: MM, *Blackberry Winter*, 14–17.

160 "a particular psychological problem": MM to Herbert E. Gregory, Dec. 20, 1926, MM Papers, Box I4, Folder 16.

161 By December she declared: Ibid.

161 "propaganda for the ethnological": MM to "Dr. Handy," Dec. 21, 1926, MM Papers, Box I4, Folder 16.

161 "THAT from Papa Franz!": MM to William Ogburn, Apr. 27, 1927, MM Papers, Box Q11, Folder 20.

161 Mead wanted something: See the original typescript of "The Adolescent Girl in Samoa," MM Papers, Box I2, Folder 2.

162 The suggested subtitle: MM to William Morrow, Jan. 25, 1928; MM to William Morrow, Feb. 11, 1928; and William Morrow to MM, Feb. 20, 1928, all in MM Papers, Box I2, Folder 1.

162 A press pamphlet: William Morrow promotional pamphlet, MM Papers, Box L3, Folder 1.

163 "In those social spheres": MM, *Coming of Age in Samoa*, 60.

164 "Romantic love as it occurs": Ibid., 105.

164 In great contrast to Americans: Ibid., 126.

164 "To live as a girl": Ibid., 109.

165 "The stress is in our civilisation": Ibid., 162.

166 "Whether or not we envy": Ibid., 160.

166 *Coming of Age in Samoa* was full of bravado: Later in Mead's career, her most dogged critic was the New Zealand anthropologist Derek Freeman, who devoted much of his life, from the mid-1960s until his death in 2001, to taking down a person he believed to be a shoddy scientist, even a charlatan. Freeman was particularly interested in Mead's Samoan work, both because it was the research that he felt had established her authority and because Freeman himself had conducted fieldwork in the islands (although mainly in Western Samoa—now called simply Samoa—rather than in American Samoa).

    Rather than being sexually free and at ease, Freeman claimed, Samoan society was highly regulated and constrained, with plenty of sexualized violence. He also contended that Mead's reliance on young female informants had skewed her data. These young people had simply been engaging in sexual joking and bravado, which Mead, a gullible foreigner, took to be fact. On these points, see Freeman, *Margaret Mead and Samoa* and *Fateful Hoaxing*.

    The reaction against Freeman was nearly as severe as his critique of Mead. Some scholars faulted him for precisely the thing he had accused Mead of doing: selectively using evidence and mishandling interview data, along with misrepresenting her original claims. Mead almost certainly overstated the case on many points of Samoan society, much like any ethnographer trying to extrapolate from a limited set of informants to an entire society. But no one who examines Mead's notebooks today could accuse her of being cavalier or naïve as a fieldworker. Nor does the tone of the subsequent letters between the Samoan girls and Mead suggest systematic trickery or falsehood. The notebooks are now fully available for consultation at the Library of Congress, so readers can judge for themselves—something that Freeman never did, since his original book on Mead was published before the papers were fully public. For a detailed treatment of the entire controversy, see Shankman, *Trashing of Mead*, and on Freeman himself, see Hempenstall, *Truth's Fool*.

166 "All these people from Fitiuta": S. T. Galeai Pulefano to MM, May 5, 1926, MM Papers, Box N1, Folder 4.

167 "seeking to prove that": Quoted in Lutkehaus, *Margaret Mead*, 50.

167 "an absolutely first-rate piece": Bronislaw Malinowski to William Morrow, Aug. 22, 1928, MM Papers, Box S9, Folder 2.

167 "While some people complain": Alfred Kroeber to MM, Oct. 11, 1929, MM Papers, Box I2, Folder 1.

167 "disturbed and rather cheap": ES to RB, Sept. 4, 1928, MM Papers, Box S15, Folder 2.

167 Within a few months of publication: William Morrow to MM, Jan. 11, 1929, MM Papers, Box I2, Folder 1.

167 She had also started to inform: MM to Stella Jones, May 24, 1928, MM Papers, Box I4, Folder 16.

168 "Philadelphia Girl Plans": "Phila. Girl Plans Cannibal Sojourn," *Philadelphia Public Ledger*, Aug. 25, 1928.

168 For some time, she had been plotting: RF to MM, June 26, 1928, MM Papers, Box S1, Folder 15.

168 "You know it's your career": MM to RF, Aug. 29, 1928, MM Papers, Box R4, Folder 6.

169 Love affairs could trundle along: MM to RB, Sept. 3, 1928, MM Papers, Box S3, Folder 4.

169 "beautiful walled palace": MM to RB, Sept. 5, 1928, and MM to RB, Sept. 4, 1928, both in MM Papers, Box S3, Folder 4.

169 She cabled Benedict: MM to RB (telegram), Oct. 15, 1928, MM Papers, Box S3, Folder 5.

169 It felt like: MM to RB, Oct. 13, 1928, ibid.

169 On a moonlit night: Mead, *Blackberry Winter*, 169.

170 "a perfect little rustic Venice": MM to RB, Nov. 29, 1928, MM Papers, Box S3, Folder 5.

170 The men wore their hair: MM, *Blackberry Winter*, 169.

170 "independent little water rats": MM to FB, Dec. 22, 1928, MM Papers, Box R7, Folder 16.

170 She took a twelve-hour: MM, draft manuscript of *Blackberry Winter*, MM Papers, Box I204, Folder 4; MM to RB, Apr. 8, 1929, MM Papers, Box S3, Folder 6.

170 The drawings soon piled up: MM, *Blackberry Winter*, 175.

171 The maker wrote back: See MM Papers, Box I1, Folder 2. She published the results of this work as MM, "Methodology of Racial Testing," one of her first scholarly articles.

171 One of the "fundamental aims": Boas, *Anthropology and Modern Life*, 206.

173 "Rather good-looking": Goddard, *Kallikak Family*, 11–12.

174 The images, it was later: See Gould, *Mismeasure of Man*.

175 "Laws restricting marriage": Davenport, *State Laws Limiting Marriage*, 7.

175 a wave of forced sterilization: Kühl, *Nazi Connection*, 17.

175 Two grand international: Black, *War Against Weak*, 236–38, 298.

176 "socially inadequate persons": See Laughlin, *Second International Exhibition of Eugenics*.

176 "It is better for all": *Buck v. Bell* (1927), at https://caselaw.findlaw.com/us -supreme-court/274/200.html.

176 By the early 1930s: Cohen, *Imbeciles*, 300.

177 By 1941: Reilly, *Surgical Solution*, 97.

177 By the 1960s: Kluchin, *Fit to Be Tied*, 17.

177 "While the stock judges": Quoted in Lovett, *Conceiving the Future*, 144.

178 "dysgenic breeding": Sanger, *Pivot of Civilization*, 283.

178 One of the most popular: It was, in fact, the method used by Margaret Mead. See MM to GB, Dec. 3, 1934, MM Papers, Box R2, Folder 6.

178 "We cannot treat": FB, *Anthropology and Modern Life*, 15.

179 "almost every anthropological": Ibid., 16.

179   "We classify the variety": Ibid., 23.
179   The mobilization of sham: Ibid., 84.
179   "parting of the ways": Ibid., 108.
180   "how easily the human": Ibid., 205.
180   Had the British: Ibid., 124.
181   He piled up hypotheses: Kroeber, "Totem and Taboo," 51.
181   Mead, too, had been: MM to William Ogburn, Apr. 27, 1927, MM Papers, Box Q7, Folder 20.
182   "They are quarrelsome": MM to Social Science Research Council, Apr. 17, 1929, MM Papers, Box I4, Folder 11.
182   "For them the dark": MM to Social Science Research Council, Feb. 12, 1929, ibid.
183   "One of the principal": Ibid.,
183   "I would suggest": MM to Social Science Research Council, Apr. 17, 1929, ibid.
184   "All social relations": MM to Committee on Research Fellowships, Social Science Research Council, Nov. 30, 1928, MM Papers, Box I4, Folder 11.
184   "experiments in what could": MM, Growing Up in New Guinea, 6.
185   Mead and Fortune arrived: MM, draft manuscript of Blackberry Winter, MM Papers, Box I204, Folder 4.
185   William Morrow, her publisher: William Morrow to MM, June 4, 1930, MM Papers, Box Q12, Folder 5.
185   She wrote quickly: MM to RF, Apr. 30, 1934, MM Papers, Box R4, Folder 10.
185   "Your book": Henry Neil to MM, Jan. 3, 1929, MM Papers, Box I2, Folder 1.
185   "It is the only book": R. F. Barton to MM, July 6, 1929, ibid.
185   She hired an agent: Contract with Harry Blake, Dec. 8, 1930, MM Papers, Box Q2, Folder 2.
185   "We can't stomach": Merritt Hulburb to MM, Dec. 9, 1930, MM Papers, Box I5, Folder 2.
186   "the last book": MM, Blackberry Winter, 199.
186   "stable, though": Ibid., 185.

Chapter Nine: Masses and Mountaintops

187   Harvard and Columbia continued: See the table of students in Darnell, Along Came Boas, 171–72.
188   "We all call him": ZNH, Dust Tracks, 140.
188   "to stand and give": Ibid., 13, 22.
188   "a dark rock": ZNH, "How It Feels to Be Colored Me," in Folklore, Memoirs, and Other Writings, 828.
188   The closest she had ever: Hemenway, Zora Neale Hurston, 17–19.
188   "paternalistic affection": Washburn, Cosmos Club, 149.
189   No one knew: ZNH, Dust Tracks, 21.
189   Zora Neale Hurston was born: Hemenway, Zora Neale Hurston, 13; Kaplan, Zora Neale Hurston, 773.
189   "a pure Negro town": ZNH, Dust Tracks, 1.
189   She was only two: Boyd, Wrapped in Rainbows, 15.

189   Jumping at the sun: ZNH, *Dust Tracks*, 13.
190   "a little colored girl": Ibid., 70.
190   When her father died: Boyd, *Wrapped in Rainbows*, 78.
190   She became part: Anderson, *White Rage*, 52.
190   "Colored" toilets: Asch and Musgrove, *Chocolate City*, 220.
191   Never jailed, Heflin: Ibid., 209.
191   A few years later: Ibid., 237.
191   After three nights: Ibid., 232–34.
191   "I felt the ladder": ZNH, *Dust Tracks*, 131.
192   "Zora's greatest ambition": *The Bison* (Howard University Yearbook, 1923), n.p.
192   In the first week of January: Hemenway, *Zora Neale Hurston*, 9; ZNH, *Dust Tracks*, 138.
193   "I became Barnard's": Hurston, *Dust Tracks*, 139.
193   "cross eyed": ZNH to Countee Cullen, Mar. 11, 1926, in Kaplan, *Zora Neale Hurston*, 83.
193   "certainly the most amusing": Hughes, *Big Sea*, 238–39.
194   "It made both faculty": ZNH to Fannie Hurst, Mar. 16, 1926, in Kaplan, *Zora Neale Hurston*, 85.
194   It seemed hard: Hemenway, *Zora Neale Hurston*, 60–61.
194   "I do not care": Du Bois, "Criteria of Negro Art," *Crisis* (October 1926), reprinted in Gates and Jarrett, *New Negro*, 259.
194   Elevation, advancement: Stewart, *New Negro*, 511.
195   "To many of her white": Hughes, *Big Sea*, 239.
195   "Negroes were supposed": ZNH, *Dust Tracks*, 171.
195   "a child that questions": Ibid., 25.
195   Hurston's story: Ibid., 140.
195   "Of course, Zora": Ibid.
196   She took to calling: ZNH to Melville Herskovits, July 20, 1926, in Kaplan, *Zora Neale Hurston*, 87.
196   "I am being trained": Hemenway, *Zora Neale Hurston*, 63; Hughes, *Big Sea*, 236.
196   Herskovits had even: Herskovits, *Anthropometry of American Negro*, 39.
196   "stop the average Harlemite": Hughes, *Big Sea*, 239.
196   It was a source: ZNH, *Dust Tracks*, 143.
196   In February 1927: "Chronology," in Kaplan, *Zora Neale Hurston*, 775.
196   "poking and prying": ZNH, *Dust Tracks*, 143.
197   On November 2, 1920: My account of the Ocoee massacre is based on Ortiz, *Emancipation Betrayed*, 220–24, which uses Hurston but corroborates her account with other sources.
197   "White children stood": Quoted ibid., 223.
198   But she knew the world: ZNH to Annie Nathan Meyer, Mar. 7, 1927, in Kaplan, *Zora Neale Hurston*, 91.
198   "the harshest and most unlovely": Ibid., 92.
198   "Flowers are gorgeous": ZNH to Lawrence Jordan, Mar. 24, 1927, ibid., 94. *Cracker* was a term in wide use for Colonial-era white cattlemen in the woods

and prairies of northern and central Florida. It was not considered a racially charged insult and is still today the common way of referring to old Floridian families whose roots go back to the eighteenth and nineteenth centuries.

198   In the time she had been: Mormino, *Land of Sunshine*, 45.

198   A combination of: Ibid., 7.

199   Between 1890 and 1930: Miller, *Crime, Sexual Violence*, 16.

199   Not a single person: Ibid.

199   "We used to own": Quoted in Sellers and Asbed, "Forced Labor in Florida Agriculture," 37.

200   "You certainly ought": FB to ZNH, Mar. 24, 1927, FB Papers (digitized).

200   But it all became: ZNH to FB, Mar. 29, 1927, FB Papers (digitized).

200   "Sassy Susie": ZNH to Carl van Vechten, Aug. 26, 1927, in Kaplan, *Zora Neale Hurston*, 103.

200   Just in case things: Boyd, *Wrapped in Rainbows*, 145.

200   "Pardon me, but": Hurston, *Dust Tracks*, 144.

201   She contemplated: ZNH to Annie Nathan Meyer, in Kaplan, *Zora Neale Hurston*, 100.

201   But she was coming: ZNH to Dorothy West, Mar. 24, 1927, ibid., 96.

201   She had even more: ZNH to FB, Mar. 29, 1927, FB Papers (digitized).

201   Their "negroness": Ibid.

201   To make sure she got: ZNH to Lawrence Jordan, May 3, 1927, in Kaplan, *Zora Neale Hurston*, 98–99.

202   Over the next few: ZNH to Carl Van Vechten, Aug. 26, 1927, ibid., 105.

202   "he tries to hold me": ZNH to Langston Hughes, Mar. 8, 1928, ibid., 114.

202   Much of the text, however: Hemenway, *Zora Neale Hurston*, 96–99; Boyd, *Wrapped in Rainbows*, 153–54.

202   She consulted Boas: ZNH, *Dust Tracks*, 144.

202   He had urged her: FB to ZNH, May 3, 1927, FB Papers (digitized).

202   Mason lived in: Kaplan, *Miss Anne in Harlem*, 197.

203   "Negro folk-lore is still": ZNH to Langston Hughes, Apr. 12, 1928, in Kaplan, *Zora Neale Hurston*, 115–16.

204   a hundred different people: ZNH manuscript (MS 7532), NAA.

204   "At last I come up": ZNH to FB, June 8, 1930, FB Papers (digitized).

204   After all, he said, Africans: Baker, *From Savage to Negro*, 121.

204   "There is nothing to prove": Boas, *Mind of Primitive Man*, 271.

204   "It is of course not fair": Kroeber, *Anthropology*, 505.

206   "The types and distribution": FB, "Mythology and Folk-Tales," 379.

207   "More than any other": RB, "Folklore," 288.

208   "The author considers": Woodson, *African Background Outlined*, v.

209   "Why did the Negro": Herskovits, "Negro in New World," 153.

209   "typically Negro": Gershenhorn, *Melville Herskovits*, 66, 69–70.

210   "my heart beneath": ZNH, *Dust Tracks*, 144.

210   Hurston once more: Boyd, *Wrapped in Rainbows*, 226.

211   "I have kicked": ZNH to RB, Dec. 4, 1933, in Kaplan, *Zora Neale Hurston*, 284.

211   Sometime later a telegram: ZNH, *Dust Tracks*, 174–75.

211   Still, the news came: Ibid., 175.

211   The Julius Rosenwald Fund: Edwin Rogers Embree to ZNH, Dec. 19, 1934, FB Papers (digitized).

211   "I might want to teach": ZNH to FB, Jan. 4, 1935, FB Papers (digitized).

211   "corn pone": ZNH, *Dust Tracks*, 213.

211   "Thanks and thanks": ZNH to RB, n.d. [winter–spring 1932], in Kaplan, *Zora Neale Hurston*, 248.

212   "I am full of tremors": ZNH to FB, Aug. 20, 1934, FB Papers (digitized).

212   "true inner life": FB, "Preface" to ZNH, *Mules and Men*, xiii.

212   "pitched headforemost": ZNH, *Mules and Men*, 1–2.

212   "the boiled-down juice": Quoted in Boyd, *Wrapped in Rainbows*, 318–19.

214   "Many a man thinks": ZNH, *Mules and Men*, 184.

214   "I think it is not saying": Quoted in Boyd, *Wrapped in Rainbows*, 285.

Chapter Ten: Indian Country

215   As many as twenty-five hundred: Jürgen Langenkämper, "Franz Boas' Correspondence with German Friends and Colleagues in the Early 1930s," in Darnell et al., *Boas as Public Intellectual*, 279.

215   "the utilitarian and aesthetic": Edward L. Bernays to FB, Oct. 8, 1930, RB Papers, Folder 1.1.

215   "the Negro race was far": Maurice Geller to FB, Mar. 15, 1939, FB Papers (microfilm), Reel 42.

215   "What your instructor": FB to Geller, Mar. 16, 1939, ibid.

215   Did Negroes make: Wilbur Wood to FB, Mar. 31, 1941, FB Papers (microfilm), Reel 44.

216   There was no evidence: FB to Wood, Apr. 3, 1941, ibid.

216   "There is something": FB to Ernst Boas, Apr. 12, 1919, BRC, Box 3, File labeled "Box 79."

216   He told Mead about one: FB, "The Dream of the Biting Mice," Feb. 27, 1928, MM Papers, Box A3, Folder 9. The day's meetings had involved a futile effort to try to get the National Research Council and the Social Science Research Council, two important scholarly funders, to coordinate their activities.

216   "He looks weak": RB to Marie Eichelberger, Apr. 23, 1932, MM Papers, Box S15, Folder 1.

216   She had been the consummate: ZNH to FB, Oct. 23, 1934, FB Papers (digitized).

216   For the entire night: Helene Boas Yampolsky, memoir, FB Prof. Papers, Box 3, File "Boas—Boas Family Life."

217   It was a moment of his life: FB to parents, Nov. 1, 1897, quoted in Cole, *Franz Boas*, 209.

217   Qisuk's seven-year-old son: Ibid.; Harper, *Minik*, 84–85.

218   Still others fell ill: Cole, *Franz Boas*, 209.

218   "a further study": Hrdlička, "Eskimo Brain," 500.

218   The Inuit men had worked: Jacknis, "First Boasian," 522.

219   Not until 1993: Harper, *Minik*, 229–32.

219   "Someone told him": George Hunt to FB, Jan. 10, 1899, FB Papers (microfilm), Reel 4. I have changed Hunt's original spelling and grammar for clarity.

220   His only regret: George Hunt to FB, Apr. 24, 1899, ibid.

220   A few years later, in 1897: Harper, *Minik*, 2.

220   Not long after that, the American Museum: See Bradford and Blume, *Ota Benga*; Newkirk, *Spectacle*.

220   "Have totally wild": Quoted in Victor Golla, "Ishi's Language," in Kroeber and Kroeber, *Ishi in Three Centuries*, 215.

221   Kroeber gave him: Kroeber, *Ishi in Two Worlds*, 128.

221   It was eventually donated: In 2000 Ishi's brain and cremated body were given to the Pit River Tribe and Redding Rancheria Indians and placed at an undisclosed burial site. Sackman, *Wild Men*, 296–98. See also Starn, *Ishi's Brain*.

221   Driven from their land: Madley, *American Genocide*, 346.

221   By the time he came: Starn, *Ishi's Brain*, 77.

221   "I killed him": Quoted in Kroeber, *Ishi in Two Worlds*, 234. On Sapir and Ishi, see also Darnell, *Edward Sapir*, 79–82.

222   "Dear friend I hope": Ignacita Suina to RB, Feb. 26, 1926, RB Papers, Folder 35.5.

222   Back in Manhattan, Melville: Melville Herskovits to MM, Aug. 23, 1923, MM Papers, Box C1, Folder 8.

222   "But just one thing": Fa'amotu to MM, Oct. 31, 1928, MM Papers, Box S11, Folder 11.

222   including the heads: Redman, *Bone Rooms*, 193.

222   "2 Pygmies, 3 Australians": Ibid.

223   "They are terribly afraid": ZNH, "The Florida Expedition," Committee on Native American Languages Collection, APS, File 46.

225   "If this is field work": MM to RB, July 31, 1930, MM Papers, Box S3, Folder 7.

226   "(but Two Crows denies)": Dorsey, *Omaha Sociology*, 347.

226   "embarrassing questions": Sapir, "Why Cultural Anthropology Needs," 2.

226   "We see now that Dorsey": Ibid., 3.

227   "a special kind": Ibid., 6.

228   "Instead, therefore, of arguing": Ibid.

228   They weren't "superorganic": Sapir, "Do We Need a 'Superorganic'?"

229   Just as Madison Grant: See Deloria, *Playing Indian*, chaps. 4 and 5.

230   The tendency of children: Bederman, *Manliness and Civilization*, 94.

230   "Most savages in most respects": Hall, *Adolescence*, 2:650.

230   Both should be given: Paris, *Children's Nature*, 28–30. See also Van Slyck, *Manufactured Wilderness*, 169–213.

230   "The power to throw": Hall, *Adolescence*, 1:206.

231   "an unsettled . . . body": Quoted in Bederman, *Manliness and Civilization*, 105.

231   "Margaret Mead and a whole group": Sargent, *Handbook of Summer Camps*, 38.

232   "I stand on middle ground": Quoted in Cotera, *Native Speakers*, 41.

232   Deloria was born: Early biographical details on Deloria are taken from her own account of her life, written for Mead. MM to ECD, Jan. 30, 1942, MM Papers, Box I58, Folder 10.

233   "He knew the race": ECD, "Indian Chief Helped to Build Kingdom," ECD Archive.

233   "In some of the countries": ECD, "The Study I Like Best; and Why" (Nov. 6, 1902), ibid.

233 She managed an A-plus: Transcript, All Saints School (1906–1910), ECD, ibid.

234 Her father had been: Deloria, *Indians in Unexpected Places*, 23.

235 She would later remember the stipend: Cotera, *Native Speakers*, 237n13.

235 "Dear comrades": ECD, "Indian Progress: A Pageant," Nov. 11, 1927, ECD Archive.

235 "She always appealed": FB to ECP, June 20, 1927, ECP Papers [unnumbered box], Folder 3.

235 She arrived in February 1928: Cotera, *Native Speakers*, 46.

235 Walker was careful: Walker, *Sun Dance*, 58–59.

237 The article appeared: Deloria, "Sun Dance of the Oglala Sioux."

238 "I cannot tell you": ECD to FB, July 11, 1932, FB Papers (digitized).

238 "to go at it": Ibid.

238 To extract the sinew: ECD to RB, Nov. 23, 1935 [1925 as written], RB Papers, Folder 28.3.

239 She became acquainted: MM to ECD, Jan. 30, 1942, MM Papers, Box C5, Folder 13.

239 She and Hurston worked: Cotera, *Native Speakers*, 47.

239 "Get nowhere": ECD, misc. notes, n.d., ECD Archive.

239 On one occasion, she reported: Susan Gardner, "Introduction," in Deloria, *Waterlily*, vi.

239 Some were for paying: ECD to MM, Jan. 28, 1942, MM Papers, Box C8, Folder 11.

240 From its establishment in 1927: Leeds-Hurwitz, *Rolling in Ditches*, 132.

241 "In all his work": RB to Roland S. Morris, Sept. 27, 1943, RB Papers, Folder 28.3.

241 "Her knowledge of the subject": FB to "Whom It May Concern," July 7, 1937, ECD Archive.

241 Margaret Mead had found: MM to RB, Sept. 2, 1930, MM Papers, Box S3, Folder 7.

241 "armchair anthropology": ECD, misc. notes, n.d., ECD Archive.

243 "Her childhood among": RB, "Special Report to the Council for Research in the Social Sciences," n.d. [likely 1934], Department of Anthropology Records, CU, Box 1, Folder "Research—CRSS, Project 35, Acculturation, 1930–1938."

243 "I am very sad today": ECD to FB, "end of 1938," FB Papers (digitized).

243 "I can't get any federal": Ibid.

243 "You will be glad": FB to ECD, July 20, 1939, ECD Archive.

243 Deloria's perfect command: FB and ECD, *Dakota Grammar*, vii.

244 "So many people are asking": ECD to FB, July 15, 1941, FB Papers (microfilm), Reel 44.

Chapter Eleven: Living Theory

245 "He is vain": RB to MM, Apr. 25, 1933, MM Papers, Box S5, Folder 7.

246 "a belligerent romanticist": ES to RB, May 11, 1926, MM Papers, Box T4, Folder "Benedict, Ruth. Correspondence. Sapir Edward, 1922–1925"; MM, *Blackberry Winter*, 159.

246 On one occasion he allegedly slipped: MM, interview by Jean Houston, 1975, transcript, MM Papers, Box Q18, Folder 4, f. 434.

246 He had praised her Samoan: Banner, *Intertwined Lives*, 281.

246 "She is . . . a loathsome bitch": ES to RB, Apr. 29, 1929, MM Papers, Box S15, Folder 2.

246 "Love having been squeezed": ES, "Observations on Sex Problem," 529.

246 Jealousy, she said: MM, "Jealousy: Primitive and Civilised," in Schmalhausen and Calverton, *Woman's Coming of Age*, 35–48; Banner, *Intertwined Lives*, 280–81.

246 "the most difficult problem": FB, "Limitations of Comparative Method," 903.

246 "People don't use": MM to RB, July 4, 1931, MM Papers, Box S3, Folder 8.

247 "It is clear that Dr. Boas'": Sapir, "Franz Boas," 278.

248 "cheap and dull": Ibid., 279.

248 "To many of us": Lynd and Lynd, *Middletown*, 5.

249 "I find I am growing": MM to RB, Dec. 2, 1932, MM Papers, Box S4, Folder 1.

249 Her salary as an assistant: MM tax documents for 1933, MM Papers, Box Q24, Folder 12.

249 Benedict at least had: Department of Anthropology Records, CU, Box 2, Folder "Administrative—Budget, 1931–1954"; and pay scales in RB Papers, Folder 42.5

249 She also wasn't allowed: Banner, *Intertwined Lives*, 378.

249 Mead worried that she herself: MM to RF, Jan. 6, 1928, MM Papers, Box R4, Folder 6.

249 "I don't think having": MM to RB, Dec. 2, 1932, MM Papers, Box S4, Folder 1.

249 "The country here": Henrietta Schmerler to FB, July 4, 1931, Department of Anthropology Records, CU, Box 1, Folder "Research—Fieldwork Expenditures. Schmerler (Henrietta) murder, correspondence, 4 July 1931–18 January 1932."

250 "as placid as kittens": MM to RB, Jan. 16, 1932, MM Papers, Box S3, Folder 8.

250 Their name, in fact: Mead, *Mountain Arapesh*, 1:111n1.

251 They would have kept: MM to RB, Jan. 16, 1932, MM Papers, Box S3, Folder 8.

251 "I'm more than ever": MM to RB, Apr. 23, 1932, MM Papers, Box S3, Folder 9.

251 "solved the sex problem": MM to RB, Apr. 25, 1932, ibid.

251 "Yes, the woman's husband": Ibid.

252 People would copulate: Mead, *Blackberry Winter*, 205–6.

252 "Yes, I have eaten": MM field notes, MM Papers, Box N101, Folder 1.

252 Mead walked around: MM to RB, Oct. 9, 1932, MM Papers, Box S4, Folder 1.

252 After three months in these conditions: MM to RB, Oct. 11, 1932, ibid.

252 "You're tired": MM, *Blackberry Winter*, 208.

253 "I've got a lot": MM to RB, "Day After Christmas 1932," Box S4, Folder 1.

253 During school holidays: GB to Martin Bateson, Sept. 4, 1921, MM Papers, Box Q1, Folder 2.

253 When his two older brothers: Lipset, *Gregory Bateson*, 70–92.

253 Shortly after Mead and Fortune: MM, *Blackberry Winter*, 217.

253 "vulnerable beauty": MM to RB, "Day After Christmas 1932," Box S4, Folder 1.

254 "any gunpowder": Ibid.

254 "I do think I've learned": Ibid.

254 The holiday season found: This account of Ambunti, the journey upriver, and the origins of the Mead-Fortune-Bateson triangle is from MM to RB, Dec. 30, 1932, MM Papers, Box S4, Folder 1; Lipset, *Gregory Bateson*, 135–38; Howard, *Margaret Mead*, 154–66; Banner, *Intertwined Lives*, 324–39; MM, *Blackberry Winter*, 208–22.

255 "I love you terribly": MM to GB, Nov. 3, 1934, MM Papers, Box R2, Folder 7; Banner, *Intertwined Lives*, 324.

255 They built large: Tchambuli description from Mead, *Sex and Temperament*, 221–28.

255 "I've climbed mountains": MM to RB, Jan. 9, 1933, MM Papers, Box S4, Folder 1.

255 "The truth of the matter": MM to GB, n.d. ("Friday"), from "Tsambuli," MM Papers, Box R1, Folder 6.

255 As they made the rounds: Ibid.

256 The language was no less: MM to GB, n.d. ("Sunday morning"), MM Papers, Box R1, Folder 6.

256 More and more, Mead: Ibid.

256 "And Reo and I go to bed": MM to RB, Feb. 23, 1933, MM Papers, Box S4, Folder 1.

256 "So I do feel": MM to RB, Feb. 14, 1933, ibid.

257 "discovery of great magnitude": MM to RB, Mar. 29, 1933, Box R7, Folder 13.

258 "We moved back and forth": Mead, *Blackberry Winter*, 216.

258 "This is the climax": MM to RB, Mar. 29, 1933, MM Papers, Box R7, Folder 13.

259 He drafted a letter: RF to LC, Apr. 9, 1933, MM Papers, Box R4, Folder 7.

259 Even Fortune and Bateson: MM to RB, June 16, 1933, MM Papers, Box S4, Folder 1; MM to GB, June 12, 1934, MM Papers, Box R2, Folder 7.

259 She had even told Bateson: RF to MM, Sept. 12, 1933, MM Papers, Box R4, Folder 7.

259 "Gregory ate our baby": MM, interview by Jean Houston, 1975, transcript, MM Papers, Box Q18, Folder 5, f. 441.

260 "There was a large amount": MM to RB, June 16, 1933, MM Papers, Box S4, Folder 1.

260 The voyage was "ghastly": Ibid.

260 He hit her: MM to RF, Sept. 10, 1933, MM Papers, Box R4, Folder 7. Mead would later say that earlier, while they were still in Tchambuli, Fortune had knocked her down and caused a miscarriage. MM, interview by Jean Houston, 1975, transcript, Box Q18, Folder 5, f. 441.

261 "forced [his] hand": RF to MM, June 25, 1934, MM Papers, Box R4, Folder 11; RF to RB, n.d. ("end of October") [pencil mark: 1934], Box R5, Folder 2.

261 But after they ate: MM to RB, Aug. 26, 1933, MM Papers, Box S4, Folder 1.

261 "Oh, Ruth": Ibid.

261 "They say there are devils": GB to "E. J.," Feb. 27, 1936, Box S1, Folder 8.

261 She took in a movie: MM to GB, n.d. [pencil mark: Oct. 2, 1933], MM Papers, Box R1, Folder 6.

261 When she finally arrived: MM to GB, n.d. [apparently Sept. 1933; second half of letter dated Sept. 28, 1933], ibid.

261 "I find that I am worried": RB to MM, July 19, 1933, MM Papers, Box S5, Folder 7.

261 "one from Hell": MM to RF, Aug. 29, 1928, MM Papers, Box R4, Folder 6.

262 "Don't make up": RF to MM, June 25, 1934, MM Papers, Box R4, Folder 11.

262 He in turn made a bonfire: Ann McLean, "In the Footprints of Reo Fortune," in Hays, *Ethnographic Presents*, 37.

262 She wondered for an instant: MM to GB, Nov. 1, 1933, MM Papers, Box R1, Folder 7.

262 He told her they would: GB to MM (telegram), Sept. 3, 1933, Box R1, Folder 6.

263 Physical intimacy might happen: Banner, *Intertwined Lives*, 272–73.

263 They had long been living: Ibid., 315.

263 She also sent along: GB, interview by Jane Howard, n.d., JH Papers, CU, Box 38.

264 "Anthropology is the study": RB, *Patterns of Culture*, 1.

264 "great arc": Ibid., 24.

264 "a mechanical Frankenstein's monster": Ibid., 49.

265 "the Procrustean bed": Ibid., 228.

266 "the great arc of potential": Ibid., 237.

266 "The recognition of cultural relativity": Ibid., 278.

266 "Ruth's book": MM to GB, Oct. 9, 1933, MM Papers, R1, Folder 6.

267 "propaganda for the anthropological": Kroeber, "Review of *Patterns of Culture*," 689.

267 "the doctrine of cultural relativity": "Review of *Patterns of Culture*," *New York Times*, Oct. 21, 1934.

267 "It's funny, you know": MM to GB, June 12, 1934, MM Papers, Box R2, Folder 7.

267 "It was of course a form": Ibid.

268 "The kind of feeling": MM to RB, Mar. 29, 1933, MM Papers, Box R7, Folder 13.

268 "We were well away": GB to RF, Jan. 22, 1935, MM Papers, Box R2, Folder 9.

269 "Before I was nothing": Ibid.

269 "You got so excited": RF to MM, n.d. [pencil mark: 1933], MM Papers, Box R4, Folder 8.

269 But just a few months after: MM to GB, Dec. 21, 1933, MM Papers, Box R1, Folder 7.

269 "our own modern cultures": Ibid.

270 "brilliant": RF to MM, July 19, 1935, MM Papers, Box R5, Folder 5.

270 It was also an effort: Banner, *Intertwined Lives*, 405.

270 "plays out the whole drama": MM, *Sex and Temperament*, xxxv.

274 "A civilization might take": Ibid., 298.

Chapter Twelve: Spirit Realms

275 "the life of the unsophisticated": Henry Lee Moon, "Big Old Lies," *New Republic*, Dec. 11, 1935, 142.

275 Fannie Hurst, the best-selling author: Boyd, *Wrapped in Rainbows*, 284.

275 The year after *Mules and Men:* MM to GB, Apr. 18, 1934, MM Papers, Box R2, Folder 5.

275 "literary science": Boyd, *Wrapped in Rainbows*, 286.

276 "a study of magic practices": Ibid.

276 "formalized curiosity": Hurston, *Dust Tracks*, 143.

276 "Just squat down": Quoted in Boyd, *Wrapped in Rainbows*, 288.

276 "Papa Franz knows": ZNH to Melville Herskovits, Apr. 15, 1936, in Kaplan, *Zora Neale Hurston*, 372.

276 She cut a dashing image: Boyd, *Wrapped in Rainbows*, 288.

276 "a land where": ZNH, *Tell My Horse*, 6.

276 "Everywhere else a person": Ibid., 7.

277 She joined a boar hunt: Ibid., 31–37.

277 On this occasion, the corpse: Ibid., 39–56.

278 Frederick Douglass, who served: Speech at Haiti Pavilion, Chicago World's Fair, 1893, text at faculty.webster.edu/corbetre/haiti/history/1844-1915 /douglass.htm.

279 "Funeral met funeral": ZNH, *Tell My Horse*, 71.

279 The country was really: Ibid., 73.

279 "a peace I have never": Ibid., 135.

279 He governed entire plantations: Ibid., 139.

280 " 'Voodoo,' or *vodun*": Herskovits, *Life in Haitian Valley*, 139.

281 "in a universe": Ibid.

281 the best thing yet written: Gershenhorn, *Melville Herskovits*, 84.

281 "uncontaminated Africanisms": Herskovits, *Life in Haitian Valley*, 268.

281 Herskovits would later rank: Herskovits, "Problem, Method and Theory in Afroamerican Studies," *Afroamerica* 1 (1945), reprinted in Herskovits, *New World Negro*, 53.

281 "If the life of the Haitian Negro": Herskovits, *Life in Haitian Valley*, 47.

282 After all, what was a white: Herskovits, "Some Next Steps in the Study of Negro Folklore," *Journal of American Folklore* 56 (1943), reprinted in Herskovits, *New World Negro*, 174.

282 "As concerns the inner life": Herskovits, *Life in Haitian Valley*, 12.

283 L. Marlow: Ibid., 13.

283 The American authorities: Renda, *Taking Haiti*, 213.

283 "Probably all the caco chiefs": Quoted in Dubois, *Haiti*, 272.

284 *The Magic Island* (1929), a best-selling: Ibid., chap. 6; Ramsey, *Spirits and Law*, chap. 3.

284 "Voodoo on Haiti": Seabrook, *Magic Island*, 12–13.

284 Hurston had read: ZNH, *Tell My Horse*, 134.

285 "a soulless human corpse": Seabrook, *Magic Island*, 93.

286 "seeps over the country": ZNH, *Tell My Horse*, 179.

286 A doctor pulled the cloth: Hurston's description of her encounter with Felix-Mentor is ibid., 179–81, 195–97.

287 But when Hurston suddenly: Boyd, *Wrapped in Rainbows*, 299–300.

288 "What is the whole truth": ZNH, *Tell My Horse*, 179.

289 Magic, Hurston had learned: RB, "Magic," 39.

289 People who "play the zig-zag": ZNH, *Dust Tracks*, 232.

289 "Gods always behave": ZNH, *Tell My Horse*, 219.

290 "dammed up": ZNH, *Dust Tracks*, 175.

290 "one for anthro.": ZNH to Henry Allen Moe, Aug. 26, 1937, in Kaplan, *Zora Neale Hurston*, 404.

290 Hurston had been in Haiti: Melville and Frances Herskovits spent a little over three months in Mirabelais. Herskovits, *Life in Haitian Valley*, 320.

290 Years earlier Margaret Mead: Howard, *Margaret Mead*, 71.

290 Now it was Millay: Boyd, *Wrapped in Rainbows*, 300, 306.

291 Some months earlier she had fallen: Ibid., 271–74, 286–87.

291 "I did not just fall": ZNH, *Dust Tracks*, 205.

292 "It's uh known fact": ZNH, *Their Eyes*, 192.

293 "Novelists know": MM to GB, Sept. 12, 1933, MM Papers, Box R1, Folder 1.

293 It was rather the ability: MM to GB, June 21, 1935, MM Papers, Box R2, Folder 9.

293 In fact, she had given up: Boyd, *Wrapped in Rainbows*, 270.

294 In the summer of 1935: MM to GB, June 7, 1935, MM Papers, Box R2, Folder 9.

294 She kept up her correspondence: See MM Papers, Box R2, Folder 8.

294 Especially given the public notice: MM to GB, May 10, 1935, MM Papers, Box R2, Folder 9.

294 The royalties would help: MM to GB, June 27, 1934, MM Papers, Box R2, Folder 7.

294 She had not spoken: MM to GB, Sept. 3, 1935, MM Papers, Box R2, Folder 9.

294 Only later that year: MM to GB, Oct. 17, 1935, ibid.

295 "In any case I think": GB to MM, Dec. 14, 1935, ibid.

295 "almost female-Darwin face": Quoted in Lipset, *Gregory Bateson*, 151.

296 In the months that followed: MM, *Blackberry Winter*, 234.

296 "the perfect intellectual": Ibid., 224.

296 That September a Chinese boat: MM, draft manuscript of *Blackberry Winter*, Box I204, Folder 4.

296 "The crises are always": MM to Eleanor Pelham Kortheuer, May 21, 1938, MM Papers, Box Q12, Folder 9.

296 "I feel like a frightful pig": MM to Eleanor Pelham Kortheuer, Dec. 16, 1936, ibid.

296 "There is no doubt": MM to Kortheuer, May 21, 1938, ibid.

297 A British edition: ZNH to Edwin Osgood Grover, Oct. 12, 1939, in Kaplan, *Zora Neale Hurston*, 422.

297 There was a return: Boyd, *Wrapped in Rainbows*, 326.

298 "folkloric fiction": Quoted in Stewart, *New Negro*, 748.

298 "I get tired": ZNH to James Weldon Johnson, Feb. 1938, in Kaplan, *Zora Neale Hurston*, 413.

298   "Negro fiction": Boyd, *Wrapped in Rainbows*, 336.

299   "The form of prayer": ZNH, "Ritualistic Expression from the Lips of Communicants of the Seventh Day Church of God, Beaufort, South Carolina" (1940), MM Papers, Box C5, Folder 13.

299   "I am sure": MM to ZNH, May 29, 1940, ibid.

300   "Girls are funny creatures!" Hughes, *Big Sea*, 332.

300   That same spring: Boyd, *Wrapped in Rainbows*, 345–46.

300   "love unselfishly": ZNH, *Dust Tracks*, 231.

301   She had named one: Boyd, *Wrapped in Rainbows*, 349.

Chapter Thirteen: War and Nonsense

302   "I am to be": RB to RF, June 8, 1936, MM Papers, Box R5, Folder 8.

302   "Being a woman": Ibid.

303   After Linton's arrival: Goldfrank, *Notes on Undirected Life*, 110. On Benedict's evolving relations with Linton and the Boas succession, see Young, *Ruth Benedict*, 47–51.

303   Boas was allowed: Ralph Linton to FB, Feb. 24, 1942, FB Papers (microfilm), Reel 44.

303   required to submit detailed memos: FB to ECP, Jan. 5, 1940, ECP Papers, Box 1.

303   Funds for his research: See Department of Anthropology Records, CU, Box 2, Folder "Administrative—Executive Officers and Chairman. Benedict, Ruth—re. Franz Boas Support Fund, 1936–1938."

303   "I'll have to get accustomed": FB to ECP, Sept. 3, 1936, ECP Papers, Box 1.

304   In the spring of 1933: Herskovits, *Franz Boas*, 117.

304   His books were pulled: "Dr. Boas on the Blacklist," *New York Times*, May 6, 1933.

304   "his dispossessed Jews": MM to GB, Nov. 14, 1933, MM Papers, Box R1, Folder 7.

304   "Intellectual freedom in many": FB, "On Democracy and Freedom."

305   "to make our schools": Ibid.

306   "My interests are for America": Gordon, *Second Coming of KKK*, 73.

306   "He will remain the master": Hitler, *Mein Kampf*, 286.

306   Heinrich Krieger, one of the major: Whitman, *Hitler's American Model*, 114.

306   In turn, German universities: Kühl, *Nazi Connection*, 86.

307   "In most of the Southern states": Quoted in Whitman, *Hitler's American Model*, 122.

307   "U.S. model": Quoted in Kühl, *Nazi Connection*, 37.

308   "National Socialism is nothing": Ibid., 36.

308   A new German translation: Ibid., 41–42.

308   "This is one of the bulwarks": MM to GB, June 12, 1935, MM Papers, Box R1, Folder 9.

308   "It will be a fortunate nation": Frederick Osborn, "The Application of Measures of Quality," in *Congrès international de la population*, 8:121–22.

308   "Our consideration of both": FB, "Heredity and Environment," ibid., 8:91.

309   "is at best a poetic": Ibid., 8:92.

309 For more than a year: FB to RB, Dec. 20, 1939, RB Papers, Folder 114.4.

309 If you looked at American: "Freedom of Mind in Schools Urged," *Baltimore Sun*, Aug. 22, 1939.

311 "I will try to clean up": "The Race Question," *New York Times*, July 5, 1936.

311 Stanley, still legally: Caffrey, *Ruth Benedict*, 286.

311 "brilliant" and "challenging": RB, "Edward Sapir," 465.

312 "corroding resentment": MM, interview by Jean Houston, 1975, transcript, MM Papers, Box Q18, Folder 4, f. 429.

312 Not long after she returned: MM to RB, Aug. 28, 1926, MM Papers, Box S3, Folder 4.

312 Miscarriages received: MM datebook for 1939, MM Papers, Box Q8, Folder 4.

312 "I shall work very moderately": MM to Caroline Beatrice Bateson, Mar. 15, 1939, MM Papers, Box R1, Folder 1.

312 "England declares war": MM datebook for 1939, MM Papers, Box Q8, Folder 4.

312 "not overfond of being held": MM to Caroline Beatrice Bateson, Feb. 27, 1940, MM Papers, Box R1, Folder 1.

312 "The slogan of 'science' ": RB, *Race: Science and Politics*, 147.

314 She learned of her: Banner, *Intertwined Lives*, 416.

314 Perhaps half of all people: Mandler, *Return from Natives*, 65.

314 The book sold briskly: Ibid., 80–84.

315 "joint household organized for wartime": MM, *Blackberry Winter*, 271.

315 "I have just learned": Leon J. Fish to FB, Feb. 5, 1942, FB Papers (microfilm), Reel 44.

315 "My dear Leon": FB to Fish, Feb. 19, 1942, ibid.

315 "now carrying into effect": "11 Allies Condemn Nazi War on Jews," *New York Times*, Dec. 18, 1942.

316 "We should never stop": Rivet, "Franz Boas." Rivet gave a slightly different account years later (Rivet, "Tribute to Franz Boas"), in 1958, but the version written in 1943, shortly after the event, is probably a more accurate recollection. Mead was the source for a more dramatic account, which had Boas beginning to announce a new theory of race just as he died. There seems to be no evidence for this statement, nor could other people later confirm it. See Goldfrank, *Notes on Undirected Life*, 121.

316 One young French visitor: Loyer, *Lévi-Strauss*, 316.

316 But Lévi-Strauss did not: Boas had never heard of Lévi-Strauss when someone inquired about a letter of reference for him in the fall of 1940. They were first introduced by Benedict in the summer of 1941. FB to Alvin Johnson, Oct. 21, 1940, FB Papers (microfilm), Reel 43; Claude Lévi-Strauss to FB, Aug. 26, 1941, FB Papers (microfilm), Reel 44.

316 "He believed the world": RB, "Franz Boas," *Nation*, Jan. 2, 1943, 15.

316 "It would have": RB to J. M. Willis, Sept. 27, 1943, RB Papers, Folder 114.10.00.

316 She was an associate professor: See the pay scales in RB Papers, Folder 42.5.

317 "touchy": Kluckhohn, *Ralph Linton*, 244.

317 "a swine": Quoted in Banner, *Intertwined Lives*, 379.

317 She was probably: Ibid.

317 "Some people have shouted": RB and Weltfish, "The Races of Mankind," in RB, *Race: Science and Politics*, 174.

317 "The negro may be": Fred Hastings to RB, Mar. 4, 1944, RB Papers, Folder 12.3.

317 "Communistic propaganda": Violet Edwards, "Note on *The Races of Mankind*," in RB, *Race: Science and Politics*, 167–68; Mandler, *Return from Natives*, 77.

317 The FBI dispatched: Price, *Threatening Anthropology*, 111.

317 Churches and civic groups: Violet Edwards, "Note on *The Races of Mankind*," in RB, *Race: Science and Politics*, 168; Mandler, *Return from Natives*, 77.

318 "You are no better": "A Citizen of Mississippi" to RB, Mar. 7, 1944, RB Papers, Folder 12.3.

318 In the fall of 1943: MM, "The Years as Boas' Left Hand," in *AAW*, 252–53.

318 "Chairborne Division": Mandler, *Return from Natives*, 66.

318 "the swift and the glib": Doob, "Utilization of Social Scientists," 655.

319 Then there were films: See Kent, "Appendix," for a reconstructed list of sources based on Benedict's private papers.

320 "In Europe we felt": Quoted in Dower, *War Without Mercy*, 78.

320 Shortly after Pearl Harbor: "How to Tell Japs from the Chinese," *Life*, Dec. 22, 1941, 81–82.

320 "The Japanese were a product": Quoted in Dower, *War Without Mercy*, 85.

321 Whatever traits Washington: Mandler, *Return from Natives*, 163–69.

322 Peeking out from: Hayashi, *Democratizing Enemy*, 92.

322 "In the war in which": U.S. Department of War, *Final Report*, 34.

322 "I think it's probable": Quoted in Daniels, *Prisoners Without Trial*, 38.

323 "I believe that we are being": Quoted ibid., 37.

323 The Census Bureau provided: Seltzer and Anderson, "After Pearl Harbor"; Steven A. Holmes, "Report Says Census Bureau Helped Relocate Japanese," *New York Times*, Mar. 17, 2000.

323 By the end of October: U.S. Department of War, *Final Report*, 362.

323 "The work areas . . . should": Quoted in Suzuki, "Overlooked Aspects," 230–31n25.

323 From the spring to the fall: "Santa Anita," *Densho Encyclopedia*, located at encyclopedia.densho.org/Santa_Anita_%28detention_facility%29/.

323 President Roosevelt's executive order: Hayashi, *Democratizing Enemy*, 57.

323 He was given a number: Documents regarding detainees such as Hashima are available on ancestry.com ("Final Accountability Rosters of Evacuees at Relocation Centers, 1942–1946: Colorado River, November 1945"), as well as in the War Relocation Authority papers at the U.S. National Archives and Records Administration.

324 "community analyst": See Starn, "Engineering Internment."

324 "Great care was exercised": U.S. Department of War, *Final Report*, 505.

324 "A mass evacuation of people": Quoted in Spicer, "Use of Social Scientists," 20.

325 "a lady, who was slender": Suzuki, "Ruth Benedict, Robert Hashima," 58.

325 The two first met: Ibid.

326 When her reports: Suzuki, "Overlooked Aspects," 219. On the role of

Hashima, see also C. Douglas Lummis, "Ruth Benedict's Obituary for Japanese Culture," in Janiewski and Banner, *Reading Benedict/Reading Mead*, 126–40; and Benedict's interview notes with Hashima in RB Papers, Folder 105.8.

326 "I wish I knew": Quoted in Suzuki, "Overlooked Aspects," 225.

326 Titles such as: Nanko Fukui, "The Lady and the Chrysanthemum: Ruth Benedict and the Origins of *The Chrysanthemum and the Sword*," in Janiewski and Banner, *Reading Benedict/Reading Mead*, 123.

326 as did *The Enameled Rod:* RB to MM, July 25, 1946, MM Papers, Box Q11, Folder 6.

326 "It embarrasses me": Ibid.

327 "The Japanese were the most": RB, *Chrysanthemum and Sword*, 1.

327 "The anthropologist has good": Ibid., 10.

327 "human society must make": Ibid., 12.

327 "geared into": Ibid., 13.

327 "the habits that are expected": Ibid., 16.

328 "Taking one's proper": Ibid., 43.

329 That decision probably flowed: Mandler, *Return from Natives*, 168–69; Price, *Anthropological Intelligence*, 171–99.

330 "Japanese men and women": RB, *Chrysanthemum and Sword*, vi.

330 "Any reader of this book": Offprint from *Book of the Month Club News*, Dec. 1946, in RB Papers, Folder 50.2.

330 "It's like a fog": Quoted in Caffrey, *Ruth Benedict*, 326.

330 It sold in the millions: Bennett and Nagai, "Japanese Critique," 404.

331 The reason was straightforward: RB to Capt. Donald V. McGranahan, Sept. 12, 1945, RB Papers, Folder 13.7; Mandler, *Return from Natives*, 169. More than a year after the war ended, in December 1946, Benedict was personally invited by MacArthur's headquarters to go to Japan on a two-to-three-month assignment. Her reply does not appear to be in her personal papers. See D. Donald Klous to RB, Dec. 26, 1946, RB Papers, Folder 13.10.

331 "Why didn't I transvestite?": RB to MM, Sept. 20, 1945, MM Papers, Box Q11, Folder 6.

Chapter Fourteen: Home

332 "I read with interest": ZNH to RB, June 19, 1945, in Kaplan, *Zora Neale Hurston*, 523.

332 "The world smells": Quoted in Hemenway, *Zora Neale Hurston*, 301.

332 "Ass-and-All of Democracy": Hurston, "Crazy for This Democracy," 45–46.

333 "I will fight for my country": Hurston, *Dust Tracks*, 261.

333 Hurston had jumped: Hemenway, *Zora Neale Hurston*, 297.

333 For Hurston, the signature: Ibid.

333 "Disturbing as our 'ethnic minorities'": Lowie, "American Contributions," 327.

333 The burden of distance: Bateson, *With Daughter's Eye*, 49.

333 The year after the war: Banner, *Intertwined Lives*, 433; Lipset, *Gregory Bateson*, 175–76.

333 "Marriage is like": Quoted in Michael Kernan, "Ringing the Tocsin," *New York Times*, Apr. 1, 1976.

334 She made field notes: See the notes in MM Papers, Box R3, Folder 9.

334 When friends went through: See RB Papers, Folder 39.8.

335 Condolences were sent: Howard, *Margaret Mead*, 281.

335 "The discovery of anthropology": Margery Freeman to MM, Sept. 18, 1948, RB Papers, Folder 117.2.

335 There was no way: ECD to MM, n.d. [late 1948], MM Papers, Box I58, Folder 10.

335 "And thank you also": ECD to MM, Dec. 28, 1958, MM Papers, Box C41, Folder 7.

336 "Together we can do": ZNH to Jane Belo, Oct. 1, 1944, in Kaplan, *Zora Neale Hurston*, 507.

336 The year Benedict died: Boyd, *Wrapped in Rainbows*, 387–90.

336 She fell into another depression: Ibid., 396–97.

336 "one of the most significant": Walker, "In Search of Hurston," 74.

336 She had shelved books: Boyd, *Wrapped in Rainbows*, 426–31.

336 Her death certificate: Hemenway, *Zora Neale Hurston*, 348.

336 Mead slipped the article: See MM Papers, Box K57, Folder 9.

337 A zealous janitor: Boyd, *Wrapped in Rainbows*, 436.

337 "Ain't it a shame": Alan Lomax to Solon Kimball, Feb. 15, 1978, MM Papers, Box K57, Folder 9.

337 Mead had once tried: MM chart of love affairs and influences, MM Papers, Box S11, Folder 1.

338 Her rooms in the rafters: Bateson, *With Daughter's Eye*, 130.

338 Her early books: Molloy, *Creating Usable Culture*, 14.

338 In turn her FBI file: Price, *Threatening Anthropology*, 255.

338 "Dear Dr. Mead": Lenora De Lusia to MM, Feb. 20, 1958, MM Papers, Box C38, Folder 4.

339 "I think you will find": MM to De Lusia, Feb. 28, 1958, ibid.

339 "The whole world": Sargeant, "It's All Anthropology," 32.

340 "cut down her own vision": Friedan, *Feminine Mystique*, 122.

340 She feared that a younger generation: Howard, *Margaret Mead*, 363–64.

340 "that comes from many years": Sargeant, "It's All Anthropology," 31.

341 "a mother who is": MM, *Blackberry Winter*, 289.

341 "Almost every student": Bloom, *Closing of American Mind*, 25.

341 "Sexual adventurers like Margaret Mead": Ibid., 33.

342 "to establish a world community": Ibid., 36.

342 "We have been the first": Clifford Geertz, "Anti-Anti-Relativism," in Geertz, *Available Light*, 65.

344 "There is no evolution": Boas, *Anthropology and Modern Life*, 227.

345 "I have seen and heard": ZNH, *Dust Tracks*, 264.

BIBLIOGRAPHY

Archives and Private Papers
American Indian Studies Research Institute, Indiana University
    Ella Deloria Archive (online)
American Philosophical Society
    American Council of Learned Societies Committee on Native American
        Languages
    Boas Family Papers
    Boas-Rukeyser Collection
    Elsie Clews Parsons Papers
    Franz Boas Field Notebooks and Anthropometric Data
    Franz Boas Papers
    Franz Boas Professional Papers
Barnard College Archives
    Alumnae Biographical Files
Columbia University, Rare Book and Manuscript Library
    Department of Anthropology Records
    Nicholas Murray Butler Papers
    Jane Howard Papers
Harvard Medical School, Center for the History of Medicine,
        Francis A. Countway Library of Medicine
    Walter B. Cannon Papers
Harvard University, Houghton Library
    Oswald Garrison Villard Papers
Harvard University, Peabody Museum
    Frederic Ward Putnam Papers
    Frederic Ward Putnam Peabody Museum Director Records
    Charles P. Bowditch Papers
    World Columbian Exposition Photograph Collection
Harvard University, Tozzer Library
    Cora Alice Du Bois Papers
The Keep, Brighton
    Geoffrey Gorer Archive

Library of Congress
    Franz Boas Papers (microfilm)
    Margaret Mead Papers and South Pacific Ethnographic Archives
Smithsonian Institution, National Anthropological Archives
    Anthropological Society of Washington Records
    Bureau of American Ethnology Records
    Esther Schiff Goldfrank Papers
    Aleš Hrdlička Papers
    Zora Neale Hurston Gulf Coast manuscript (MS 7532)
    Ruth Schlossberg Landes Papers
Vassar College, Archives and Special Collections
    Ruth Fulton Benedict Papers

Published Sources

Adams, William Y. *The Boasians: Founding Fathers and Mothers of American Anthropology*. Lanham, Md.: Hamilton Books, 2016.

Allen, John S. "Franz Boas' Physical Anthropology: The Critique of Racial Formalism Revisited." *Current Anthropology* 30, no. 1 (Feb. 1989): 79–84.

Anderson, Carol. *White Rage: The Unspoken Truth of Our Racial Divide*. New York: Bloomsbury, 2016.

Annual Reports of the Bureau of Ethnology to the Secretary of the Smithsonian Institution. 15 vols. Washington, D.C.: U.S. Government Printing Office, 1881–97.

Asch, Chris Myers, and George Derek Musgrove. *Chocolate City: A History of Race and Democracy in the Nation's Capital*. Chapel Hill: University of North Carolina Press, 2017.

Baker, Lee D. *Anthropology and the Racial Politics of Culture*. Durham, N.C.: Duke University Press, 2010.

———. "The Cult of Franz Boas and His 'Conspiracy' to Destroy the White Race." *Proceedings of the American Philosophical Society* 154, no. 1 (Mar. 2010): 8–18.

———. "Franz Boas Out of the Ivory Tower." *Anthropological Theory* 4, no. 1 (2004): 29–51.

———. *From Savage to Negro: Anthropology and the Construction of Race, 1896–1954*. Berkeley: University of California Press, 1998.

Banner, Lois W. *Intertwined Lives: Margaret Mead, Ruth Benedict, and Their Circle*. New York: Vintage, 2003.

Barnes, R. H. *Two Crows Denies It: A History of Controversy in Omaha Sociology*. Lincoln: University of Nebraska Press, 1984.

Bateson, Gregory. *Naven*. 2nd ed. Stanford, Calif.: Stanford University Press, 1958.

Bateson, Mary Catherine. *With a Daughter's Eye: A Memoir of Margaret Mead and Gregory Bateson*. New York: William Morrow, 1984.

Bederman, Gail. *Manliness and Civilization: A Cultural History of Gender and Race in the United States, 1880–1917*. Chicago: University of Chicago Press, 1995.

Benedict, Ruth. "Animism." In *Encyclopedia of the Social Sciences*, edited by Edwin R. A. Seligman, 2:65–67. New York: Macmillan, 193.

————. *The Chrysanthemum and the Sword: Patterns of Japanese Culture.* Boston: Houghton Mifflin, 2005 [1946].

————. "Edward Sapir." *American Anthropologist* 41, no. 3 (July–Sept. 1939): 455–77.

————. "Folklore." In *Encyclopedia of the Social Sciences*, edited by Edwin R. A. Seligman and Alvin Johnson, 6:288–93. New York: Macmillan, 1931.

————. "Franz Boas." *Nation* (Jan. 2, 1943): 15–16.

————. "The Future of Race Prejudice." *American Scholar* 15, no. 4 (Autumn 1946): 455–61.

————. "Human Nature Is Not a Trap." *Partisan Review* 10, no. 2 (Mar.–Apr. 1943): 159–64.

————. "Magic." In *Encyclopedia of the Social Sciences*, edited by Edwin R. A. Seligman, 10:39–44. New York: Macmillan, 1933.

————. *Patterns of Culture.* Boston: Houghton Mifflin, 2005 [1934].

————. *Race: Science and Politics.* Rev. ed. New York: Viking, 1959 [1940].

————. "Racism Is Vulnerable." *The English Journal* 35, no. 6 (June 1946): 299–303.

————. "Tales of the Cochiti Indians." *Bureau of American Ethnology Bulletin*, no. 98. Washington, D.C.: U.S. Government Printing Office, 1931.

————. "Transmitting Our Democratic Heritage in the Schools." *American Journal of Sociology* 48, no. 6 (May 1943): 722–27.

————. "Victory Over Discrimination and Hate: Differences vs. Superiorities." *Frontiers of Democracy* 9 (Dec. 15, 1942): 81–82.

————. "The Vision in Plains Culture." *American Anthropologist* 24, no. 1 (Jan.–Mar. 1922): 1–23.

————. "The Younger Generation with a Difference." *New Republic*, Nov. 28, 1928.

————. *Zuni Mythology.* 2 vols. New York: Columbia University Press, 1935.

Bennett, John W., and Michio Nagai. "The Japanese Critique of the Methodology of Benedict's 'Chrysanthemum and the Sword.'" *American Anthropologist* 55, no. 3 (1953): 404–11.

Benton-Cohen, Katherine. *Inventing the Immigration Problem: The Dillingham Commission and Its Legacy.* Cambridge, Mass.: Harvard University Press, 2018.

Berkhofer, Robert F., Jr. *The White Man's Indian: Images of the American Indian from Columbus to the Present.* New York: Alfred A. Knopf, 1978.

Berman, Marshall. *All That Is Solid Melts into Air: The Experience of Modernity.* New York: Penguin, 1988.

Black, Edwin. *War Against the Weak: Eugenics and America's Campaign to Create a Master Race.* New York: Four Walls Eight Windows, 2003.

Bloom, Allan. *The Closing of the American Mind.* New York: Simon and Schuster, 1987.

Boas Anniversary Volume: Anthropological Papers Written in Honor of Franz Boas. New York: G. E. Stechert and Co., 1906.

Boas, Franz. "The Aims of Anthropological Research." *Science* 76, no. 1983 (Dec. 30, 1932): 605–13.

————. "An Anthropologist's Credo." *Nation*, Aug. 27, 1938, 201–4.

―――. "Anthropology." *Science* 9, no. 212 (Jan. 20, 1899): 93–96.

―――. *Anthropology*. New York: Columbia University Press, 1908.

―――. *Anthropology and Modern Life*. New York: Dover, 1986 [1928].

―――. "Are the Jews a Race?" *World Tomorrow* 6 (January 1923): 5–6. Reprinted as "The Jews" in Franz Boas, *Race and Democratic Society*, 38–42. New York: J. J. Augustin, 1945.

―――. *Aryans and Non-Aryans*. New York: Information and Service Associates, n.d.

―――. *The Central Eskimo*, in *Sixth Annual Report of the Bureau of Ethnology to the Secretary of the Smithsonian Institution, 1884–1885* (Washington, D.C.: U.S. Government Printing Office, 1888): 399–670.

―――. "Changes in the Bodily Form of Descendants of Immigrants." *American Anthropologist* 14, no. 3 (July–Sept. 1912): 530–62.

―――. "The Coast Tribes of British Columbia." *Science* 9, no. 216 (Mar. 25, 1887): 288–89.

―――. "Cumberland Sound and its Eskimos." *Popular Science Monthly* (Apr. 26, 1885): 768–79.

―――. "The Eskimo of Baffin Land." *Transactions of the Anthropological Society of Washington* 3 (Dec. 2, 1884): 95–102.

―――. "Eskimo Tales and Songs." *Journal of American Folk-Lore* 7, no. 24 (Jan.– Mar. 1894): 45–50, and 10, no. 37 (Apr.–June 1897): 109–15.

―――. "An Eskimo Winter." In *American Indian Life by Several of Its Students*, edited by Elsie Clews Parsons, 363–80. New York: Viking Press, 1922.

―――. "Evolution or Diffusion?" *American Anthropologist* 26, no. 3 (July–Sept., 1924): 340–44.

―――, ed. *General Anthropology*. Boston: D.C. Heath & Co., 1938.

―――, ed. *Handbook of American Indian Languages*. Part 1. Washington, D.C.: U.S. Government Printing Office, 1911.

―――. "History and Science in Anthropology: A Reply." *American Anthropologist* 38, no. 1 (Jan.–Mar. 1936): 137–41.

―――. "The History of Anthropology." *Science* 20, no. 512 (Oct. 21, 1904): 513–24.

―――. "Human Faculty as Determined by Race." *Proceedings of the American Association for the Advancement of Science* 43 (Aug. 1894): 301–27.

―――. *Indian Myths & Legends from the North Pacific Coast of America: A Translation of Franz Boas' 1895 Edition of Indianische Sagen von der Nord-Pacifischen Küste Amerikas*. Vancouver: Talonbooks, 2006 [1895].

―――. "Individual, Family, Population, and Race." *Proceedings of the American Philosophical Society* 87, no. 2 (Aug. 1943): 161–64.

―――. "Introductory." *International Journal of American Linguistics* 1, no. 1 (July 1917): 1–8.

―――. "Inventing a Great Race." *New Republic* (Jan. 13, 1917): 305–7.

―――. "A Journey in Cumberland Sound and on the West Shore of Davis Strait in 1883 and 1884." *Journal of the American Geographical Society of New York* 16 (1884): 242–72.

―――. "The Limitations of the Comparative Method of Anthropology." *Science* 4, no. 103 (Dec. 18, 1896): 901–8.

————. "The Method of Ethnology." *American Anthropologist* 22, no. 4 (Oct.–Dec. 1920): 311–21.

————. *The Mind of Primitive Man*. New York: Macmillan, 1922 [1911].

————. "Museums of Ethnology and Their Classification." *Science* 9, no. 228 (June 17, 1887): 587–89, and no. 229 (June 24, 1887): 614.

————. "Mythology and Folk-Tales of the North American Indians." *Journal of American Folklore* 27, no. 106 (Oct. 1915): 374–410.

————. "Nationalism in Europe." In *Germany and the Peace of Europe*, edited by Ferdinand Schevill, 3–15. Chicago: Germanistic Society of Chicago, 1915.

————. "Notes on the Ethnology of British Columbia." *Proceedings of the American Philosophical Society* 24 (July–Dec. 1887): 422–28.

————. "The Occurrence of Similar Inventions in Areas Widely Apart." *Science* 9, no. 224 (May 20, 1887): 485–86.

————. "On Alternating Sounds." *American Anthropologist* 2, no. 1 (Jan. 1889): 47–53.

————. "On Democracy and Freedom of Thought." WNYC broadcast, May 3, 1939, http://www.wnyc.org/story/leader-american-anthropology-launches-wnyc-series/.

————. "Poetry and Music of Some North American Tribes." *Science* 9, no. 220 (Apr. 22, 1887): 383–85.

————. "The Problem of the American Negro." *Yale Review* 10 (May 1921): 392–95. Reprinted as "The Negro in America" in Franz Boas, *Race and Democratic Society*, 70–81. New York: J. J. Augustin, 1945.

————. "The Problem of Race." In *The Making of Man: An Outline of Anthropology*, edited by V. F. Calverton, 113–41. New York: Random House, 1931.

————. "Psychological Problems in Anthropology." *American Journal of Psychology* 21, no. 3 (July 1910): 371–84.

————. "The Question of Racial Purity." *American Mercury* (Oct. 1924): 163–69.

————. *Race, Language, and Culture*. New York: Macmillan, 1940.

————. "The Race-War Myth." *Everybody's Magazine* 31 (July–Dec. 1914): 671–74.

————. "Remarks on the Theory of Anthropometry." *Publications of the American Statistical Association* 3, no. 24 (Dec. 1893): 569–75.

————. *The Social Organization and the Secret Societies of the Kwakiutl Indians*. Washington, D.C.: Smithsonian Institution, 1897 [1895].

————. "Some Philological Aspects of Anthropological Research." *Science* 23, no. 591 (Apr. 27, 1906): 641–45.

————. "Some Recent Criticisms of Physical Anthropology." *American Anthropologist* 1, no. 1 (Jan. 1899): 98–106.

————. "The Study of Geography." *Science* 9, no. 210 (Feb. 11, 1887): 137–41.

————. "A Year Among the Eskimo." *Bulletin of the American Geographical Society* 19, no. 4 (1887): 383–402.

Boas, Franz, and Ella Deloria. *Dakota Grammar*. Memoirs of the National Academy of Sciences. Washington, D.C.: U.S. Government Printing Office, 1941.

————. "Notes on the Dakota, Teton Dialect." *International Journal of American Linguistics* 7, nos. 3–4 (Jan. 1933): 97–121.

Boas, Franz, and Elsie Clews Parsons. "Spanish Tales from Laguna and Zuñi, N. Mex." *Journal of American Folklore* 33, no. 127 (Jan.–Mar. 1920): 47–72.

Boyd, Robert. *A Different Kind of Animal.* Princeton: Princeton University Press, 2017.

Boyd, Valerie. *Wrapped in Rainbows: The Life of Zora Neale Hurston.* New York: Scribner, 2003.

Bradford, Phillips Verner, and Harvey Blume. *Ota Benga: The Pygmy in the Zoo.* New York: St. Martin's Press, 1992.

Browman, David L. *Cultural Negotiations: The Role of Women in the Founding of Americanist Anthropology.* Lincoln: University of Nebraska Press, 2013.

———. "The Peabody Museum, Frederic W. Putnam, and the Rise of U.S. Anthropology, 1866–1903." *American Anthropologist* 104, no. 2 (Jun. 2002): 508–19.

Browman, David L., and Stephen Williams. *Anthropology at Harvard: A Biographical History, 1790–1940.* Cambridge, Mass.: Peabody Museum Press, 2013.

Bruinius, Harry. *Better for All the World: The Secret History of Forced Sterilization and America's Quest for Racial Purity.* New York: Alfred A. Knopf, 2006.

Buettner-Janusch, John. "Boas and Mason: Particularism Versus Generalization." *American Anthropologist* 59, no. 2 (Apr. 1957): 318–24.

Caffrey, Margaret M. *Ruth Benedict: Stranger in This Land.* Austin: University of Texas Press, 1989.

Caffrey, Margaret M., and Patricia A. Francis, eds. *To Cherish the Life of the World: Selected Letters of Margaret Mead.* New York: Basic Books, 2006.

Clark, Christopher. *Iron Kingdom: The Rise and Downfall of Prussia, 1600–1947.* Cambridge, Mass.: Belknap Press of Harvard University Press, 2006.

———. *The Politics of Conversion: Missionary Protestantism and the Jews in Prussia, 1728–1941.* Oxford: Clarendon Press, 1995.

Cohen, Adam. *Imbeciles: The Supreme Court, American Eugenics, and the Sterilization of Carrie Buck.* New York: Penguin, 2016.

Cole, Douglas. *Franz Boas: The Early Years, 1858–1906.* Seattle: University of Washington Press, 1999.

Cole, Douglas, and Ludger Müller-Wille. "Franz Boas' Expedition to Baffin Island, 1883–1884." *Études/Inuit/Studies* 8, no. 1 (1984): 37–63.

Cole, Sally. *Ruth Landes: A Life in Anthropology.* Lincoln: University of Nebraska Press, 2003.

Congrès international de la population. 8 vols. Paris: Hermann et Cie., 1938.

Conklin, Alice L. *In the Museum of Man: Race, Anthropology, and Empire in France, 1850–1950.* Ithaca, N.Y.: Cornell University Press, 2013.

Côté, James E. "Was *Coming of Age in Samoa* Based on a 'Fateful Hoaxing'? A Close Look at Freeman's Claim Based on the Mead-Boas Correspondence." *Current Anthropology* 41, no. 4 (2000): 617–20.

Cotera, María Eugenia. *Native Speakers: Ella Deloria, Zora Neale Hurston, Jovita González, and the Poetics of Culture.* Austin: University of Texas Press, 2008.

Cressman, Luther S. *A Golden Journey: Memoirs of an Archaeologist.* Salt Lake City: University of Utah Press, 1988.

Cushing, Frank Hamilton. *My Adventures in Zuñi.* Palo Alto: American West Publishing Company, 1970.

Dain, Bruce. *A Hideous Monster of the Mind: American Race Theory in the Early Republic.* Cambridge, Mass.: Harvard University Press, 2002.

Daniels, Roger. *Guarding the Golden Door: American Immigration Policy and Immigrants Since 1882.* New York: Hill and Wang, 2004.

————. *Prisoners Without Trial: Japanese Americans in World War II.* New York: Hill and Wang, 1993.

Darnell, Regna. *And Along Came Boas: Continuity and Revolution in Americanist Anthropology.* Amsterdam: John Benjamins Publishing Co., 1998.

————. *Edward Sapir: Linguist, Anthropologist, Humanist.* Lincoln: University of Nebraska Press, 1990.

————. *Invisible Genealogies: A History of Americanist Anthropology.* Lincoln: University of Nebraska Press, 2001.

Darnell, Regna, and Frederic W. Gleach. *Anthropologists and Their Traditions Across National Borders.* Lincoln: University of Nebraska Press, 2014.

Darnell, Regna, Michelle Hamilton, Robert L. A. Hancock, and Joshua Smith, eds. *Franz Boas as Public Intellectual: Theory, Ethnography, Activism.* Franz Boas Papers, Vol. 1. Lincoln: University of Nebraska Press, 2015.

Darwin, Charles. *The Descent of Man.* New ed. Lovell, Coryell and Co., 1874 [1871].

Davenport, Charles B. *State Laws Limiting Marriage Selection Examined in the Light of Eugenics.* Cold Spring Harbor, N.Y.: Eugenics Record Office, 1913.

Davis, W. M. *Biographical Memoir of John Wesley Powell, 1834–1902.* Washington, D.C.: National Academy of Sciences, 1915.

Deacon, Desley. *Elsie Clews Parsons: Inventing Modern Life.* Chicago: University of Chicago Press, 1997.

Deloria, Ella Cara. *Dakota Texts.* New York: G. E. Stechert and Co., 1932.

————. *Speaking of Indians.* New York: Friendship Press, 1944.

————. "The Sun Dance of the Oglala Sioux." *Journal of American Folklore* 42 (Oct.–Dec., 1929): 354–413.

————. *Waterlily.* New ed. Lincoln: University of Nebraska Press, 1988.

Deloria, Philip J. *Indians in Unexpected Places.* Lawrence: University Press of Kansas, 2004.

————. *Playing Indian.* New Haven: Yale University Press, 1998.

————. "Thinking About Self in a Family Way." *Journal of American History* 89, no. 1 (June 2002): 25–29.

Dobrin, Lise M., and Ira Bashkow. "'Arapesh Warfare': Reo Fortune's Veiled Critique of Margaret Mead's *Sex and Temperament.*" *American Anthropologist* 112, no. 3 (2010): 370–83.

————. "'The Truth in Anthropology Does Not Travel First Class': Reo Fortune's Fateful Encounter with Margaret Mead." *Histories of Anthropology Annual* 6 (2010): 66–128.

Doerries, Reinhard R. "German Emigration to the United States: A Review Essay on Recent West German Publications." *Journal of American Ethnic History* 6, no. 1 (Fall 1986): 71–83.

Doob, Leonard W. "The Utilization of Social Scientists in the Overseas Branch of the Office of War Information." *American Political Science Review* 41, no. 4 (1947): 649–67.

Dorsey, James Owen. *Omaha Sociology*. Washington, D.C.: U.S. Government Printing Office, 1885.

Douglas, Bronwen. *Science, Voyages, and Encounters in Oceania, 1511–1850*. London: Palgrave Macmillan, 2014.

Douglas, Bronwen, and Chris Ballard, eds. *Foreign Bodies: Oceania and the Science of Race, 1750–1940*. Canberra: Australian National University Press, 2010.

Dower, John W. *Embracing Defeat: Japan in the Wake of World War II*. New York: W. W. Norton, 1999.

———. *War Without Mercy: Race and Power in the Pacific War*. New York: Pantheon, 1986.

Dubois, Laurent. *Haiti: The Aftershocks of History*. New York: Metropolitan Books, 2012.

Embree, John F. *Suye Mura: A Japanese Village*. Chicago: University of Chicago Press, 1939.

Engels, Friedrich. *The Origin of the Family, Private Property, and the State*. New York: Pathfinder Press, 1972 [1884].

Federal Writers' Project. *WPA Guide to Florida*. New York: Pantheon Books, 1984 [1939].

Fortune, Reo. *Omaha Secret Societies*. New York: Columbia University Press, 1932.

———. "The Social Organization of Dobu." Ph.D. dissertation, Columbia University, 1931.

———. *Sorcerers of Dobu: The Social Anthropology of the Dobu Islanders of the Western Pacific*. New York: E. P. Dutton, 1932.

Frazer, J. G. *The Golden Bough: A Study in Comparative Religion*. 2 vols. London: Macmillan, 1890.

Freed, Stanley A. *Anthropology Unmasked: Museums, Science, and Politics in New York City*. 2 vols. Wilmington, Ohio: Orange Frazer Press, 2012.

Freeman, Derek. *The Fateful Hoaxing of Margaret Mead: A Historical Analysis of Her Samoan Research*. Boulder, Colo.: Westview Press, 1999.

———. *Margaret Mead and Samoa: The Making and Unmaking of an Anthropological Myth*. Cambridge, Mass.: Harvard University Press, 1983.

Friedan, Betty. *The Feminine Mystique*. New York: W. W. Norton, 2013 [1963].

Gates, Henry Louis, Jr. *Stony the Road: Reconstruction, White Supremacy, and the Rise of Jim Crow*. New York: Penguin, 2019.

Gates, Henry Louis, Jr., and Gene Andrew Jarrett, eds. *The New Negro: Readings on Race, Representation, and African American Culture, 1892–1938*. Princeton: Princeton University Press, 2007.

Gay, Peter. *The Enlightenment: An Interpretation*. London: Weidenfeld and Nicolson, 1966.

Geertz, Clifford. *Available Light: Anthropological Reflections on Philosophical Topics*. Princeton: Princeton University Press, 2000.

———. *Works and Lives: The Anthropologist as Author*. Stanford, Calif.: Stanford University Press, 1988.

Gershenhorn, Jerry. *Melville J. Herskovits and the Racial Politics of Knowledge*. Lincoln: University of Nebraska Press, 2004.

Gildersleeve, Virginia Crocheron. *Many a Good Crusade*. New York: Macmillan, 1954.

Gilkeson, John S. *Anthropologists and the Rediscovery of America, 1886–1965.* Cambridge, U.K.: Cambridge University Press, 2010.

Goddard, Henry Herbert. *The Kallikak Family: A Study in the Heredity of Feeble-Mindedness.* New York: Macmillan, 1912.

Goldfrank, Esther S. *Notes on an Undirected Life: As One Anthropologist Tells It.* Flushing, N.Y.: Queens College Press, 1978.

Goldschmidt, Walter, ed. *The Anthropology of Franz Boas: Essays on the Centennial of His Birth.* Washington, D.C.: American Anthropological Association, 1959.

Gordon, Linda. *The Second Coming of the KKK: The Ku Klux Klan of the 1920s and the American Political Tradition.* New York: Liveright, 2017.

Gould, Stephen Jay. *The Mismeasure of Man.* Rev. ed. New York: W. W. Norton, 1996.

Grant, Madison. *The Passing of the Great Race; or, The Racial Basis of European History.* New York: Charles Scribner's Sons, 1916.

Gravlee, Clarence C., H. Russell Bernard, and William R. Leonard. "Heredity, Environment, and Cranial Form: A Reanalysis of Boas' Immigrant Data." *American Anthropologist* 105, no. 1 (2003): 125–38.

———. "Boas' *Changes in Bodily Form*: The Immigrant Study, Cranial Plasticity, and Boas' Physical Anthropology." *American Anthropologist* 105, no. 2 (2003): 326–32.

Hall, G. Stanley. *Adolescence: Its Psychology and Its Relations to Physiology, Anthropology, Sociology, Sex, Crime, Religion, and Education.* 2 vols. New York: D. Appleton and Co., 1904.

———. *Life and Confessions of a Psychologist.* New York: Arno Press, 1977 [1923].

Hammond, Joyce D. "Telling a Tale: Margaret Mead's Photographic Portraits of Fa'amotu, a Samoan *Tāupou.*" *Visual Anthropology* 16 (2003): 341–74.

Harper, Kenn. *Minik: The New York Eskimo.* Hanover, N.H.: Steerforth Press, 2017.

Harris, Marvin. *The Rise of Anthropological Theory: A History of Theories of Culture.* Updated ed. Walnut Creek, Calif.: AltaMira Press, 2001.

Hayashi, Brian Masaru. *Democratizing the Enemy: The Japanese American Internment.* Princeton: Princeton University Press, 2004.

Hays, Terrence E., ed. *Ethnographic Presents: Pioneering Anthropologists in the Papua New Guinea Highlands.* Berkeley: University of California Press, 1992.

Hemenway, Robert E. *Zora Neale Hurston: A Literary Biography.* Urbana: University of Illinois Press, 1977.

Hempenstall, Peter. *Truth's Fool: Derek Freeman and the War over Cultural Anthropology.* Madison: University of Wisconsin Press, 2017.

Herrnstein, Richard J., and Charles Murray. *The Bell Curve: Intelligence and Class Structure in American Life.* New York: Free Press, 1994.

Herskovits, Melville J. *The Anthropometry of the American Negro.* New York: Columbia University Press, 1930.

———. *Franz Boas: The Science of Man in the Making.* New York: Charles Scribner's Sons, 1953.

———. *Life in a Haitian Valley.* New York: Alfred A. Knopf, 1937.

———. *Man and His Works: The Science of Cultural Anthropology.* New York: Alfred A. Knopf, 1948.

———. *The Myth of the Negro Past.* Boston: Beacon Press, 1958 [1941].

————. "The Negro in the New World: The Statement of a Problem." *American Anthropologist* 32, no. 1 (1930): 145–55.

————. *The New World Negro.* Edited by Frances S. Herskovits. Bloomington: Indiana University Press, 1966.

Herskovits, Melville J., and Frances S. Herskovits. *Rebel Destiny: Among the Bush Negroes of Dutch Guiana.* New York: Whittlesey House, 1934.

Hermann, Elfriede, ed. *Changing Context, Shifting Meanings: Transformations of Cultural Traditions in Oceania.* Honolulu: University of Hawai'i Press, 2011.

Higham, John. *Strangers in the Land: Patterns of American Nativism, 1860–1925.* 2nd ed. New York: Atheneum, 1975.

Hinsley, Curtis M. *The Smithsonian and the American Indian: Making a Moral Anthropology in Victorian America.* Washington, D.C.: Smithsonian Institution Press, 1981.

Hinsley, Curtis M., and Bill Holm. "A Cannibal in the National Museum: The Early Career of Franz Boas in America." *American Anthropologist* 78, no. 2 (June 1976): 306–16.

Hinsley, Curtis M., and David R. Wilcox, eds. *Coming of Age in Chicago: The 1893 World's Fair and the Coalescence of American Anthropology.* Lincoln: University of Nebraska Press, 2016.

Hitler, Adolf. *Mein Kampf.* Translated by Ralph Manheim. Boston: Houghton Mifflin, 1971.

Hobsbawm, E. J. *The Age of Revolution, 1789–1848.* Cleveland: World Publishing Co., 1962.

Holmes, W. H. "The World's Fair Congress of Anthropology." *American Anthropologist* 6, no. 4 (Oct. 1893): 423–34.

Howard, Jane. *Margaret Mead: A Life.* New York: Simon and Schuster, 1984.

Hrdlička, Aleš. "An Eskimo Brain." *American Anthropologist* 3, no. 3 (July–Sept. 1901): 454–500.

Hughes, Langston. *The Big Sea.* New York: Hill and Wang, 1993 [1940].

Huhndorf, Shair M. "Nanook and His Contemporaries: Imagining Eskimos in American Culture, 1897–1922." *Critical Inquiry* 27, no. 1 (2000): 122–48.

Hurston, Zora Neale. "Crazy for This Democracy." *Negro Digest* 4 (Dec. 1945): 45–48.

————. "Dance Songs and Tales from the Bahamas." *Journal of American Folklore* 43 (July–Sept. 1930): 294–312.

————. *Dust Tracks on a Road.* New York: Harper Perennial Modern Classics, 2006 [1942].

————. *Every Tongue Got to Confess: Negro Folk-Tales from the Gulf States.* New York: HarperCollins, 2001.

————. *Folklore, Memoirs, and Other Writings.* Edited by Cheryl A. Wall. New York: Library of America, 1995.

————. "Hoodoo in America." *Journal of American Folk-Lore* 44, no. 174 (Oct.–Dec. 1931): 317–417.

————. *Jonah's Gourd Vine.* New York: Harper Perennial Modern Classics, 2008 [1934].

————. *Moses, Man of the Mountain.* New York: Harper Perennial Modern Classics, 2009 [1939].

————. *Mules and Men*. New York: Harper Perennial Modern Classics, 2008 [1935].

————. "My Most Humiliating Jim Crow Experience." *Negro Digest* 2 (June 1944): 25–26.

————. "The 'Pet Negro' System." *American Mercury* 56 (Mar. 1943): 593–600.

————. *Seraph on the Sewanee*. New York: Harper Perennial Modern Classics, 2008 [1948].

————. *Tell My Horse: Voodoo and Life in Haiti and Jamaica*. New York: Harper Perennial Modern Classics, 2009 [1938].

————. *Their Eyes Were Watching God*. Harper Perennial Modern Classics, 2013 [1937].

Jacknis, Ira. "The First Boasian: Alfred Kroeber and Franz Boas, 1896–1905." *American Anthropologist* 104, no. 2 (June 2002): 520–32.

————. "Margaret Mead and Gregory Bateson in Bali: Their Use of Photography and Film." *Cultural Anthropology* 3, no. 2 (May 1988): 160–77.

Janiewski, Dolores, and Lois W. Banner, eds. *Reading Benedict/Reading Mead: Feminism, Race, and Imperial Visions*. Baltimore: Johns Hopkins University Press, 2004.

Jefferson, Thomas. *Notes on the State of Virginia*. Richmond: J. W. Randolph, 1853 [1785].

Kaplan, Carla. *Miss Anne in Harlem: The White Women of the Black Renaissance*. New York: HarperCollins, 2013.

————, ed. *Zora Neale Hurston: A Life in Letters*. New York: Doubleday, 2002.

Keller, Phyllis. *States of Belonging: German-American Intellectuals and the First World War*. Cambridge, Mass.: Harvard University Press, 1979.

Kendi, Ibram X. *Stamped from the Beginning: The Definitive History of Racist Ideas in America*. New York: Nation Books, 2016.

Kent, Pauline. "An Appendix to *The Chrysanthemum and the Sword*: A Bibliography." *Japan Review* 6 (1995): 107–25.

————. "Japanese Perceptions of *The Chrysanthemum and the Sword*." *Dialectical Anthropology* 24, no. 2 (1999): 181–92.

————. "Ruth Benedict's Original Wartime Study of the Japanese." *International Journal of Japanese Sociology* 3, no. 1 (1994): 81–97.

Kluchin, Rebecca M. *Fit to Be Tied: Sterilization and Reproductive Rights in America, 1950–1980*. New Brunswick: Rutgers University Press, 2009.

Kluckhohn, Clyde. *Ralph Linton, 1893–1953*. Washington, D.C.: National Academy of Sciences, 1958.

Kroeber, A. L. *Anthropology*. New York: Harcourt, Brace and Co., 1923.

————. "Review of *Patterns of Culture*." *American Anthropologist* 37 (new ser.), no. 4, pt. 1 (Oct.–Dec. 1935): 689–90.

————. "The Superorganic." *American Anthropologist* 19, no. 2 (Apr.–June 1917): 163–213.

————. "Totem and Taboo: An Ethnologic Psychoanalysis." *American Anthropologist* 22, no. 1 (Jan.–Mar. 1920): 48–55.

Kroeber, A. L., Ruth Benedict, Murray B. Emeneau, Melville J. Herskovits, Gladys A. Reichard, and J. Alden Mason. *Franz Boas, 1858–1942*. Special issue of *American Anthropologist* 45, no. 3, pt. 2 (July–Sept. 1943).

Kroeber, A. L., and Clifton Kroeber, eds. *Ishi in Three Centuries*. Lincoln: University of Nebraska Press, 2003.

Kroeber, Theodora. *Ishi in Two Worlds*. Berkeley: University of California Press, 1961.

Kuechler, Manfred. "The NSDAP Vote in the Weimar Republic: An Assessment of the State-of-the-Art in View of Modern Electoral Research." *Historical Social Research/Historische Sozialforschung* 17, no. 1 (1992): 22–52.

Kühl, Stefan. *The Nazi Connection: Eugenics, American Racism, and German National Socialism*. Oxford: Oxford University Press, 1994.

Kuklick, Henrika, ed. *A New History of Anthropology*. Oxford: Blackwell, 2008.

Laland, Kevin N. *Darwin's Unfinished Revolution*. Princeton: Princeton University Press, 2017.

Lapsley, Hilary. *Margaret Mead and Ruth Benedict: The Kinship of Women*. Amherst, Mass.: University of Massachusetts Press, 1999.

Laughlin, Harry H. *The Second International Exhibition of Eugenics*. Baltimore: Williams and Wilkins Co., 1923.

Laurière, Christine. "Anthropology and Politics, the Beginnings: The Relations Between Franz Boas and Paul Rivet (1919–42)." *Histories of Anthropology Annual* 6 (2010): 225–52.

Leavitt, John. "The Shapes of Modernity: On the Philosophical Roots of Anthropological Doctrines." *Culture* 11, nos. 1–2 (1991): 29–42.

Leeds-Hurwitz, Wendy. *Rolling in Ditches with Shamans: Jaime de Angulo and the Professionalization of American Anthropology*. Lincoln: University of Nebraska Press, 2004.

Leighton, Alexander H. *The Governing of Men: General Principles and Recommendations Based on Experience at a Japanese Relocation Camp*. Princeton: Princeton University Press, 1945.

Leonard, Thomas C. *Illiberal Reformers: Race, Eugenics, and American Economics in the Progressive Era*. Princeton: Princeton University Press, 2016.

Lévi-Strauss, Claude. *Tristes Tropiques*. Translated by John and Doreen Weightman. New York: Penguin, 1992 [1955].

Lewis, Herbert S. "Boas, Darwin, Science, and Anthropology." *Current Anthropology* 42, no. 3 (June 2001): 381–406.

———. "The Misrepresentation of Anthropology and Its Consequences." *American Anthropologist* 100, no. 3 (Sept. 1998): 716–31.

———. "The Passion of Franz Boas." *American Anthropologist* 103, no. 2 (June 2001): 447–67.

Linton, Ralph. *The Study of Man: An Introduction*. New York: D. Appleton-Century Company, 1936.

Lipset, David. *Gregory Bateson: The Legacy of a Scientist*. Boston: Beacon Press, 1982.

———. "Rereading *Sex and Temperament*: Margaret Mead's Sepik Triptych and Its Ethnographic Critics." *Anthropological Quarterly* 76, no. 4 (2003): 693–713.

Lombardo, Paul A. *Three Generations, No Imbeciles: Eugenics, the Supreme Court, and* Buck v. Bell. Baltimore: Johns Hopkins University Press, 2008.

Longerich, Peter. *Holocaust: The Nazi Persecution and Murder of the Jews*. Oxford: Oxford University Press, 2010.

Lovett, Laura L. *Conceiving the Future: Pronatalism, Reproduction, and the Family in the United States, 1890–1938.* Chapel Hill: University of North Carolina Press, 2007.

Lowie, Robert H. "American Contributions to Anthropology." *Science* 100, no. 2598 (Oct. 13, 1944): 321–27.

———. *Franz Boas, 1858–1942.* Washington, D.C.: National Academy of Sciences, 1947.

———. "Review of *Coming of Age in Samoa.*" *American Anthropologist* 31 (1929): 532–34.

Loyer, Emmanuelle. *Lévi-Strauss.* Paris: Flammarion, 2015.

Luebke, Frederick C. *Bonds of Loyalty: German-Americans and World War I.* DeKalb: Northern Illinois University Press, 1974.

Lutkehaus, Nancy C. *Margaret Mead: The Making of an American Icon.* Princeton: Princeton University Press, 2008.

Lynd, Robert S., and Helen Merrell Lynd. *Middletown: A Study in Contemporary American Culture.* New York: Harcourt, Brace & Co., 1929.

Lyons, Andrew P., and Harriet D. Lyons. *Irregular Connections: A History of Anthropology and Sexuality.* Lincoln: University of Nebraska Press, 2004.

Madley, Benjamin. *An American Genocide: The United States and the California Indian Catastrophe, 1846–1873.* New Haven: Yale University Press, 2016.

Malinowski, Bronislaw. *Argonauts of the Western Pacific.* New York: Routledge, 2014 [1922].

Mandler, Peter. *Return from the Natives: How Margaret Mead Won the Second World War and Lost the Cold War.* New Haven: Yale University Press, 2013.

Martin, Susan F. *A Nation of Immigrants.* Cambridge: Cambridge University Press, 2011.

Mason, Otis T. "The Occurrence of Similar Inventions in Areas Widely Apart." *Science* 9, no. 226 (June 3, 1887): 534–35.

McCaughey, Robert A. *Stand, Columbia: A History of Columbia University in the City of New York, 1754–2004.* New York: Columbia University Press, 2003.

Mead, Margaret. *And Keep Your Powder Dry: An Anthropologist Looks at America.* New York: William Morrow, 1942.

———. *An Anthropologist at Work: Writings of Ruth Benedict.* Boston: Houghton Mifflin, 1959.

———. "An Anthropologist Looks at Our Marriage Laws." *Virginia Law Weekly Dicta* 2, no. 3 (Oct. 6, 1949): 1, 4.

———. "Are Children Savages?" *Mademoiselle*, July 1948, 33, 110–11.

———. *Blackberry Winter: My Earlier Years.* New York: Simon and Schuster, 1972.

———. "Broken Homes." *Nation* (Feb. 27, 1929): 253–55.

———. *The Changing Culture of an Indian Tribe.* New York: Columbia University Press, 1932.

———. *Coming of Age in Samoa: A Psychological Study of Primitive Youth for Western Civilization.* New York: Perennial Classics, 2001 [1928].

———. "An Ethnologist's Footnote to *Totem and Taboo.*" *Psychoanalytic Review* 17, no. 3 (July 1930): 297–304.

———. *Growing Up in New Guinea: A Comparative Study of Primitive Education.* New York: Perennial Classics, 2001 [1930].

———. "Jealousy: Primitive and Civilised." In *Woman's Coming of Age*, edited by S. D. Schmalhausen and V. F. Calverton, 35–48. New York: Liveright, 1931.

———. "A Lapse of Animism Among a Primitive People." *Psyche* 33 (July 1928): 72–77.

———. *Letters from the Field, 1925–1975*. New York: Perennial, 2001 [1977].

———. "Life as a Samoan Girl." In *All True! The Record of Actual Adventures That Have Happened to Ten Women of Today*. New York: Brewer, Warren, and Putnam, 1931.

———. *Male and Female*. New York: Perennial, 2001 [1949].

———. *The Maoris and Their Arts*. American Museum of Natural History Guide Leaflet Series, No. 71 (May 1928).

———. "Melanesian Middlemen." *Natural History* 30, no. 3 (Mar.–Apr. 1930): 115–30.

———. "The Methodology of Racial Testing: Its Significance for Sociology." *American Journal of Sociology* 31, no. 5 (Mar. 1926): 657–67.

———. "More Comprehensive Field Methods." *American Anthropologist* 35, no. 1 (Jan.–Mar. 1933): 1–15.

———. *The Mountain Arapesh*. 2 vols. New Brunswick: Transaction, 2002 [1938].

———. "Must Marriage Be for Life?" *'47: The Magazine of the Year* 1, no. 9 (Nov. 1947): 28–31.

———. "Review of *Patterns of Culture* by Ruth Benedict." *Nation*, Dec. 12, 1934, 686.

———. *Sex and Temperament in Three Primitive Societies*. New York: Harper Perennial, 2001 [1935].

———. "Social Change and Cultural Surrogates." *Journal of Educational Sociology* 14, no. 2 (Oct. 1940): 92–109.

———. *Social Organization of Manua*. Honolulu: Bernice P. Bishop Museum, 1930.

———, et al. "Culture and Personality." *American Journal of Sociology* 42, no. 1 (July 1936): 84–87.

Menand, Louis. *The Metaphysical Club: A Story of Ideas in America*. New York: Farrar, Straus and Giroux, 2001.

Meyer, Annie Nathan. *Barnard Beginnings*. Boston: Houghton Mifflin, 1935.

———. *It's Been Fun: An Autobiography*. New York: Henry Schuman, 1951.

Meyerowitz, Joanne. "'How Common Culture Shapes the Separate Lives': Sexuality, Race, and Mid-Twentieth-Century Social Constructionist Thought." *Journal of American History* 96, no. 4 (Mar. 2010): 1057–84.

Mikell, Gwendolyn. "When Horses Talk: Reflections on Zora Neale Hurston's Haitian Anthropology." *Phylon* 43, no. 3 (1982): 218–30.

Miller, Vivien M. L. *Crime, Sexual Violence, and Clemency: Florida's Pardon Board and Penal System in the Progressive Era*. Gainesville: University Press of Florida, 2000.

Millman, Chad. *The Detonators: The Secret Plot to Destroy America and an Epic Hunt for Justice*. New York: Little, Brown, 2006.

Molloy, Maureen A. *On Creating a Usable Culture: Margaret Mead and the Emergence of American Cosmopolitanism*. Honolulu: University of Hawai'i Press, 2008.

Morgan, Lewis Henry. *Ancient Society; or, Researches in the Lines of Human Progress from Savagery Through Barbarism to Civilization.* Cleveland: World Publishing Co., 1963 [1877].

———. *League of the Ho-de'-no-sau-nee or Iroquois.* 2 vols. New ed. New York: Burt Franklin, 1966 [1851].

Mormino, Gary R. *Land of Sunshine, State of Dreams: A Social History of Modern Florida.* Gainesville: University Press of Florida, 2005.

Morris, Aldon D. *The Scholar Denied: W. E. B. Du Bois and the Birth of Modern Sociology.* Berkeley: University of California Press, 2015.

Mukherjee, Siddhartha. *The Gene: An Intimate History.* New York: Scribner, 2016.

Müller-Wille, Ludger. *The Franz Boas Enigma: Inuit, Arctic, and Sciences.* Montreal: Baraka Books, 2014.

———, ed. *Franz Boas Among the Inuit of Baffin Island, 1883–1884: Journals and Letters.* Translated by William Barr. Toronto: University of Toronto Press, 1998.

Murray, Stephen O. *American Anthropology and Company: Historical Explorations.* Lincoln: University of Nebraska Press, 2013.

Nadel, Stanley. *Little Germany: Ethnicity, Religion, and Class in New York City, 1845–1880.* Urbana: University of Illinois Press, 1990.

Newkirk, Pamela. *Spectacle: The Astonishing Life of Ota Benga.* New York: Amistad, 2015.

Nott, Josiah Clark, and George R. Gliddon, eds. *Types of Mankind: Ethnological Researches Based Upon the Ancient Monuments, Paintings, Sculptures, and Crania of Races, and Upon Their Natural, Geographical, Philological, and Biblical History.* 4th ed. Philadelphia: Lippincott, Grambo, 1854.

Ortiz, Paul. *Emancipation Betrayed: The Hidden History of Black Organizing and White Violence in Florida from Reconstruction to the Bloody Election of 1920.* Berkeley: University of California Press, 2005.

Painter, Nell Irvin. *The History of White People.* New York: W. W. Norton, 2010.

Paris, Leslie. *Children's Nature: The Rise of the American Summer Camp.* New York: New York University Press, 2008.

Parsons, Elsie Clews. *Fear and Conventionality.* New York: G. P. Putnam's Sons, 1914.

———. *Social Freedom: A Study of the Conflicts Between Social Classifications and Personality.* New York: G. P. Putnam's Sons, 1915.

Paxson, Margaret. *Solovyovo: The Story of Memory in a Russian Village.* Bloomington: Indiana University Press, 2005.

Powell, John Wesley. *The Exploration of the Colorado River.* Garden City, NY: Anchor Books, 1961 [1875].

———. "From Barbarism to Civilization." *American Anthropologist* 1, no. 2 (Apr. 1888): 97–123.

———. "Museums of Ethnography and Their Classification." *Science* 9, no. 229 (June 24, 1887): 612–14.

Prahlad, Sw. Anand. "Africana Folklore: History and Challenges." *Journal of American Folklore* 118, no. 469 (2005): 253–70.

Price, David H. *Anthropological Intelligence: The Deployment and Neglect of American Anthropology in the Second World War.* Durham, N.C.: Duke University Press, 2008.

———. "Anthropologists as Spies." *Nation* (Nov. 2, 2000): Online.

————. *Cold War Anthropology: The CIA, the Pentagon, and the Growth of Dual Use Anthropology*. Durham, N.C.: Duke University Press, 2016.

————. *Threatening Anthropology: McCarthyism and the FBI's Surveillance of Activist Anthropologists*. Durham, N.C.: Duke University Press, 2004.

Ramsey, Kate. *The Spirits and the Law: Vodou and Power in Haiti*. Chicago: University of Chicago Press, 2011.

Rapport, Mike. *1848: Year of Revolution*. New York: Basic Books, 2008.

Redman, Samuel J. *Bone Rooms: From Scientific Racism to Human Prehistory in Museums*. Cambridge, Mass.: Harvard University Press, 2016.

Reilly, Philip R. *The Surgical Solution: A History of Involuntary Sterilization in the United States*. Baltimore: Johns Hopkins University Press, 1991.

Renda, Mary A. *Taking Haiti: Military Occupation and the Culture of U.S. Imperialism, 1915–1940*. Chapel Hill: University of North Carolina Press, 2001.

Reports of the Immigration Commission: Abstracts of Reports of the Immigration Commission. 2 vols. Washington, D.C.: U.S. Government Printing Office, 1911.

Reports of the Immigration Commission: Changes in Bodily Form of Descendants of Immigrants. Washington, D.C.: U.S. Government Printing Office, 1911.

Reports of the Immigration Commission: Dictionary of Races or Peoples. Washington, D.C.: U.S. Government Printing Office, 1911.

Ripley, William Z. *The Races of Europe: A Sociological Study*. New York: D. Appleton & Co., 1899.

————. *A Selected Bibliography of the Anthropology and Ethnology of Europe*. New York: D. Appleton & Co., 1899.

Rivet, Paul. "Franz Boas." *Renaissance* 1, no. 2 (1943): 313–14.

————. "Tribute to Franz Boas." *International Journal of American Linguistics* 24, no. 4 (1958): 251–52.

Rohner, Ronald P., ed. *The Ethnography of Franz Boas: Letters and Diaries of Franz Boas Written on the Northwest Coast from 1886 to 1931*. Chicago: University of Chicago Press, 1969.

Roscoe, Paul. "Margaret Mead, Reo Fortune, and Mountain Arapesh Warfare." *American Anthropologist* 105, no. 3 (Sept. 2003): 581–91.

Rosenberg, Rosalind. *Changing the Subject: How the Women of Columbia Shaped the Way We Think About Sex and Politics*. New York: Columbia University Press, 2004.

Rosenthal, Michael. *Nicholas Miraculous: The Amazing Career of the Redoubtable Dr. Nicholas Murray Butler*. New York: Columbia University Press, 2015.

Ross, Dorothy. *G. Stanley Hall: The Psychologist as Prophet*. Chicago: University of Chicago Press, 1972.

Ryback, Timothy W. *Hitler's Private Library: The Books That Shaped His Life*. New York: Alfred A. Knopf, 2008.

Sackman, Douglas Cazaux. *Wild Men: Ishi and Kroeber in the Wilderness of Modern America*. Oxford: Oxford University Press, 2010.

Sanger, Margaret. *The Pivot of Civilization*. New York: Brentano's, 1922.

Sapir, Edward. "Culture, Genuine and Spurious." *American Journal of Sociology* 29, no. 4 (Jan. 1924): 401–29.

————. *Culture, Language, and Personality: Selected Essays*. Edited by David G. Mandelbaum. Berkeley: University of California Press, 1949.

————. "Do We Need a 'Superorganic'?" *American Anthropologist* 19, no. 3 (July–Sept. 1917): 441–47.

————. "Franz Boas." *New Republic*, Jan. 23, 1929, 278–79.

————. *Language: An Introduction to the Study of Speech.* New York: Harcourt, Brace & Co., 1921.

————. "Observations on the Sex Problem in America." *American Journal of Psychiatry* 85, no. 3 (1928): 519–34.

————. *Time Perspective in Aboriginal American Culture: A Study in Method.* Canada Department of Mines, Geological Survey Memoir no. 90. Ottawa: Government Printing Bureau, 1916.

————. "Why Cultural Anthropology Needs the Psychiatrist." *Psychiatry* 64, no. 1 (2001) [1938]: 2–10.

Sargeant, Winthrop. "It's All Anthropology." *New Yorker*, Dec. 30, 1961.

Sargent, Porter. *A Handbook of Summer Camps.* 12th ed. Boston: Porter Sargent, 1935.

Schmalhausen, Samuel D., and V. F. Calverton, eds. *Woman's Coming of Age: A Symposium.* New York: Horace Liveright, 1931.

Schmerler, Gil. *Henrietta Schmerler and the Murder That Put Anthropology on Trial.* Eugene, Ore.: Scrivana Press, 2017.

Seabrook, W. B. *The Magic Island.* New York: Literary Guild of America, 1929.

Sellers, Sean, and Greg Asbed. "The History and Evolution of Forced Labor in Florida Agriculture." *Race/Ethnicity: Multidisciplinary Global Contexts* 5, no. 1 (Autumn 2011), 29–49.

Seltzer, William, and Margo Anderson. "After Pearl Harbor: The Proper Role of Population Data Systems in Time of War." Unpublished paper, 2000, https://margoanderson.org/govstat/newpaa.pdf.

Settle, Dionyse. *Laste Voyage into the West and Northwest Regions.* New York: Da Capo Press, 1969 [1577].

Shankman, Paul. "The 'Fateful Hoaxing' of Margaret Mead." *Current Anthropology* 54, no. 1 (Feb. 2013): 51–70.

————. *The Trashing of Margaret Mead: Anatomy of an Anthropological Controversy.* Madison: University of Wisconsin Press, 2009.

Simpson, George Eaton. *Melville J. Herskovits.* New York: Columbia University Press, 1973.

Sinclair, Upton. *The Goose-Step: A Study of American Education.* Pasadena, Calif.: Published by the author, 1923.

Singer, Audrey. "Contemporary Immigrant Gateways in Historical Perspective." *Daedalus* (Summer 2013): 76–91.

Smith, J. David. *Minds Made Feeble: The Myth and Legacy of the Kallikaks.* Rockville, Md.: Aspen Systems Corp., 1985.

Sparks, Corey S., and Richard L. Jantz. "A Reassessment of Human Cranial Plasticity: Boas Revisited." *Proceedings of the National Academy of Sciences* 99, no. 23 (Nov. 2002): 14636–39.

————. "Changing Times, Changing Faces: Franz Boas' Immigrant Study in Modern Perspective." *American Anthropologist* 105, no. 2 (June 2003): 333–37.

Spicer, Edward H. "The Use of Social Scientists by the War Relocation Authority." *Applied Anthropology* 5, no. 2 (Spring 1946): 16–36.

Spiller, G., ed. *Papers on Inter-Racial Problems Communicated to the First Universal Races Congress.* London: P. S. King & Son, 1911.

Spindel, Carol. *Dancing at Halftime: Sports and the Controversy over American Indian Mascots.* New York: NYU Press, 2000.

Spiro, Jonathan Peter. *Defending the Master Race: Conservation, Eugenics, and the Legacy of Madison Grant.* Burlington: University of Vermont Press, 2009.

Starn, Orin. "Engineering Internment: Anthropologists and the War Relocation Authority." *American Ethnologist* 13, no. 4 (Nov. 1986): 700–720.

———. *Ishi's Brain: In Search of America's Last "Wild" Indian.* New York: W. W. Norton, 2004.

Stern, Alexandra Minna. *Eugenic Nation: Faults and Frontiers of Better Breeding in America.* Berkeley: University of California Press, 2005.

Stern, Fritz. *Five Germanys I Have Known.* New York: Farrar, Straus and Giroux, 2006.

Steward, Julian H. *Alfred Kroeber.* New York: Columbia University Press, 1973.

Stewart, Jeffrey C. *The New Negro: The Life of Alain Locke.* Oxford, U.K.: Oxford University Press, 2018.

Stocking, George W., Jr., ed. *American Anthropology, 1921–1945.* Lincoln: University of Nebraska Press, 1976.

———, ed. *Bones, Bodies, Behavior: Essays on Biological Anthropology.* Madison: University of Wisconsin Press, 1988.

———. *The Ethnographer's Magic and Other Essays in the History of Anthropology.* Madison: University of Wisconsin Press, 1992.

———, ed. *Functionalism Historicized: Essays on British Social Anthropology.* Madison: University of Wisconsin Press, 1984.

———, ed. *Malinowski, Rivers, Benedict, and Others: Essays on Culture and Personality.* Madison: University of Wisconsin Press, 1986.

———, ed. *Observers Observed: Essays on Ethnographic Fieldwork.* Madison: University of Wisconsin Press, 1983.

———, ed. *Romantic Motives: Essays on Anthropological Sensibility.* Madison: University of Wisconsin Press, 1989.

———, ed. *The Shaping of American Anthropology, 1883–1911: A Franz Boas Reader.* New York: Basic Books, 1974.

———, ed. *Volksgeist as Method and Ethic: Essays on Boasian Ethnography and the German Anthropological Tradition.* Madison: University of Wisconsin Press, 1996.

Sussman, Robert Wald. *The Myth of Race: The Troubling Persistence of an Unscientific Idea.* Cambridge, Mass.: Harvard University Press, 2014.

Suzuki, Peter T. "Anthropologists in Wartime Camps for Japanese Americans: A Documentary Study." *Dialectical Anthropology* 6, no. 1 (1981): 23–60.

———. "Overlooked Aspects of *The Chrysanthemum and the Sword.*" *Dialectical Anthropology* 24, no. 2 (1999): 217–32.

———. "Ruth Benedict, Robert Hashima, and *The Chrysanthemum and the Sword.*" *Research: Contributions to Interdisciplinary Anthropology* 3 (1985): 55–69.

Taylor, C. J. "First International Polar Year, 1882–83." *Arctic* 34, no. 4 (Dec. 1981): 370–76.

Taylor, Yuval. *Zora and Langston: A Story of Friendship and Betrayal*. New York: W. W. Norton, 2019.

Tcherkézoff, Serge. "A Long and Unfortunate Voyage Towards the 'Invention' of the Melanesia/Polynesia Distinction, 1595–1832." *Journal of Pacific History* 38, no. 2 (Sept. 2003): 175–96.

Teslow, Tracy. *Constructing Race: The Science of Bodies and Cultures in American Anthropology*. Cambridge, U.K.: Cambridge University Press, 2014.

Thomas, Caroline. "Rediscovering Reo: Reflections on the Life and Anthropological Career of Reo Franklin Fortune." *Pacific Studies* 32, nos. 2–3 (June–Sept. 2009): 299–324.

Toulmin, Stephen. "The Evolution of Margaret Mead." *New York Review of Books*, Dec. 6, 1984.

Tozzer, Alfred M. *Biographical Memoir of Frederic Ward Putnam, 1839–1915*. Washington, D.C.: National Academy of Sciences, 1935.

Tylor, Edward Burnett. *Anthropology*. New York: D. Appleton & Co., 1920 [1881].

———. *Primitive Culture: Researches into the Development of Mythology, Philosophy, Religion, Language, Art and Custom*. 3rd American ed. 2 vols. New York: H. Holt, 1883 [1871].

United States Department of War. *Final Report: Japanese Evacuation from the West Coast, 1942*. New York: Arno Press, 1978 [1943].

Valentine, Lisa Philips, and Regna Darnell, eds. *Theorizing the Americanist Tradition*. Toronto: University of Toronto Press, 1999.

Van Slyck, Abigail A. *A Manufactured Wilderness: Summer Camps and the Shaping of American Youth, 1890–1960*. Minneapolis: University of Minnesota Press, 2006.

Vaughan, Alden T. *Transatlantic Encounters: American Indians in Britain, 1500–1776*. Cambridge, U.K.: Cambridge University Press, 2006.

Vermeulen, Han F. *Before Boas: The Genesis of Ethnography and Ethnology in the German Enlightenment*. Lincoln: University of Nebraska Press, 2015.

Walker, Alice. "In Search of Zora Neale Hurston." *Ms. Magazine*, Mar. 1975, 74–89.

Walker, James R. *Lakota Belief and Ritual*. Edited by Raymond J. DeMallie and Elaine A. Jahner. Lincoln: University of Nebraska Press, 1980.

———. *Lakota Myth*. Edited by Elaine A. Jahner. New ed. Lincoln: University of Nebraska Press, 1983.

———. *Lakota Society*. Edited by Raymond J. DeMallie. Lincoln: University of Nebraska Press, 1982.

———. *The Sun Dance and Other Ceremonies of the Oglala Division of the Teton Dakota*. New York: American Museum of Natural History, 1917.

Washburn, Wilcomb E. *The Cosmos Club of Washington: A Centennial History, 1878–1978*. Washington, D.C.: Cosmos Club, 1978.

Weiss-Wendt, Anton, and Rory Yeomans, eds. *Racial Science in Hitler's New Europe, 1938–1945*. Lincoln: University of Nebraska Press, 2013.

Weitz, Eric D. *Weimar Germany: Promise and Tragedy*. New ed. Princeton: Princeton University Press, 2013.

Westbrook, Laurel, and Aliya Saperstein. "New Categories Are Not Enough:

Rethinking the Measurement of Sex and Gender in Social Surveys." *Gender and Society* 29, no. 4 (2015): 534–60.

White, Leslie A. "The Ethnography and Ethnology of Franz Boas." *Bulletin of the Texas Memorial Museum* 6 (Apr. 1963): 1–76.

White, Marian Churchill. *A History of Barnard College*. New York: Columbia University Press, 1954.

White, Richard. *The Republic for Which It Stands: The United States During Reconstruction and the Gilded Age, 1865–1896*. Oxford, U.K.: Oxford University Press, 2017.

Whitman, James Q. *Hitler's American Model: The United States and the Making of Nazi Race Law*. Princeton: Princeton University Press, 2017.

Winkler, Allan M. *The Politics of Propaganda: The Office of War Information, 1942–1945*. New Haven: Yale University Press, 1978.

Woodbury, Richard B., and Nathalie F. S. Woodbury. "The Rise and Fall of the Bureau of American Ethnology." *Journal of the Southwest* 41, no. 3 (Autumn 1999): 283–96.

Woodson, Carter G. *The African Background Outlined*. Washington, D.C.: Association for the Study of Negro Life and History, 1936.

Wulf, Andrea. *The Invention of Nature: Alexander von Humboldt's New World*. New York: Knopf, 2015.

Young, Michael W. *Malinowski: Odyssey of an Anthropologist, 1884–1920*. New Haven: Yale University Press, 2004.

Young, Virginia Heyer. *Ruth Benedict: Beyond Relativity, Beyond Pattern*. Lincoln: University of Nebraska Press, 2005.

Yudell, Michael, et al. "Taking Race Out of Human Genetics." *Science* 351, no. 6273 (Feb. 5, 2016): 564–65.

Zeidel, Robert F. *Immigrants, Progressives, and Exclusion Politics: The Dillingham Commission, 1900–1927*. DeKalb: Northern Illinois University Press, 2004.

Zumwalt, Rosemary Lévy. *Wealth and Rebellion: Elsie Clews Parsons, Anthropologist and Folklorist*. Urbana: University of Illinois Press, 1992.

Zumwalt, Rosemary Lévy, and William Shedrick Willis. *Franz Boas and W. E. B. Du Bois at Atlanta University, 1906*. Philadelphia: American Philosophical Society, 2008.

INDEX

AMNH = American Museum of Natural History

Illustration Credits

Margaret Mead wading in the surf (title page): Margaret Mead Papers, Library of Congress

Franz Boas aboard the Germania: Franz Boas Papers, American Philosophical Society

Boas with his wife, Marie Krackowizer: Franz Boas Papers, American Philosophical Society

John Wesley Powell, ca. 1890: Library of Congress Prints and Photographs Division

Anthropology Building at the Chicago World's Fair: Gift of Frederic Ward Putnam, 1893. Courtesy of the Peabody Museum of Archaeology and Ethnology, Harvard University, PM93-1-10/100266.1.17

Kwakiutl dancers at the Chicago World's Fair: Gift of Frederic Ward Putnam, 1893. Courtesy of the Peabody Museum of Archaeology and Ethnology, Harvard University, PM93-1-10/100266.1.37

Boas demonstrating the Kwakiutl hamatsa: National Anthropological Archives, Smithsonian Institute

Franz Boas's anthropometry inventory sheet: National Anthropological Archives, Smithsonian Institution

Ruth Benedict in 1924: Margaret Mead Papers, Library of Congress

A page from Boas's report for the Dillingham Commission: U.S. Government Printing Office

Tabletop display used by the American Eugenics Society: American Eugenics Society Records, American Philosophical Society

Madison Grant: Library of Congress Rare Book and Special Collections Division

Adolf Hitler's copy of The Passing of the Great Race: Library of Congress Rare Book and Special Collections Division

A dedication to Hitler from the publisher: Library of Congress Rare Book and Special Collections Division

Margaret Mead as a girl: Margaret Mead Papers, Library of Congress

Margaret Mead as a student: Margaret Mead Papers, Library of Congress

Edward Sapir: Margaret Mead Papers, Library of Congress

The house of the Holt family: Margaret Mead Papers, Library of Congress

Margaret Mead with Fa'amotu: Margaret Mead Papers, Library of Congress

Reo Fortune with boys of Pere village: Margaret Mead Papers, Library of Congress

Margaret Mead with children in the lagoon of Pere village: Margaret Mead Papers, Library of Congress

Zora Neale Hurston with car: Zora Neale Hurston Papers, Special and Area Studies Collections, George A. Smathers Libraries, University of Florida, Gainesville, Florida

Gregory Bateson: Margaret Mead Papers, Library of Congress

Ella Deloria: The Indian Leader, Sept. 25, 1925. Courtesy of Haskell Indian Nations University Library

Bateson, Mead, and Fortune in an Australian newspaper: Margaret Mead Papers, Library of Congress

Felicia Felix-Mentor in Life: Life, Dec. 13, 1937

Zora Neale Hurston by Carl Van Vechten: Margaret Mead Papers, Library of Congress

Bateson and Mead eating in New Guinea, 1938: Margaret Mead Papers, Library of Congress

Hurston with musicians, 1935: Margaret Mead Papers, Library of Congress

Boas on the cover of Time: Time, May 11, 1936

Benedict, ca. 1931: Ruth Benedict Papers, Archives and Special Collections, Vassar College Library

Interned Japanese Americans at Santa Anita racetrack, 1942: Library of Congress Prints and Photographs Division

Map of Mead's relationships in the Boas circle: Margaret Mead Papers, Library of Congress

Mead in her office in the American Museum of Natural History: Image #338667, American Museum of Natural History Library

BEYOND CULTURE
by Edward T. Hall

For too long, people have taken their own ways of life for granted, ignoring the vast, international cultural community that surrounds them. Humankind must now embark on the difficult journey beyond culture, to the discovery of a lost self and a sense of perspective. By holding up a mirror, Hall permits us to see the awesome grip of unconscious culture. With concrete examples ranging from James Joyce's *Finnegans Wake* to the mating habits of the bowerbird of New Guinea, Hall shows us ourselves. *Beyond Culture* is a book about self-discovery; it is a voyage we all must embark on if mankind is to survive.

Anthropology

A HISTORY OF HISTORIES
Epics, Chronicles, and Inquiries from Herodotus and Thucydides to the Twentieth Century
by John Burrow

Treating the practice of history not as an isolated pursuit but as an aspect of human society and an essential part of the culture of the West, John Burrow magnificently brings to life and explains the distinctive qualities found in the work of historians from the ancient Egyptians and Greeks to the present. With a light step and graceful narrative, he gathers together over 2,500 years of the moments and decisions that have helped create Western identity. This unique approach is an incredible lens with which to view the past. Standing alone in its ambition, scale, and fascination, Burrow's history of history is certain to stand the test of time.

Historiography

THE EAST, THE WEST, AND SEX
A History
by Richard Bernstein

Richard Bernstein explores the connection between sex and power as it has played out between Eastern cultures and the Western explorers, merchants, and conquerors who have visited them. This illuminating book describes the historical and ongoing encounter between these travelers and the morally ambiguous opportunities they found in foreign lands. Bernstein's narrative teems with real figures, from Marco Polo and his investigation into the harem of Kublai Khan; the nineteenth-century American missionary Isabella Thoburn and her efforts to stamp out the "sinfulness" of the Mughal culture of India; Gustave Flaubert and his dalliances with Egyptian prostitutes; to modern-day sex tourists in Southeast Asia, as well as the women that they both exploit and enrich. Provocative and insightful, *The East, The West, and Sex* is a lucid look at a pervasive and yet mostly ignored subject.

History

THE GIRL AT THE BAGGAGE CLAIM
Explaining the East-West Culture Gap
by Gish Jen

Drawing on a trove of personal accounts and cutting-edge research, Gish Jen shows how our worldviews are shaped by what cultural psychologists call "independent" and "interdependent" models of selfhood. Coloring what we perceive, remember, do, make, and tell, imbuing everything from our ideas about copying to our conceptions of human rights, these models help explain why the United States produced Apple while China created Alibaba—and what that might mean for our shared future. As engaging as it is fascinating, *The Girl at the Baggage Claim* is a book that profoundly transforms our understanding of ourselves and our time.

Social Science

THE CHILDREN OF SANCHEZ
Autobiography of a Mexican Family
by Oscar Lewis

A pioneering work from a visionary anthropologist, *The Children of Sanchez* is hailed around the world as a watershed achievement in the study of poverty—a uniquely intimate investigation, as poignant today as when it was first published. It is the epic story of the Sánchez family, told entirely by its members—Jesus, the fifty-year-old patriarch, and his four adult children—as their lives unfold in the Mexico City slum they call home. Weaving together their extraordinary personal narratives, Oscar Lewis creates a sympathetic but ultimately tragic portrait that is at once harrowing and humane, mystifying and moving. *The Children of Sanchez* reads like the best of fiction, with the added impact that it is all, undeniably, true.

Anthropology/Sociology

THE COLOR COMPLEX (REVISED)
The Politics of Skin Color in a New Millennium
by Kathy Russell-Cole, Midge Wilson, PhD,
and Ronald E. Hall, PhD

The Color Complex is a provocative exploration of how Western standards of beauty are influencing cultures across the globe and impacting personal, professional, romantic, and familial relationships. Processes like skin lightening in India, hair smoothing in Black America, eyelid reconstruction in China, and plastic surgery worldwide continue to rise in popularity for men and women facing discrimination from both within and outside of their own increasingly fluid ethnic groups. Now including a wealth of new information since the first edition, the authors, through a historical and sociological lens, have measured the impact of recent pop culture events effecting race relations to determine whether colorism has gotten better or worse over time.

Sociology

GENDER AND OUR BRAINS
How New Neuroscience Explodes the
Myths of the Male and Female Minds
by Gina Rippon

We live in a gendered world, where we are ceaselessly bombarded by messages about sex and gender. On a daily basis, we face deeply ingrained beliefs that sex determines our skills and preferences, from toys and colors to career choice and salaries. But what does this constant gendering mean for our thoughts, decisions, and behavior? And what does it mean for our brains? Drawing on her work as a professor of cognitive neuroimaging, Gina Rippon unpacks the stereotypes that surround us from our earliest moments and shows how these messages mold our ideas of ourselves and even shape our brains. By exploring new, cutting-edge neuroscience, Rippon urges us to move beyond a binary view of the brain and to see instead this complex organ as highly individualized, profoundly adaptable, and full of unbounded potential. Rigorous, timely, and liberating, *Gender and Our Brains* has huge implications for women and men, for parents and children, and for how we identify ourselves.

Science

VINTAGE BOOKS & ANCHOR BOOKS
Available wherever books are sold.
www.vintagebooks.com
www.anchorbooks.com